OXFORD
Children's
Encyclopedia

OXFORD
Children's
Encyclopedia

Oxford University Press

Oxford University Press, Walton Street, Oxford OX2 6DP

Oxford   New York   Toronto
Delhi   Bombay   Calcutta   Madras   Karachi
Petaling Jaya   Singapore   Hong Kong   Tokyo
Nairobi   Dar es Salaam   Cape Town
Melbourne   Auckland
and associated companies in
Berlin   Ibadan

Oxford is a trade mark of Oxford University Press
© Oxford University Press 1991
Reprinted 1991

ISBN 0 19 910139 6 (complete set)

Volume 1: 0 19 910132 9 (not for sale separately)

A CIP catalogue record for this book is available from the British Library

Printed in Great Britain by
William Collins Sons and Company Ltd, Glasgow

Editor	Mary Worrall
Design and art direction	Richard Morris
Cover design	Philip Atkins
Assistant editors	Jane Bingham
	David Burnie
	Tony Drake
	Deborah Manley
	Sarah Matthews
	Pamela Mayo
	Stephen Pople
	Andrew Solway
	Catherine Thompson
Copy preparation	Eric Buckley
	Richard Jeffery
Proof reader	Richard Jeffery
Index	Radmila May
Photographic research	Catherine Blackie
	Libby Howells
	Linda Proud
	Suzanne Williams

Introduction

An encyclopedia is a book, or a set of books, which gives information on many different subjects. The word comes from Greek and means 'all round education'.

The sum total of all human knowledge is, of course, far too great to be included in a set of seven books. Even if we had chosen to produce an encyclopedia of 100 volumes, it would still contain only a tiny part of all known facts.

We have planned the encyclopedia to be a starting point from which you can begin to find out about animals, plants, people, places, science, technology, the Earth, the universe, history, religions, music, painting and many other topics. As you search for the article you want, you may come across subjects that you had not even thought of. These volumes are full of surprises.

What to put in and what to leave out

It took a team of people, each an expert in a different subject, several months to draw up the final list of articles. A physicist, Professor Charles Taylor, made a list of science topics. Joyce Pope, lecturer at the Natural History Museum in London, made a zoology list. A geographer, Patrick Wiegand, did the same for the earth sciences. Peggy Morgan, a lecturer at Westminster College, Oxford prepared a list that covered the religions of the world. Historians argued over which historical events were most important.

As well as experts, children were consulted. We asked them to note down the topics they wanted to read about. There was a lot of interest in science and technology and so there are many detailed articles on these subjects. Children's choices also helped the team to decide which articles should be the longer ones. The final list was a balance between what the experts thought was important and what children wanted to know. The lists were put in alphabetical order using a computer.

Why alphabetical?

The articles are arranged alphabetically, not thematically under subjects, with the exception of Volume 6: Biography. We planned it this way because librarians, teachers, parents and children all said they found it easier to use than a set of books divided by subjects. It is easier, for instance, to find Radio under R than to have to decide whether it comes in a volume on Communication or Science. As everyone knows who a person is, the biographies are all collected in Volume 6.

Authors and artists

One hundred and twelve writers contributed the articles. Jacqueline Mitton, Public Relations Officer to the Royal Astronomical Society, wrote the astronomy articles. Mike Corbishley, an archaeologist on the staff of English Heritage, wrote the entries on the ancient world and prehistory. Gillian Wolfe, of the Dulwich Picture Gallery, London, prepared the articles on painting and sculpture. Peter Holden, chairman of the Young Ornithologists Club, wrote about birds. Contributions also came from Australia, Canada, Japan, New Zealand and other countries.

Almost all the illustrations, diagrams and maps have been specially drawn for this encyclopedia. One artist painted all the birds; another illustrated the human body. A team of artists prepared diagrams on science and technology. Three researchers looked at thousands of photographs from many picture agencies in Britain and from museums and galleries in Europe and North America. They selected the best and most appropriate.

Changing knowledge

Work on this encyclopedia began early in 1987. During the four and a half years which it has taken to plan, design, write, illustrate and print, there have been many changes in world events and in technology. When we started, Germany was two separate countries. So was Yemen. Cambodia was called Kampuchea. Roald Dahl was alive. Nelson Mandela was in prison. Compact disc players were rare and most supermarket tills could not read bar codes. The final proofs are being checked in February and March 1991. You the reader, may be reading this several months or years later. We hope it will start you off on the search for important and exciting ideas; a beginning to your 'all round education'.

Mary Worrall *Editor*   March 1991

Principal consultants

John Brown
Flexible learning adviser,
South-West Region

Dr Henry Bennet-Clark
University Lecturer in Invertebrate
Zoology, Oxford University

Joyce Pope
Formerly Senior Lecturer,
Natural History Museum, London

Professor Charles Taylor
Emeritus Professor, University of
Wales. Formerly Professor of
Experimental Physics at the
Royal Institution

Peter Teed
Formerly Headmaster, Goole
Grammar School, Goole,
Humberside

Patrick Wiegand
Lecturer in Geographical
Education, University of Leeds

The editors acknowledge with
thanks the queries, criticism and
help from the children and staff of:

Blunsdon St Andrew School,
Blunsdon, Wiltshire

Courthouse Green Primary School,
Coventry
Henry Bellairs Middle School,
Bedworth, Warwickshire
St Edwards School,
Paddington, London
Stonesfield County Primary School,
Stonesfield, Oxfordshire
Woodstock C E Primary School,
Woodstock, Oxfordshire

Contributors

Dr R E Allen
Tom Arkell
Toni Arthur
Dr Stephen Ashton
Peter Aykroyd
Jill Bailey
Professor Chris Baines
Dr Christopher Baldick
Peter Ball
Penny Bateman
Brian S Beckett
Dr John Becklake
Sue Becklake
H C Bennet-Clark
Dr Michael J Benton
Jane Bingham
Johnny Black
Alan Bloomfield
Dr Brian Bowers
Professor Adrian Brockett
John R Brown
Ben Burt
Gerald Butt
Arthur Swift Butterfield
Richard C Carter
Kate Castle
Professor Joan M Chandler
Mary Cherry

Jean Cooke
Jeremy Coote
Mike Corbishley
Judith Court
Hilary Devonshire
Tony Drake
Professor Michael Dummett
Professor T H Elkins
David Fickling
Elizabeth Foster
John L Foster
Dr Bernard J Freedman
Nigel Frost
Gib Goodfellow
Susan Goodman
Dr Alastair McIntosh Gray
J M Gullick
Bridget Hadaway
Gerald Haigh
Michael Harrison
Margaret Hebblethwaite
Peter Hebblethwaite
Sonya Hinton
John Hodgson
Peter Holden
Janet E Hunter
Michael Hurd
Paul James

Christopher Jarman
Rob Jeffcoate
Dr Terry Jennings
Astley Jones
Stephen Keeler
Rosemary Kelly
Margaret Killingray
Ann Kramer
Clive A Lawton
Dr Conrad Leyser
Vivienne M Little
Ann Low-Beer
Keith Lye
Vicki Mackenzie
Dr Nicholas Mann
Sarah Matthews
Kenneth and Valerie McLeish
Haydn Middleton
Dr N J Middleton
Dr Jacqueline Mitton
Peggy Morgan
Dr Roger Neich
Paul C Noble
John O'Connor
Catherine O'Keefe
Dr Stuart Owen-Jones
Tony Pawson
Dr David Pimm

Henry Pluckrose
Joyce Pope
Stephen Pople
Philip Pullman
Jeremy Purseglove
Judy Ridgway
Professor James Riordan
R J Ritchie
John Robottom
Lois Rock
Theodore Rowland-Entwistle
Ann Schlee
Daljit Sehbai
Imogen Stewart
Derek Strange
John N Stringer
Professor Charles Taylor
Peter Teed
Dr Nicholas Tucker
Pauline Vincent
John N Walker
Roger Watson
Dr Philip Whitfield
Patrick Wiegand
Mark Wilson
Gillian A Wolfe
Jenyth Worsley
Jill A Wright

Other consultants

Dr Terry Allsop
Dr Stephen Ashton
Dr Christopher Baldick
Rev John Barton
Dr G T Bath
Marigold Best
Dr John Blair
Jean Bolam
Professor Keith Branigan
Professor Adrian Brockett
Dr Peter Carey
Professor William Chafe
Ian Chilvers
Mike Farr

Dr Honor Gay
Dr David Gellner
Dr Andy Gosler
Dr Daniel Greenstein
Narayana Gupta
Gerald Haigh
Michael Harrison
Peggy Heeks
Michael Hurd
M Mashuq ibn Ally
Dr Brian Keeble
Dr Margaret Kinnel
Dr Katherine Krebs

Clive A Lawton
Helen Lewins
Henrietta Leyser
Professor James Lydon
Shirley Matthews
Dr Euan McKendrick
Professor W H McLeod
Professor Clyde A Milner II
Professor Kenneth O Morgan
Dr Chandra Muzatfar
Dr Beth Okamura
Dr Judith Okely
Quentin Oliver

Padraig O'Loingsigh
Professor J H Paterson
Chris Powling
Jan Powling
Judith Salmon
Dr Ian Scargill
Dr Andrew Sherratt
Dr Harry Shukman
Professor Harvard Sitkoff
Margaret Spencer
Janet Stevenson
John Stringer
Anita Tull

How to use the Oxford Children's Encyclopedia

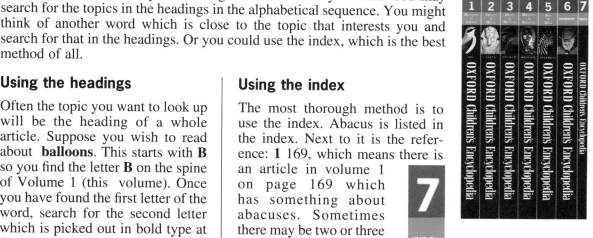

There are three main ways of finding the information you want. You may search for the topics in the headings in the alphabetical sequence. You might think of another word which is close to the topic that interests you and search for that in the headings. Or you could use the index, which is the best method of all.

Using the headings

Often the topic you want to look up will be the heading of a whole article. Suppose you wish to read about **balloons**. This starts with **B** so you find the letter **B** on the spine of Volume 1 (this volume). Once you have found the first letter of the word, search for the second letter which is picked out in bold type at the top of the page like this: **Ba**lloons and airships.

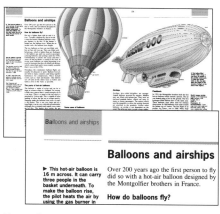

Balloons and airships

▶ This hot-air balloon is 16 m across. It can carry three people in the basket underneath. To make the balloon rise, the pilot heats the air by using the gas burner in

Over 200 years ago the first person to fly did so with a hot-air balloon designed by the Montgolfier brothers in France.

How do balloons fly?

People

If you are looking for an article about a person, go straight to Volume 6: the Biography. These articles are in alphabetical order, listed under the surname (family name) as in a telephone directory: **Curie**, Marie.

Think of another word

If you cannot find what you want under the main headings, think of another word or topic that is very close to what you need. Suppose you want to look up **abacus**. You search in the **A**s and there is no article. But you know that an abacus is a type of calculator. So find **Calculators**; there is a section on the abacus towards the end.

In ancient times and in the Middle Ages surnames were not common and so you will find many people under their first names: **Boudica**, **Francis** of Assisi, **Muhammad**.

Spellings of historical characters vary and you may have to search over a few pages.

Using the index

The most thorough method is to use the index. Abacus is listed in the index. Next to it is the reference: **1** 169, which means there is an article in volume 1 on page 169 which has something about abacuses. Sometimes there may be two or three articles which have something on the subject you want.

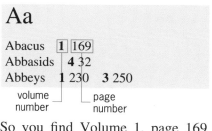

Aa

Abacus   **1** 169
Abbasids   **4** 32
Abbeys   **1** 230   **3** 250

volume number   page number

So you find Volume 1, page 169 which is the second page of the article on **Calculators**.

Calculators

Electronic calculators in use

A simple calculator is useful for checking bills or helping with your mathematics at school. But for some jobs, more advanced calculators are needed. Often, these are specially designed to suit particular jobs. Scientists and engineers use specially designed calculators; so do accountants. The electronic checkouts in supermarkets are calculators specially designed to work out customers' bills. On some, you do not even have to press the buttons. The price labels are read automatically by a laser light beam.

Flashback

The **abacus** (counting frame) was probably the first calculating machine. It is an oblong frame holding wires on which beads are strung. On a Chinese abacus there are seven beads on each wire: two above and five below a crossbar. Each bead above the crossbar represents five. Each bead below the crossbar represents one. The thirteenth wire represents trillions. To add you move the beads to the bar, and to subtract you move them away. When you run out of beads, you swap five ones for a five, or two fives for a one in the next column. The abacus is still used in China and Japan today. Skilled operators can work it almost as fast as an electronic calculator.

some, if you wanted to multiply by five, you had to turn a handle five times. Later versions had electric motors to speed things up, but they

▲ On an abacus, calculating is done by sliding beads along

Cross references

Almost every article leads on to many more. Look for the red **See also** bar in the margin at the end of an article. This lists other articles which have more information related to what you have read.

This list appears at the end of the article on **Balloons and airships**.

Suppose you want to read about Cuchulain, the ancient Irish hero. He is not listed in the Biography. The index gives the reference: **1** 205. Turn to Volume 1, page 205. Cuchulain is in the article on **Celtic myths and legends**.

 See also

Air
Atmosphere
Flight
Helium

Biography
Montgolfier brothers

Contents

Aborigines of Australia

The Aborigines are the original inhabitants of Australia. The word 'aboriginal' comes from the Latin *ab origine* meaning 'from the beginning'. They have lived in Australia for an immensely long period. Scientists have found stone tools dating back at least 45,000 years.

The Aborigines probably moved southwards from Asia to Australia, island-hopping in their canoes. They spread over the country in large family groups known as tribes. The tribes developed varied customs and many different languages. However, all the Aborigines lived off the land, hunting animals and gathering plants. They did not create farms, buildings or permanent villages.

The Aborigines' beliefs

The first European explorers and settlers thought the Aborigines were primitive because they had no permanent settlements. However, the Aborigines were very skilled in their chosen life-style of living off the land. They worshipped the land, because they believed the spirits of their ancestors had created its features back in a period they called the Dreamtime. They held ceremonies at places made sacred by visits from the ancestral spirits. They acted in songs and danced stories about the Dreamtime.

◄ Aborigines making music with a didgeridoo (a wind instrument), and with percussion instruments.

Effects of European settlement

After the Europeans arrived over 200 years ago, conflicts with the Aborigines soon began. The Aborigines resented the settlers taking over their land, especially the sacred sites. The settlers destroyed the Aborigines' hunting grounds and killed them in large numbers. The Aborigines' spears and boomerangs were no match for the settlers' guns. Aborigines also suffered from diseases, carried to Australia by Europeans, to which they had no resistance.

The Aboriginal population has been greatly reduced since European settlement and most Aborigines have lost their traditional way of life. Family ties were lost, sacred sites were lost, native languages died out. Many now live in big cities, or on the fringes of country towns. Some live on church or government missions in the outback.

Languages
Over 300 different languages were spoken by Aborigines before European settlement. Far fewer are spoken now.

⊙ See also
Australia's history
Boomerangs
Creation myths
Hunter-gatherers

Aborigines today

Today Aborigines prefer to be known as Kooris. Individuals and groups are working hard to maintain an identity to be proud of. Australians have acknowledged the contribution of many Kooris to politics, religion, law, sport and the arts; and governments are working towards restoring some Aboriginal sacred sites and returning to original Aboriginal names. Ayers Rock is now known as Uluru. ■

► Bark painting, probably by Yirawala, depicting the rainbow serpent, Njalyod, giving birth to Aboriginal people. This painting comes from the Northern Territory of Australia.

▼ Demonstration by Aborigines and their supporters demanding recognition by white Australians of their rights to ownership of land.

FGD equipment is fitted to some power-stations to help reduce acid rain.
FGD stands for Flue Gas Desulphurization.

▼ Over the years acid rain has slowly dissolved parts of this statue.

See also
Acids
Fuel
Gases
Pollution

Acid rain

Acid rain is caused by air pollution. When coal, oil and petrol are burned, the smoke given off contains the gases sulphur dioxide and nitrogen dioxide. These gases escape into the atmosphere, where they dissolve in water droplets to form weak acids. These acids then fall to the ground in rain, snow or sleet.

Acid rain is harmful to plants and animals. It is hard to control because it may be blown by the wind, falling thousands of kilometres from where it was first formed. For example, much of the acid rain in Canada is caused by smoke from factories and power-stations in the USA; the acid rain in Scandinavia may come from Britain.

The effects of acid rain

Acid rain has many different effects. It has killed fish in the lakes of North America, Scandinavia, Scotland and Wales. Vast areas of forest in northern and central Europe are dying because of it, while in many European cities statues and stone buildings are being eaten away by the acid. It corrodes metalwork such as steel bridges and railings, and it attacks some types of concrete. Even the water we drink is slowly being polluted by it.

How acid rain produces its effects

No one knows for certain exactly how acid rain produces its effects. Scientists believe that acid rain in the soil washes away important plant foods. It also changes certain metals, particularly aluminium, in the soil into a poisonous form. The aluminium then damages tree roots. When the aluminium is washed into lakes it affects the gills of fish and kills them.

Preventing acid rain

Most of the acid gases which produce acid rain probably come from power-stations and factories. The exhaust fumes from motor vehicles also make some of the acid. Building tall chimneys reduces the effects near by, but passes the pollution on to other areas.

There are ways of stopping acid rain. They include using types of coal and oil which contain little sulphur, and cleaning the waste gases before they pass out of factory and power-station chimneys. Cars can be fitted with devices to clean their exhaust smoke. These methods are all expensive. Some governments and companies would prefer not to spend the extra money if they can avoid it. Others say they are waiting until cheaper methods of control can be found. Still others are worried that 'cures' may have harmful side effects. ■

Acids

An acid is a sour-tasting substance. Lemons taste sour because they contain citric acid. The sour taste of vinegar is due to acetic acid, while sour milk contains lactic acid. All these are weak acids.

Strong acids are far too dangerous to taste or touch. They are corrosive, which means that they can eat into skin, wood, cloth and other materials. Three of the best-known strong acids are sulphuric, hydrochloric and nitric acids.

Hundreds of acids have been discovered. Not all of them are liquids; many are solids. Acids react with both alkalis and metals to form salts. All acids contain hydrogen, and this gas is given off when acids react with some metals. To detect an acid, scientists use indicators. These are chemicals that change colour when mixed with an acid. Litmus is one indicator. An acid turns blue litmus red. These acids are often added to water and used in a diluted form. Acids with almost no water in them are called concentrated acids.

Uses of acids

Acids have many uses. Sulphuric acid, for example, is used to make fertilizers, explosives, plastics, paints, dyes, detergents and many other chemicals. It is also used in car batteries. In fact, without sulphuric acid, many of the things we use every day would not exist.

Scientists measure the strength of acids (and alkalis) on a scale of numbers called the pH scale. The strongest acid has a pH of 0. Pure water, with no acid effect at all, has a pH of 7. The strongest alkali has a pH of 14.

Acids in the body

Rather surprisingly, your body contains some acids. Hydrochloric acid, made in the stomach, kills most of the germs that you swallow with your food. It also makes the conditions right for the food in your stomach to be digested. If you eat a lot of sugary food, lactic acid, made by bacteria feeding on the sugars, may give you tooth decay. ■

See also
Alkalis
Chemicals

Acupuncture

There are up to 1,000 acupuncture points in the human body.

Acupuncture is a very ancient Chinese form of healing. It uses no medicines or surgery, only very fine needles. These needles are used to prick the skin at particular points on the patient's body, either to stimulate or to damp down the energy which flows through the body. Acupuncturists believe that there are meridians, paths of energy (something like a mild electric current), which run through the body and can be tapped at different acupuncture points.

A person falls ill when the energy flow in the body becomes blocked, because of too little or too much energy in the heart, lungs, liver or other vital organs. A healthy person is balanced, with sufficient energy flowing along all fourteen meridians.

In Western countries there are now some trained acupuncturists. They offer an 'alternative' or 'complementary' way of healing people alongside doctors trained in Western medicine.

Chinese acupuncturists have treated every kind of illness, from deafness to heart failure, for over 2,000 years. Recently they have used acupuncture instead of anaesthetics to prevent patients feeling pain during operations. ■

Addiction

Some narcotic drugs, like heroin, create a physical dependence, where the body will not function properly if the drug is withdrawn. Other substances, like tobacco, are addictive only because the user cannot break the habit of using them. However, it is very hard to draw the line between those drugs which create physical dependence and those which do not.

Addiction is a habit that people find very hard to stop. They get so used to having something that they feel they cannot do without it. They have a constant urge to have more and without it feel ill or lost. Taking drugs like heroin and cocaine is addictive and extremely dangerous to the body.

Smoking, drinking alcohol and sniffing glue and other substances can easily become addictions. These habits all damage people's health. Even drinking too much coffee can become an addiction. It is possible to change a habit but it takes a lot of determination. Many people need professional help to overcome an addiction. ■

👁 See also
Alcoholics
Drugs
Smoking

Adolescence

Adolescence is the stage in between being a child and being an adult. From being looked after by other people (dependence) you become able to look after yourself (independence). Many changes take place in the body. This time of physical change is called puberty.

Adolescents have more freedom and more responsibilities than children. They have to make choices about their future, their education and their jobs. Adolescents try to make up their own minds about things, and their feelings often become very strong and variable.

Adolescence hardly exists in many societies. Children take part in adult activities as soon as they are able to do so. ■

In most cases adolescence corresponds to the teenage years from about twelve to about sixteen or seventeen.

👁 See also
Children
Puberty

Adoption

There are two ways in which a child becomes part of a family. The child can be born into one, or adopted. Babies or children who lose their natural parents may be adopted by other couples, or in some cases a single person. Their new, adoptive parents bring them up as if they were their natural children. Being adopted is like being in an ordinary family. You take that family's name and are part of it for ever.

Adoption only became legal in Britain in 1926.

Not just anyone can adopt children. In many countries there are very careful laws about the choice of adoptive parents. Social workers spend a lot of time checking that adults who want to adopt are going to be able to love and look after their new child properly. They also try to make sure that they understand the child's special needs.

Adopted people over the age of 18 have the right in Britain to obtain a full certificate of birth so that they can find out who their natural parents are.

After all these checks, a judge in a law court makes the adoption order. This order makes someone the adoptive child of new parents. From that moment onwards the child has a new family. ■

👁 See also
Families
Foster children

Advertising

It costs a great deal of money to advertise in best-selling magazines or on television. When the American Football Superbowl is being shown live on television it costs more than half a million dollars to run an advertisement for 30 seconds.

The people who check advertisements in Britain are known as the Advertising Standards Authority.

Advertising brings information to people. Most advertising is from producers telling people about the things they make so that they can sell more. Shopkeepers who put their goods on display in the shop window are advertising. People also advertise by posters in the street, by putting notices in newspapers and by short films (commercials) on the television. Much advertising is by direct mail: letters sent to peoples' homes, often including details of competitions and free offers. Advertising is not common everywhere. Some governments discourage competition between manufacturers and consider advertising to be a waste of resources and money.

▲ **The 1989 Tour de France is an example of how sports events are sponsored by companies who pay for their name to be displayed on clothing and equipment.**

▶ **A Cadbury's chocolate advertisement from the year 1900.**

In 1988 Pepsi Cola paid Michael Jackson millions of dollars to do four short television advertisements.

⊙ See also
Businesses
Capitalists
Posters
Shops
Victorian Britain

Advertising agencies

People who sell goods and services often use advertising agencies to bring their products to the attention of the public. First, the agency has to understand the product. Suppose it is a breakfast cereal. The advertising team have to decide what is special about it, what sort of people are likely to buy it and what other cereals there are. They then have to think of an idea that will persuade people to buy this cereal. Perhaps people will eat the cereal if it is recommended by a famous sportsperson, or if the healthy nature of the ingredients is emphasized. Perhaps it would be a good idea to make a short television advert showing the sports star enjoying a happy family breakfast. If the cereal manufacturer likes the idea, the agency must arrange for the script to be written, actors and

camera crew hired, and the film to be made. The agency must then decide when the film is to be shown: in the late afternoon for children to see, or in the evening? Finally, the agency makes sure that the advert is actually shown and they send their client the bill.

Control of advertising

Advertisements have often been criticized for persuading people to buy things they do not want or cannot afford. Advertisers say that they only provide information about the choices that people have. Advertisers have to follow a code of practice. In Britain advertisements have to be 'legal, decent, honest and truthful'. Products that can be harmful, such as cigarettes, have to carry health warnings. Advertising can be very powerful, and the slogans that are used to tell people about products often become part of everyday language.

CADBURY'S MILK CHOCOLATE

Flashback

Advertising has been used for hundreds of years. Before most people could read, shopkeepers had signs outside their shops to show what type of business they ran. Some of these can still be seen today, like the hairdresser's red and white striped pole. ■

Aerosols

Paints, polishes, deodorants, air-fresheners, fly-killers, shaving creams and oven cleaners are just some of the substances that can be sprayed by aerosol cans. They are even used to spray liquid bandages that turn solid when they touch the skin.

Inside an aerosol can

An aerosol can consists of a metal container with a concave base. The base is shaped like this to withstand the high pressure of the substances inside the can. In the top of the can is a plastic nozzle, connected to a valve and a plunger. A narrow tube passes from these almost to the bottom of the can. The can contains the substance to be sprayed together with a liquid known as a propellant. The propellant is unusual because it turns into a gas when it is released. When the nozzle is pressed, the pressure of this gas forces the paint,

polish, or whatever else the can contains, through the hole in the nozzle. It is this that creates the spray.

Aerosols and the ozone layer

In recent years scientists have become worried that some of the propellants used in aerosol cans may be polluting our world. In particular, they believe that some of the most commonly used propellants: substances known as chlorofluoro-carbons (CFCs for short), may be damaging the ozone layer in the upper atmosphere. This thin layer protects us from the harmful ultraviolet rays in sunlight. If the ozone layer is badly damaged, it could make humans more prone to skin cancer. Scientists have developed safer propellants, and some countries have banned the use of CFCs in aerosol cans. Aerosol cans that contain safe propellants often have 'Ozone Friendly' written on them. ■

Before the word 'aerosol' came to be used as a spray, it had a similar meaning to scientists. When tiny liquid or solid particles are held in a gas, that is an aerosol. So smoke, fog and clouds are all really examples of aerosols.

See also
Atmosphere
Ozone
Pollution

Afghanistan

▲ A Pathan woman milks her goat while her son holds it steady.

Afghanistan is a mountainous country in south-west Asia. One of the highest mountain ranges in the world, the Hindu Kush, lies in the centre of the country. North of these rugged, windswept mountains lies a plain where fruit, wheat and vegetables grow well. The southern edge of the Hindu Kush is mostly desert. Here temperatures are high and terrible dust storms blow in summer. The overland route from Europe to India goes through Afghanistan and over the Khyber Pass.

Afghanistan is one of the world's poorest countries. Only about one person in ten can read or write and the average age that an Afghan can expect to live to is 36 years for a man, 39 for a woman.

Afghan people come from many different ethnic groups, though

almost all are Muslims. In recent centuries both the British and Russians have invaded and tried to rule Afghanistan, but their troops have found it impossible to control the mountainous regions against the very independent tribespeople. The latest invasion ended when Russian troops withdrew in 1989. ■

Area
652,090 sq km
(251,773 sq miles)
Capital
Kabul
Population
10,000,000
Language
Pashto, Dari
Religion
Muslim
Government
Republic
Currency
1 afghani = 100 puls

See also
Asia
Muslims
Russia's history

Biography
Gorbachev

Africa

Area
30,334,592 sq km
(11,712,252 sq miles)
Highest peak
Mount Kilimanjaro 5,895 m
Lowest point
Lake Assal 155 m below
sea-level
Largest lake
Victoria 68,800 sq km
(26,560 sq miles)
Longest rivers
Nile, Zaïre, Niger, Zambezi
Largest country (by area)
Sudan 2,505,813 sq km
(967,500 sq miles)
Largest country (by
population)
Nigeria 105,000,000

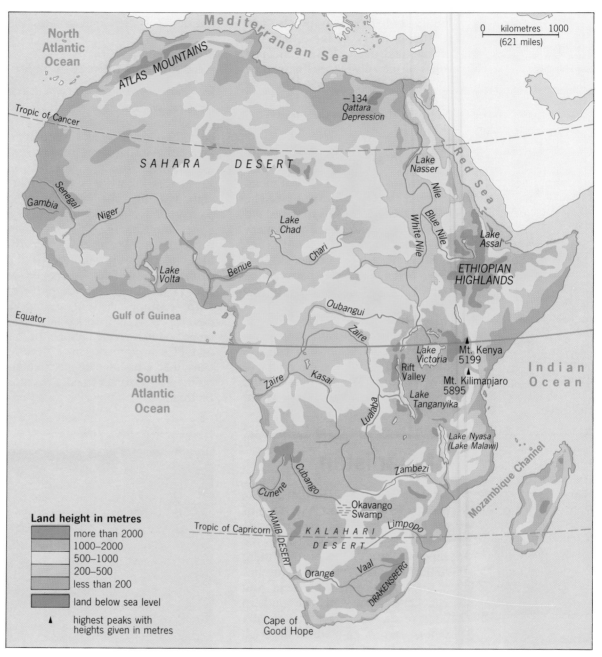

Land height in metres

more than 2000
1000–2000
500–1000
200–500
less than 200

land below sea level

▲ highest peaks with
heights given in metres

Africa is the world's second largest continent. Apart from the narrow strip of land at Suez which joins it to Asia, the continent is completely surrounded by sea. Its chunky shape gives it far less coastline than western Europe and there are few natural harbours. Fourteen of the 47 countries of Africa have no sea coast.

Landscapes

Much of the south and east of Africa is high plateau country. Mount Kilimanjaro and Mount Kenya are extinct volcanoes. Most of the north and west, with the exception of the Atlas Mountains in Morocco, is lower. The area around Lake Chad is an inland basin. Instead of flowing to the sea, rivers empty themselves in the lake.

In the north lies the Sahara Desert, the largest area of sand and bare rock in the world. In the south-west of Africa lie two other deserts: the Kalahari and the Namib. Lakes Tanganyika and Malawi (Nyasa) lie in a great split in the earth's surface, a rift valley. A similar valley is filled by the Red Sea and stretches across to the lakes in Kenya.

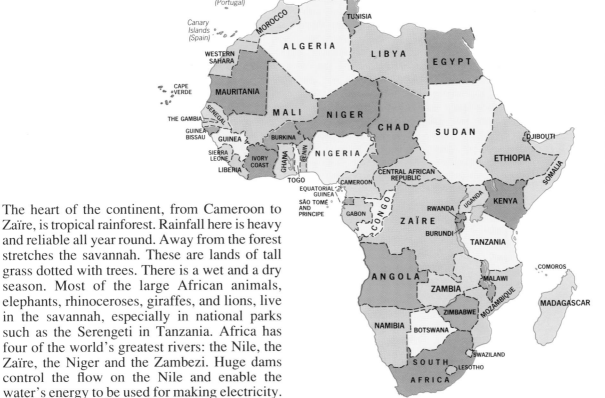

Madeira
(Portugal)

Canary
Islands
(Spain)

MOROCCO
TUNISIA
ALGERIA
LIBYA
EGYPT
WESTERN
SAHARA
CAPE
VERDE
MAURITANIA
MALI
NIGER
CHAD
SUDAN
DJIBOUTI
THE GAMBIA
SENEGAL
GUINEA-
BISSAU
GUINEA
BURKINA
NIGERIA
ETHIOPIA
SIERRA
LEONE
IVORY
COAST
GHANA
BENIN
TOGO
CENTRAL AFRICAN
REPUBLIC
SOMALIA
LIBERIA
CAMEROON
EQUATORIAL
GUINEA
SÃO TOMÉ
AND
PRINCIPE
GABON
CONGO
ZAÏRE
RWANDA
UGANDA
KENYA
BURUNDI
TANZANIA
COMOROS
ANGOLA
ZAMBIA
MALAWI
MADAGASCAR
MOZAMBIQUE
ZIMBABWE
NAMIBIA
BOTSWANA
SWAZILAND
SOUTH
AFRICA
LESOTHO

The area called Western Sahara was a Spanish colony until 1975. It was then divided between Morocco and Mauritania (which gave up its claim in 1979), but the Polisario guerrillas fought for independence until 1988, when they agreed on a ceasefire till a referendum was held.

The heart of the continent, from Cameroon to Zaïre, is tropical rainforest. Rainfall here is heavy and reliable all year round. Away from the forest stretches the savannah. These are lands of tall grass dotted with trees. There is a wet and a dry season. Most of the large African animals, elephants, rhinoceroses, giraffes, and lions, live in the savannah, especially in national parks such as the Serengeti in Tanzania. Africa has four of the world's greatest rivers: the Nile, the Zaïre, the Niger and the Zambezi. Huge dams control the flow on the Nile and enable the water's energy to be used for making electricity.

Climate

Almost all of Africa is warm or hot. The countries which lie on the Equator are wet all year round. July is the wet season for a group of countries further north, from Guinea to Ethiopia. January is the wet season for the rest of the continent, from Zaïre to South Africa. The driest parts of Africa are the Sahara, Namib and Kalahari deserts. These have long hours of hot, bright sunshine. The Mediterranean shores and the tip of South Africa have warm, wet winters and hot, dry summers.

People and languages

Some African countries have never had an accurate census and so population statistics can be unreliable. The coast of West Africa, the Nile Valley and the area around Lake Victoria are crowded. But these areas are separated by up to 2,000 km (1,250 miles) of desert or forest where very few people live.

Over 1,300 languages are spoken in Africa, and very many Africans are able to speak not only their mother tongue but often as many as six other languages. They are multilingual. In North Africa most people speak Arabic. In West Africa, Hausa, Yoruba, Akan and Malinke are important languages spoken by millions of people. East

Africans can mostly speak Swahili. South of the Equator people speak one or other of the Bantu languages.

In the late 19th century, several European nations divided up and ruled most of the continent of Africa. French, Portuguese and English are spoken in the areas which those countries used to rule. The boundaries between African nations today are often the same as the lines drawn on the map by European administrators. In many parts of Africa you will find people in neighbouring countries speaking the same language and belonging to the same tribal group.

Religion

The Arabic-speaking people of the north are Muslims, as are the majority of the people of Mali, Sudan and northern Nigeria. About half of all Africans are Muslims and their religion, Islam, is the fastest growing religion. Christian churches are strong, too. As well as Roman Catholics and Anglicans there are many independent African churches. Traditional African religions have their own rituals and ways of getting advice and guidance from the supreme god. Africans worship with dance and music, and these are important art-forms throughout the continent. ∎

Swahili is a Bantu language, but it is simpler then the other Bantu languages and contains a great many Arabic words. It developed on the coast and islands near Zanzibar in Tanzania, which for centuries were ruled by Arabs. *Swahili* comes from an Arabic word meaning 'coast'.

See also

African history
African music
Arabs
Christians
Dance
Deserts
Drums
Grasslands
Mediterranean
Muslims
Nile
Sahara

African history

Archaeologists have found more hand axes and other stone tools in East Africa than anywhere else on Earth. Fragments of fossils of early humans have also been discovered. So scientists believe that human beings evolved in Africa and spread out from there to other parts of the world. It was in Africa that prehistoric people developed skills of shaping tools, hunting, learning to use fire and living in groups.

See also
British empire
Commonwealth
Egyptian ancient history
Slaves
Slave trade
The flashback sections of articles on African countries

Biography
Kenyatta
Kruger
Livingstone
Luthuli
Mandela
Mugabe
Nkrumah
Nyerere
Park
Rhodes
Shaka
Smuts
Tutu

Egypt, Meroe and Ethiopia

Most Africans, over the centuries, lived in small settlements and villages and very little is known in detail of prehistoric times. From about the year 4000 BC powerful empires grew up by the River Nile, because the soil along its banks was rich and fertile. The most famous was Egypt of the Pharaohs. Further south, Meroe grew rich, trading up and down the river. Its people smelted iron, built cities and buried their kings under pyramids. The Meroitic language was engraved on walls and stones, but today no one can understand what is written. Meroe's rule ended when other trading kingdoms from Ethiopia invaded. These kingdoms became Christian, and one, in the highlands of Ethiopia, lasted into the 20th century.

Cities and kingdoms

Trade was important in West Africa, too, and increased when traders began to use camels to cross the Sahara Desert with gold, salt and slaves. In the grasslands south of the Sahara, city states grew rich and powerful. Many of their kings adopted the Muslim religion which traders and scholars brought with them from North Africa. Mansa Musa, the king of Mali, went to the holy city of Mecca in Arabia in the 14th century, paying everyone with gold on the way.

◀ The royal court of Benin in West Africa produced quantities of bronze casts from the 16th to the 19th centuries. This head is of a queen mother.

Other states grew up in the forest areas nearer to the coast. These were also rich, from trading in gold, slaves, leather goods and cloth. In Benin richly clothed kings ruled from a magnificent palace and craftsmen and artists produced fine ivory carvings and bronze sculptures.

City states on the east coast, such as Kilwa and Sofala, sent ivory, gold, copper and gum by sea to Arabia, India and China. The gold came from the powerful inland state of Zimbabwe. Its great drystone granite buildings, over a thousand years old, still remain. Kilwa had grand houses and a large Muslim mosque built of coral stone. During the 16th century Portuguese guns and ships destroyed the wealth of these coastal states.

Slavery and wars

Slavery had long existed in African societies. Slaves were also exported, north across the Sahara to the Mediterranean and east to Arabia and India. But the slave trade grew during the

▼ This impressive mosque in the Muslim city of Mopti (now in Mali) was built of local materials in traditional style.

16th, 17th and 18th centuries, when European ships took large numbers of Africans across the Atlantic to the cotton and sugar plantations of the Americas and the Caribbean. In this period the Dutch, English and French, as well as the Portuguese, sent their ships to buy and sell on the West African coast, building forts to control the trade.

In the 19th century there were serious wars and disturbances in various parts of Africa. Passionate Muslims fought to control states in the interior of western Africa, wanting Islam to be the only faith of the people. In southern Africa the Zulu people conquered neighbouring African groups and also fought the Dutch (Boers) and British who were settling on their lands.

European rulers

In the late 19th century most parts of Africa were conquered and divided up by France, Britain, Portugal, Germany and Belgium. For over 60 years Africa was under European rule. The white colonists imposed new systems of law, government, language and education on the African people and often tried to stamp out their religion and culture. The boundaries Europeans drew on the map ignored the shapes of former kingdoms and empires. Artificial frontiers separated people who spoke the same language. Some colonies, including Uganda and Nigeria, were made of groups of people (tribes) who had nothing in common and were hostile to one another. A few African kings survived, in Buganda and Swaziland for instance, but they had lost their power.

Resistance and independence

Many Africans continued to resist colonial rule, but they were not at first strong enough to free their lands. Nationalist groups were formed to campaign for independence and from 1956 onwards one by one the states of Africa achieved their freedom. Some had to fight the colonial powers, who did not want to lose their African colonies, and there were long wars in Algeria against the French, and in Mozambique and Angola against Portugal.

Most of Africa became politically independent of European rule, but problems remained. The newly independent countries kept the territorial boundaries which the European colonists had drawn, and these did not correspond with the territories of ethnic groups (tribes). In South Africa the white minority kept political power for itself.

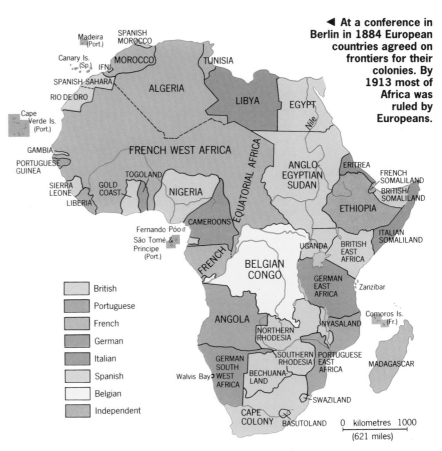

◀ At a conference in Berlin in 1884 European countries agreed on frontiers for their colonies. By 1913 most of Africa was ruled by Europeans.

British
Portuguese
French
German
Italian
Spanish
Belgian
Independent

In the years after independence cities grew, railways and roads were improved and new industries began. The countries of Africa sent their representatives to the United Nations and took part in world politics. But although politically independent, they were dependent on the prices that other countries gave them for the products they were able to export. Difficult climates, fast growing populations, lack of resources and local wars and rebellions have caused widespread famine and unrest in parts of Africa since independence. ■

▲ Zimbabwe, which had been the colony of Southern Rhodesia, became an independent republic in 1980. Here the people are celebrating in the capital city, Harare. Its name in colonial times was Salisbury.

African music

▶ The singer Youssou N'Dour is popular with Western audiences as well as with people all over Africa. In 1989 he toured the world to help raise money for the charity Amnesty International.

mbira

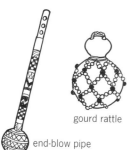

gourd rattle

end-blow pipe

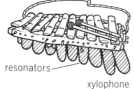

resonators

xylophone

slit drum

👁 See also
Drums
Pop and rock music
Singing and songs

In Africa, music has always been a part of everyday life. There are political songs, love songs, storytelling songs, music for ceremonies, music to sing along with, and music which dazzles you with its amazing rhythms and brilliant technique. None of it is written down, so the songs and ways of playing instruments have been passed down through families and the community.

African music is based on the rise and fall of the human voice. Singers and instrumentalists often follow and imitate each other in turn. In many songs a leader sings one sentence and a chorus replies, rather as in sea shanties and work songs. The chorus often move or dance as they sing, and they accompany the song with rhythmic handclaps.

Traditional music

The sound is very different from European music. The music of North African countries is Arabic in style. Singers use a very high part of their voice and they make up their own version of a tune with warbles and trills in long musical phrases. Most tunes have a percussion accompaniment.

Further south, the first thing you notice is the brilliant rhythm and rhythmic patterns: sometimes in song, sometimes played on a set of tuned drums or xylophones. No two performances of a piece of music are the same, because the musicians improvise on the tunes, making up new versions and adding new ideas to the music as they play.

Afro-rock and pop

African music today is part of the world music scene. It is a mixture of traditional music with Western styles such as rock, soul, and jazz. In West Africa, popular music called highlife has a Latin American beat.

One of Africa's most brilliant musicians, Youssou N'Dour from Senegal, plays a type of music called *mbalax*. Rich-sounding brass instruments and guitars with a complex syncopated beat accompany N'Dour's high-pitched vocals, which may be a call and response musical conversation.

Black musicians from Zimbabwe and southern Africa are best known for their choral singing, for example in Paul Simon's album *Graceland*, featuring the Ladysmith Black Mambazo choir.

Flashback

Until this century, most African people lived their daily lives in the open air and musicians used the natural materials around them to make their instruments. A set of talking drums is made from different sizes of hollow tree-trunk, each covered by an animal skin. A single-stringed fiddle is made from a hunting bow. Gourds, clay pots and hollow reeds with seeds or pebbles inside are used as rattles. Thin bones or bamboo shoots are carved into flutes and pan-pipes. Other common instruments are xylophones and the little *mbira*, also called a hand piano, which is made from strips of metal fixed to a piece of wood and tuned to different notes. ■

Afro-Americans

Many citizens of the United States are descended from West Africans who were taken to America during the 17th and 18th centuries and the early 1800s as slaves. They used to be called Negroes, but now prefer to be known as Afro-Americans, African Americans, or blacks.

Most of the slaves worked on farms in the Southern states. The importation of slaves ended in 1808 when the slave trade was abolished in the USA. In 1863, during the American Civil War, slaves were made free by law. But after that war many Southern states passed segregation laws, which provided that black Americans should live in separate districts, go to separate schools, and be segregated from whites in public places. As a result of these oppressive laws, many black people were not able to get a proper education or good jobs.

World Wars I and II brought a big change in Afro-American fortunes. Thousands served in the armed forces and several million moved from the South to the North to work in factories. As a result, there are now more blacks in the North than in the South.

After World War II, black people pressed still more strongly for civil rights, including the desegregation of schools. Martin Luther King led the Civil Rights movement but was assassinated for his beliefs in 1968. In that same year there were riots in northern cities; people protested that although laws had changed, white people's attitudes had not. The 'Black Power' movement demanded that discrimination against blacks should end. During the 1970s and 1980s racial barriers were steadily broken down.

African Americans play a big part in American culture, especially in jazz music, literature, dance and sport. Many now hold senior jobs in the armed services, in businesses and as government officials. ■

In Harlem, New York, there was a renaissance of black music and culture in the 1920s.

The National Association for the Advancement of Coloured People was founded in 1909. It worked to prevent lynching and other violent acts against blacks and for equal rights in employment.

See also
Jazz
Slaves
USA: history

Biography
Armstrong, Louis
Ellington
Fitzgerald
Holiday
Jackson, Jesse
King
Parker
Robeson
Tubman
Washington, Booker
Pop and rock special
Sports special

Afro-Caribbeans

Afro-Caribbean is the name sometimes given to people whose ancestors were among the 5 million taken as slaves from West Africa to work in the sugar plantations of European colonies in the Caribbean islands. When slavery was completely abolished in British colonies in 1838, many of the ex-slaves became farmers, traders and craftsmen. But jobs and land were scarce in the West Indies, so many others sought work in other countries. Up to the middle of the 20th century most went to other Caribbean islands, such as Cuba, to the USA, or to South and Central America, often returning home when a season's work was finished. Only small numbers went to Britain. They were mostly students, sailors, or men who joined the British army in the world wars.

After World War II, Britain was short of workers and advertised jobs and recruited workers in the Caribbean islands. Each year several thousands migrated to Britain, mostly to posts in transport, the hospitals and other vital public services. Some carried on the Caribbean tradition of staying only for a short while, but the majority settled permanently.

From 1962, a series of immigration rules made it difficult for people to enter Britain from any of her ex-colonies. Today many of the approximately half million Afro-Caribbean people of Britain are the children or grandchildren of the settlers of the 1950s and early 1960s. Prejudice and discrimination have been continuing problems in spite of the fact that it is illegal to discriminate on the grounds of racial differences. Other people with the same ancestry live in France and The Netherlands, which once owned sugar-growing islands in the Caribbean. There are now large communities of Afro-Caribbean origin in the United States and Canada. Most people who leave the Caribbean today travel to North America. ■

An act abolishing slavery was passed by the British Parliament in 1833 and became law the following year. The act stated that those over the age of six should serve as apprentices to their former owners for seven years. This did not work and slavery was finally abolished in the British Caribbean in 1838.

The Race Relations Act of 1976 made it illegal to discriminate on grounds of race, colour or ethnic origin in the provision of all goods and services.

In 1981 young black people were involved in street riots in Toxteth, Liverpool and Brixton, London. In 1985 there was a riot in Handsworth, Birmingham. Unemployment and police harassment were among the causes.

See also
Caribbean
Caribbean history
West Indies

Agricultural revolutions

For thousands of years farmers used to sow their seed broadcast; that is, they scattered it by the handful. This was a very inefficient and wasteful process.

In 1701, Jethro Tull, an Oxfordshire barrister and farmer, invented a seed drill. A blade made a small furrow, and the seed was fed into the furrow at an even rate down a tube. Modern seed drills work in much the same way.

◉ See also
Agriculture
Domestication
Enclosures
Farming
Farm machinery
Highland clearances
Irrigation
Prehistoric people

▼ This threshing machine is driven by a steam-engine. Engines like this were used on farms in Britain and North America in the second half of the 19th century.

When we think of revolutions we may picture people in street fighting. But some of the world's most important revolutions happened peacefully, on the farm. About 11,000 years ago, prehistoric people were beginning to grow crops and keep animals. That was the first 'agricultural revolution'. Archaeologists have given the name neolithic, meaning new stone age, to the period when people first started to settle down in one place and farm, rather than gather wild crops and hunt.

Revolution and evolution

After the neolithic revolution there was a long period of evolution in farming skills and methods. The plough had its origin in the digging stick. People soon fitted handles, so that it could be pulled or pushed. In about 4500 BC people harnessed oxen to the plough, the first step towards applying power to agriculture.

The next stage was irrigation: taking water through canals to land that was otherwise dry. This enabled more crops to be grown. The Romans noticed that the land seemed to yield less after several crops had been grown on it, so they started leaving half of it fallow (idle) each year, to recover.

A minor revolution occurred when the horse collar, invented in Asia, came into general use in Europe about AD 900. The harness previously used pressed on the windpipes of horses, so that they could not pull hard. The collar throws all the weight on the horse's shoulders. Horses could

pull ploughs faster than oxen. Even so, oxen continued to be used on farms in Europe. Horses were valuable and were used to pull carts and coaches.

The 18th-century agricultural revolution

A new agricultural revolution began in Britain in the 18th century. Over the years between 1750 and 1870 there was a huge increase in farm output.

Farmers learned (partly from Dutch engineers) how to drain their fields and enclose them in hedges. They found that by growing turnips, clover, barley and wheat in successive years, they could use the land all the time, instead of having it lie fallow for a year. One great advantage of this was that people could now grow enough clover and turnips (fodder) to keep their animals fed through the winter months. At the same time, stock breeders developed larger and fatter animals. But some people suffered from these changes. In Scotland, sheep-farming led to the Highland clearances, and in England the enclosure of fields deprived cottagers of grazing rights on common land.

The mechanical revolution

Farm machinery developed during the late 18th and early 19th centuries, much of it in the rapidly growing United States of America. Reapers, threshers and combine harvesters followed in succession. Steam-engines were used to power the traction engines used for ploughing and threshing. In the early 20th century petrol-driven tractors appeared. All these machines meant that more food could be grown by fewer people.

Even such well-tried devices as the plough were improved. The invention of the all-steel plough in 1837 by John Deere, a blacksmith of Illinois, in the USA, reduced the power needed to pull it through the soil. Deere's invention has been called 'the plough that broke the plains', because it was capable of breaking up the heavy soil of the North American prairies for cultivation. As a result, the USA and Canada became the biggest grain-producing area of the world.

The Green Revolution

The latest agricultural revolution began in the 1960s and is still going on. It is called the 'Green Revolution'. Plant breeders have produced new varieties of grains such as rice, wheat and maize that have increased food production in India, the Philippines, Mexico and many other countries. ■

Agriculture

The word agriculture is often used instead of farming, but strictly speaking agriculture only refers to growing crops, not rearing animals. The types of crops grown depend on where in the world the farm is. Wheat is grown in Argentina, the USSR, North America and Europe. Farmers in hot, wet parts of the tropics produce crops such as rice. In drier tropical areas of Africa cassava and millet are the main crops. In most parts of the world fields are ploughed and planted by hand or with animals. In other countries, machines such as tractors and combine harvesters are used. ∎

⊙ See also
Agricultural revolutions
Farming

Aid agencies

Aid agencies are organizations which work with people in the poor countries of Africa, Asia, Latin America and, to a lesser extent, the Middle East. These organizations have two main priorities. The first is to try to meet the immediate needs of families affected by emergencies such as famine, drought or flood.

The second important area of their work involves helping people in longer-term ways. People in poor countries often lack many of the things which those in richer countries take for granted, such as food, shelter, clean water, education and health care. The aid agencies try to enable people to improve their own lives by providing training, tools and equipment for improving farming methods and water supplies, and education about health and nutrition. They also help groups who want to learn to read and write. These are often adult men and women who could not go to school when they were young.

Some agencies in Europe and North America try to make people in their own countries aware of the causes of poverty and hardship overseas. Many of the aid agencies are chari-ties and some were established by the churches. For example, CAFOD is the official aid agency of the Roman Catholic Church in England and Wales, and Christian Aid is the agency of the Council of Churches in Britain and Ireland. ∎

Some aid agencies around the world
Australia Community Aid Abroad
Canada Canadian University Service Overseas
France Frères des Hommes International
Germany Brot für die Welt
Ireland Trocaire
Italy Mani Tese
Japan Japan International Volunteer Centre
Spain Manos Unidas
United Kingdom Save the Children
USA CARE

⊙ See also
Charities
Drought
Famine
Floods
Oxfam

AIDS

The letters A I D S stand for 'Acquired Immune Deficiency Syndrome'. AIDS is caused by a virus called HIV-1. This virus attacks some of the white blood cells which help kill the germs that cause disease. When this happens the body cannot fight infections, and victims may die of diseases that would not normally be serious.

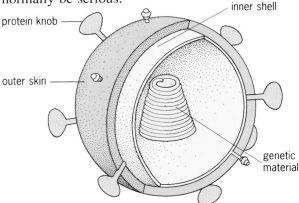

protein knob — inner shell — outer skin — genetic material

The AIDS virus is not caught like other virus diseases such as colds and flu. You cannot get AIDS by breathing the same air as AIDS victims, by touching them, or by using the same shower, cutlery, furniture, swimming pool or toilet. The AIDS virus must pass straight into the body to infect someone. This may happen when someone has sexual intercourse with an infected person; if they get a blood transfusion that is infected; or if they inject themselves with a needle used by someone with the AIDS virus. If a mother has AIDS her baby will probably be born with AIDS.

Scientists and doctors all over the world are trying to make a medicine or vaccine to protect people against this illness. ∎

▲ Diagram of the AIDS virus magnified about 200,000 times. The viruses enter white blood cells and change them into factories for making new viruses.

⊙ See also
Blood
Diseases
Vaccinations
Viruses

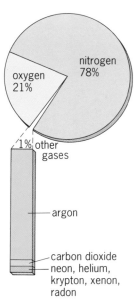

▲ **Gases in the air.**

In 1777 the French scientist Lavoisier showed that air was a mixture of gases and about ⅕ of it was oxygen.

A method for liquefying air on a large scale for commercial use was developed in 1895 by two scientists working separately: William Hampson, an Englishman, and Karl von Linde, a German.

In 1892 James Dewar invented special flasks for maintaining the liquefied gases of air at low temperatures. We call them thermos flasks and use them for keeping things hot.

Air can be changed into a colourless liquid under pressure, at about −200˚C.

▶ **Mountaineer wearing oxygen mask.**

◐ See also
Atmosphere
Barometers
Greenhouse effect
Jet engines
Mountains
Oxygen
Photosynthesis
Pollution
Pressure
Respiration

Biography
Lavoisier

Air

You are surrounded by a mixture of gases you breathe called air. You cannot see, smell or taste air, but you can feel it moving when the wind blows. Without air our planet would be a waterless, empty desert without any living creatures.

Air mainly consists of two gases: oxygen (21 per cent) and nitrogen (78 per cent). There is a small amount (less than 1 per cent) of argon and an even smaller amount of carbon dioxide. Carbon dioxide is very important as it is the main food of green plants. The Sun shines on the plants and by a process called photosynthesis helps the plants to use the carbon dioxide to produce oxygen. There are all sorts of other things in the air: dust, water vapour, pollen, seeds, tiny microscopic animals, bacteria and pollution from factory chimneys.

Mountain air

On mountains the air is much cleaner with less dust and pollution. But as you climb up a mountain the air becomes thinner, with less gases and not so much oxygen. Above 3,000 m (10,000 ft) you have to walk slowly until your body gets used to working with less oxygen. On very high mountains there is so little oxygen that climbers must carry their own supply in cylinders.

Weight and pressure

A bucketful of air weighs about the same as two pages of this book. This may not sound very much. But it means that in a space as big as your school hall there is probably more than a tonne of air. That is more than the weight of a small car!

The weight of the air above is always pressing on us. At sea-level, air pressure is equivalent to the weight of about 1 kilogram pressing on every square centimetre (15 lb on every square inch). However, we are not squashed by this pressure because we have air inside us as well as outside. Air pressure can be measured with a barometer. The reading is often given in millibars (mb) or in kilopascals (kPa). At sea-level, air pressure is just over 1,000 mb (100 kPa) on average, but this varies slightly from day to day depending on the temperature and the amount of moisture in the atmosphere. A fall in pressure warns you that rain may be on the way. Higher pressure usually means fine weather.

Air pressure can be increased by pumping more and more air into the space available. Tyres are filled with extra air so that they can support bicycles, cars and even aircraft. Air under pressure operates fast-acting brakes on trains and lorries. Pneumatic drills are driven by compressed air. Jet engines also rely on air. They get their thrust by sucking in a huge mass of air and pushing it out behind at high speed.

Air-conditioning

An air-conditioning system keeps the temperature and moisture of the air in a room at levels which are comfortable for people to live and work in (usually between 20°C and 25°C (68°F to 77°F) and a relative humidity of 35–70 per cent). The process takes place in an air-conditioning unit, which is no more than a large box for an average room. Here fresh air and air taken from the air-conditioned room are mixed; dust and smoke are removed by passing the air through filters; some of the air is warmed by passing over pipes containing hot water or steam and the rest of the air is cooled when it passes over cold water pipes. The warm and cold air is mixed to produce the required temperature and a fine spray of tiny water particles can be added if the air is too dry. ■

Something to do

Try this to prove that air really does have weight. Blow up two balloons. Get a stick or ruler about 50 cm (20 in) long and hang one balloon from each end using thread. Tie another piece of thread near the middle of the stick and position it so that when you hold this thread, the balloons balance and the stick is level. Now prick one balloon with a needle. Do this right next to the rubber knot so that the balloon leaks without popping. When the air has escaped and the balloons have settled, what has happened to the stick?

Aircraft

Aircraft is the name we use for flying machines. Most have wings to keep them in the air but helicopters and hot-air balloons are really aircraft as well.

During the 19th century, short gliding flights were made in craft built by Sir George Cayley in England and Otto Lilienthal in Germany. However, it was not until 1903 that powered flight was achieved by the Wright brothers in the USA. In 1909, Louis Blériot flew across the English Channel. Ten years later, Alcock and Brown made the first non-stop flight across the Atlantic.

Passenger flying developed after World War I. During the 1920s, passengers often flew aboard mail planes, sometimes with the mailbags on their laps! By the late 1930s, flying was a much more luxurious affair. People could travel between Europe and the Far East aboard large flying boats which took off and landed on water.

The first jet aircraft, the Heinkel HE178, flew in 1939. However, jets were mainly developed after World War II. The first jet airliner, the De Havilland Comet, entered service in 1952. Today, nearly all long-distance international travel is by jet.

▲ The Handley Page HP42 entered service with Britain's Imperial Airways in 1931. It could carry up to 38 passengers. Safe and reliable, it had a maximum speed which was less than the take-off speed of a modern jet.

▲ The *Wright Flyer* makes the first-ever powered flight in 1903. Orville Wright is at the controls. His brother Wilbur is running alongside. The flight lasted just 12 seconds.

▼ In 1927, Charles Lindbergh flew solo from New York to Paris in this Ryan monoplane. The flight took 33½ hours. Lindbergh used a periscope to see over the huge fuel tank in front of his cabin.

◀ The first international passenger service, from London to Paris, was started in 1919. Early passenger aircraft were often adapted bombers from World War I.

▼ The Boeing 747 'jumbo jet' was the first of the wide-bodied jets. Latest 'stretched' versions can carry over 600 passengers and fly a third of the way round the world non-stop.

◀ A Concorde prototype makes its first flight at Bristol, England, in 1969. Concorde was the first supersonic (faster-than-sound) airliner to enter service. It can carry up to 144 passengers at twice the speed of sound and can cross the Atlantic in 3 hours.

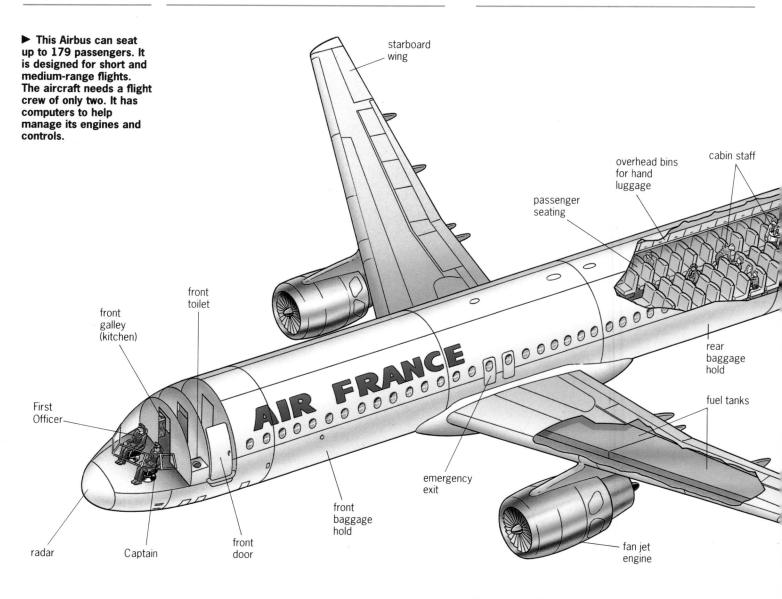

► This Airbus can seat up to 179 passengers. It is designed for short and medium-range flights. The aircraft needs a flight crew of only two. It has computers to help manage its engines and controls.

starboard wing

overhead bins for hand luggage

cabin staff

passenger seating

front toilet

front galley (kitchen)

rear baggage hold

First Officer

fuel tanks

AIR FRANCE

radar

Captain

front door

front baggage hold

emergency exit

fan jet engine

Shapes

Most aircraft have a central body called a fuselage, with wings near the middle and a smaller tailplane and fin at the back. Straight wings work best for carrying heavy loads at low speed, but swept-back wings give a better airflow for fast flying. Some military jets, such as the Panavia Tornado, have 'swing wings' which swing further back for high-speed flight. Some aircraft do not have a tailplane. Instead, the wings form a triangular shape, called a delta, which goes all the way to the back. Concorde is like this. Delta wings are good for high-speed flight but do not perform well at low speed. When Concorde lands, its wings are set at such a steep angle that the nose has to be lowered to give the pilot a forward view. A few aircraft have their wings at the back and their 'tailplane' at the front. This is called a canard arrangement.

Construction

Aircraft normally have a frame made from a light alloy such as duralumin. This frame is covered with a skin of light metal which acts as a shell and makes the fuselage very strong, like a tube. The wings are built in a similar way. Building aircraft with a rigid shell is called monocoque construction. Before it was developed in the 1920s, aircraft had wood or metal frames covered in fabric and braced by wires.

Power

Most modern aircraft use jet engines in one form or another. Even where a propeller is fitted, the power may come from a turboprop engine which is based on the jet. Until the 1950s, most aircraft had propellers turned by piston engines. Some small aircraft still do. These engines work in the same basic way as a motor car engine.

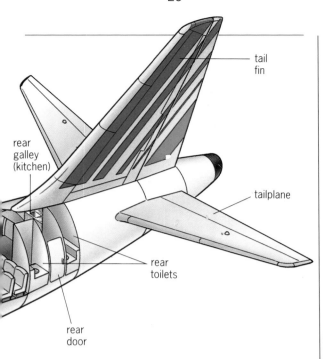

tail
fin

rear
galley
(kitchen)

tailplane

rear
toilets

rear
door

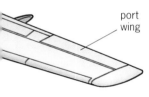

port
wing

The changing face of design

Concorde was designed in the 1960s. Nowadays, airlines are more interested in economy than speed, and other airliners travel at less than half Concorde's speed. Using computers, designers have developed wings which slip more easily through the air, and engines which are quieter and burn their fuel more efficiently. A 'jumbo jet' can carry four times as many passengers as Concorde using only the same amount of fuel.

Computers are an important part of a modern airliner. The autopilot is a computer which can navigate and fly the aircraft for most of its journey. On some aircraft, the pilot does not directly control the plane. Instead, the pilot's controls send instructions to a computer and the computer works out the best way to fly the plane. This system is known as fly-by-wire. ■

Air forces

Military aircraft are used in both defence and attack in time of war, to bomb enemy soldiers or warships, to carry troops and supplies into battle, to destroy attacking enemy bombers, and for reconnaissance (looking to see what the enemy is doing). In addition, aircraft can attack a country's industries, roads and railways, and so make it less able to wage war. In some countries aircraft form a part of army and naval equipment. In others, including Britain and the USA, there is a separate air force.

The two biggest air forces in the world are that of the United States of America and that of the Soviet Union. In the late 1980s each had about half a million men and 5,000 aircraft. But most of the men and women never actually fly. A large proportion of an air force's personnel is needed to put the aircraft in the air.

Air forces use many different kinds of aircraft. Bombers are designed to fly long distances and to carry heavy bomb-loads. They also launch guided missiles, but these have been increasingly replaced by intercontinental rockets. Fighters are small, very fast planes designed to intercept and shoot down enemy bombers, and to fire at targets on the ground or at sea. Reconnaissance planes are very fast. They carry cameras, radar and other devices to detect enemy defence systems. Transport planes are the largest of all. They are built to ferry troops and supplies to wherever they are needed. ■

▲ These Harrier jets are flying fast but they can slow right down and hover.

The air force of the USA consists of: US Command, Air Force Europe, Pacific Air Forces, Alaska Air Command, Caribbean Air Command.

The world's oldest air force is Britain's Royal Air Force, founded in 1918.

Officers of the Royal Air Force (equivalent army ranks in brackets)

Pilot Officer (2nd Lieut.)
Flying Officer (Lieut.)
Flight Lieutenant (Captain)
Squadron Leader (Major)
Wing Commander (Lieut.-Col.)
Group Captain (Colonel)
Air Commodore (Brigadier)
Air Vice-Marshal (Major-General)
Air Marshal (Lieut.-General)
Air Chief Marshal (General)
Marshal of the Royal Air Force (Field Marshal)

See also
Aircraft
Bombs
Helicopters

Airports

If you have flown abroad on holiday, or been to meet friends from a plane, you will have been to an international airport. These airports are bustling noisy places with a huge area for aeroplanes to take off or land. Many airport buildings are open 24 hours a day, providing service for aeroplanes landing day and night, and for passengers arriving, waiting for planes, or departing.

Passengers

Most airports have good train and bus services to bring in or carry away passengers. Other travellers going to catch a plane may drive, and park in vast car parks, and travel to other parts of the airport on buses. Some airports, such as Los Angeles, California, USA, have people movers – giant conveyor belts to carry passengers to other airport buildings, or to a departure gate where they board the aircraft. Even so, because airports are so vast, most passengers still have to do a lot of walking. Airports usually provide trolleys for passengers' baggage.

Passengers waiting for a plane can shop, use a bank, or have a meal at most airports. There are usually huge areas of seats where passengers, or people meeting them, can wait.

▲ Passengers show their ticket at the check-in desk, where the clerk gives them a boarding card and takes their baggage.

▼ At the end of the journey, passengers collect their baggage from a conveyor belt before going through customs.

▼ Phoenix International Airport in Arizona. Passengers have walked from the departure lounge to their plane. The tall building in the background is the control tower.

▶ Special containers full of cargo, being loaded on to a Boeing 747 at Changi airport, Singapore.

▲ Air traffic controllers in the airport control tower direct planes taking off and landing, and control their movement on the ground.

Cargo

A large part of the work of an airport is handling increasing amounts of goods flown to foreign markets as air freight. Warehouses store goods to be loaded into aircraft. Bonded warehouses hold arriving goods for inspection by customs officers. Duty-free airports, such as Shannon in the Irish Republic, assemble products from goods air freighted in, and then fly the finished products out again to foreign markets. Some freight is flown in special holds in passenger aircraft. Most air freight travels in specially designed aircraft with an almost empty fuselage and huge doors for loading freight containers.

Airport staff

Thousands of people work at an international airport, though not many of them are seen by the travelling public. Jobs related directly to aeroplanes include cleaning, refuelling, maintaining, and moving aircraft; loading them with freight and baggage; and preparing and packing food and other items needed to serve passengers in flight. Jobs relating to passengers include providing all the goods and services needed while people wait for planes, plus many specialist services peculiar to airports. These include immigration and passport control, customs, emergency services such as firefighters and medical staff in case of an accident, and security. Because of terrorist attacks on airports and planes, security has become especially important since the 1960s. Security staff at airports search passengers and other staff, and open or X-ray all baggage, watching out for bombs, guns, and other weapons.

Types of airport

Problems such as noise, and needing room for expansion, mean that most major airports are located away from city centres. Generally only small feeder or short-haul airports are in cities, serving helicopters or quieter STOL (short take-off and landing) aircraft, like the airport in London's dockland.

Hong Kong airport is unusual, because lack of space has led to the international airport being built, near the city centre, on land reclaimed from the sea. The world's busiest airport, in terms of international flights and passengers, is London Heathrow, which has more than half a million passengers arriving or departing each week. ■

Largest airport
King Khalid International, Saudi Arabia
221 sq km (85 sq miles)

Longest runway
Pierre van Ryneveld, South Africa 4.89 km (3.04 miles)

Busiest airports
Chicago International Airport, Illinois, USA: over 56 million passengers a year

Hartsfield Atlanta, Georgia, USA: over 50 million passengers a year

Heathrow Airport, London, UK: over 38 million passengers a year

▲ The pilot lands the plane with the help of the ILS (Instrument Landing System). The aircraft descent is controlled using signals from the ground. This means that planes can fly at night and in bad weather.

◄ Aerial photograph of Schiphol Airport, near Amsterdam in The Netherlands.

◄ All airports have special firefighting equipment in case of accidents.

See also

Aircraft   Radar
Flight   Transport

Alaska

Population
About 521,000
Highest mountain
Mount McKinley 6,194 m
Capital
Juneau

Alaska is the largest state of the USA but it is the most sparsely populated. The northernmost parts lie within the Arctic Circle; there is light 24 hours a day in midsummer and darkness at midday in winter. The capital, Juneau, is further south and therefore warmer than the other major, and larger, towns, Anchorage and Fairbanks. Mount McKinley, North America's highest mountain, is in Alaska. There are many active volcanoes and the state has suffered several bad earthquakes. To the west across the Bering Strait is the USSR, at the narrowest point only 82 km (51 miles) distant.

Alaska was bought from Russia in 1867 for about 7 million dollars or two cents an acre. Soon after the USA bought it, gold was discovered. Alaska is also rich in oil, natural gas and other valuable minerals. It became a full state of the USA in 1959. ■

See also
Arctic Ocean
Glaciers
United States of America

Albania

Area
28,748 sq km
(11,101 sq miles)
Capital Tirana
Population 3,080,000
Language Albanian
Religion Muslim
Government Republic
Currency
1 lek = 100 qintars

Albania is a tiny, mountainous country in Europe sandwiched between Yugoslavia and Greece. The mountains, many of them over 2,000 m (6,500 ft) high, form an almost complete defensive wall around the country's land borders. Near the coast, the climate is warm enough to grow palm trees, oranges and lemons. Further east, as the land rises, it is rather colder. Albania is a poor country.

The communist government has allowed very little contact between Albania and the rest of the world.

Albania won its independence from the Turkish Ottoman empire in 1912. In 1939 it was occupied by Italy, but after World War II the Albanian Communist Party took control of the country. In 1946 they declared Albania to be a People's Socialist Republic. ■

See also
Communists
Europe
Muslims
Ottoman empire

Albinos

Albino animals and people have white hair, and their skin and eyes are pink. This is because they lack a substance called melanin which normally gives colour to skin, eyes and hair. Albinos' skin and eyes are pink because of red blood vessels near the surface. When hair and skin contains a lot of melanin, it is black. When there is little, it is brown. When there is very little, it is fair.

Albinos inherit this appearance from their parents and there is no cure. As melanin in skin normally cuts out the harmful rays in sunlight, albinos are prone to severe sunburn. ■

◀ This albino rabbit is almost certainly a pet. Albino animals are very rarely found in the wild, as they are easy to see and so get hunted down quickly.

See also
Hair
Skin

Alchemists

For hundreds of years alchemists tried to find a substance that could change the cheap metal lead into gold. They also searched for a magic potion, the 'Elixir of Life', that would make people live for ever. Arabs gave the name alchemy to this subject, which began thousands of years ago in Egypt and China. In the 12th century, people in Europe learnt about alchemy from translations of old Arabic writings.

Nowadays, it is possible to make very tiny amounts of some rare metals in a nuclear reactor, but it is much more expensive than buying the natural metals.

Work in alchemy helped form the subject we now call chemistry. ■

The great Sir Isaac Newton was fascinated by alchemy and spent many months trying to produce the magic 'elixir' which could turn ordinary metals into gold.

Queen Elizabeth I imprisoned in the Tower of London an alchemist who failed to make the gold he promised.

See also
Chemists
Gold
Metals

Alcohol

Alcohol comes from the Arabic words *al kuhl* meaning 'the kohl', a kind of powder used as eye-shadow. In English it first meant a powder made by heating; later it came to mean alcohol, which is made in the same sort of way by distilling.

There are many different kinds of alcohol. They are clear, colourless liquids. They all burn easily and evaporate quickly. The best-known is ethanol. It is the chemical that makes drinks 'alcoholic' and is so common that it is often just called 'alcohol'. A mixture of ethanol with another alcohol called methanol is sold as 'methylated spirits'. Because methanol is very poisonous, a dye and a nasty taste are added to stop people from drinking it.

Uses

Alcohols dissolve many things that will not dissolve in water, and are used as a solvent in paints, glues, printing inks, perfumes and aftershaves. Solvents are important in cleaning, and alcohols are used as a safe cleaner in making and maintaining electrical goods such as computers. In homes, alcohols are often used for cleaning paintbrushes. Alcohols are also ingredients in making other important chemicals such as detergents and plastics. The liquid used as an antifreeze in cars, ethylene glycol, is an alcohol.

Some countries, such as Brazil, are short of oil from which to make petrol and so they use alcohol, made from plants like sugar cane or maize, as a cheap ingredient of petrol.

Alcoholic drinks

Ethanol is a very simple carbohydrate, with two carbon and two oxygen atoms and six hydrogen atoms in each molecule. Methanol is even simpler, with one carbon, two oxygen and four hydrogen atoms.

The ethanol in alcoholic drinks is made from parts of plants by a process called fermentation. Yeast gradually turns sugar into ethanol. Drinks such as beer and lager are made using barley malt. Things like hops or oatmeal are added to give flavour. Beer and lager contain very little alcohol.

Drinks such as wine and cider are made from juice squeezed from fruit; wine is made from grapes, cider from apples. About one-tenth of these drinks is alcohol, and most of the rest is water. Spirits, such as brandy, gin, whisky, or vodka, are made by distilling a liquid such as wine. The liquid is boiled, and most of the alcohol evaporates first, and moves away. In a condenser it is cooled and becomes liquid again as almost pure alcohol. This alcohol is mixed with some of the original liquid to give it flavour, and to dilute it. Less than half of a spirit is alcohol.

Drinking laws

Alcohol is a drug that has a powerful effect on the human body. It changes people's behaviour, and can lead to aggressive or anti-social actions. In most countries, laws limit the use of alcohol, to prevent the effects of over-use. For example, shops may be prevented from selling alcohol without a licence, and children are generally banned from buying alcohol or drinking it in public. The religion of Islam (Muslims) bans anyone from drinking alcohol, and it is completely illegal in Saudi Arabia and other states ruled in accordance with Islamic law. ■

See also
Alcoholics
Beer
Fuel
Wine

Alcoholics

Alcoholics are people who have got so used to drinking beer, wine or spirits that they cannot do without alcohol. Alcoholics are addicted and need to drink alcohol constantly. Without it they feel anxious and ill and cannot face life's everyday problems. Often people who are alcoholics try to hide their habit of drinking too much.

Drinking too much alcohol regularly damages the liver and kidneys and can harm the brain. Alcoholism changes people's behaviour which can be very distressing for their families. It is an expensive habit and so alcoholics may get into debt and cause further difficulties for their families. When alcoholics are determined to stop drinking they can do it but they usually need help to overcome their addiction. Doctors and special organizations like Alcoholics Anonymous can help both alcoholics and their families. ■

See also
Addiction

Algae

Algae are the simplest plants. Nearly all grow in water and the best-known are seaweeds. Some grow in moist places on land, like the green scum on damp ground and the powdery green layer on the bark of some trees. Some live inside corals and other water animals, and others live with fungi to form a group called lichens. Algae vary in size from microscopic plants which have only one cell to giant sea kelps, brown seaweeds which can grow up to 45 m (150 ft) long.

Algae are divided into groups by colour. Blue-green algae can be microscopic or occur in clumps or long threads. They can live in freezing Antarctic lakes, near boiling hot springs and even on bare rock. Green algae live mainly in fresh water and include blanket weed, which can cover ponds and streams which are polluted with fertilizer washed out of the soil by rain. Brown and red algae include the seaweeds found on most rocky shores.

Microscopic algae form part of the sea's plankton, the beginning of a food chain which keeps most sea creatures alive. Plankton is eaten by tiny sea animals which are then eaten by a chain of other animals including fish, whales, sea birds and humans. ■

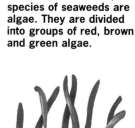

▼ Almost all of the 7,000 species of seaweeds are algae. They are divided into groups of red, brown and green algae.

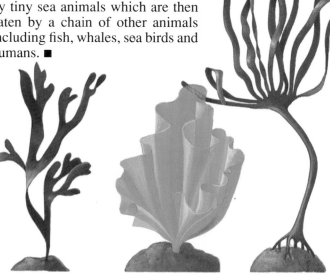

See also

Food chains and webs
Lichens
Plankton
Seaweeds

Algebra

Think of a number. Double it. Add six. Divide that number by two and then take away the number you first thought of. You will be left with three. Always! Does it matter which number you choose to begin with? How can you be certain? Let's try a couple of examples:

Your number	times 2	add 6	divide by 2	subtract your number
5	10	16	8	3
7	14	20	10	3
16	32	38	19	3

We could go on with dozens more examples, to try to prove that the answer always comes to 3. But mathematicians have a different way of going about solving a problem like this. They might write this table as an equation:

number x 2 + 6 ÷ 2 − **number** = 3

using the word **number** to show 'the number you first thought of'. Generally, though, this gets a bit long-winded and they prefer to write just a single letter, such as 'n' or 'x' to mean 'unknown'.

Using words (or letters) to represent numbers whose values are not known, enables mathematicians to prove whether or not results like this are always true, no matter what number you choose to begin with.

The answer to the equation is always 3, because **number** is first doubled, then added, then halved again, and finally taken away. In other words, exactly what is 'put in' is later 'taken out' again. The answer of 3 has nothing to do with the 'number you first thought of' at all. It is simply the '6' you added, and later divided by '2'.

Algebra often involves the use and rearranging of equations. These are just a compact way of writing down how one thing relates to another. ■

Divide 100 loaves among 10 men including a boatman, a foreman and a doorkeeper, who receive double portions. What is the share of each?

This problem comes from ancient Egypt. It is on the Rhind Papyrus, written in about 1650 BC and now in the British Museum. It can be solved using algebra.

An unknown Egyptian, writing about algebra nearly 4,000 years ago, used the word *hau* (a heap) where we might use the letter x for the unknown amount.

We get the word algebra from the Arabic word *al-jabr*, meaning 'bone-setting', in the sense of 'binding the broken bones together again'. It was used in the title of a book by Muhammad ben Musa about 1,200 years ago, meaning 'putting together' the parts of an equation.

See also

Arithmetic
Equations
Mathematics

Algeria

Algeria is one of the Arab countries in North Africa. It is very big. If you imagine the size of Britain, Algeria is the size of ten Britains put together. But you could travel around much of it without seeing another person. You would have to be careful, though, not to get lost because most of Algeria is desert, where there are no roads or towns.

The country stretches from the Mediterranean Sea in the north to the middle of the Sahara Desert in the south. Nearly all Algerians live close to the sea because this is where the soil is good for growing food. In the winter this northern area can be chilly and rainy. But in the summer the country is extremely hot and dry. About 200 km (124 miles) from the coast the vast Sahara Desert begins. Here temperatures are high all the year and rain is scarce. Nothing much grows in the desert, but there is a wealth of oil and natural gas below it. Algeria earns most of its money from selling oil and gas.

Algiers, the capital, is also a busy port, and is built on hills overlooking a bay. In some of the older winding streets you can see buildings with blue wooden shutters and small balconies similar to houses in the south of France. But on the skyline you can see the minarets of mosques, for Algeria is a Muslim country.

Many Algerians, boys and girls as well as men and women, wear the traditional loose-fitting robe, called *jallaba*. The favourite food in Algeria is *couscous*, made of steamed grains of wheat, with sauces added.

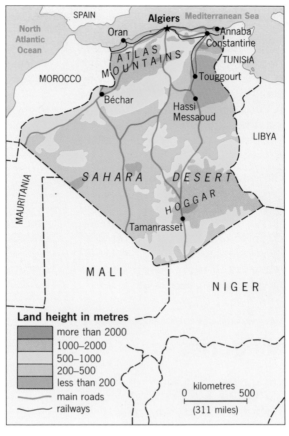

Area
2,381,741 sq km
(919,595 sq miles)
Capital
Algiers
Population
22,971,500
Language
Arabic, Berber, French
Religion
Muslim, Christian
Government
Republic
Currency
1 dinar = 100 centimes

Land height in metres
more than 2000
1000–2000
500–1000
200–500
less than 200
— main roads
— railways

kilometres
0   500
(311 miles)

◀ Inhospitable mountains rise above their desert surroundings near Tamanrasset in Algeria.

Flashback

Algeria became an independent Arab state in 1962. But for 90 years before that it was considered by the French, who had conquered it, as a district of France. Many French families had settled in Algeria.

Algerians fought a long and costly war for their independence and more than one million people died in the fighting. After independence most French settlers left, but the strong influence of France on Algerian life remained. Many Algerians speak French as well as Arabic, and tens of thousands of them have travelled to France in search of jobs. ■

◀ A palm-tree grove provides a welcome contrast to the desert sands at the oasis at El Golea in Algeria.

⊙ See also
Africa
Arabs
Mediterranean
Muslims
Sahara

Alkalis

Alkalis are chemicals which feel soapy. They can be strong enough to burn your skin, just like strong acids. But if you mix an alkali and an acid together in the right quantities the substance they make is neutral; it is neither acid nor alkali and will not burn.

The word alkali is Arabic for ashes. Long ago people burned plants and used the ashes in making soap and glass. The ashes contained the alkalis soda and potash. The modern chemical industry, which began 200 years ago, was based on the manufacture of alkalis. ■

See also
Acids
Chemicals

Allergies

Your body has defences to protect it against invading germs. Unfortunately, sometimes the defences react violently to harmless things that get into the body. When your body over-reacts in this way to dust in your house, grass pollen in the air, the long hair of a cat or something similar, you are allergic to those things.

Allergies like these mean that when you come into contact with dust, pollen or hair you become unwell. You might have a runny nose, sore eyes, a rash on the skin or find it difficult to breathe. ■

See also
Asthma
Eczema
Hay fever

Allegories

An allegory is a story or picture that can be enjoyed for itself but which has a deeper meaning if we look for it.

George Orwell wrote a novel called *Animal Farm* in 1945. It tells of a lazy, cruel farmer, Mr Jones. His animals dream of a better world in which all animals will be equal. One day they rebel and drive the humans off the farm. At first all goes well, but gradually the pigs take over and give the orders. At the end, everything is just as bad as it was at the beginning.

▼ The medieval legend of the hunting of the unicorn is an allegory of the crucifixion and resurrection of Christ. The innocent unicorn is captured and killed, but miraculously comes back to life. This scene from a 16th-century tapestry shows the unicorn's cruel death.

Animal Farm is not just a good story; it is an allegory. The farm represents Russia and Mr Jones is the tsar (emperor). The rebellion of the animals is the Russian Revolution of 1917 and the head pig is Stalin. As leader of the Soviet Union, he inflicted great suffering on the Russian people during the 1930s. Orwell wanted to warn people of Stalin's cruelties, but many would not listen to direct criticism since Stalin was an ally in the war against Hitler. *Animal Farm* is a book we can still appreciate today because it is an allegory about how a powerful leader can become cruel.

Allegories often have religious meanings. *The Pilgrim's Progress* by John Bunyan is an allegory of a Christian journey through life. In *The Lion, the Witch and the Wardrobe* the author, C. S. Lewis, retells the Christian message. Narnia has fallen under the spell of the White Witch. By his willingness to die, Aslan the lion breaks the witch's power, just as Christ's death, Christians believe, breaks the power of the devil over people. Aslan comes back to life and this is an allegory for the Christian belief that Christ rose from the dead. ■

See also
Biography
Bunyan
Lewis
Orwell

Alligators

Alligators and their close relatives the caymans are short-snouted members of the crocodile family. True alligators seem to be able to survive in colder conditions than their relatives. They live further north and may hibernate during the winter. The Chinese alligator spends much time in a burrow dug into a river bank where its eggs are laid.

We know more about the American alligator than other alligators, as it is one of the most intensively studied of all reptiles. But probably other species of alligators live and develop in much the same way. The skin of alligators and caymans makes valuable leather, and many have been destroyed because of this. In some cases the disappearance of the alligators has led to ecological disaster, as the insects, rodents and fish that were the alligator's food have increased in number and become pests. ■

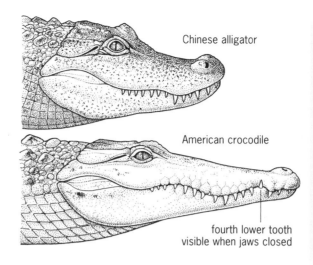
Chinese alligator

American crocodile

fourth lower tooth visible when jaws closed

▲ **Alligators have shorter, blunter snouts than crocodiles. When a crocodile's mouth is closed, the large tooth fourth from the centre on** the lower jaw still shows near the front of the mouth and fits into a notch in the upper jaw. No lower teeth can be seen when an alligator shuts its mouth.

Distribution
American alligator is found in the warm parts of South America and as far north as Carolina in the USA. Chinese alligator lives by the lower Chang Jiang (Yangtze) river. Caymans live in tropical America.

Largest about 5·8 m
Number of eggs 25–55
Lifespan
56 years in captivity

Subphylum
Vertebrata
Class Reptilia
Order Crocodilia
Number of species
Alligators 2, caymans 4

The American alligator is likely to be seen by visitors to the Florida Everglades. At one time it was very rare, but because of conservation its numbers have now increased.

◄ **Alligators swim by moving their long, powerful tails from side to side.**

See also
Crocodiles
Reptiles

Alloys

Most pure metals are weak and soft. But if other substances are added to them, the mixture, which is known as an alloy, may be very different.

Bronze, the first alloy

Alloys have been made for thousands of years. Copper was the first pure metal to be worked. Because it is soft, copper knives and other tools had poor cutting edges. Before 4000 BC, people in Mesopotamia had discovered that by adding tin to molten copper they could make a much harder metal. It did not rust or corrode, but still melted at a low temperature. The alloy, which we now call bronze, was made into bowls, cups and cooking utensils, axe-heads and arrowheads.

Today bronze is still used for statues, ornaments and church bells.

Brass is an alloy of copper and zinc, and the alloy of copper and nickel is known as cupro-nickel. It is used to make most coins. Iron has been used since about 2000 BC and it remains one of the most important metals. It can be converted into the tough metal we call 'steel' by taking out some of the carbon that makes cast iron very brittle. If chromium is added we have 'stainless' steel, an alloy that does not rust. Many other alloys have been produced in recent years for the car and aircraft industries and for space research. Duralumin, for example, is an alloy of aluminium and copper. It is light and strong, and is used to make aircraft bodies. ■

In China and Thailand bronze objects were made before 2700 BC.

See also
Copper
Iron and steel
Metals
Prehistoric people

Alphabets

About 50 different alphabets are used in the world today.

Most alphabets have between 20 and 30 letters in them, but the Sinhalese alphabet (Sri Lanka) has more than 50 letters.

Not everyone uses alphabets for their languages. The Chinese do not write down the sounds of their words. They draw out in shapes the whole ideas of their words. These 'idea shapes' are called ideograms. The Japanese use a combination of these ideograms with symbols for sounds.

See also

Anglo-Saxons (runes)
Calligraphy
Languages
Writing systems

To write down what we say (our language) we use an alphabet. The word itself is made up from the first two letters of the ancient Greek alphabet, pronounced alpha (= a) and beta (= b). We put letters together to form sounds. Try S and H. Then add AKE to the sound of S and H and you have a word. The alphabet for the English language has 26 letters beginning with A and B and ending in Z. But other alphabets have different numbers of letters.

The Roman alphabet

The alphabet we use today is the one the Romans used for writing their language, Latin. The ancient Roman alphabet had 23 letters. In England during the Middle Ages the letters J, U, and W were added. Although there were many different languages and dialects in the huge Roman empire, Latin was the official language. After the collapse of the Roman empire the Latin language survived in changed forms in many countries in Europe. In Britain, France, Italy, Spain, Portugal and other countries people still use the Roman alphabet to read and write their language. It is the most widely used alphabet in the world today.

Other alphabets

Below are some of the alphabets used today, apart from the Roman one. The letters in each alphabet have different shapes and there are different numbers of letters which make up the sounds and words of the languages.

Flashback

Some historians think that all the alphabets we use today came from one called the North Semitic alphabet. The first true alphabet was probably developed by the Canaanite people of the town of Ugarit on the coast of Syria in the 15th century BC. They used an alphabet of 32 letters.

The Phoenicians, who were descended from the Canaanites, developed an alphabet of 22 letters and spread it through the Mediterranean. It is from the Phoenicians that the Greek, Roman, Arabic and Hebrew alphabets developed.

The letter H came from the Phoenician letter for *heth*, meaning 'gate'.

The letter T came from the Phoenician letter for *taw*, meaning 'mark'. ■

► **The ancient Greek alphabet has 24 letters. People in Greece use it.**

► **The Cyrillic alphabet grew out of the Greek alphabet and is used today by people in the USSR, Bulgaria and parts of Yugoslavia.**

► **The Devanagari alphabet has 46 letters. It is the main alphabet of northern India and is used for writing Hindi and other Indian languages.**

► **The Hebrew alphabet is used by people in Israel and by Jews in other countries and has 22 letters. It is written and read from right to left across the page.**

► **The Arabic alphabet has 28 letters and is used by people all over the Arab world. It is written and read from right to left across the page.**

Alps

The Alps are a large range of mountains curving for 1,200 km (750 miles) from the Mediterranean Sea in south-east France north-eastwards into Austria. They are really several separate mountain ranges close together.

The mountains have steep slopes and jagged snow-capped peaks. In places there are huge limestone cliffs and canyons. The Alps began to be formed between 2,500,000 and 65 million years ago, as two parts of the Earth's surface squeezed together, pushing up the crust in between into great folds. This is still happening.

During the ice ages of the Quaternary Period, glaciers carved out deep U-shaped valleys. The heads of the valleys were cut back to form steep-sided peaks like the Matterhorn. Today permanent snowfields and glaciers still cover about 4,000 sq km (1,500 sq miles).

The weather is often moist and humid, but the outer mountains receive more rain than the inner ones. The temperature falls with altitude. Winters are longer and frosts more frequent. Deep valleys, overshadowed by the mountains, have a short growing season.

Settlement

Most villages are in the valleys, which also provide routes for roads and railways. There are many mountain passes linking the valleys and many tunnels have been cut. Alpine life centres around the farms, which are mainly for dairy cattle. In summer the cattle graze on the meadows, in winter they are brought back to the valley and fed on hay. Goats are kept for milk and cheese. Crops are grown in the sunnier valleys. Rivers are used for hydroelectric power.

Wildlife

No plants can grow on the bleak slopes of the highest mountains, but above the meadows is a zone of alpine plants, cushion-shaped and low-growing to escape the wind. Below the meadows are dark conifer woods and on the lower slopes broad-leaved woodlands of beech and birch.

Ibex, chamois and marmots live among the rocks. In winter the marmots hibernate. Mountain hares and ptarmigan (a kind of grouse) develop white winter coats for camouflage against enemies like golden eagles. The alpine meadows in summer are full of wild flowers, while the woods provide shelter for woodpeckers, squirrels and other animals.

Tourism

However, the skiing industry is causing problems for the environment. The scenery is being spoiled by ski-lifts and cable cars. Trees are felled to make new slopes, causing erosion and removing barriers to avalanches and mudslides. ■

◄ Alpine valley towns like this one in Austria profit from the tourist industry. But fewer people want to live in farming areas as there is more work available in the towns.

The Alps cover an area of over 80,000 sq km (30,000 sq miles). They include parts of France, Italy, Switzerland, Austria, Yugoslavia and Germany.

Highest mountain
Mont Blanc 4,807 m

Largest glacier
Aletsch Glacier in south-west Switzerland, covering over 130 sq km (50 sq miles)

3,500,000 cubic m of snow fell in an avalanche in the Italian Alps in 1885.

The greatest mountain climbing challenge in the Alps is the north face of the Eiger (Ogre). It was first climbed in 1938 by Austrian and German mountaineers.

See also
Austria
Avalanches
Glaciers
Hydroelectric power
Mountains
Plate tectonics
Skiing
Switzerland
Valleys

Aluminium

Aluminium is one of the lightest metals in everyday use. You are most likely to see it rolled out into thin sheets and used to wrap chocolate bars or made into cans for soft drinks. Other uses of aluminium include parts of cars, trains and ships as well as doors and windowframes.

Aluminium is a good conductor of heat, and originally its main use was for saucepans and other cooking utensils. Because aluminium conducts electricity easily, it is now often used

to make electric cables. Pure aluminium is not very strong, but it can be made much tougher by mixing it with other metals. These alloys are used in all kinds of machines from racing bicycles to aircraft.

Aluminium is the most abundant metal in the Earth's crust. It occurs in most kinds of rock, but is mainly extracted from the ore known as bauxite. Because aluminium never rusts, it is easy to recycle. It simply has to be melted and reused. ■

See also
Alloys
Metals

Amazon River

► Several rivers join together in the highlands of Peru to flow into the main Amazon River.

Length
6,440 km (4,000 miles)

The Amazon is about 240 km (150 miles) wide when it flows into the Atlantic. Every second, the river discharges an average of 120,000 cubic metres (160,000 cubic yards) of water into the Atlantic Ocean.
The river basin is the largest in the world, covering about 7,045,000 sq km (2,720,000 sq miles).

See also
Brazil
Forests
Rivers
South America

The Amazon River in South America contains more water than any other river in the world: about 25 per cent of all the water that runs off the Earth's surface.

The Amazon rises high up in the Andes Mountains in Peru, and is fed by about 15,000 tributaries and sub-tributaries on its way to the sea on the coast of Brazil.

The river contains over 2,000 different kinds of fish, including piranhas, catfish, electric eels and the giant arapaima. The nutrient-rich silt, deposited by the river, supports vast tropical forests which line its banks, home to millions of animals and plants. ■

Amazons

The Amazons lived in an area in what is now Turkey.

The legendary Greek hero Hercules was said to have killed the Amazon Queen Hippolyta.

Amazons were warrior-women in Greek myths. In the stories, they were so fierce that even the Sun was afraid and refused to visit them so their country was dark and icy. They broke the legs of all male babies, to cripple them; only females were allowed to grow up to become warriors. The Amazons cut off their right breasts to make it easier to throw spears and shoot with bows and arrows. They ate raw meat and drank mares' milk and fresh, warm blood.

To the ancient Greeks, Amazons existed only in stories. They were as unreal as monsters, giants or witches. But 2,000 years later, when the first European explorers landed in South America, they faced female and male warriors armed with arrows, spears and blowpipes. The warriors never fully showed themselves, vanishing into the forests before they could be caught. The Europeans thought that their enemies must be descendants of the ancient Amazons, so they called the area Amazonia, and its swirling waterway the River Amazon. ■

During the Trojan War, the Amazons fought on the side of Troy against the Greeks.

See also
Hercules
Trojan War

Ambulances

Ambulances are large vehicles used to carry people who are sick or hurt. Some are mainly used for carrying people who are infirm to and from hospital for treatment. Such ambulances often have a tailgate lift to enable people in wheelchairs to be loaded in.

Ambulances used for accidents and other emergencies are equipped to carry people on stretchers. These ambulances carry special life-saving equipment, such as oxygen and machines with which the ambulance crew can revive patients with heart attacks. Ambulances are fitted with sirens and flashing lights to warn other traffic to get out of the way when they are dealing with an emergency. Ambulance drivers on emergency work are allowed to break speed limits and other traffic controls. Ambulances are generally painted white, and carry special markings.

Ambulances used by the armed forces may be painted in camouflage colours. They can be identified by large red crosses on the sides and roof.

Air ambulances are aeroplanes and helicopters fitted out to carry patients. They are used in places such as the Australian outback where people live a long way from the nearest hospital, and in wartime to pick up casualties. ■

Cornwall was the first county in Britain to have an air ambulance service.

The first ambulances were wagons drawn by horses which carried wounded soldiers from the battlefield. The first flying ambulances were also used in wartime.

See also
Red Cross

American Civil War
1861–1865

The American Civil War divided the young American nation. It caused hundreds of thousands of deaths and a great deal of grief and hardship. It split friends and families. Fathers and sons and brothers fought on opposite sides. But it did also result in the ending of slavery in the United States.

The war lasted for four years, from April 1861 to April 1865. It began when some Southern states led by South Carolina seceded (withdrew) from the United States. They set up their own nation and called it the Confederate States of America.

Slavery was a major cause of the war. Before the war began there were 33 states in the United States. In the eighteen Northern states all the people, black and white, were free. But in the fifteen Southern states black people were slaves.

The parents and grandparents of the slaves had been brought across the Atlantic Ocean from Africa to work on farms. Some of the farms were very big and were known as plantations.

Lincoln's opposition

People in the South depended on their slaves to work on the plantations and wanted to extend slavery to new territories in the west. People in the North had factories as well as farms, but did not own slaves. Many Northerners felt that slavery was evil. In 1860 they helped to elect Abraham Lincoln as President of the United States. Southerners thought that he was a threat to their way of life and as a result, seven Southern states withdrew from the Union and formed the Confederacy. Four more states withdrew later.

Early battles

In July 1861 the Confederates won the first big battle of the Civil War. It took place near a small river in Virginia called Bull Run. The next year both sides won several battles, but both lost many men killed and wounded.

Early in 1863 the Southern armies, under their general Robert E. Lee, seemed to be winning the war. Lee invaded the Northern states with an army of 75,000 men. In July he met an army of 90,000 men at the little town of Gettysburg in Pennsylvania.

The two armies fought for three days. Lee lost 20,000 men killed or wounded. He had to retreat.

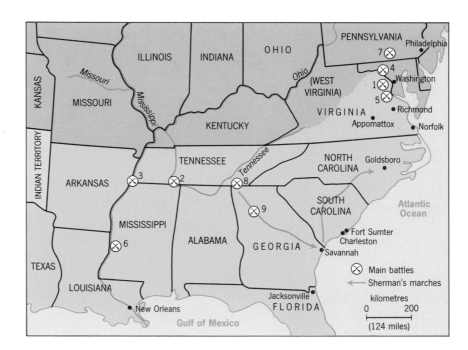

The battle was a turning point in the war. The Confederates no longer had the strength to attack the North. It was all they could do to defend their own territory.

The end of the war

As the war went on the Northern armies became stronger and the Southern armies became weaker. The Northern armies were led by two generals, Ulysses S. Grant and William T. Sherman. Grant attacked from the north, while Sherman marched in from the west.

Sherman's troops burned or destroyed everything in their path: crops, houses, factories and railways. This ruthless campaign made it impossible for the South to carry on the fight. Lee surrendered to Grant in the Court House of the little village of Appomattox, Virginia, on 9 April 1865. A few days later President Lincoln was assassinated in Washington, DC.

In time, all the Southern states rejoined the Union. But people in the South remained bitter for many years. ■

▲ This map shows which states were on the Union and Confederate sides in the American Civil War. The 11 Confederate states are coloured pink. These are the names of the main battles.

1 Bull Run
2 Shiloh
3 Memphis
4 Antietam
5 Fredericksburg
6 Vicksburg
7 Gettysburg
8 Chattanooga
9 Atlanta

Casualties
Altogether 529,332 soldiers from both sides died in the Civil War. That is more than the total number of Americans killed in World Wars I and II.

◀ A wounded soldier is given water. This and other photographs by Mathew Brady showed the reality of suffering in the war.

◉ See also

Battles | Biography
Slaves | Custer
USA: history | Grant
| Lee
| Lincoln

American colonial history

▶ Painting of a house built for a wealthy plantation owner next to the Mississippi River. The families who lived on these Southern estates enjoyed a very high standard of living. Black slaves worked as servants as well as in the cotton and sugar fields.

The first European colonists in North America were the Spaniards, who had already begun to explore the Caribbean and South America. During the 16th century Spaniards settled in Florida and other southern parts of what is now the United States.

At this time the French were establishing settlements in Canada and along the Mississippi River valley.

Almost 100 years later some English adventurers began settling along the eastern coast. Dutch and Swedish settlers also formed small colonies there.

The thirteen colonies

The first permanent English settlement was by 100 men at Jamestown, Virginia, in 1607. The Jamestown settlers were sent out by a company of London merchants. They had to hack clearings out of the forests, try to grow crops and build their own houses. Many died from starvation, disease and attacks by American Indians, who resented the 'white man' taking their land.

The company sent out more men and supplies, and later some 'young and handsome' girls as wives for the men. The settlement flourished after the women arrived. The Jamestown settlers made a living by growing tobacco for sale to Britain.

The second colony, Plymouth Colony which became part of Massachusetts, was established by a band of Puritan farmers and craftsmen and their families. They called themselves 'Pilgrims' because they were seeking a place where they could follow their religion without persecution. The Plymouth Colony flourished when Indian farmers taught them how to grow corn (maize).

North and South

The first settlers built their houses of wood, of which there was plenty. They made roofs of thatch, and later of shingles (thin sheets of hardwood). The first chimneys were of stone, but later the colonists made bricks.

Colonists in the North had to make most of their furniture and clothing. They spun thread, wove cloth, made candles from fat or beeswax, tanned leather and made their own shoes. Life was often hard. But they were free, and they had plenty of land to grow their crops.

The 13 colonies, with the dates they were founded

Connecticut	1633
Delaware (Swedish 1638)	
	British 1664
Georgia	1733
Maryland	1634
Massachusetts	1620
New Hampshire	1623
New Jersey (Dutch 1660)	
	British 1664
New York (Dutch 1624)	
	British 1664
North Carolina	1653
Pennsylvania	1643
Rhode Island	1636
South Carolina	1670
Virginia	1607

◑ See also

American Indians
American Revolution
Pilgrim Fathers
Puritans
Slaves
Spanish colonial history
USA: history

Biography
Penn

The wealthy colonists, from aristocratic English families, tended to settle in the South, where they had good farm land. They imported black Africans to work the land for them. At first the blacks, like many white servants, were indentured, bound to serve for a number of years.

But the Africans were regarded as inferior, and by 1660 blacks shipped over in appalling conditions were made to serve unpaid as long as they lived. Slavery had begun. The rich landowners created a new aristocracy. They lived in big mansions and bought fine furniture and clothes from England.

In the North the land was less good and the climate harsher. Although most people farmed, some turned to fishing, trade and industry. Many were Quakers, Puritans and other Protestants who led sober, hard-working lives.

A rich land

By 1760 the colonies were growing prosperous. Immigrants had flocked in, lured by the prospect of owning land and making a new life for

themselves. Most were from the British Isles, including a great many Scots and Irish. Others migrated from Germany, the Netherlands and France, escaping from poverty or religious and political persecution in Europe.

The Northern colonies, forming New England, were most like Britain. The Southern colonies contained huge estates, the plantations, where black slaves toiled in the heat of the Sun to grow cotton and tobacco.

Towns and cities grew up, but the majority of people still lived on the land. Stage coaches ran along well-kept dirt roads. A postal service was operating, and there were several newspapers. Schools were set up, although many children were taught at home. There were six colleges for men students. British laws applied in all the colonies, but each colony had a governor, and a legislature to pass local laws.

For many people, particularly new settlers and those in the outskirts of the colonies, life was as hard and primitive as ever. Yet this encouraged the spirit of sturdy independence which led in time to the American Revolution. ∎

American Constitution

The American Revolution ended in 1783 when the thirteen colonies became independent states. They soon found that they needed a federal (joint) government in order to work together. The states called a conference and its members decided to write a new constitution. The Constitution of the United States is one of the world's most important documents.

The three powers

Basically, the Constitution provides for three balanced powers: the legislature (Congress), which makes the laws; the executive (the President and his government departments), which carries out the laws; and the judiciary (the courts), which decides what the laws mean. It also ensures that power is divided between the federal government and the governments of the individual states.

Although the Constitution is now more than 200 years old, and has been amended several times, its basic principles still hold good.

Amendments

Twenty-six amendments to the Constitution have been approved so far, the latest in 1971. The first ten, known as the Bill of Rights, were agreed in 1791. They guarantee certain basic rights, such as freedom of speech. Other particularly important amendments were Amendment 13 (1865), which abolished slavery; Amendment 15 (1870), which guaranteed the rights of black Americans to vote; Amendment 19 (1920), which gave women the vote; and Amendment 26 (1971), which gave the vote to 18-year-olds. Amendment 18 (1919), the Prohibition Amendment, banned the sale of liquor; Amendment 21 (1933) repealed it. ∎

⊙ **See also**

American Revolution
USA: history

Biography
Jefferson

▼ The original document of the US Constitution is displayed in the National Archives Building in Washington, DC. It begins: 'We, the People of the United States, in order to form a more perfect union . . . do ordain and establish this Constitution for the United States of America.'

American Indians

► These Sioux Indians from the Fort Peck Reservation have jobs as firefighters in Yellowstone National Park, USA.

Indian is a name given to the original people of North and South America by European explorers who thought they had arrived in the East Indies. The people known as American Indians or Amerindians speak many different languages and have very different customs and ways of making a living. Before contact with Europeans, Indians had their own political systems and national boundaries. They depended on their environment for food and materials to make clothing, shelter, tools and transportation. Their religions taught respect for all of nature. Many Indian nations had no concept of ownership. No one owned land, but they respected the right of villages and families to farm certain fields and hunt in certain areas. Farmers asked forgiveness for cutting down trees to plant crops, and after a few years let the land return to forest. Hunters apologized for killing animals and killed only for food.

Central and South America

In the mountainous countries from Mexico south to Bolivia, Indians developed large empires. Efficient agriculture supported the city populations of the Mayan, Aztec and Inca empires. They had lengthy trade routes and large armies to control their people. Most of the people were peasant farmers who grew food for their own families, sold a small surplus at village markets and gave the rest to government officials.

After the Spanish conquest, life changed very little for the farmers. Roman Catholic missionaries converted them to Christianity but they kept their languages, dress and even most of their holidays. Today, many are moving to cities to make a better life. However, they earn low wages if they are able to find work, and live in shanty towns on steep slopes where no one else wants to live.

► A Yanomami woman and child in their home in the Amazon forest of Brazil.

Some Indian nations

South and Central America
Aztec
Chimu
Chichimec
Inca
Maya
Yanomami

Caribbean
Arawak
Carib

Diseases, carried by Europeans, had tragic effects on the Indians. In Europe, measles and smallpox were diseases suffered mainly by children. But in America they killed native people of all ages. So many Indians died that Europeans often mistook neglected lands for unused wilderness.

The Indian people of the tropical forests are also farmers. They grow cassava root and vegetables in small clearings in the forest. Their villages are small and scattered to give each family a large enough area to hunt for meat and gather plants for food and medicine. In the 1980s settlers from the coast of Brazil burnt down huge areas of the forest along the Amazon River to create large cattle farms. Some even killed the Indians so they could lay claim to their lands. The same thing happened in the Caribbean during the 16th and 17th centuries when the European plantation owners wanted to get rid of the Arawak and Carib peoples.

Forests of eastern North America

Before contact with Europeans, Indians grew maize, trapped small animals, fished and hunted deer. They travelled by canoe to trade. Some lived in villages where two families shared one long house.

At first, both Indians and Europeans benefited from contact. The Indians wanted to trade for iron pots and knives. They led the Europeans on their explorations and provided them with food. Every autumn, Americans celebrate Thanksgiving and remember the assistance given to the Pilgrim Fathers when the Indians brought maize, sweet potatoes, pumpkin, squash and wild turkey.

Beginning with George Washington, the first president of the United States, some government leaders questioned whether Indians and white people could live together. Many Indians were forced from their homelands and moved westwards during the 1830s. The Cherokee Indians called the route they followed 'The Trail of Tears'. Today, very few Indians live east of the Mississippi River.

◀ Totem pole displayed in Stanley Park, Vancouver, on the north-west coast of Canada.

▲ This photograph was taken in about 1900 in South Dakota, USA. The woman and her children are from the Blackfoot nation. The children are carried in a *travois*.

The Great Plains of central North America

The Indians of the grasslands followed the buffalo herds and lived in buffalo-hide tipis which could easily be moved. They wore eagle feathers in their hair and war bonnets for special occasions. The young men trained as skilful riders and proved their bravery by stealing horses, using stealth rather than bloodshed. When the buffalo were slaughtered by the new white settlers, their livelihood was destroyed. Indians were forced to live on reservations, land set aside for their use only. Few of the Plains Indians were farming people and most could not survive on the poor reservation lands. They received some assistance from the government, but not enough to provide a better way of life.

Western North America

Along the north-west coast many families lived together in large log houses. People such as the Haida of the Queen Charlotte Islands carved totem poles to tell their family history. They went to sea in dug-out canoes to hunt whales, and speared salmon in the rivers. Today, they live on isolated reserves and try to maintain their traditional life-style.

In the deserts, mountains and cold northern regions, many Indians have been successful in maintaining the old ways. These lands were not valued by the European settlers. The Navajo of New Mexico raise sheep on the largest reserve (65,000 sq km,

25,000 sq miles) in the USA. It is desert. Today the American and Canadian governments are making deals to use Indian lands for mines, roads and pipelines. Damage to the environment and increased contact with new technology make it difficult to maintain traditions.

In the past, small bands of Indians have been powerless against the governments of Canada and the USA. But today some Indians are using the law to negotiate better deals with the government. Others are using aggressive methods to enforce their land claims, causing such disruptions as roadblocks. Tribal governments on reservations are demanding the right to control their own schools.

At the same time Indians everywhere are learning their native languages and practising the skills of their ancestors. Native artists, authors and song writers are popularizing Indian ideas.

North American society is beginning to appreciate many of the Indian values. The Indians have always known that they are part of nature, not in control of it. Indian councils have always tried to represent all the people in a tribe. The Indians know that people keep to decisions if they are part of the deciding. ■

Some Indian nations

Eastern North America
Beothuk
Cherokee
Cree
Iroquois
Micmac

Central North America
Apache
Blackfoot
Cheyenne
Comanche
Pawnee
Sioux

Western North America
Haida
Hopi
Navajo (pronounced Navaho)
Nootka
Kwakiutl

See also

Aztecs
Canada's history
Caribbean history
Guatamala
Hiawatha
Honduras (photo)
Incas
Mexico
Peru

Biography
Atahualpa
Moctezuma
Pocahontas

American Revolution
1775–1783

British historians have called the Revolution the American War of Independence.

The reason the militia were waiting for the British soldiers at Lexington was that Paul Revere, a silversmith, had ridden through the night to warn them that the British were coming.

👁 **See also**
American colonial history
USA : history

Biography
Franklin, Benjamin
Jefferson
Revere
Washington, George

In the 18th century Britain ruled thirteen colonies along the eastern coast of North America. But although each of the colonies had its own local government, Britain made all the major decisions from the other side of the Atlantic Ocean. In particular, the British taxed the colonists to pay for their defence against the French, who also had colonies in North America. The colonists wanted to make their own decisions. They objected to being taxed when they were not represented in the British Parliament. Eventually they rebelled.

The start of the war

On the night of 18 April 1775, British troops went to seize a stock of arms held by the colonists at Concord, Massachusetts. They were met at Lexington, on the way there, by an armed militia (a colonial defence force). A shot was fired, and war began.

The colonists organized their militias into an army, under the command of an experienced soldier, General George Washington. The British won the first major battle, at Bunker Hill near Boston, Massachusetts, but suffered such heavy losses that they had to withdraw from Boston.

The years of struggle

For over a year the colonists struggled on. They then decided that they could never make peace with Britain, and so on 4 July 1776 all thirteen colonies declared themselves independent.

In the bitter cold winter of 1777–1778 the main American army under Washington nearly starved in its camp at Valley Forge, near Philadelphia. Meanwhile in the summer of 1777 a British army under General John Burgoyne began a major attack southward from Canada. He expected to be joined by other British troops. But he was surrounded by a larger American force under General Horatio Gates, and had to surrender at Saratoga.

The defeat led the British government to offer the rebels semi-independent status. But it also induced the French to join in the war on the side of the Americans. With French aid, the Americans had a better chance of winning the war.

The final campaigns

In 1779 Spain joined in the war on the American side, and in 1780 the Netherlands also joined in. The British had to fight a war on several fronts, especially at sea.

There were no more major campaigns in the North, because neither side was strong enough to mount them. In the Southern colonies, the British won victories at Charleston and Camden and seemed to be in a powerful position. Then the main British army was besieged at the port of Yorktown, in Virginia, by a larger American force on land and a French fleet at sea. On 19 October 1781, the British commander, Lord Cornwallis, surrendered.

This surrender convinced the British they could no longer win, and peace talks began in 1782. Peace was signed in Paris on 15 April 1783, giving the new United States of America their independence. ■

Battles won by British		Battles won by Americans	
Bunker Hill	1775 (2)	Princeton	1777 (4)
New York	1776 (3)	Bennington	1777 (5)
Brandywine	1777 (6)	Saratoga	1777 (7)
Charleston	1780 (8)	Kings Mountain	1780 (10)
Camden	1780 (9)	Yorktown	1781 (11)

Lexington (1) was not a battle.

American West

◀ Photograph of the gold-mining town of Goldhill, Nevada in 1868.

When the thirteen American colonies gained their independence in 1783, their western frontier ran along the Appalachian Mountains. Land stretching to the Mississippi River was thrown open to any citizens or new immigrants from Europe who wanted to settle it. The next century saw the western frontier pushed back to the Pacific.

Moving westwards

Westward movement was led by pioneers such as Daniel Boone, who opened up the Wilderness Trail through the Cumberland Gap, a pass through the Appalachians. Settlers poured through this and other passes, hacking out farms in the woodlands and building settlements and towns. By 1819 almost all the lands between the Appalachians and the Mississippi had been settled and formed into member states of the Union.

Meanwhile, when Jefferson was president, the United States had bought from France the Louisiana Territory, a huge area that doubled the size of the country. This was known as the Louisiana Purchase. Settlers used rowboats and rafts to cross the Mississippi into the new land, until the development of steamboats turned the river into a major highway. The next stage was the admission of Texas, a former Mexican territory, to the Union. This led to war with Mexico, which brought the USA all the land between Texas and California.

Gold and cattle

The discovery of gold in California in 1848 led to a huge rush of prospectors and settlers to the West. The following year the 'Forty-Niners' travelled from all over North America to make their fortune and tens of thousands more followed from all over the world.

Railways had been extending further and further in that direction. In 1869 the first line to the Pacific coast was completed. This greatly speeded up the progress of westward movement.

Ranchers began grazing huge herds of cattle on the open range of the Great Plains, and driving them to rail depots for shipment east. This was the period of the romantic 'Wild West', of cowboys and gun law. It lasted less than 20 years. By 1890 farmers had moved in and fenced the range, and the Wild West ceased to exist.

The pioneer spirit

The true pioneer spirit of the American West was not to be found in the tough, greedy gold prospectors. It lay in the hardy men and women who built their homes in the forest and plains, in spite of the hostility of the American Indians whose lands they took. These settlers drove westwards in covered wagons, or later by train, taking all their household goods with them, prepared to rough it to make a home and a living. Women and children played an equal part with men in settling the West. ■

For 18 months, beginning in 1860, daring riders galloped across the lonely trails from Missouri to California carrying letters. This service was the Pony Express, and it carried the US mail in just nine days, faster than the stage coaches could. It came to an end when the building of the telegraph meant that messages could be sent by wire within a few hours.

See also
American colonial history
American Indians
Cowboys
USA: history

Biography
Boone
Jackson, Andrew
Jefferson

Amnesty International

Amnesty means a pardon or forgiveness especially for political offences.

Amnesty International is a worldwide organization dedicated to fighting for the release of people whom it terms 'prisoners of conscience'. By this it means anyone who is imprisoned because of their political or religious beliefs, provided they have not been members of a terrorist group. Amnesty International also fights against the imposition of the death penalty, the use of torture, and abuses of basic human rights.

The organization was founded in 1961. It has its headquarters in London, but has sectional offices in many countries of the world. It depends on donations from ordinary people for its funds. ■

Amoebas

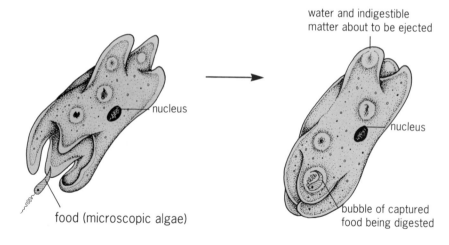

water and indigestible matter about to be ejected

nucleus

nucleus

food (microscopic algae)

bubble of captured food being digested

▲ An amoeba surrounds and traps its food in a bubble called a food vacuole. Digestive juices dissolve the food so it can be absorbed into the cell.

Phylum
Sarcomastigophora

An amoeba is a tiny animal made up of a single cell. Under a microscope it looks like a blob of jelly. It lives in watery places such as lakes and streams, the sea and wet soil.

The largest amoebas are half a millimetre across and can just be seen without a microscope. The smallest amoebas are one-hundredth of a millimetre across.

An amoeba constantly changes shape to move and feed. It feeds on bacteria, algae and other organisms smaller than itself. The amoeba traps the food and swallows it by changing shape. An amoeba can also move around its habitat by changing shape.

Amoebas are neither male nor female animals. This means that all amoebas can reproduce, and they do this simply by splitting in half. ■

 See also

Algae
Bacteria

Amphibians

Amphibians are animals with backbones and, usually, a soft, moist skin. Their name comes from two Greek words, and means 'two (both) ways of life'. This is because most amphibians start their lives in water and later change so they are able to live on land.

Life history

Most amphibians mate in the water, which is where the females lay their eggs. They may lay up to several thousand eggs each year. The eggs are not protected by a shell, but soon after they are laid the outside swells to make a jelly-like surround. The eggs hatch quite quickly, but the baby that emerges is unlike its parents. Instead it resembles a little fish, with a big head and a wriggly tail. This is a tadpole. At first the tadpole breathes with gills and feeds on minute plants that live in the water. As it grows its body changes. It loses its gills and grows lungs and legs, so that it can live on land. Its diet changes too. Adult amphibians eat flesh, feeding on many sorts of small animals. This change in body and way of life is called a metamorphosis.

How they breathe

Although adult amphibians are able to live on land, they must keep moist. Although they have lungs these are usually not very big, and so amphibians breathe through their skin as well. They can only do this if their skins are damp, so they rarely move far away from water.

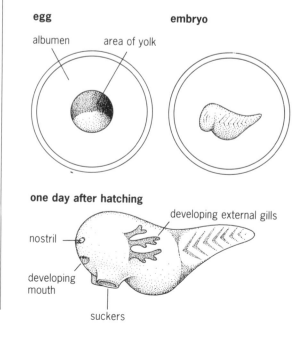

egg

embryo

albumen

area of yolk

one day after hatching

developing external gills

nostril

developing mouth

suckers

Cold-blooded

Amphibians are 'cold-blooded' animals. This means that their body temperature depends on the warmth of the air or water in which they are living. When the weather is cold they become very sluggish, and in the cooler parts of the world, such as Britain, they hibernate in the winter months. Most kinds of amphibians live in warm countries.

Kinds of amphibians

There are three main kinds of amphibians. **Blind worms** are strange creatures found only in the tropics. Although they have backbones, they have no legs and look very much like worms. **Newts** and **salamanders** look like lizards. Some kinds, such as axolotls, can remain in the tadpole stage for all of their lives and live entirely in water. **Frogs** and **toads** have no tails, but usually have very long hind legs, which they use for jumping. All amphibians are small animals. They defend themselves by hiding during the daytime and being active mainly at night. They are also protected by poison glands in the skin. These make them taste so nasty that hunting animals such as foxes usually leave them alone. ■

👁 **See also**

Frogs
Newts
Salamanders
Tadpoles
Toads

▲ Blind worms are unusual amphibians as only one species lives in water. All the others burrow underground and are rarely seen on the surface. Many do not even need water to breed.

Biggest amphibian
Japanese giant salamander, which grows to a length of 1·6 m
Smallest amphibian
One of the South American arrow poison frogs, which measures up to 1·3 cm

Subphylum Vertebrata
Class Amphibia
Number of species
167 species of blind worms
Over 300 species of newts and salamanders
2,600 species of frogs and toads

▶ This Kenyan leopard toad, like most toads, has very drab colouring making it difficult to see against its natural background.

◀ A frog hatches out as a tadpole, with gills for breathing and a tail for swimming. At first it uses yolk inside its body for food. Later it eats water plants, and finally it changes to a diet of small water animals.

three weeks old

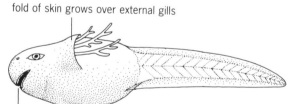

fold of skin grows over external gills

hard, rough lips

one month old

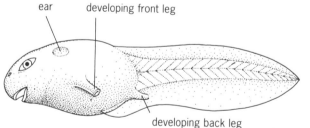

ear   developing front leg

developing back leg

two months old

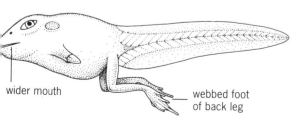

wider mouth   webbed foot of back leg

three months old

remains of tail

adult

Anaemia

Anaemia is a disease which can occur when there are not enough red blood cells in the blood. These cells hold a substance called haemoglobin which gives blood its red colour. Haemoglobin is a special iron-containing protein and its function is to carry oxygen around the body. The body's tissues need oxygen to function properly. If there are not enough red blood cells or enough haemoglobin, there will be a poor oxygen supply to the body. People with anaemia look pale, and feel tired and ill because they are suffering from oxygen starvation.

Anaemia can be caused by a lack of iron in the diet. A person who bleeds for a long time, or has a disease of the bone marrow, in which the new blood cells are made, can also suffer from anaemia. It can sometimes be inherited.

Some kinds of anaemia can be treated by eating foods such as liver or black treacle because they contain a lot of iron. There are also medicines that can supply the iron the body is lacking. ■

See also
Blood
Diets
Proteins

In ancient times people were anaesthetized by making them very drunk on wine or strong beer. The first true anaesthetics were ether, chloroform and nitrous oxide. They were introduced in the 1840s.

A doctor who specializes in giving anaesthetics is called an anaesthetist.

Anaesthetics

Anaesthetics are drugs that are used to stop pain while a doctor or dentist does something that would otherwise hurt.

Local anaesthetics are used to make only a small area of the body numb, so a tooth can be taken out or a stitch put in without causing pain. The patient stays awake during a local anaesthetic.

General anaesthetics are more powerful drugs that actually put a patient to sleep. Large operations can be carried out without the patient feeling any discomfort. Anaesthetics are given as gases which you breathe in, or liquids which are injected or sprayed onto the skin. ■

See also
Drugs
Operations
Surgeons

Anansi

Anansi was a trickster-god. He tricked everyone: other gods, human beings, animals, birds and insects. He could take any shape he liked, but he usually went about as a spider. That way, the creatures he was tricking never noticed him, or thought him harmless, until it was too late.

The Asante people of West Africa told the first stories about Anansi, and Africans who were taken as slaves to America and the Caribbean took the stories with them.

One of the best tells how the stories began. Anansi asked Nyankopon the sky-god to sell him a bag of stories, and the sky-god set what he thought was an impossible price: a hornet, a python, a leopard, a ghost and Anansi's own aged mother. But Anansi tricked his mother, a ghost, a leopard, a python and a nest of hornets into an old corn-sack and took them to Nyankopon. As soon as Nyankopon handed over the bag of stories, Anansi took them out one by one, changed the hero's name to Anansi and scattered them on the ground like seeds. However many Anansi stories people tell, hundreds more grow every day.

Stories about tricksters, like Anansi, are common in many countries. The trickster is a joker, a cunning fool and a prankster who does things that seem foolish but often turn out to be wise and clever. ■

Spider stories
Anansi means 'spider' in the Asante language. Among the Asante, it is said, these spider stories are only told at night, perhaps because they have power.
Before the story is told the teller may begin with something like:
'We do not really mean, we do not really mean that what we say is true.'
And then the teller will end the story by saying something like:
'This, my spider story, which I have told, if it is sweet, if it is not sweet, take some somewhere else and let some come back to me.'

English and Irish tricksters
Robin Goodfellow is the trickster of England. In Ireland he is to be found in the stories of Finn MacCool.

Other tricksters
The Winnebago Sioux, natives of North America, have a trickster called Hare. Brer Rabbit of the deep south of the USA is a trickster of a sort. In New Zealand the Maoris have Mauii.

See also
Brer Rabbit

Anatomy

Anatomy is the study of the ways in which the bodies of animals are built. During training, doctors use X-rays and dissection to study human anatomy.

This helps them to understand the positions of the muscles, heart, lungs, kidneys and all the other organs of the human body. ■

See also
Human body

Ancient world

Seven wonders of the ancient world
Pyramids of Egypt
Hanging gardens of Babylon
Temple of Artemis, Ephesus
Statue of Zeus, Olympia
Mausoleum of
 Halicarnassus
Colossus of Rhodes
Pharos (lighthouse) of
 Alexandria

Historians have dated Egyptian history from 3100 BC when the first king is recorded, but their civilization must have begun long before that.

When historians talk about the 'ancient world', they usually mean the great civilizations of Mesopotamia, Egypt, Greece and Rome.

People first discovered how to domesticate animals and crops in Mesopotamia and were building cities there by 3800 BC. It had the right climate for a settled farming existence in the rich valleys of its rivers. By 2300 BC another civilization was emerging along the River Indus in what is now Pakistan. Egyptian civilization developed along the fertile valley of the Nile.

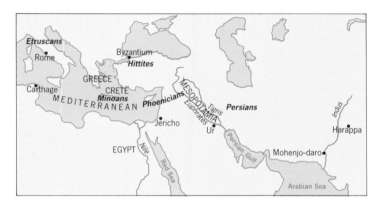

▲ The map shows some of the most important cities and people of the Mediterranean and west Asia.

European civilization developed around the shores of the Mediterranean Sea, first on Crete, where by about 2000 BC the Minoans were building cities and palaces; then by Phoenicians and other Semitic peoples in the east and Greeks to the north. Greek civilization flourished for hundreds of years. Gradually the Romans extended their power all around the Mediterranean, including Greece.

Chinese civilization began in the valleys of the Huang He (Yellow River) and Chang Jiang (Yangtze). The earliest evidence is from about 2000 BC but it may be much older.

In Central America and the Andes people had been cultivating crops, keeping animals and living in villages since about 5000 BC. The great civilizations of the Maya, Incas and Aztecs developed many centuries later. ■

See also

Aztecs
China's history
Egyptian ancient history
Etruscans
Greek ancient history
Hittites
Incas
Mesopotamia
Minoans
Phoenicians
Roman ancient history

Andes

The Andes are a large series of mountain ranges stretching 8,900 km (5,500 miles) down the whole west side of South America. There are many snow-capped peaks over 6,700 m (22,000 ft). In parts of the Andes, mountain ranges are separated by high plateaux, containing lakes such as Lake Titicaca. From the high, jagged peaks in the south, capped with permanent snowfields, glaciers push down to the Pacific Ocean. The formation of the Andes began about 80 million years ago and the mountains are still rising. There are many active volcanoes. The western slopes are desert or semi-desert in much of Peru and northern Chile, but forested further south. ■

▲ The Andes range of mountains is the second largest mountain system in the world. It was formed when the floor of the Pacific Ocean was thrust under the South American continental plate.

The Andes run through the countries of Venezuela, Colombia, Ecuador, Peru, Bolivia, Chile and Argentina.

Highest Andean peak
Mt Aconcagua in Argentina, 6,960 m

See also

Mountains
Plate tectonics
South America

Andorra

Andorra is a small state in the eastern Pyrenees, between France and Spain. Winters are cold and summers mild and sunny in the mountainous countryside where peaks reach heights up to 3,000 m (9,800 ft). Andorrans live in six valleys which are also very popular with tourists who come to ski in the winter. Most Andorrans are Roman Catholics and speak Catalan (the official language), Spanish and French. ■

Area
465 sq km (180 sq miles)
Capital
Andorra la Vella
Population
42,712
Language
Catalan, Spanish, French
Religion
Christian
Government
Self-governing French/Spanish co-principality
Currency
Spanish peseta and French franc

See also
Europe

Anglo-Saxons

Today we use this name to describe a number of different peoples from Germany and Scandinavia called Angles, Saxons and Jutes. Two other peoples, Franks and Frisians, came to live in what is now France, Holland and parts of Germany. The English language spoken today comes from the one the Anglo-Saxons spoke 1,500 years ago. These Anglo-Saxons were skilled craftspeople and traders.

▲ This coin shows the head of Offa, who was King of Mercia from 757 to 796. He built a great bank of earth 192 km (119 miles) long between his kingdom and Powys in Wales.

Moving to new lands

There were some Anglo-Saxons in Britain even while the Romans ruled the country. In the late 4th and early 5th centuries AD, Anglo-Saxon soldiers, with their families, were brought over as paid fighters to help defend the south and east coasts, against pirates and other Saxons.

By about AD 410 the last Roman troops had left Britain and local councils had to look after their own citizens. Although some people managed to live in a Roman way, many places began to change and become Anglo-Saxon, as more and more new settlers came from across the English Channel and the North Sea.

Towns and settlements

The Anglo-Saxon immigrants to Britain gradually began to take over more land and to build farms, villages and towns. In 200 years, from about 450 to 650, they moved further west in Britain and established kingdoms. Some of the names survive, like East Anglia, the kingdom of the East Angles. We can still recognize Anglo-Saxon names today. A *ford* is a river crossing: Bradford or Chelmsford, for example. *Ton* meant a farm or village. You will find a lot of place names ending in *-ton* on a map of England.

Archaeologists have discovered some Anglo-Saxon villages. One, called West Stow, has been completely excavated. People lived at West Stow from about 400 to about 650. They kept sheep, cattle and pigs. They also hunted deer and caught fish and wild birds to eat.

In 597 the Pope sent Augustine to convert the people of Britain to Christianity. Churches were built, most of wood but some of stone, and a few can still be seen today. By the 9th century towns, called *burhs*, were being built. These towns were protected by strong banks so that the townspeople and those who lived in the countryside around could take refuge. The Anglo-Saxons were by now threatened by new immigrants: the Vikings.

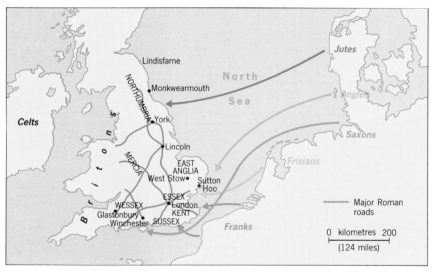

▲ The boundaries between Anglo-Saxon kingdoms were always changing as the kings fought one another for territory. The Britons (Celts) were pushed back to Cornwall and Wales.

▶ Houses were built of wood, so none have survived. Even the kings lived in wooden buildings. This picture is by a modern artist who has reconstructed some village homes.

◄ The Sutton Hoo ship did not survive, only its traces. Archaeologists, working very carefully, found the impressions of the ship's timbers and the iron nails which held it together.

► This warrior's helmet, which may have been made for King Raedwald, was placed next to his body in the ship. It is finely decorated with scenes of fighting and made of bronze, silver and gold.

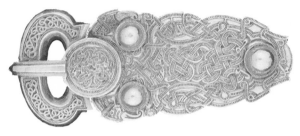

◄ A number of precious objects were carefully arranged around the king. This is a gold buckle, about 13 cm long, for a leather belt for his sword. The criss-cross decoration, called interlace, is often found on jewellery and on stone carving.

Clothes and possessions

We know quite a lot about the Anglo-Saxons from the remains which archaeologists have discovered. Rich Anglo-Saxons were usually buried with some precious possessions and, of course, the bodies were dressed. From very small fragments of cloth surviving in graves, archaeologists have been able to reconstruct what people wore. Women often wore long, flowing gowns fastened at the shoulders with big brooches. On their belts they might hang a purse. Jewellery such as brooches, necklaces, pins and bracelets has been found too. Men usually wore short tunics over leggings, and cloaks for warmth. Some men were buried with a shield and sword.

Writing

The Anglo-Saxons used an alphabet with 33 special letters called *runes*. It was often used to inscribe pots or special objects made of bone or metal jewellery. Christianity introduced Latin to the Anglo-Saxons and some of their handwritten books (called manuscripts) survive today. Some of these manuscripts have drawings too, another piece of evidence about the Anglo-Saxons.

The Sutton Hoo burial

A most remarkable discovery was made in 1939 near Woodbridge in Suffolk. The owner of farmland on which there were some mounds began an excavation. Under one of the mounds were the remains of a ship.

Although the soil had rotted away the wood of the boat, archaeologists discovered a large number of objects inside. Among them were a helmet, a sword, a shield and a number of spears. Where a body had originally been were the metal remains of a sword strap and belt, and a purse. Archaeologists also found the remains of buckets, bowls, spoons and coins. Recently, archaeologists have begun some more investigations at Sutton Hoo.

Which Anglo-Saxon could have been buried with so much wealth? Some of the objects show that he was a king. Archaeologists think that it may have been the grave of Raedwald, who was not only King of East Anglia but was also High King of Britain. We know that King Raedwald died in 624 or 625. The most famous Saxon king, Alfred, lived over 200 years later. ■

Kings of Wessex and all England

Alfred	871–899
Edward the Elder	899–925
Athelstan	925–939
Edmund	939–946
Eadred	946–955
Eadwig	955–959
Edgar	959–975
Edward the Martyr	975–978
Ethelred the Unready	978–1016

Danish (Viking) kings

Cnut	1016–1035
Harold I	1035–1040
Hardicanute	1040–1042

Kings of England

Edward the Confessor	1042–1066
Harold II	1066

See also

Archaeologists
Dark Ages
English language
Roman Britain
Vikings

Biography

Alfred
Augustine of Canterbury

Angola

Angola is a big country in south-western Africa. A small area, called Cabinda, is cut off from the rest of Angola by a thin strip of land belonging to Zaïre. Angolans use the Portuguese language for official business, because Portugal once ruled the country. In everyday life, most people speak one of the local African languages. The largest ethnic group is the Ovimbundu who live on the central plateau.

Area
1,246,700 sq km
(481,350 sq miles)
Capital
Luanda
Population
8,754,000
Language
Portuguese, Umbundu, Kimbundu, Kongo, others
Religion
Christian, Traditional
Government
Republic
Currency
1 kwanza = 100 lwei

Behind the narrow coastal plain are high grasslands and forests. It is warm throughout the year and most places have plenty of rain. The rain feeds Angola's many rivers. Only the south-west, which is a rocky desert, is dry.

Three out of every four Angolans live in small farming villages where they grow little more than they need to feed their families. The main foods are cassava (a root crop like potatoes) and maize. The most valuable crop, coffee, is sold abroad. Angola also earns money by selling oil and diamonds and there are large reserves of minerals.

Flashback

Portuguese sailors landed in Angola about 500 years ago. From the 16th century, many Angolans were taken to the Americas to work as slaves. Later on, Portuguese farmers settled in Angola. In the 1950s, black Angolans demanded independence from Portugal and a civil war began. When Angola became independent in 1975, most of the white people left. But a civil war continued between the government and the people of southern Angola until a ceasefire was announced in 1988. ■

◐ **See also**
Africa

Animal behaviour

Animals can move about, using their muscles to swim, walk or fly. This means that animals can obtain food by hunting or foraging, and can avoid climatic extremes by migration or hibernation. In these ways animals differ from plants.

Animal behaviour helps animals in four essential tasks: finding food, avoiding enemies, obtaining a mate, and caring for the young. When we observe animal behaviour we can try to discover what task the animal is engaged in. Sometimes this is obvious, but sometimes you have to do a little detective work.

Black-headed gulls remove broken eggshells from the nest after the chicks have hatched. To do this they have to fly away with the eggshell, leaving the nest unguarded. Why do they endanger their young in this way? Experiments with artificial nests and eggs show that the white insides of the broken eggshell make the nest conspicuous to predators. Crows stole more eggs from nests containing broken eggshells than from nests with only whole eggs. By removing the eggshells the parent bird is taking a small risk to obtain better camouflage for the nest.

Instinct and learning

Some animal behaviour is instinctive and some is learnt. The behaviour of newborn animals is due to instinct, and is inherited from the parents. Newly hatched mallard ducklings instinctively follow nearby moving objects. In nature they usually follow their mother, but they will follow any moving object, even a person. As they follow the mother, the ducklings learn what she looks like. As they grow up, they learn the differences between their mother and other ducks. When they are adult, they direct their courtship towards birds that look like their mother.

If they are raised by a foster parent of another species, then they will often court members of the other species in later life. The courtship behaviour is instinctive, but the birds have to learn what type of animal to direct it towards. In nature, they do this by following and learning about their parents. This process is called imprinting.

◄ Gannets communicating by a display on their nest.

Communication

Animals communicate in many different ways. Like us, they use sounds, scents and touch. They also use visual signals like facial expressions, and body movements called displays.

Gannets are large sea birds which nest on cliff ledges. The nests are closely spaced, and each sitting bird is just beyond pecking distance of its neighbours. A gannet who lands at the wrong nest is viciously attacked and must quickly retreat. Paired gannets have elaborate displays, which look as though they are fencing with their bills. This is the way they show each other that they are friendly.

When a worker honey bee finds a new patch of flowers rich in nectar, she flies back to the hive and communicates her discovery to her fellow workers. To do this, she must tell them about the direction and distance of the flowers, so that they can fly out and find them for themselves.

The bee passes on her message by performing a dance on the vertical surface of the comb inside the hive. If the flowers are near by she performs a simple round dance, but if the flowers are far away she performs a more complicated waggle dance. The other bees gather round and feel the shape of the dance in the darkness of the hive.

The waggle dance is like a figure 8 in which the bee waggles her tail in the middle part. The number of waggles indicates the distance of the flowers from the hive. The direction that the bee is heading when doing the waggles signals the direction of the flowers. An upwards direction

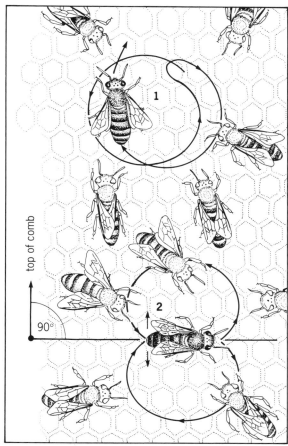

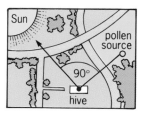

◄ A worker bee communicates to her fellow workers with a waggle dance. Her dance shows the direction of the food in relation to the Sun.

indicates that the flowers are in the direction of the Sun. If the dance is angled clockwise from the vertical, this indicates to the workers that they should maintain this clockwise angle to the Sun when they fly out of the hive to find the flowers. ■

See also

Bees
Instinct
Migration

Animals

Animals are living things that feed by eating other living things. Plants, which are also alive, do not need to eat. They are able to harness the Sun's energy and use water, carbon dioxide and minerals from the earth to make their own food. Animals must also breathe, taking oxygen from the air or from water. There are many other differences between animals and plants, including details in their cells and in the ways that they are able to move, but the great dividing line between plants and animals is in how they obtain their food.

There are at least 1 million different species (sorts) of animals, and more are discovered every day. Most animals, such as jellyfish, worms or insects, do not have backbones. The majority of them are small. Over 99 per cent are smaller than human beings.

Animals live almost everywhere. Some live in forests, on plains or on high mountains. Some live in rivers, in the sea or in dark caves. They eat many things. Some feed on plants. These are called herbivores. Some feed on the flesh of other animals. These are called carnivores. Only a few feed on both plants and flesh. These are called omnivores. Some creatures feed on plants and animals which may have been dead for some time. These are called scavengers. Some, which are called parasites, live in the bodies of other animals that are still alive.

Animals are many different shapes. A few, like sea anemones or starfish, do not have a head or a tail end or any sides. If you divide them in half from above the halves will always be more or less identical. We call this being radially symmetrical. Such animals can get food from any direction.

Most animals are bilaterally symmetrical. This means that they have a left and a right side and a head and a tail end. The head contains the brain and the main sense organs. Bilaterally symmetrical animals are usually more active than radially symmetrical ones.

An animal's legs can often give a clue to its way of life. Long-legged creatures are usually fast runners; short-legged creatures tend to move slowly.

Most animals have short lives. Some animals without backbones live for only a few months. Few kinds of animals survive for many years, although a very big old tortoise or crocodile may be as much as 200 years old.

radial symmetry

sea anemone

bilateral symmetry

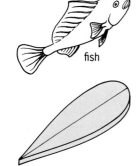

fish

The animal kingdom can be divided into groups of animals that are related to each other. Each division is called a phylum, and the main ones are shown here.

Protozoa (more than 30,000 species) These have only one cell, and most live in water, or damp places. They reproduce by splitting in half. Many are important scavengers.

Sponges *Porifera* (over 20,000 species) These are built up of many cells which make a network of tubes. The cells do not form organs, but feed and breathe individually.

Jellyfish and their relatives *Cnidaria* (about 10,000 species) These have a radially symmetrical simple sack-shaped body, with a mouth surrounded by tentacles with sting cells on them.

Flatworms *Platyhelminthes* (about 5,500 species) These are flat-bodied creatures, which live in water or moist places. Most feed on other animals.

Roundworms *Nematoda* (over 10,000 species) These are tiny worms with cylindrical bodies. They are common almost everywhere. Some are pests or parasites, attacking plants and animals and causing diseases.

Moss animals *Bryozoa* (about 4,000 species) These are small but they have complex bodies surrounded by a hard skin. They are usually found in the sea, and live in colonies.

Lamp shells *Brachiopoda* (about 260 species) These sea-living animals resemble clams on the outside but are very different inside. They are now rather rare, but are common as fossils.

Snails and their relatives *Mollusca* (over 45,000 species) These soft-bodied animals are usually protected by a shell. They live on land, in fresh water or in the sea.

Segmented worms *Annelida* (over 7,000 species) These have soft bodies made up of segments. They can be found in the soil, in fresh water and even in the sea.

Jointed-legged animals *Arthropoda* (over one million species) These have segmented bodies which are protected by hard armour, and some have wings. They are widespread and include crustaceans, insects and spiders.

Starfish and their relatives *Echinodermata* (about 5,500 species) These are radially symmetrical. They have a tough, often spiny, outer skin, and some have an internal skeleton.

Rod-backed animals *Chordata* (about 43,000 species) These nearly all have backbones and belong to the subphylum Vertebrata. There are about 21,000 species of fish, 4,000 of amphibians, 5,200 of reptiles, 8,700 of birds and 4,000 of mammals. ∎

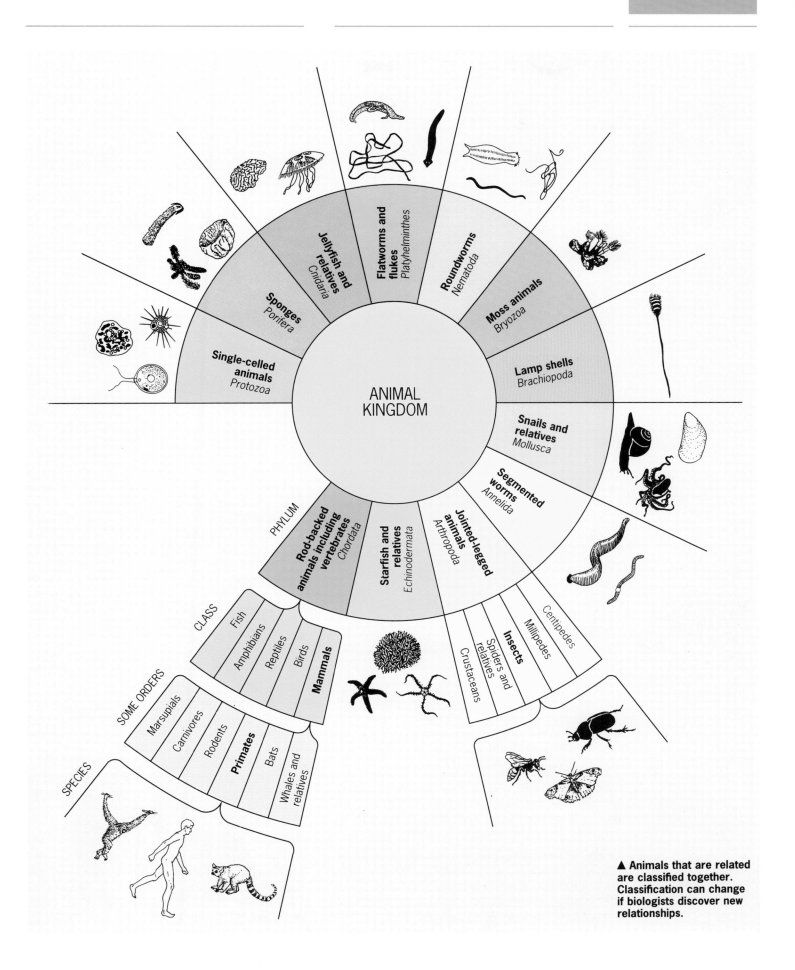

Flatworms and flukes
Platyhelminthes

Jellyfish and relatives
Cnidaria

Roundworms
Nematoda

Sponges
Porifera

Moss animals
Bryozoa

Single-celled animals
Protozoa

Lamp shells
Brachiopoda

ANIMAL KINGDOM

Snails and relatives
Mollusca

Segmented worms
Annelida

PHYLUM

Rod-backed animals including vertebrates
Chordata

Starfish and relatives
Echinodermata

Jointed-legged animals
Arthropoda

CLASS

Fish

Amphibians

Reptiles

Birds

Mammals

Centipedes

Millipedes

Insects

Spiders and relatives

Crustaceans

SOME ORDERS

Marsupials

Carnivores

Rodents

Primates

Bats

Whales and relatives

SPECIES

▲ Animals that are related are classified together. Classification can change if biologists discover new relationships.

Antarctica

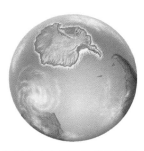

Highest point
Vinson Massif 5,140 m
Lowest point
2,538 m below sea-level
(ice-filled)
World's longest glacier
Lambert Glacier 400 km
(250 miles)
Most active volcano
Mount Erebus 3,743 m
Area
13,340,000 sq km
(5,149,000 sq miles)

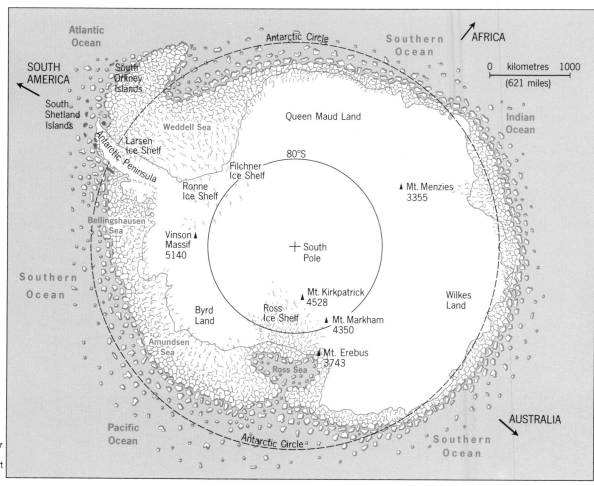

Key:
- Land not covered by ice
- Ice cap (up to 4000 metres thick)
- Sea covered by ice all year
- Sea covered by ice for part of the year

Antarctica has 90 per cent of all the ice in the world. If all the ice in Antarctica melted, the world's sea-level would rise by 70 m.

▶ **Scientists from the USA at the South Pole with flags of some of the nations which signed the Antarctic Treaty.**

The Earth's fifth largest continent is at the South Pole. Nearly all of the huge area is covered with ice over three kilometres thick. The ice has built up from snow that has fallen over millions of years. The sheet of ice spreads out onto the sea, where huge pieces break off to make icebergs.

There are whole mountain ranges buried under the ice. Just the very tops poke through. The tallest peak is called the Vinson Massif and is 5,140 m (16,860 ft) high.

Geologists who study the rocky areas that are not under ice have discovered coal and the fossils of plants and animals. These finds show that Antarctica once had a warm climate. It began to get cold about 150 million years ago.

Antarctica is now the coldest continent. The world's lowest temperature recorded is –89·2°C (–128°F) at Vostok, Antarctica. The climate is made worse by very strong winds. Except in summer, the sea around the continent is full of ice.

Exploration

One of the first explorers to sight Antarctica may have been Captain James Cook, who sailed south in 1774. Soon after, hunters who had heard stories about the many seals and whales in the Southern Ocean started to venture further south in their ships.

The first people to set foot on the continent were probably seal hunters in about 1820. But the cold and the ice made exploration too difficult for

them. By 1895, though, people were keen to find out what Antarctica was like. Members of a Belgian party that sailed in 1897 were the first people to spend a winter on the ice.

Captain Robert F. Scott led a British expedition in the years 1901 to 1904. In 1910 he returned, hoping to be the first to reach the South Pole, but his attempt ended in tragedy. Roald Amundsen, a Norwegian explorer, reached there first, on 14 December 1911, and returned successfully. Scott and his companions arrived a month later, but their expedition had not been so well planned and they all died on the way back.

Since then, many countries have sent scientific expeditions to study Antarctica and have set up permanent stations where scientists can live and work safely.

A continent for research

In 1956 twelve countries, including the United States, the Soviet Union and the United Kingdom, took part in an international research effort in the Antarctic. It was so successful that the countries later signed the Antarctic Treaty in 1959. They agreed not to make rival claims to territory but to use the Antarctic only for peaceful research.

Now there are 32 countries that have accepted the treaty. Their flags stand in a ring round the South Pole where the Amundsen-Scott station is run by the United States.

Living in the Antarctic

The Antarctic climate is so harsh that no land animals can live there. The penguins and seals of Antarctica are really sea creatures. They depend on the sea for their food and live in the sea or at its edge.

People who go there have to take absolutely everything they need. That includes food, special warm clothing, sledges and tractors for travelling around on the ice, and fuel oil. The supplies are taken during the southern summer by ship or aircraft.

Most of the research is done in the summer, and scientists usually spend a few months there doing experiments. The geologists often set up camps with tents in the remote areas where they want to collect rocks. Then they go home to finish their work. Some people stay all winter to look after the stations. They are usually people with special skills, like builders, electricians and mechanics.

Antarctic stations today are comfortable places to live, but it is still very dangerous for people travelling and working outside. There are very strict rules about clothing and equipment, and everyone has to be specially trained in first aid and safety. ■

⊙ See also

Continents
Ice
Icebergs and ice-caps
Penguins
Seals
Snow
Whales

Biography
Amundsen
Cook
Scott, Robert
Shackleton

◀ ▼ **Modern transport and clothing of today's British Antarctic Survey team contrast vividly with the equipment of Sir Ernest Shackleton and Frank Hurley, pictured in the 1914–1916 expedition.**

Anteaters

Largest
Giant anteater: head and body length up to 120 cm; tail up to 90 cm; weight up to 39 kg
Smallest
Silky anteater: head and body length up to 23 cm; tail up to 29 cm
Number of young 1

Subphylum Vertebrata
Class Mammalia
Order Edentata
Number of species 4 true anteaters

Anteaters feed on ants and termites and sometimes other sorts of insects, such as beetle grubs. An anteater uses the long claws on its front feet to tear open the nests of its prey. Its wormlike tongue is covered with tiny backward-pointing spines which are made gummy with sticky saliva. There is no escape for the scurrying insects, and a giant anteater (whose tongue is over 60 cm/24 in long) may mop up as many as 30,000 in a day.

Giant anteaters live on the ground, travelling slowly by day or night through the damp forests and savannahs. They are usually alone, although babies stay with their mothers for up to two years, often riding on their backs.

Other species of anteaters live in trees. They have prehensile tails which help them to climb and hold

on securely. The smallest of them, the silky anteater, lives mainly in silk cotton trees. It rarely comes to the ground, and is difficult to see because it looks like a newly opened silk cotton pod.

Other kinds of animals also rely on ants and termites for their food. Spiny anteaters from Australia and pangolins from Africa and tropical Asia have large claws and long, sticky tongues like the anteaters of South America although they are not related. ■

▲ The lesser anteater, or southern tamandua, usually lives in a hollow tree. It emerges at night to feed on ants, termites and bees. If it is attacked, it protects itself with its large, sharp claws.

⊙ See also
Ants
Termites

Antelopes

⊙ See also
Cattle
Domestication
Goats
Horns and antlers

▼ Herd of impala, usually made up of as many as a hundred females and their young. During the mating season single males will join the herd.

Antelopes may be as big as cows or as small and delicate as new-born lambs. They are all long-legged, cloven-hoofed animals that feed on plants. Like cows they chew the cud.

Most antelopes live in large herds. Often a herd consists of only females and calves, as males form other groups. Males ready to mate

generally live alone and will fight other males for territory. Their horns are usually spiral or notched so that the rivals' horns lock together when fighting. This results in a trial of strength as they push each other backwards and forwards. Although the fights look fierce, the loser can easily break free and injuries are rare.

A baby antelope can stand within minutes of being born, and is soon an active member of the herd. It becomes independent quickly, for its mother will produce a new calf in the next year.

Antelopes are the prey of many flesh eaters, but humans are their most dangerous enemy. Many species have now become very rare through over-hunting, or destruction of their habitat. Attempts have been made to domesticate some kinds of antelope, and they may become important farm animals in the future. ■

Distribution
African grasslands mainly, but also forests, deserts and swamps and the cold steppes of Asia
Largest antelope
Eland, shoulder height up to 1.8 m; weight up to 1,000 kg
Smallest antelopes
Royal and Bates's pygmy antelopes, which are about 30 cm at the shoulder and weigh about 3 kg
Number of young
1 per year in the larger species; smaller antelopes breed more often.
Lifespan
Over 23 years for eland, over 10 years for one of the small species

Subphylum Vertebrata
Class Mammalia
Order Artiodactyla (cloven-hoofed animals)
Family
Bovidae (cattle family)
Number of species
About 105

Anthems

An anthem is the name for a piece of music sung by a church choir. It is a hymn, but sung by the choir alone, without the rest of the congregation. Sometimes an organ or piano plays an accompaniment.

Anthem composers often write music that mirrors the feelings in the words of the anthem. So for triumphant words they write march-like music, or for sorrowful words sad music. When the words talk about musical instruments, such as harps, trumpets, or drums, the composers make the music imitate the sounds.

Anthems first became popular in the 16th century, when English replaced Latin as the language used in church services. Composers were keen to show off the new English translations of the services. They took care to choose especially fine verses. When the Bible was translated into English, many composers used verses from the Book of Psalms in their anthems. A favourite was Psalm 150. ■

A famous anthem, by Hubert Parry, was sung by the choir of Westminster Abbey at the coronation of Queen Elizabeth II in 1953. The anthem was originally written for Edward VII's coronation in 1902.

Motet is another word for anthem.

See also
Choirs
National anthems

Anthropologists

Anthropologists are people who study other people. Some anthropologists study the development of people's bodies and how they have evolved since prehistoric times. But most anthropologists study the ways of life of different groups of people in order to understand what makes us all human. To do this they usually look at ways of life different from their own. Most anthropologists have come from Western countries, so they usually concentrate on non-Western peoples but this is changing as anthropologists become interested in how people live in urban, technological societies too. Learning about other ways of life helps us to understand our own society. ■

The word comes from two Greek words: *anthropos* meaning 'human being' and *logia* meaning 'study'. As a subject for study anthropology began in the 19th century.

Antibiotics

An antibiotic is a type of medicine that doctors may use to try and cure disease. Antibiotics are all natural products of moulds, fungi and other tiny living things. These organisms make the antibiotic substances to defend themselves against the germs called bacteria.

Diseases in humans such as boils, food poisoning, pneumonia and typhoid fever are all caused by bacteria. A person with a bacterial disease can usually pass it to someone else: this means it is infectious.

Antibiotics damage or kill bacteria in different ways. Many stop the bacteria from building a protective wall around themselves. Without this layer, the bacteria explode. Other antibiotics stop the bacteria from making proteins. Without these they die.

Before antibiotics were discovered, bacterial diseases killed and harmed thousands of people. Now many of these diseases can be cured, but because the drugs are expensive, only wealthy countries can afford to use them in large quantities.

Flashback

Sir Alexander Fleming discovered the first antibiotic, penicillin, by accident when he was growing bacteria in the laboratory. Some spores of the mould *Penicillium* floated into his bacteria by mistake. He noticed that where the mould grew, the bacteria were killed. ■

See also
Bacteria
Germs
Penicillin

Biography
Fleming

Antipodes

The 'Antipodes' is the place which is on exactly the opposite side of the world to where you are standing. To find the antipodes, look at a globe and pretend you are standing at one place. You can then see which spot is on the other side of the globe. ■

The word comes from Greek meaning 'having the feet opposite'. *Podes* means 'feet' in Greek.

Australasia is known as the antipodes by Europeans.

Ants

▲ Ants are protected in some parts of the world because they kill and eat some insects which are forest pests. These weaver ants are tearing a beetle apart.

See also
Animal behaviour
Aphids
Honeydew
Insects

Ants are insects which always live in groups or colonies. There may be 100,000 ants in a colony but they all have the same mother. She is called the queen ant. The ants that you are most likely to see are called workers. These are all females, yet they are unable to lay eggs, for their sex organs are not fully developed.

Most ants do not have wings, as they live in sheltered nests, where wings would get in the way. But for a short time each year, usually on a warm, muggy day, the air is full of flying ants. These are the males and the egg-laying females, leaving the nest for their mating flight. After mating, the males die, but the females begin to make new nests to lay eggs in. Their wings break off

and the muscles which enabled them to fly are used to give them energy until the first young workers hatch. From then on the workers collect food for themselves, their young sisters and the queen. Some of the later workers may become soldiers, growing large and helping to protect the nest, by biting and squirting acid at enemies.

Ants feed on many kinds of food. Some hunt other animals, some feed on seeds and some eat a kind of fungus that they grow on a compost of leaves especially gathered. Most ants like sweet things and some 'milk' aphids of their honeydew. In most of the things that ants do their behaviour is innate, which means they do not have to think about it, or learn how to do it. ∎

Distribution
Worldwide
Largest ant
Bulldog ant, 2·5 cm long
Smallest ant
Some Argentine ants are less than 2 mm

Phylum
Arthropoda
Class
Insecta
Order
Hymenoptera
Number of species
About 14,000

▼ Red ant worker collecting honeydew from aphids on a nettle stem. The ant will actually carry the aphids to suitable plants.

Apartheid

See also
South Africa

Biography
Luthuli
Mandela
Tutu

South Africa's government has been dominated by white people, although there are nearly five times as many people of other races: blacks, coloureds (people of mixed race) and Asians. The government has had a policy of segregation, called *apartheid*: meaning 'apart-ness' or 'separate development'.

Effectively this has denied the blacks, who form 70 per cent of the

population, any say in what happens to them. The white government has created ten so-called 'Bantustans' or homelands for the blacks, and says four of them are independent countries. The United Nations has not recognized them as independent. There has been widespread opposition to apartheid and parks and beaches and other public places are no longer segregated. But there are still restrictions on the rights of non-white people. ∎

Since 1990 the apartheid laws have been gradually removed.

Apes

Distribution
Great apes found in tropical forests in Africa, Sumatra and Borneo, lesser apes in south-east Asia
Lifespan
Great apes about 50 years, lesser apes 30–40 years

Subphylum Vertebrata
Class Mammalia
Order Primates
Number of species 13 (9 lesser apes, 4 great apes)

◀ **Rwandan mountain gorillas grooming each other. Unusually it is the dominant male, the silverback, that is doing the grooming.**

Apes are our nearest relatives in the animal kingdom. Like humans they are intelligent, long-lived animals, which generally travel in family parties. There are two main groups of apes. Gibbons and siamangs are the lesser apes, and gorillas, chimpanzees and orang-utans are the great apes. The great apes have bodies much like ours. Like us they have no visible tail, and they have 32 teeth. Vision is their most important sense and, unlike most mammals, they can see colours much as we can.

There are many other similarities between apes and humans. Some of the blood proteins of chimpanzees are exactly the same as ours, and, as with human families, ape females normally have one baby at a time.

Young apes develop slowly. Ape mothers, unlike many humans, do not have another baby until the last young one is several years old, by which time it is fairly independent. A baby chimpanzee, for example, is not weaned until it is about four years old. Until then it is cared for by its mother, often riding on her back. Even after the birth of her next young one, earlier members of the family often stay with their mother. They learn many things from her such as how to make

nests and use a twig as a 'fishing rod' to catch termites. Like all intelligent animals, they continue to learn throughout their lives.

Apes and humans

There are some obvious differences between apes and humans. The apes all have far more hair covering their bodies than we do. Also their arms are much longer and stronger, while their legs tend to be shorter and weaker. Apes can climb very well and often swing about in the branches of trees, but adult great apes are too heavy for the higher, weaker branches.

Apes usually walk on all fours. This is known as knuckle walking, as they put their weight on their knuckles. They are able to walk upright, but usually do so only for a few paces.

In spite of the fact that the apes are our nearest relatives, we have not treated them well. We have killed them, imprisoned them in zoos and experimented on them in laboratories. Worse, much of the forests in which they live have been destroyed. The orang-utan and the gorilla are both endangered species, and chimpanzees are much less common than they were. ■

▲ **Chimpanzees and other apes have long toes so they can grasp things with their feet. Like us their hands have a thumb which can be pressed against a finger to pick up small items.**

◯ ▮ See also
Chimpanzees
Gibbons
Gorillas
Human beings
Monkeys
Orang-utans
Primates

Aphids

► **Winged female giving birth to live young.**

Aphids are often called 'greenflies'. This is not a good name for them, as they are not true flies but bugs. Many kinds of aphid are not even green!

During the summer-time all aphids are female. These do not lay eggs, but without mating are able to give birth to live young, all females. This process is called parthenogenesis. In about ten days time these daughters can start producing families of their own. This means that the number of aphids can soon become very large. The first young to be born cannot fly, but as the numbers grow greater, some develop wings and fly to other plants. As autumn approaches and the days become shorter and colder, some males are born. These mate with the females which now lay eggs and then die. The eggs hatch next spring into females, which are the start of that year's population of aphids.

Because aphids are small and defenceless, they are eaten by many kinds of creatures, including insects such as ladybirds and hoverflies and many kinds of birds. However, only one needs to survive for the population to build up again quite quickly. ■

Distribution
Worldwide, mainly in cooler countries
Largest aphid
About 4 mm in length
Lifespan
About 3 months
Number of young born
About 100 to each aphid

Phylum
Arthropoda
Class
Insecta
Order
Hemiptera
Number of species
About 4,000

See also
Bugs
Honeydew
Insects
Ladybirds

Apostles

The apostles were the twelve men Jesus chose as his assistants from among all the disciples (followers) who believed in him. We know very little about most of them. Four of them were fishermen: Peter and his brother Andrew, James and his brother John. One, Matthew, was a tax-collector. The others were: Philip, Bartholomew, Thomas, James (who is often called 'the Less' to distinguish him from the other James), Thaddaeus (also called Jude), Simon and Judas Iscariot. After Jesus was crucified, Judas hanged himself because he had betrayed Jesus for 30 pieces of silver. Matthias replaced him. ■

See also
Christians
Biography
Jesus
Peter, Saint

Appendix

Inside your body, at the join between the small intestine and the large intestine, you have a small, worm-shaped organ called an appendix. It is 1 cm (½ in) wide and up to 10 cm (4 in) long, and is found in the lower right-hand corner of the abdomen. Most mammals have similar organs, and in some, such as horses, they may be quite large and used in digestion.

In humans the appendix does not seem to have any function. It may have had a use once that has been lost through evolution.

If the connection between the appendix and the rest of the gut becomes blocked, for instance by a fruit stone, the appendix can become infected and inflamed. This is the disease called appendicitis. It is quite common in children and young adults.

The inflamed appendix causes a bad pain in the abdomen, at first round the navel and then lower down on the right. This usually has to be treated by an operation, called an appendectomy, which removes the appendix. ■

Appendicitis occurs mainly between the ages of 10 and 25 years. It is much more common in males than females. There has been a considerable increase in the number of people with appendicitis over the past 30 years in Western countries. This probably has a lot to do with the foods we now eat. It is still hardly known in Africa and Asia.

See also
Digestive systems

Aquariums

An aquarium is a tank in which water plants and animals are kept. It may be of any size, ranging from one which can hold only a few water snails or insects, to some which are large enough to house dolphins and killer whales. Some people keep cold water aquariums for creatures which come from chilly climates. But many aquariums are heated, to make suitable homes for brilliantly coloured fish from the tropics. It is also possible to keep a salt water aquarium for sea dwellers, such as corals or crabs.

If you want to keep fish and water animals, you should make a home for them which is as natural as possible. There should be plants and places where the animals can hide or rest. The bottom should be covered with gravel, like the bed of a stream or pool. The water must be kept clean and must contain plenty of oxygen for the animals to breathe. The best way to do this is to have a pump which bubbles air into the water, and a filter which removes any waste matter.

Setting up an aquarium

Decide where your aquarium is to be kept. It should be out of direct sunlight, for this will cause green plants to make a curtain of slime on the glass. An aquarium is heavy and you may need a special table or stand for it.

Buy your tank, the gravel, plants, and heating, filter and cleaning equipment from an aquarium shop. The larger the tank you can afford, the more fish you can keep, and the better home you will be able to make for them. For a permanent home for fish, it should be at least about 60 cm (24 in) long, 30 cm (12 in) wide and 38 cm (15 in) high.

Set up your tank and equipment in the place where you have decided to keep it. Once full, it will be very heavy and should not be moved, for that could strain the joints of the

An aquarium 60 cm long will make a home for about 25 fish 3–4 cm long when they are full grown. If you have bigger fish, you cannot keep so many in the space. To avoid overcrowding allow 20 square cm of water surface area to each centimetre of fish (excluding tail).
Most tropical fish need to be kept at a temperature of 23–26°C.

glass and make it leak. Let the water stand for several days before getting your fish, and check that all of the equipment works properly.

Choose the fishes that you want. The shop will probably sell you young ones, but you should check that they will not grow too big. Also make certain that you have got fish that will live together. It is no use if one kind attacks all of the others. Try to get some which will swim near to the surface of the water and others which will live lower down.

Put your fish gently into the water still in their container and leave them for half an hour, so when you release them there will be no temperature change. They will settle down quite quickly. Watch and feed them every day, but do not give them too much to eat, for this will only go to waste and make the tank dirty. ■

Some suitable aquarium fish
For a cold water aquarium goldfish are best. For a heated aquarium some of the most brightly coloured are tiny fishes, such as the neon tetra, or the cardinal tetra. Other beautiful fishes are the barbs and the danios. Angelfishes and pearl gouramis are larger. Live-bearing fishes produce living babies. They are easy to keep and include guppies, platies, swordtails and mollies.

See also
Fish
Pets

Aqueducts

An aqueduct is a bridge which carries water across a valley or low ground.

All towns and cities use vast amounts of water. Often a reservoir is built in the nearest mountains or hills to trap the rain-water. This is then carried by pipes or aqueducts to where it is needed.

In the United States of America the Colorado River Aqueduct has large channels with aqueducts that carry water for 390 km (240 miles) across mountain ranges to serve several cities. In Britain, much of Birmingham's water supply is carried more than 110 km (68 miles) from reservoirs in the Elan Valley in Wales.

▼ Pont du Gard, near Nîmes in southern France.

Flashback

Aqueducts were first built and used at least 2,000 years ago. The greatest of them was the aqueduct of Carthage, in what is now Tunisia. It was nearly 141 km (88 miles) long and was built by the Romans during the 2nd century AD. Scientists have calculated that the aqueduct would have carried 32 million litres (7 million gallons) of water a day. Perhaps the finest example of a Roman aqueduct, though, was the one built in AD 19 by the Roman general Agrippa and still standing today. It is the Pont du Gard in southern France. This aqueduct is 270 m (885 feet) long and more than 47 m (154 feet) high. ∎

See also
Roman ancient history
Water supplies

Arabia

Arabia is the name given to a vast area about half the size of Europe at the heart of the Arab world. It has no exact boundaries, but it is generally considered to be centred on the country of Saudi Arabia and to include some of the smaller states on its edges.

In the Red Sea coastal strip, formerly called Hejaz, are the two cities of Mecca and Medina. Arabia is mostly desert and not many people live there; most of them until recently were nomads. The area is now one of the richest in the world because of the huge reserves of oil and natural gas that lie beneath the surface. The wealth has been used to build a network of ultra-modern cities, roads and airports. ∎

See also
Arabs
Middle East
Muslims
Nomads
Saudi Arabia
United Arab Emirates
Yemen

Arabian Nights

The Arabian Nights' Entertainment is the full name of a book of stories. People first enjoyed them in the Middle East a thousand years ago. Some tell of magic: genies in bottles, flying carpets, birds big enough to carry off pirate ships. Others tell of the tricks and jokes of ordinary people's lives. Three of the best-known stories are *Sinbad the Sailor, Aladdin's Wonderful Lamp* and *Ali Baba and the Forty Thieves.*

Legend says that a young woman, Scheherazade, first collected all the stories. Her husband, a cruel tyrant, had married a new wife each night, and had her executed in the morning.

To save herself, Scheherazade told him stories, one each night for 1,001 nights; her husband was so eager to hear the tales that he spared her life and ended up by falling in love with her.

This legend explains the *Arabian Nights'* alternative title, *A Thousand and One Nights.* ∎

The original stories were written in Arabic. The stories were first translated into French and introduced to the West by Antoine Galland in the 17th century.

Not children's stories
The original stories were not intended for children. In fact they contain a lot of material that has never been considered polite in the Arab world.

A famous explorer
One of the most famous translators of *The Arabian Nights* was the English explorer Sir Richard Burton. Burton was the first Englishman to enter Mecca, the first to explore Somaliland and the first to discover the great lakes of central Africa.

Arabs

There are over 200 million Arabs living in the 21 countries which stretch from the Atlantic Ocean in the west to the borders of Iran in the east. The countries differ greatly in size and in the way people live. Some, such as the desert country of Saudi Arabia and its tiny neighbours, are immensely rich because of oil. Others, such as Egypt, have difficulty finding the money to feed a huge and rapidly growing population.

The people, with all their variety, are brought together by three things: language, religion and history. They all speak Arabic, although there are some differences in dialect. A person from Iraq, for example, might find it difficult having a conversation in Morocco. Most Arabs are Muslims, although there are some Christian and Jewish communities. All Arabs share a pride in the achievements of their ancestors who conquered the lands they now live in more than a thousand years ago.

The original Arabs were a bedouin people in Arabia. In the 7th century they were inspired by the message of the Prophet Muhammad, the founder of the Muslim religion, and began a series of invasions into neighbouring lands. Two hundred years later, at the height of the empire, they had a civilization stretching from Spain to India that was centuries in advance of Europe. The Arabs were responsible for introducing into Europe many new ideas in astronomy, chemistry, medicine and mathematics. The word 'algebra', for example, was originally an Arabic one.

◄ **Saudi Arabian men feasting on a traditional dish of rice and lamb.**

In the centuries since they spread from Arabia the Arabs have intermarried with many different peoples, so their complexions range from black to fair. The last century, which included a long period of European rule over most of the Arab world, has seen enormous changes in the way people live. An Arab city today looks much like one anywhere else, with its traffic jams, neon advertising signs and office blocks. But many customs survive. For example, you can still see Arab men and women wearing the traditional loose robes. Also, the Arabs still live within large and close family groups. In times of trouble the family protects and cares for its members. ■

League of Arab States
Algeria
Bahrain
Djibouti
Egypt
Iraq
Jordan
Kuwait
Lebanon
Libya
Mauritania
Morocco
Oman
Qatar
Saudi Arabia
Somalia
Sudan
Syria
Tunisia
United Arab Emirates (UAE)
Yemen

The Palestine Liberation Organization is a member of the League.

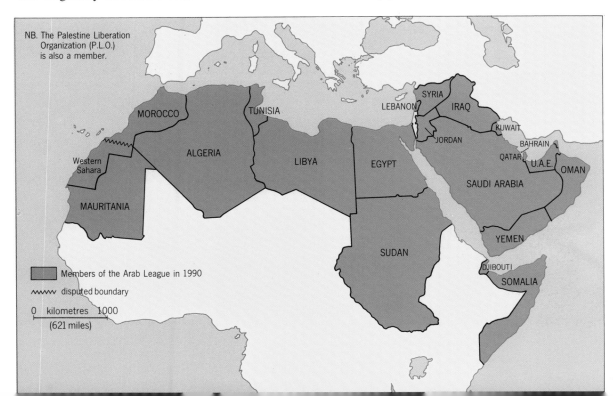

NB. The Palestine Liberation Organization (P.L.O.) is also a member.

MOROCCO
TUNISIA
LEBANON
SYRIA
IRAQ
Western Sahara
ALGERIA
LIBYA
EGYPT
JORDAN
KUWAIT
BAHRAIN
QATAR
U.A.E.
OMAN
SAUDI ARABIA
MAURITANIA
YEMEN
SUDAN
DJIBOUTI
SOMALIA

▨ Members of the Arab League in 1990

⌇⌇⌇ disputed boundary

0   kilometres   1000
(621 miles)

⊙ See also
Alphabets
Middle East
Muslims
Nomads

Archaeologists

Archaeologists are like detectives investigating what happened in the past. They look for clues, make careful records and then write the 'story' of their investigation. They look for their clues among the remains of past peoples. These remains might be small objects thrown away, such as bones from a meal or a broken jar. But they might also be the large ruins of a house or even a whole town, like Pompeii. Archaeologists usually work in teams of specialists; each uses a different technique to unravel the story of the past.

Discovering where to look

Archaeologists must find where the past is hidden before they can investigate it. Sometimes the remains are so large that they can easily be seen, like the Inca city of Machu Picchu in Peru. Quite often, though, archaeologists must hunt out the clues in buildings, on the landscape, below the ground or under the sea.

Aerial photography is probably the most important technique archaeologists have for finding out where the remains of the past are to be found. Crops, such as wheat, barley or sugar beet, will grow in different ways if their roots are over some disturbance, such as a buried wall or a filled-in ditch. Sometimes even grass shows the 'crop marks' of an archaeological site hidden below ground. Archaeologists use hundreds of photographs taken from aeroplanes each year.

Field surveying means taking careful measurements of any remains which can be seen, perhaps on the surface of a field. Burial mounds, for example, are usually plotted in detail using tapes and measuring instruments. Some archaeologists spend their time making records (drawings, photographs and notes) of buildings or other remains in towns.

Field walking is sometimes the next stage in investigating and plotting the past. This means collecting the bits and pieces from an archaeological site hidden under the surface of a field. Ploughing usually brings to the surface broken pottery, bones and building material such as roof tiles. Careful collection and plotting on a map will show where people used to live in the past.

This word comes from two Greek words: *archaia* meaning 'ancient things' and *logos* meaning 'theory or science of'.

The first archaeologists were Italian Popes, cardinals and noblemen who began collecting items from ancient Greek and Roman times in the 16th century.

In 1798 Napoleon took French archaeologists with him on his conquest of Egypt to record the ancient civilization there. Then in 1822, Jean-François Champollion became the first person to decipher ancient Egyptian writing.

▶ This aerial photograph was taken over the site of a Roman city at Silchester. This is now farmland and the only Roman remains visible at ground level are of the city wall. On the photograph the line of the wall is mostly marked by a line of trees. In the fields inside the city wall differences of growth in the crops reveal the Roman street plan and the shapes of the forum and other buildings. (The regular pattern of dots in the bottom part of the picture is made by modern farming: they are pig shelters.)

Excavation

Today, archaeological records from survey work are kept by teams of archaeologists. Sometimes archaeologists want to find out much more about a particular place or people. They do this by excavating the remains. Quite often, in all parts of the world, rescue excavations have to be carried out because the sites are to be disturbed by new roads, redevelopment of a city centre, or just by ploughing deeply. Most archaeologists today work on rescue sites.

Excavation of a site means that the archaeologists must actually destroy most of the site to understand it. Careful records, plans and photographs are very important. Archaeologists will investigate the remains of buildings, industry or burial places but they will also discover the little things left behind. Archaeologists call these 'finds'.

It is not possible to excavate a site properly on your own. Archaeologists work in teams. There are specialists in excavating, making drawings, surveying, taking photographs and looking after the finds.

Analysing what has been found

Work does not stop when the excavation is finished. Specialists must examine the records of the excavation and write a report. People who are expert in identifying and dating different types of animal bone, fragments of pottery, or seeds from plants, and many other experts are all needed to put together the 'story' of the site. In 1948 an American, Willard F. Libby, developed radioactive carbon dating which made it possible to date findings accurately over a period of 40,000 years. Even with the most up to date scientific methods it is a difficult job to reconstruct the past because not everything will have survived. Not all sites are as well preserved as Pompeii or as an Egyptian mummy!

Displaying the past

Usually the remains (or at least some of them) of an archaeological investigation are displayed in a museum. The objects found must be looked after and preserved for others to study and enjoy. Some museums will show you objects in glass cases. Others will put a number of things together to show you the story of what the archaeologists found. A few places, like the Jorvik Viking Centre in York or West Stow Anglo-Saxon Village, have made reconstructions of the past to give people a better idea of what actually went on. ■

◀ Archaeologists are working in an Iron Age Celtic grave at Welwyn Garden City, England. A gas-pipe runs through the site and the trench made for the pipe had destroyed part of the grave. But the archaeologists were able to draw up a plan of the complete grave and they found a great many objects. The two *amphorae* (pottery jars) were excavated later and are displayed in the bottom photograph.

◀ In a laboratory, conservation workers piece together storage jars found on a site in what is now Jordan in the Middle East. The jars had been broken and crushed on the floor of a storeroom before 1150 BC.

◯ **See also**
Anglo-Saxons
Aztecs
Burial mounds
Carbon (carbon dating)
Celtic history
Egyptian ancient history
Greek ancient history
Hillforts
Incas
Prehistoric people
Roman ancient history
Vikings

◀ These are some of the finds from the Celtic chieftain's grave which is shown in the process of being excavated in the top photograph. The display in the British Museum shows five amphorae for storing wine, a silver cup and other pots and bowls.

Archaeopteryx

Archaeopteryx means
'ancient wing'.

Number of specimens
Five
First specimen found
1861
**Age of rocks containing
the fossil**
Upper Jurassic (145 million
years ago)
Specimens on show
Natural History Museum,
London; Jura Museum
(Eichstätt, Germany)

One of the most famous fossils is *Archaeopteryx*, the earliest known fossil of a bird. This fossil is very well known because it is a 'missing link' between the dinosaurs and the birds as we know them today. The first fossil of *Archaeopteryx* was found in Germany in 1861. This showed an almost complete skeleton of a small animal with very slender bones. It was about the size of a pigeon, and had teeth and a long tail. However, there were also feathers to be seen pressed into the fine mud-stone which contained the bones. This showed that *Archaeopteryx* was partly like a bird and partly like dinosaurs. Since 1861, only a few more specimens have been found.

Bird-like and reptile-like

Archaeopteryx is a link because it had some bird-like features, such as its feathers and a wishbone. However, *Archaeopteryx* had teeth and a long bony tail, so in that way it was like living reptiles and not at all like modern birds. ∎

◐ **See also**
Birds
Dinosaurs
Evolution of living things
Fossils
Geological time

▲ *Archaeopteryx* was quite similar to small dinosaurs like *Compsognathus*, except that it had feathers.

◀ The fossils of *Archaeopteryx* have been found in rocks in Germany. You can see clearly the bones and the feathers.

▶ The New Zealander, Neroli Fairhall, competes in an archery contest at the Commonwealth Games in 1982.

◐ **See also**
Weapons (longbow)

Archery

The sport of shooting at a target with bow and arrows is called archery. The modern bow is made of layers of woods specially selected to make the bow strong, supple and light.

An archery competition consists of 'rounds' of arrows shot from varying distances (a 'round' is a specified number of arrows). The winner is the archer with the highest total score after the rounds have been completed.

The bow is a killing weapon, and has been used in war and in hunting since prehistoric times. The sport of target archery was used to keep archers on top form. ∎

Other kinds of archery
As well as target archery there is field archery, which is intended to be like hunting. A course is laid out in wooded land, and you shoot at targets which look like various animals. There are also competitions for distance shooting.

Other kinds of bow
The crossbow is drawn by a mechanism turned by a handle, and it shoots a short arrow, called a bolt. The footbow is braced by the feet and you use it in a sitting position.

Arches

An arch is a type of support for a bridge or building. It is usually curved in shape and forms an opening or gap between two upright parts of a wall. An arch has to be strong, since it usually has to support the weight of a wall or roof above.

Lintels

Until people learned how to build an arch, openings or gaps had to be spanned with a large, flat piece of stone or wood. This was called a lintel. Modern buildings still have lintels, usually made of steel or reinforced concrete, to support the walls above doors and windows. Such lintels can span quite a large gap because they are long, strong and relatively light. But before these materials were available, builders were never able to make a very wide rectangular doorway or window, because it was difficult to find a piece of stone or wood large enough and strong enough.

Building an arch

An arch can be made to any size. Every building-block used in the early arches had to be narrower at the bottom than at the top. In this way, no spaces were left between the blocks when they were arranged in a curve. The central block of an arch is called the keystone. Often it is larger than the other blocks, because it has the greatest pressures acting upon it.

When building an arch there is nothing to support the building-blocks until they are all in place. So the arch is made on a temporary wooden frame. The builder constructs the curve from both sides, but it is not until the last block, the keystone, is pushed into place that the arch can stand alone. A temporary wooden framework is still used when building modern concrete arches, but it is not necessary when building iron, steel or pre-stressed concrete ones.

Strengthening an arch

When an arch has been completed, the stresses tend to squeeze the blocks outwards. If the arch is not firmly supported, or buttressed, on each side, it may collapse. Often in churches and cathedrals,

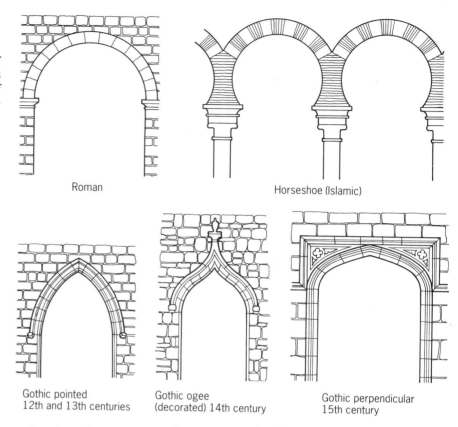

Roman

Horseshoe (Islamic)

Gothic pointed
12th and 13th centuries

Gothic ogee
(decorated) 14th century

Gothic perpendicular
15th century

the stone buttresses used to support the huge roof arches are on the outside of the building.

Flashback

The ancient Egyptians knew how to make arches, although they did not use them in their buildings. The Etruscans used arches in their buildings but the Romans were the first to use arches as major architectural features. Spectacular examples of Roman arches are to be seen in aqueducts such as the three-tiered Pont du Gard. These arches were round. This shape was used until medieval builders developed the pointed arch. Pointed arches had been used in Mesopotamia in the 7th century AD, and the idea was probably brought back to Europe by the crusaders. Pointed arches formed the basis of the Gothic style of architecture. At first the Gothic arch was narrow. Later a wider shape was used, and from this many of the more complicated kinds of arches, including the vaulted roofs of many churches and cathedrals, were developed. ■

▲ Some different styles of arch.

Everyday arches

Arches can be seen in doorways, windows, brick-lined railway tunnels and the vaulting of cathedrals and churches. In big buildings, arches provide a large open space unobstructed by columns.

◖ See also
Aqueducts
Bridges
Gothic architecture

Something to do

Make an arch with Plasticine. Cut it into 'bricks' and try to build the arch standing up, without sticking the bricks together. You may need a cardboard frame.

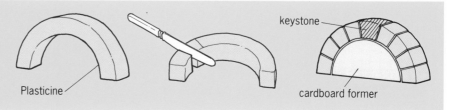

Plasticine

keystone

cardboard former

Architects

Architects create designs for buildings. The difference between a den and a designed building is that the architect has planned the design and made drawings and models before any building work can begin. A building may be a home for one family, or a block of apartments for families of different sizes. It may be a school, an ice rink, a bus station, a hotel, a church, a shopping precinct, an airport. Each kind of building and every new site presents a problem.

▲ Children sometimes build huts or dens in trees, on wasteland, or underneath a table. The construction and the size are limited by what materials can be found and by the site.

▼ 'Falling Water' is a house designed by Frank Lloyd Wright for Edgar Kaufmann and his family in Pennsylvania, USA in 1936.

Architects and space

Architects work with building materials and with space, shape and light. The shapes of a building are made by walls, floors, ceilings, stairways and doors, and with furniture and other fittings. Light can be both natural and artificial. By using light and shape the architect plans to create a building that is good to live in or work in and visit. The spaces within a building may have different functions and create certain feelings. Successful buildings may have pleasing spaces both inside and out.

◄ The 'Unité d'Habitation' was designed by Le Corbusier as apartments for 1,600 people in Marseille, France, in 1947.

'Falling Water' and the 'Unité d'Habitation' are both made mainly from concrete, but the setting and the space are completely different.

▲ The British architect, Michael Hopkins, used teflon-coated glass fibre to create a central canopy for the Schlumberger Research Building in Cambridge, England in 1985.

▼ Housing designed by the Dutch architect, Piet Blom, and built in The Netherlands. The design was partly inspired by tree housing; the homes are elevated from ground level and the shapes are unusual.

Architects and technology

Modern building materials such as roof tiles, roof trusses, doors, windows, drain-pipes and guttering are manufactured in factories, to standard sizes. Bricks also can be made identical in size and texture. Any amount of concrete can be poured on the site.

Architects need to know which kind of material will work best in a building and what the components will cost. They must design buildings using the latest developments in material technology. Sometimes an architect helps to develop a new solution to a problem, such as how to span a large open area with a lightweight structure and without a lot of heavy supports.

Opinions

Buildings last for a long time and changes may happen to the inside and outside for very many reasons. The attitude of people to buildings changes too. When highrise flats were first built in the 1950s and 1960s, architects and town planners in Britain thought they were a good solution to the problem of providing space for people to live in the cities. But they were not so convenient for some of the families who lived in them. Old Victorian terrace houses seemed shabby and dark inside. But these could be renovated. Interior

▲ The Lloyds Building in the City of London, designed by Richard Rogers and completed in 1986, provides accommodation for offices. It has a central core up to 12 storeys high, a central light well, and six service towers. The lifts and stairways, waste pipes and air conditioning systems are all visible from the outside.

walls could be taken down to make more light and space. So they became valued again.

Fashions for school buildings, factories, churches, shops and other categories of buildings have changed many times. If we understand why we feel a building is a success or not, then we know something about architecture. First impressions may not tell us the whole story behind the present level of the success of a building. We may need to study its history and find out what it was intended for in the first place. ■

See also
Arches
Bricks
Buildings
Concrete
Gothic architecture
Greek ancient history
Renaissance
Temples

Biography
Gropius
Le Corbusier
Wren
Wright, Frank Lloyd

Arctic Ocean

The Arctic Circle is at latitude 66½° North; the North Pole is at 90° N.

Area of Arctic Ocean
14,200,000 sq km
(5,500,000 sq miles)

Depth of ocean at North Pole
4,087 m

Two Americans claimed to be the first to reach the North Pole: Frederick Cook in 1908, and Robert Peary in 1909.

The Arctic is the area inside the Arctic Circle around the North Pole. Most of the Arctic is a huge frozen ocean, surrounded by islands and by the northern coasts of Norway, the USSR, Alaska and Canada. The largest island is Greenland, which is covered with a thick ice-sheet. Cold water flows out from the Arctic into the Atlantic and Pacific Oceans, carrying icebergs with it.

The weather is very cold in winter, and it is dark for most of the time. The sea is completely frozen over. In summer, temperatures creep above freezing point in four months of the year, and the Arctic is the land of the midnight Sun. Then, the edge of the Arctic Ocean melts. One famous sea-route is the North-West Passage from the Bering Strait to Baffin Island, between the

islands of the far north of Canada. It can be navigated in the summer, but drifting ice is a constant danger. Many explorers have died here.

The centre of the Arctic Ocean remains frozen all year round, although in summer the ice may crack. The ice floating on the deep ocean is called sea-ice or pack-ice. It can break apart or move together into ridges. Travelling is dangerous and difficult.

It is possible to navigate right under the North Pole by submarine. In 1958, the nuclear-powered submarine USS *Nautilus* crossed the Arctic Ocean. In 1959 the USS *Skate* managed to break through the ice and surface at the North Pole.

The land around the Arctic Ocean is bleak and treeless. For most of the year the soil is frozen and covered with snow. In summer, the snow melts and the top few inches of soil thaw out. Deeper down the soil is still frozen, so the surface is very marshy and lots of flies and mosquitoes breed in the pools. The plants that grow here can stand the severe cold and can grow in shallow, wet soil.

Some animals graze these plants, such as the reindeer of northern Europe and the caribou and musk ox of North America. The Arctic Ocean is rich in plankton and fish. These are food for millions of sea birds which nest here in summer, and for the seals, whales and other sea creatures. Arctic foxes and polar bears survive by hunting. Thick fur protects them from the cold, and the bears are excellent swimmers.

The Inuit (Eskimo) have survived here because there are animals to hunt and fish to catch. Oil has been discovered in Alaska, and other minerals have been found, so recently people have come from further south to work in the Arctic. ■

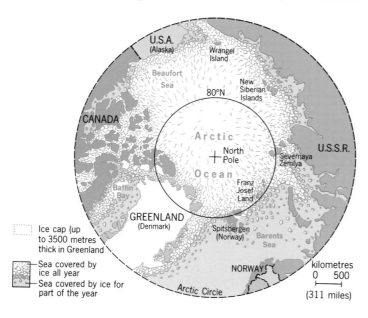

Ice cap (up to 3500 metres thick in Greenland)

Sea covered by ice all year

Sea covered by ice for part of the year

◀ **Summer in west Greenland. The ice floes have broken up enabling ships to come in close to the shore.**

Argentina

Argentina means 'Land of Silver'. The Spanish explorers who named it hoped to find silver there but were disappointed. It is the second largest country in South America, after Brazil, and is five times the size of France. On the western bank of the Río de la Plata ('River of Silver') stands the great capital city of Buenos Aires.

The land

Argentina covers most of south-eastern South America. To the west, the Andes Mountains separate Argentina from Chile. Patagonia in the south is a windswept semi-desert, with large oil reserves. It extends to the southern tip of South America. In the north is a huge region of subtropical plains and forests, called the Gran Chaco. In the centre lie the vast grassy plains of the pampas with their rich soil. The plains produce about three-quarters of Argentina's wealth. Ranchers grow millions of tonnes of wheat and maize there. They also rear cattle, sheep, and pigs and export their meat, hides and wool to many countries.

During the first half of the 20th century Argentina became an industrial as well as an agricultural society. But the economy has been through many hard times, including periods of massive inflation.

People

Most Argentinians are descended from Europeans and there are very few Indians in the country. An exception is the *gaucho*, the cowboy hero of Argentina and a symbol of horsemanship, adventure and romance. Most gauchos are descended from Spanish conquerors and Indians.

Flashback

Argentina was freed from Spanish colonial rule in 1816 by their national hero, José de San Martín. Since 1930 there have been a number of military dictators. The most famous was Juan Perón who ruled after World War II. But under the dictators many thousands of Argentinians lost their lives or were tortured. In 1982 Argentina invaded the British Falkland Islands, Islas Malvinas, which Argentina claimed as her territory. After a ten-week war Argentina was defeated at a cost of 655 lives. ∎

Area
2,766,889 sq km
(1,068,302 sq miles)
Capital
Buenos Aires
Population
30,564,000
Language
Spanish
Religion
Christian
Government
Federal republic
Currency
1 Argentine austral = 100 centavos

The musical *Evita* was written about Eva Perón, who had been very popular among some Argentinians.

◀ The gaucho uses his skill with a lasso to rope a young calf from the herd.

◉ See also

Andes
Falkland Islands
Grasslands
South America
Spanish colonial history

Aristocrats

Aristocrats were members of the noble families, the rich and privileged people who ruled the countries of Europe for hundreds of years. Aristocratic families still survive. But they do not have so much power in countries where everyone has the right to vote. In theory there are no aristocrats in republics such as France or the United States. But most countries have groups of families with power and privilege, as well as wealth, such as the Brahmins in India, or people of pure Portuguese or Spanish descent in South America. ∎

This word comes from two Greek words: *aristos* meaning 'best' and *kratos* meaning 'strength'.
In Britain in 1990 there were, in addition to the Royal Family, over 800 Dukes, Marquesses, Earls, Viscounts and Barons.

Arithmetic

In arithmetic, there are many different ways of carrying out the four basic operations (adding, subtracting, multiplying and dividing) which combine whole numbers together.

Simple sums – like '2 times 13', or '35 add 19' – we can usually do in our heads; we call this 'mental arithmetic'. It is important to be able to do this, even in an age when electronic calculators are widely available. Some more complicated arithmetic calculations may require some method of recording – fingers or pencil and paper, perhaps – while others are so difficult we might prefer an abacus, a calculator or a computer to do them.

At its simplest, **adding** is nothing more than counting on from one number to another; adding 3 and 3 is the same as starting at 3 and counting on 3 more (3...4, 5, 6). And **multiplication** is just repeated adding. For example, 7 times 3 is really just the same as

$$3 + 3 + 3 + 3 + 3 + 3 + 3 \quad (\text{or}, 7 + 7 + 7).$$

Subtraction is really just addition in reverse. To find out the answer to '15 take away 6' is just the same as asking, 'What number would I have to add to 6, to get an answer of 15?' And in its turn, **division** is simply multiple subtraction.

This is very important. Computers and electronic calculators rely very much on this fact that all complex arithmetic calculations can be reduced to doing a long series of simple additions. At the heart of every computer lies the Arithmetic Logic Unit.

Multiplication

Many things in life depend on the accurate multiplication of large or awkward numbers: for instance, navigation, astronomy, making machinery or calculating energy needs. Before computers were invented, people had devised lots of ways of multiplying. The simplest of these is a table of multiplications.

1	2	3	4	5	6	7	8	9	10
2	4	6	8	10	12	14	16	18	20
3	6	9	12	15	18	21	24	27	30
4	8	12	16	20	24	28	32	36	40
5	10	15	20	25	30	35	40	45	50
6	12	18	24	30	36	42	48	54	60
7	14	21	28	35	42	49	56	63	70
8	16	24	32	40	48	56	64	72	80
9	18	27	36	45	54	63	72	81	90
10	20	30	40	50	60	70	80	90	100

The table gives the answers to all multiplications between 1 x 1 and 10 x 10. To multiply 4 x 6, find the column with 4 at the top and the row with 6 at the side. The answer, 24, is where the column and row cross.

When we need an answer that is roughly correct, we can estimate. For example, 21 times 39 is very roughly the same as 20 times 40, which gives 800.

Estimating is all right so long as we do not need an exact answer. The beauty of Egyptian multiplication (more than 2,000 years old) is that it is almost as easy as estimating, but gives exact answers every time. We usually break down a multiplication such as 21 times 39 into several steps. The Egyptians broke it down in a rather different way. Their system relied on doubling and then adding.

First, write down a table in which each line doubles the line before, but do not go beyond the number you want to multiply.

```
 1 x 39 =  39
 2 x 39 =  78
 4 x 39 = 156
 8 x 39 = 312
16 x 39 = 624 . . .  and stop! (because the
                      next one would be 32).
```

Then, select only those left-hand numbers that combine to make 21 (in this case, 1, 4 and 16). Cross out the rest (2 and 8). Add up the totals on the right and you have the exact answer, 819.

```
 1 x        39
 2̶ ̶x̶       7̶8̶
 4 x       156
 8̶ ̶x̶      3̶1̶2̶
16 x       624
          ─────
           819
```

Something to do

Mathematicians are always on the look-out for patterns in arithmetic and they use them to find short cuts in calculations. Patterns are very obvious with some calculations with numbers like eleven and nine. For example,

11 x 11 = 121	the *middle* number in
12 x 11 = 132	each answer can be made
13 x 11 = 143	by adding the two
14 x 11 = 154	*inside* numbers.
2 x 9 = 18	the two numbers of the
3 x 9 = 27	answer can be added
4 x 9 = 36	together to give 9
5 x 9 = 45	each time.

Mental arithmetic

Some people can do as 'mental arithmetic' the kind of calculations that would have most of us reaching for the electronic calculator. Often their technique depends on noting a variety of patterns like the ones below. They break the task down into small steps, just as a computer does.

The fastest of them can keep up with and sometimes even beat opponents with hand-held calculators. In the same way, the fastest abacus users can beat most ordinary people who are using a calculator!

A quick method for multiplying by nine

Open both hands out in front of you. Count from the left the number you want to multiply by nine. Fold down that finger. Count the number of fingers to the left of the one you have folded down. This gives you the tens digit of the answer. Now count the number of fingers to the right of the finger you have folded down. This gives you the number of units in the answer.

See also
Calculators
Computers
Fractions
Mathematics
Numbers

Biography
Napier

Armada

The Spanish Armada was a huge fleet of ships which Philip II of Spain sent to invade England in 1588. The two countries had been at war for three years. Catholic Philip was the richest and most feared monarch in Europe. He decided to crush the Protestant English with a single blow. So he put together a mighty sea-borne army, and in May 1588 this 'invincible' Armada was sent to conquer England. Philip wanted it to join forces with another Spanish army which was standing by in the Netherlands.

Disasters strike

The link-up was never made. First the Armada was delayed by storms. Then it was subjected to harassing attacks as the English fleet pursued it cautiously up the Channel. The English commander was a nobleman, Lord Howard of Effingham, and among his captains were Francis Drake, Martin Frobisher and John Hawkins. Bad weather and treacherous currents forced the Armada to anchor off the French port of Calais. Here, on the night of 7 August, the English floated some burning ships (fireships) in among the Spanish fleet, which scattered to avoid them. Next day, the Armada was pounded by the English gunners off Gravelines. Seriously menaced by weather and tides, it faced total destruction.

Suddenly, a strong wind blowing from the south-west enabled sea-worthy Spanish vessels to escape into the North Sea. Abandoning their enterprise, they sailed on round the north of Scotland, suffering more losses from shipwreck and disease as they made for home. In the end, fewer than half the ships of the great Armada got back to Spain. ■

▶ An unknown Dutch artist painted this picture of the naval battle between the Armada and the English. The English vessels are those which are flying the red-cross flag of Saint George, the country's patron saint. Some of the larger Spanish galleons are already shown to be sinking.

Official number of ships
130
Total weight of ships
58,000 tons
Number of sailors
About 8,000
Number of soldiers
About 19,000
Commander
The Duke of Medina Sidonia
Cost of launching the Armada
10 million ducats (equal to Elizabeth I's total income for five or six years)

See also

Spain's history
Tudor England

Biography
Drake
Elizabeth I
Hawkins
Philip II

Armadillos

The name armadillo means 'little armoured one'. All armadillos are shielded with plates of bone and horn set in the skin of their backs, heads and tails. When attacked some can curl up into a ball. Those which are not able to roll up defend themselves with the huge claws on their front feet. But they are not aggressive and whenever possible prefer to escape danger by burrowing.

Armadillos are slow-moving animals, mainly active at night, when they hunt for insects, worms and carrion. Some armadillos produce a single young one each year, but most have a litter of identical cubs, all developed from a single fertilized egg. Most species of armadillos are now rare, partly because they have been hunted for food, and partly because of the destruction of their habitat. ■

Distribution
All of South America, Central America, and some parts of North America
Largest armadillo
Giant armadillo: head and body length up to 100 cm; tail length about 50 cm; weight up to 60 kg
Smallest armadillo
Fairy armadillo: head and body length up to 15 cm; tail about 2·5 cm
Number of young
Up to 12, usually less
Lifespan
12–15 years in the wild. Most species do not thrive in zoos and die very quickly, but a six-banded armadillo lived for nearly 19 years in captivity.

Subphylum Vertebrata
Class Mammalia
Order Edentata
Family Dasypodidae
Number of species 20

◀ As the nine-banded armadillo walks, the only part of its front feet to touch the ground is its huge claws, which it uses to dig for ants and termites.

See also

Anteaters
Armoured animals
Nocturnal animals
Sloths

Armies

Every man or woman who serves in an army has a rank, from private soldier to general; and everyone is assigned to a particular unit.

Units of an army

A modern army has many different units. **Infantry** units operate on foot, but are often equipped with sophisticated missile weapons, as well as machine-guns and grenades. **Signals** units gather information and pass on orders. **Artillery** units support infantry, providing bombardment with shells, which may have nuclear warheads.

Engineers build roads, bridges and railways, clear minefields, organize river crossings and mine besieged positions. **Tank** units are the main means of attack in a major war; many of these units in the British army were horse cavalry until after World War I.

There are **Airborne** and **Parachute** units, and in addition **Medical**, **Catering**, **Intelligence** and **Military Police**. **Ordnance** units are responsible for all supplies. **Transport** units are responsible for moving troops when needed, using troop carriers, helicopters, amphibious landing craft and fleets of lorries.

Supplies

Supplies and transport are the keys to success in modern armies. When armies were small they used to 'live off the country', buying or taking food and other provisions and turning their horses out to graze.

An army today needs good roads, railways and air transport; petrol, water and mechanical spares; food, clothing, weapons and ammunition, and workers in factories to make these munitions.

Recruiting and conscripting

In peacetime many countries, including Britain and the USA, rely on volunteers for their armies. Other countries, including Switzerland, China, Italy, France and Israel, conscript all fit young people into the armed forces for a year or more as well as having a professional army. Afterwards they spend a number of years in the reserve. This compulsory duty is called conscription, enlistment, the draft, or national service. The first country to have used conscription was ancient Egypt. In wartime most countries use it.

National armies

The word 'army' is used to describe all of a country's soldiers, for example 'the French army'. Large countries such as the USA and USSR have several 'armies' made up of a number of corps. Each army may be stationed in a different part of the world. The army of the USA consists of men and women who enlist voluntarily.

The People's Liberation Army of China has millions of conscripted soldiers in 191 divisions. Their duties are to guard the thousands of miles of frontier, but also to impose order upon the people of China, sometimes brutally. The USSR also has a huge army of conscripted soldiers defending long frontiers east and west. This 'Red Army' won many important battles in World War II, using powerful tanks. The largest African army is that of Nigeria, with some 250,000 regular soldiers.

Politics and armies

In times of political confusion, armies sometimes take over the government of a country, with a leading general in charge. This happened in England in the 17th century when a general, Oliver Cromwell, became ruler after the execution of King Charles I.

In this century the army has taken control in many countries, including Pakistan, Egypt, Sudan, Iran, Iraq, Nigeria and Chile. The aim is always to restore civilian rule when order has been imposed.

Flashback

The Greek armies of Alexander the Great were highly disciplined. They were copied by the Roman armies, which conquered the lands of the Mediterranean and beyond.

In the Middle Ages some military leaders used to form small private armies and hire them out to anyone who could pay. Such troops were called mercenaries.

In the 17th and 18th centuries wars were fought mostly by 'standing armies' of professional soldiers serving under aristocratic officers. The armies of Louis XIV of France were the first to be divided into divisions and brigades.

The first modern conscript armies were raised in France at the time of the Revolution, and since then armies have become equipped with more and more deadly weapons. ■

Ranks

Second Lieutenant
Lieutenant
Captain
Major
Lieutenant-Colonel
Colonel
Brigadier
Major-General
Lieutenant-General
General
Field Marshal

Units of the British army

Squad About 12 men
Platoon Four squads
Company Two or more platoons
Troop Cavalry equivalent of a company
Battalion Three or more companies
Regiment Two or more battalions plus headquarters and supply units
Brigade Three or more battalions or regiments plus headquarters and supply units
Division Headquarters, specialized companies, and up to 15 combat battalions
Corps Two or more divisions with headquarters and other units
Army Two or more corps

The number of officers and men in an army varies greatly between countries and between wartime and peacetime.

In 1990 the British army had about 160,000 men and women. Large numbers were stationed in Northern Ireland and West Germany.

See also

Armour
Battles
Cavalry
Guns
Tanks
Weapons

Biography
Alexander the Great
Cromwell
Napoleon Bonaparte

Armour

Buff coat
Thick leather jacket
Cuirass
Breastplate and backplate
fastened together
Cuisse
Thigh guard
Flak jacket
British term for a bullet-
proof vest
Gauntlet
Metal glove
Half armour
Armour for the body only
Helm
A large helmet covering the
whole head
Morion
An open helmet
Pauldron
Plate to guard the shoulder
Vambrace
Plate armour for the arm

Warriors have worn armour for thousands of years. The ancient Greeks wore linen or leather shirts with metal plates sewn on to protect the heart and shoulders. The hoplites (armed foot-soldiers) wore a breastplate of bronze shaped to fit the body. Greaves (shin guards) protected the legs, and bronze helmets were worn on the head. Each soldier carried a shield.

Roman foot-soldiers and the legionary cavalry wore armour of iron hoops protecting the back as well as the front of the body. Romans also used mail, at first small metal plates sewn on a leather jerkin, overlapping like tiles on a roof, and later made of metal links, known as chain armour.

In the early Middle Ages, European soldiers wore armour made of chain mail. From about 1330 knights wore heavy armour made of jointed steel plates. After the development of guns, armour was gradually reduced to a cuirass and helmet. By the 20th century only the helmet remained.

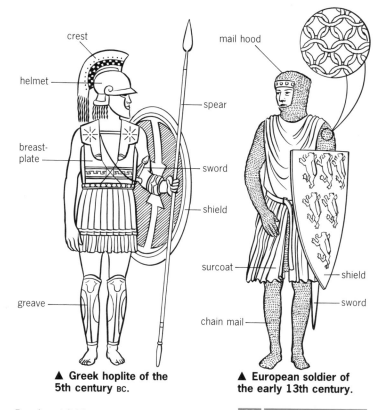

crest
helmet
breast-plate
greave

mail hood
spear
sword
shield

surcoat
chain mail
shield
sword

▲ **Greek hoplite of the 5th century** BC.

▲ **European soldier of the early 13th century.**

In the 1940s a new kind of body armour made of nylon, other plastics and glass fibres came into use. The most common form is the bullet-proof vest. ■

See also
Battles
Cavalry
Knights
Weapons

Armoured animals

Hermit crabs use the abandoned shells of other sea animals as protection.

The spines of some animals, such as sea urchins, are tipped with poison.

Many animals, such as crocodiles and alligators, have bodies covered in hard plates of 'armour' to protect them from enemies. The armadillo can roll itself up in a ball with only its hardest armour exposed, and so can tiny woodlice. Insects have hard shiny outer shells for protection, with joints between the plates to allow them to move, as do crustaceans. Sea horses, trunkfish and boxfish have such stiff armoured bodies that they cannot bend, and rely solely on their fins for swimming. Shells are used as protection by snails, shellfish and hermit crabs. Porcupines, hedgehogs, pufferfish and some caterpillars are protected by stiff sharp spines. ■

See also
Armadillos
Crabs
Crocodiles
Crustaceans
Insects
Slugs and snails
Woodlice

Arthritis

If you have arthritis, the joints of your body become swollen, stiff and painful.

When a joint bends, the ends of two bones rub together. Normally the end of each bone is covered with a smooth gristle called cartilage, and is bathed in oily joint fluid so the joint moves easily.

If the gristle is damaged, it becomes rough and this irritates the joint. The roughness stimulates the joint to make more joint fluid, which in turn swells the joint and causes more inflammation.

There are different causes of arthritis, including infections and just getting old. ■

People who take lots of exercise are less likely to suffer from arthritis when they get old.

See also
Rheumatism
Skeletons

Arthur and his knights

About 1,400 years ago a Celtic warrior-chief called Arthur may have lived and fought against the invading Anglo-Saxons. Around him gathered a great collection of stories and legends. If the real King Arthur came back to life, and heard the tales people tell of him, he might be very surprised.

Arthur and Merlin

Arthur was the baby son of King Uther Pendragon. Uther gave the child to a wizard, Merlin. 'Teach him everything,' he said. As Arthur grew up, Merlin taught him all that a prince needed to know: riding, sword-fighting, shooting with bow and arrows, dancing, reading, singing. He also taught Arthur magic. He changed him into a salmon, to explore the rivers and seas. He changed him into a hawk, to soar in the sky. He changed him into an ant, to tunnel underground. He changed him into a lizard, a cat, a bee. By the time Arthur was fifteen, he had learnt all Merlin had to teach him. He was ready to be king.

The sword in the stone

When King Uther died, no one remembered Arthur. 'Who is to be king?' they cried. Merlin stuck a sword, Excalibur, into a block of stone. 'This sword is held in the stone by magic,' he told the people. 'Only the true king will be able to pull it out.' Everyone laughed. 'What nonsense!' people jeered. 'Any fool can loosen it.' But although they tried till the muscles knotted on their arms and the blood pounded in their veins, they all failed. Then Arthur pulled the sword from the stone as easily as a knife from cheese. 'God save the King!' the people cried.

See also

Celtic history
Dark Ages

Biography
Arthur

King Arthur

Arthur's court was in Camelot Castle. His queen was Guinevere. Lancelot, his best friend, led the courtiers. They sat in council at a huge round table in the palace hall, and there Arthur ruled with justice and peace. His followers, the Knights of the Round Table, fought the wicked, helped the weak, and rescued ladies in distress. Arthur led his armies to conquer other countries. Soon he ruled everyone from the trolls of the frozen north to the mermen and mermaids of the southern seas. His enemies sent fire-snorting dragons and tree-sized giants to challenge him, and he beat them all.

The Once and Future King

For all Arthur's glory, the life of Camelot was short. While he was away, his friend Lancelot and his queen Guinevere fell in love. When Arthur heard of it, he banished Lancelot from Camelot. Many Round Table lords supported Lancelot, and went into exile with him. Only a few lords stayed loyal to Arthur, and when Arthur's wicked son Mordred saw how few supporters Arthur had, he plotted to snatch the throne. Arthur had to gather an army against his own son. He and Mordred fought hand-to-hand and Arthur killed Mordred. But Arthur too was fatally wounded. His faithful Lord Belvedere threw the sword Excalibur into a misty lake and a hand rose from the depths to grasp it. Then the Lady of the Lake took Arthur in a magic boat to the Islands of the Blessed. His lords built a tomb in his memory and wrote on it 'Arthur, the Once and Future King'. They believed that he and his soldiers had not passed from the world for ever, but lay sleeping in a secret cave. When Britain's need was greatest, Merlin would wake them with a horn-call, and they would gallop out on warhorses to save their country. ■

Artificial limbs

Artificial limbs are special devices made to replace arms, legs or hands that have been seriously damaged through disease, injury or birth defect. They are also called prostheses. All artificial limbs are made individually to fit the person who needs one. After the limb has been amputated (removed) by surgery and the wound has healed, the remaining stump is wrapped in bandages soaked with plaster of paris. A cast is made from the stump. This is used to produce a plaster and fibreglass socket onto which the artificial limb is fixed. Plastics, light metals and various fibres are used to make artificial limbs. A person wearing an artificial leg can walk without help. A person using an artificial hand can grasp, hold and perform delicate or heavy work.

Scientists are developing limbs controlled by microcomputers. These will pick up weak electrical impulses from nerves in the severed stump and use them to work tiny electric motors attached to wires and pulleys. These would move fingers, twist the wrist and make other delicate movements. The owner of such a 'bionic' limb would only have to think of a movement and the computer would perform it. Pressure-sensitive electronic skin is also being developed to give bionic limbs a sense of touch. ■

Asbestos

Asbestos is a mineral. But instead of being hard and solid, it is made up of soft, silky fibres. It is an extremely poor conductor of heat and does not burn or char, so it is very useful for insulating things from intense heat or fire. Asbestos is woven into the protective clothing worn by fire-fighters. It is also used to make the brake-pads, brake-shoes and clutch linings of motor cars. These get very hot because they rub against other moving parts. Boilers are often lined with asbestos to prevent the spread of fire and heat.

Asbestos can be very harmful to health and strict safety precautions have to be followed wherever it is made or used. Breathing in asbestos dust can cause the lung disease, asbestosis.

Asbestos is mined in Canada, the USSR, China, Italy and South Africa. ■

○ See also
Brakes
Insulation
Minerals

Asia

Each of the continents has a great variety of landscapes and people, but Asia's great size gives it the greatest contrasts. It covers one-third of the land surface of the planet and has half the world's people. The border with Europe is the Ural Mountains in the USSR. The Middle East is usually counted as part of Asia.

Landscapes

Flat frozen plains of mosses and lichens cover much of northern Siberia. Further south are coniferous forests. The grasslands of the steppes have rich black fertile soils. Much of Asia from the Red Sea to Mongolia is desert. The greatest desert is the Gobi. Much of this is bare rock, but swirling winds have piled up dunes of sand on the desert edge.

The Himalayas are the world's highest mountains. Many peaks are over 8 km (5 miles) high. Some rivers to the north of the Himalayas never reach the sea. They flow across hundreds of kilometres of desert and evaporate. Near the Equator are damp jungles and swampy sea-shores. The western Pacific coast has frequent earthquakes. Many of these occur under the sea, and there is danger from tidal waves.

Climate

Asia is so large that some parts of the continent are more than 2,500 km (1,500 miles) from the sea. In winter the land lies under a great cushion of cold heavy air. Cold, dry winds blow out from the centre of the continent. In summer the winds blow in the opposite direction. The land heats quickly and air in central Asia rises. Wet winds from the sea blow in. These winds bring the monsoon rain, which comes suddenly in torrential downpours. Only the mountains stop the wet winds from reaching the continent's interior, keeping western China and Mongolia dry.

Countries

Much of Asia's land and many of its people live in the giant countries of India, China, and the USSR. Japan, Singapore and South Korea are wealthy nations. Japan is the world's third largest industrial power. Almost every country in south-east Asia has suffered from wars since World War II. There have been large-scale civil wars in Burma, Cambodia, Korea and Vietnam. Most countries have seen clashes between the government and rebels, often resulting in many deaths. There has also been violence between peoples with different languages and customs.

People

The largest number of Asians live in India, Bangladesh and the eastern half of China. Other great centres of population are Japan, Indonesia and Sri Lanka. There are also vast areas where few people live, for example Mongolia, the western half of China and Siberia in the USSR. The most crowded areas are on the coasts and along the flood-plains of rivers such as the Huang He (Yellow) and Chang Jiang (Yangtze) in China and the Ganges and Brahmaputra in India and Bangladesh. Many of the world's worst disasters have occurred when these rivers have flooded.

With more than one-half of the world's population, it is not surprising that there is a great variety of ways of life in Asia. To be Asian means only that you come from the world's biggest continent. The way of life of a Siberian miner has little in common with a Vietnamese rice-farmer.

Most Asians live in the country and make their living from farming. Rice is the main crop in most parts of India, China and south-east Asia. The Soviet Union, however, has vast areas of land that are used for growing wheat and the

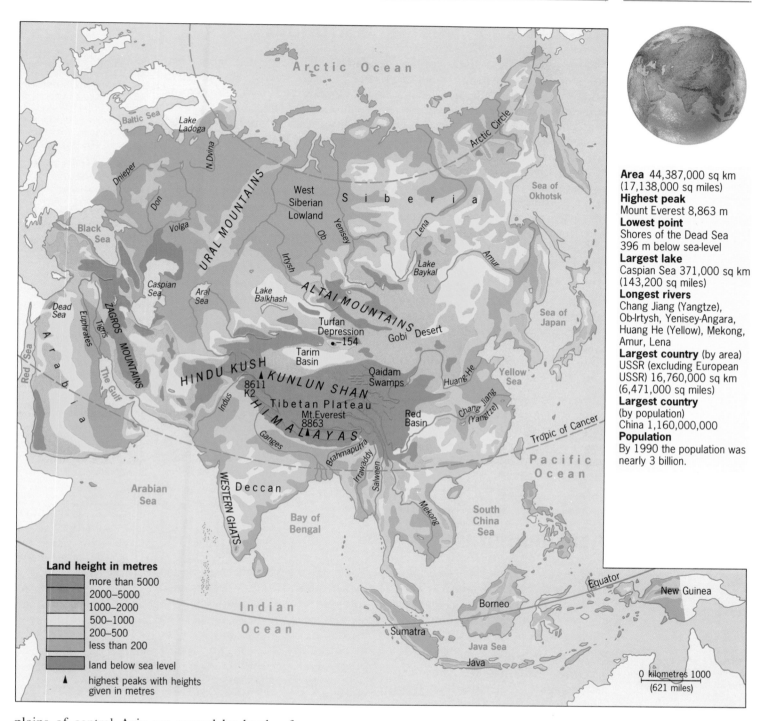

Land height in metres
- more than 5000
- 2000–5000
- 1000–2000
- 500–1000
- 200–500
- less than 200
- land below sea level
- ▲ highest peaks with heights given in metres

0 kilometres 1000
(621 miles)

Area 44,387,000 sq km (17,138,000 sq miles)
Highest peak Mount Everest 8,863 m
Lowest point Shores of the Dead Sea 396 m below sea-level
Largest lake Caspian Sea 371,000 sq km (143,200 sq miles)
Longest rivers Chang Jiang (Yangtze), Ob-Irtysh, Yenisey-Angara, Huang He (Yellow), Mekong, Amur, Lena
Largest country (by area) USSR (excluding European USSR) 16,760,000 sq km (6,471,000 sq miles)
Largest country (by population) China 1,160,000,000
Population By 1990 the population was nearly 3 billion.

plains of central Asia are grazed by herds of cattle, goats or yaks.

Asia is rich in minerals and energy reserves but only a few countries have widespread industry. These include the Soviet Union and Japan. Other Asian countries such as South Korea and the Philippines are developing industry fast.

The quality of life among Asian people varies greatly. South Asian countries have fewer doctors per person and many people do not have a balanced diet. The average life expectancy in Laos for example is about 40 years whereas people in Japan usually live to be more than 70. More babies die in Cambodia than in any other country in the world.

City life is becoming more and more attractive to many people. Seoul, Bangkok, Jakarta and many other Asian cities are growing rapidly. Over a dozen cities in Asia have more than 5 million inhabitants. ■

See also
Ganges
Himalayas
Middle East
Monsoon

Asthma

Asthma is a common disease of the respiratory (breathing) system which can affect people of all ages. Some people have mild asthma which needs little treatment, whilst in others it is quite severe. When people are troubled by asthma, they are said to be suffering from an asthma attack. In an asthma attack the air passages to the lungs become very narrow, and sufferers wheeze and have great difficulty in breathing. This can be very frightening and they may panic. An asthma sufferer should be kept calm.

Asthma attacks can be caused by many different things, but in children and young people the attack usually occurs when they have a viral infection like the common cold, which affects the air passages.

Some mild attacks of asthma will clear on their own if the person rests and relaxes. Sometimes it is necessary to use an inhaler containing a drug which opens up the air passages. ■

People who suffer from asthma throughout their lives usually do so because they are allergic to something, such as dust or animal fur.

See also
Breathing
Human body
Lungs
Respiration

Astronauts

Astronauts are people who leave the Earth and travel into space. In the USSR they are known as cosmonauts. The first was Yuri Gagarin, who orbited once round the Earth in his spacecraft on 12 April 1961.

The Moon is the furthest that any astronauts have travelled from Earth so far. Neil Armstrong and Edwin 'Buzz' Aldrin of the USA were the first to land there, on 20 July 1969. Ten other astronauts have travelled to the Moon since, the last in 1972. Missions to Mars are now being planned.

Before they go into space, astronauts have to practise all the things they will need to do when they are there. To get used to weightlessness, they fly in an aircraft which climbs and then dives in a special curved path so that the astronauts can float about in their cabin. To practise control of their spacecraft, they use a full-size working model, called a simulator, which stays on the ground. ■

First person in space
On 12 April 1961 Yuri Gagarin of the USSR circled the Earth once at a height of about 400 km (250 miles), and a speed of 29,000 km/h (18,000 mph). The whole trip lasted 108 minutes.

Dangers of space flight
In June 1971, three cosmonauts died while their spacecraft was re-entering the Earth's atmosphere. In January 1986 the *Challenger* space shuttle blew up just after launch, killing all seven people on board.

First 'space walk'
Alexei Leonov left his spacecraft for 12 minutes on 18 March 1965.

In December 1987, Yuri Romanenko of the USSR completed a stay of 326 days aboard the MIR space station.

See also
Moon
Planets
Satellites
Solar System
Space exploration

Astronomers

Astronomy comes from two Greek words: *astron* meaning 'star' and *nomia* meaning 'arrangement'.

Before the 16th century astronomers were mainly working out complicated geometrical designs involving lots of circles in an attempt to describe the way planets moved round the Earth.

Astronomers are scientists who study the planets, stars and galaxies. They try to explain all the things that you can see in the night sky and they usually work at observatories.

Some astronomers specialize in making observations. They use telescopes to gather the light from objects that are too faint to see just by eye. As well as light, stars and galaxies send out other kinds of radiation, such as X-rays and radio waves. Astronomers detect these rays with special telescopes and equipment.

Some of this equipment has to be on satellites orbiting round the Earth because the rays cannot get through the atmosphere to ground level. Satellites have helped astronomers make many discoveries.

To work out what their observations mean, astronomers often use computers. You need to know a lot about science and mathematics to do astronomy as a job, but amateur astronomers can make useful observations as well as have fun with a pair of binoculars or a small telescope.

We know from ancient records that people have been noting down what they could see in the sky for thousands of years. But when the telescope was invented, astronomy changed dramatically. In 1610, Galileo became the first person to turn a telescope on the sky. Perhaps the greatest observers of all time were Caroline and William Herschel, who lived in the 18th century. ■

From the 16th century astronomers started to study the real structure of the universe. Their ideas were not readily accepted and in 1633 Galileo Galilei was arrested and imprisoned for his ideas about the Earth moving round the Sun.

See also
Observatories
Telescopes

Biography
Brahe
Copernicus
Galilei
Halley
Herschel
Hooke
Kepler
Newton

Athletics: field

In athletics, field events are those in which competitors try to outdo each other in throwing and jumping. All athletes must be fit and strong. A field athlete must also do hours of practice to perfect his technique. There are four throws, all for distance, and four jumps. ■

See also
Olympic Games

Biography
Sports special

Good **long jumpers** are good sprinters. The jump is measured from the take-off board to the nearest mark made by the jumper in the sand-filled landing area. (men and women)

The **triple jump** is a three phase long jump. Its old name, 'hop, step and jump', describes it exactly. A good jumper tries for about an equal distance on each of the three parts. (men only)

In the **high jump** each competitor has three attempts to clear the bar. When all have tried, failed jumpers drop out and the bar is moved up for the next round of jumps. (men and women)

The **pole vault** is a high jump with the aid of a vaulting pole. The modern pole is made of fibreglass. It bends when the jumper 'plants' it at the end of his run-up, and then unbends as he rises, feet first, to the bar. At present, this is an event for men only.

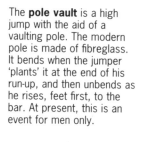

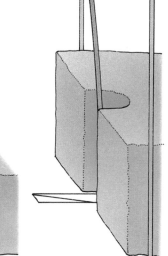

The **hammer** is a heavy metal ball joined by a wire to a handle. The athlete spins it, and himself, within the throwing circle. The spin must be aggressively fast and yet perfectly under control, so that the hammer is released at the right moment for maximum distance. (men only)

The **discus** thrower also spins in a fast and controlled way, with dancing footwork across the circle. The athlete delivers the flat and heavy discus so that it skims through the air. (men and women)

The **shot** is a heavy metal ball. It is 'put' from close to the neck, rather than thrown. The putter must have enormous strength and agility to develop speed and power within the small throwing circle. (men and women)

The **javelin** is simply a spear, thrown from a run-up. The skill is to throw with great strength and speed without slowing down at the end of the run. The point of the javelin must strike the ground first for the throw to be measured. (men and women)

Athletics: track

Track events are running races on an athletics track. The track is usually oval in layout and 400 m (1,310 ft) round. One side will be extended to make a long straight for the sprint races. There are races for men and women separately over many distances. The shortest outdoor track race is usually 100 m (330 ft); the longest 10,000 m (6¼ miles). Some races include hurdles which have to be jumped.

Getting a good start is always important, but this is especially so in sprint races. A sprinter uses starting blocks to avoid slipping, and practises concentrating on the starter's commands: 'Get to your marks!' 'Set!' and then the sound of the gun.

Although all runners are very fit, different kinds of fitness are needed for different length races. A sprinter, who runs distances up to 400 m (1,310 ft), wants his body to produce huge amounts of strength and energy in a very short time. A middle or long distance runner has a body which steadily and efficiently changes breathed-in oxygen into energy. Each does the kind of training which best suits his or her event.

A distance runner must be able to judge pace so that he knows how much energy he has left at any time. And he must be good at making decisions; for example, whether to go off after someone who has sprinted ahead, or leave him to burn himself out. A hard-fought distance race will include some short sprints as runners try to leave each other, and there may be a quick finish. For this reason the long distance runner must also have some sprinting strength. ■

▼ Athletes rise over hurdles in the men's 110 m race. The hurdles are designed so that they can be knocked over without injuring the runners. Hurdling takes its name from the sheep hurdles (movable fences) once used as the obstacles in such races.

◄ In sprint races a good start is important, so the runners use starting 'blocks' to prevent them slipping. The angled foot rests of the blocks help the runners to propel themselves forward with maximum strength.

◉ See also
Marathon
Running
Biography
Sports special

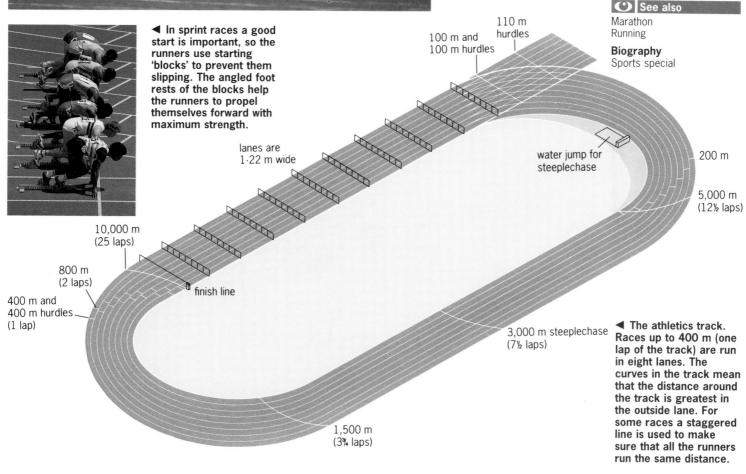

110 m hurdles

100 m and 100 m hurdles

lanes are 1·22 m wide

water jump for steeplechase

200 m

5,000 m (12½ laps)

10,000 m (25 laps)

800 m (2 laps)

finish line

400 m and 400 m hurdles (1 lap)

3,000 m steeplechase (7½ laps)

1,500 m (3¾ laps)

◄ The athletics track. Races up to 400 m (one lap of the track) are run in eight lanes. The curves in the track mean that the distance around the track is greatest in the outside lane. For some races a staggered line is used to make sure that all the runners run the same distance.

Atmosphere

The Earth is surrounded by a layer of air called the atmosphere. Imagine the Earth as an orange. Then the atmosphere is rather like the peel wrapped around the orange. The air itself is a mixture of gases, mainly nitrogen and oxygen. The atmosphere makes it possible for us to live on this planet.

Troposphere

This is the layer in which we live. It contains 90 per cent of the air in the atmosphere. Here clouds are formed and carried by winds over the Earth's surface. To help prepare weather forecasts, special balloons carrying instruments to measure weather conditions are sent up through the troposphere. The measurements are beamed back to Earth by radio. As you move up through this layer, the air becomes thinner and on high mountains there is not enough oxygen to breathe easily. The temperature drops and at about 10 km (6 miles) above sea-level it is always as cold as winter at the South Pole about $-55°C$ ($-67°F$).

Stratosphere

Here the air is much thinner than in the troposphere below. Long-distance aircraft fly in the lower part of the stratosphere so as to take advantage of the lack of air resistance. Sometimes they are also helped by the high-speed 'jet-stream' winds of up to 300 km per hour (190 mph). Among the gases in the stratosphere is a type of oxygen called ozone. It absorbs much of the harmful ultraviolet radiation from the Sun.

Ionosphere

Within the ionosphere there are layers of particles called ions which carry electricity. These layers are very important in bouncing radio signals around our planet. A transmitter at a radio station sends radio waves up through the atmosphere and they bounce off layers in the ionosphere and return to Earth many hundreds of kilometres from where they started.

Exosphere

The exosphere has hardly any gas in it at all. There are only a few molecules of hydrogen and helium floating about. The exosphere is where the Earth's atmosphere really becomes part of space. ■

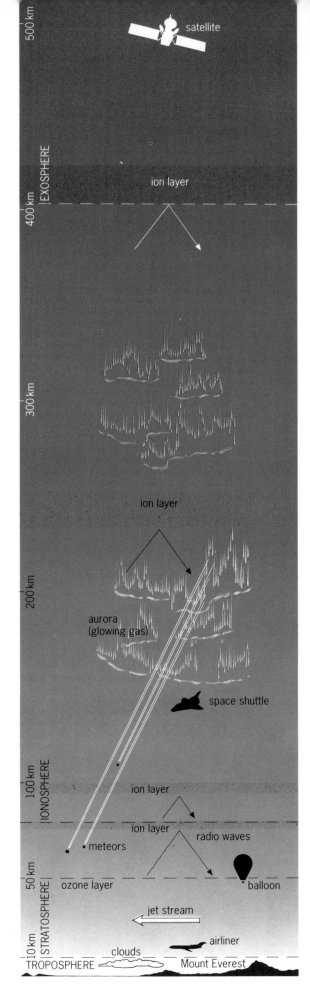

◀ **This diagram shows the structure of the atmosphere. The heights given for the different layers cannot be exact. One layer merges into another and the altitudes vary depending on the time of year, the latitude, and activities of the Sun such as sunspots and solar flares. Space shuttles can orbit as high as 300 km.**

Atmospheric pressure
The weight of the atmosphere is really quite considerable. There is more than a kilogram of air in each cubic metre of the air surrounding us. And we have the weight of all the air above pushing down on us. This atmospheric pressure is like having a kilogram pressing on every square centimetre of our bodies.

 **See also**

Air
Aurora
Ozone
Pressure
Radio
Weather

Atoms

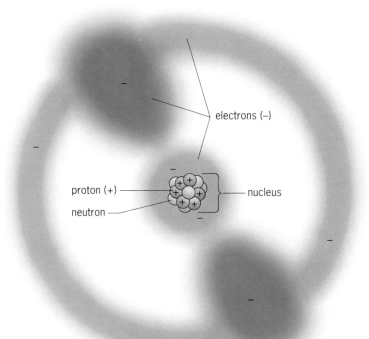

electrons (–)

proton (+)

neutron

nucleus

▲ **Model of a carbon atom. Electrons behave like smeared out clouds of electric charge as they move at high speed around a nucleus made up of neutrons and protons. The electrons are all the same, but different colours have been used to show different types of movement.**

Protons and neutrons are each 2,000 times heavier than electrons.

Proton numbers:
Hydrogen	1
Carbon	6
Nitrogen	7
Oxygen	8
Iron	26
Gold	79
Lead	82
Uranium	92

All matter is made from about 100 simple substances called elements. Elements are made up of atoms, a single atom being the smallest amount of an element you can have. Atoms are by far too small to be seen with any ordinary microscope. More than 4000,000,000 would fit across the dot on this letter i.

Your body is mainly made from atoms of carbon, oxygen, hydrogen and nitrogen. However, you do not look like any of these elements. That is because atoms can form completely different materials depending on the way they are joined together.

Inside atoms

Atoms are themselves made up of smaller particles called protons, neutrons and electrons. Strong forces bind the protons and neutrons together to form a nucleus at the centre of the atom. The electrons, which are much lighter, move around this nucleus at very high speed. Atoms usually behave like tiny, solid bits of matter, but they are largely empty space. If an atom were the size of a concert hall, its nucleus would be no bigger than a grain of salt. Yet most of the mass is concentrated on the nucleus.

The different types of particle in an atom have different electrical charges. Electrons have a negative (-) charge; protons have a positive (+) charge, while neutrons have no charge. A single atom has the same number of electrons as protons. So, overall, it is uncharged. However, some atoms gain or lose electrons when joined to other atoms. This leaves them either positively or negatively charged. Charged atoms are called ions.

Drawings of atoms often show electrons orbiting a nucleus rather like planets orbiting the Sun. This can be a useful way of thinking about an atom (scientists call it a model) but it is not really a true picture. Electrons behave more like smeared-out clouds of charge, and there is no way of telling exactly where they are at any one instant. A model like this is illustrated on this page. However scientists know that they cannot really describe atoms with pictures. Instead, they have to use the mathematical equations of quantum mechanics.

Different types of atom

All atoms are roughly the same size, but they do not all have the same number of particles. For example, atoms of hydrogen, the lightest element, have just one proton in the nucleus. Atoms of uranium have 92. All atoms of a particular element have the same number of protons (called the proton number or atomic number). However, they may have different numbers of neutrons. These different versions of

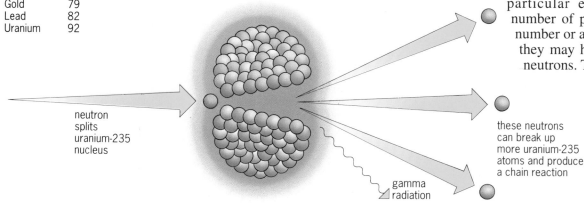

neutron splits uranium-235 nucleus

these neutrons can break up more uranium-235 atoms and produce a chain reaction

gamma radiation

◄ **Nuclear fission: the two parts of the nucleus, the gamma radiation and the neutrons all shoot off carrying enormous amounts of energy.**

the same element are known as isotopes. Scientists name isotopes by putting a number after the name of the element, for example: uranium-235. In this case, the total number of neutrons and protons in the nucleus is 235.

Energy from the nucleus

Some types of atom have arrangements of neutrons and protons which are unstable. In time, their nuclei change by shooting out tiny particles and, sometimes, bursts of gamma waves as well. Scientists say that these atoms are radioactive. The particles and gamma waves they then shoot out are called nuclear radiation. Nuclear radiation carries energy which was originally stored in the nucleus. A single atom does not release much energy, but billions of them can heat up materials which absorb their radiation. The high temperatures deep in the Earth are mainly due to radioactivity in the rocks there.

In a nuclear reactor, neutrons are used to 'unlock' the energy stores in nuclei of uranium-235 atoms. The process works like this. A neutron strikes a uranium-235 nucleus and makes it split. As the nucleus splits, it shoots out more neutrons (and some gamma radiation). These neutrons may split other uranium-235 nuclei...and so on in a chain reaction. The splitting process is called fission. It releases energy which makes the materials in the reactor heat up. In a nuclear power station, a carefully controlled chain reaction gives a steady supply of heat. In nuclear weapons, an uncontrolled chain reaction gives an almost instant release of energy. During fission, each split nucleus becomes the nuclei of two new atoms.

Particle research

Scientists use huge accelerators to study the particles in atoms. Often these accelerators are circular tunnels many kilometres long in which magnetic coils speed up particles (such as electrons) and crash them into other particles or atoms. The particles shot out from these collisions are far too small to be seen, but they leave tracks, rather as high-flying aircraft leave vapour trails. The tracks give scientists clues about the structure of atoms and their particles. It is experiments like these that make scientists think that neutrons and protons are themselves made of even smaller particles called quarks.

Flashback

The idea of atoms is not new. The ancient Greeks invented the word 'atom' (which means 'unsplittable') to describe their idea of the smallest particles of matter. In the 18th and 19th centuries scientists developed different theories about atoms to account for their observations in physics and chemistry. The Danish physicist Niels Bohr was the first to have the idea that atoms consisted of a tiny nucleus surrounded by orbiting electrons. ■

▲ **Mushroom cloud from an American atom bomb test in January 1962.**

⊙ See also

Chemists
Elements
Matter
Molecules
Nuclear power
Particles
Physicists
Radiation
Relativity

Biography
Bohr
Dalton
Einstein
Rutherford

Aurora

People who live in northern countries, such as Norway, Canada and Scotland, sometimes see shimmering curtains of light and huge glowing patches in the night sky. The popular name for this display is the 'Northern Lights', but scientists call it the aurora. The lights can be white, or coloured red, green, yellow and blue. The patterns they make are sometimes like rays from a searchlight, twisting flames or curtains blowing in a wind. Just occasionally, an aurora can be seen from further south, in England, for instance. There are many old records dating back thousands of years that talk about these lights in the sky. Captain James Cook reported seeing an aurora in the far southern sky when he was on one of his great voyages of discovery in 1773. We now know that they happen just as often in the southern hemisphere. But what causes them?

In the 18th century, people began to notice that there was a connection with the Sun. When there are big sunspots on the Sun, we are more likely to see an aurora. Atomic particles that burst off the Sun travel across space to the Earth. When they collide with atoms in our atmosphere, the different coloured lights are given off. This all happens very high up in the atmosphere, between 80 and 600 km (50 to 370 miles) above the ground. ■

The word *aurora* is Latin for 'dawn'. The glowing light near the horizon during an aurora makes it look as if the Sun is about to rise. The word aurora was first used for the northern lights in 1621.

⊙ See also

Atmosphere
Sun

Biography
Cook

◀ **An aurora in the starry sky over Antarctica. The lights move constantly, sometimes rippling like the curtain in this picture, sometimes shooting out like streamers.**

Australia

Australia is the sixth largest country in the world. Its climate ranges from hot and tropical in the north, to cool and wet in the far south. It is one of the flattest countries on Earth. This is because its landforms are extremely ancient. Once, they were part of a larger southern continent. About 65 million years ago the part which became Australia broke away and drifted north.

The mountains have been worn down by wind and water over millions of years. They are now rounded rather than steep. The highest ranges have snow in the winter and people enjoy skiing on them.

The outback

Australians call the vast, inland region 'the outback'. It is hot and dry and a large part of it is desert. The first European explorers, dismayed by endless barren plains, called the central interior 'the dead heart'.

However, this was misleading: even the deserts are full of life. After heavy rain, many species of flowering plants bloom, flocks of birds such as cockatoos and budgerigars arrive and there are fish in normally dry rivers. Kangaroos hop over the plains, and emus, which are large birds like ostriches, graze. The people who live in the outback have to rely on 'Flying Doctors' for medical help.

Unique animals and plants

There are many species of animals which are only found in the wild in Australia. As well as kangaroos, there are koalas, wombats, possums and wallabies, all belonging to a group of animals called marsupials, which keep their young in pouches.

The eucalypts are the most famous native Australian trees. They grow in all shapes and sizes from the deserts to the mountain snows. They used to be unique to Australia but are now grown in other parts of the world.

Area
7,682,300 sq km
(2,966,150 sq miles)
Capital
Canberra
Population
16,676,800
Languages
English, Aboriginal
languages, Greek, Italian,
Vietnamese, others
Religion
Christian
Government
Federal parliamentary
monarchy
Highest mountain
Mount Kosciusko 2,228 m

See also
Aborigines of Australia
Australia's history
Boomerangs
British empire
Commonwealth
Deserts
Marsupials
Oceania
Tasmania

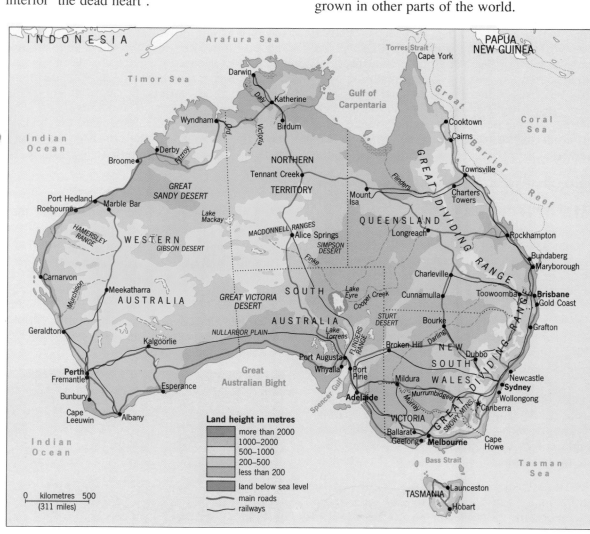

Land height in metres
- more than 2000
- 1000–2000
- 500–1000
- 200–500
- less than 200
- land below sea level
- main roads
- railways

0 kilometres 500
(311 miles)

Coastal cities and inland farms

Most Australians, including the Aborigines, do not see much of the outback. Eighty per cent of them live in cities and towns along the coasts, because the vast majority of jobs are to be found in the cities, not in the rural areas. The two largest cities, Melbourne and Sydney, are on the coast. Sydney, which is famous for its great harbour, has over 3 million people, one-fifth of the total population of Australia.

A smaller number of people live in the country towns or on farms scattered all over the country. The farms produce mostly beef, mutton and wool from sheep, and wheat. Australia exports these products all over the world.

In the outback, where the soil is too poor to graze many animals in small areas, the farms are enormous. Some of these 'stations', as they are called, are as large as an English county. In some places their sheep and cattle have done much damage to the fragile soil.

System of government

Australia is a democracy where everyone has the right to vote. Because the nation is so large, it has a federal system of government: that is, it is divided into states, each of which has its own state government. But there is also a central Federal government which runs the affairs of the whole nation. The state governments are dependent on the Federal government for finance. Voting is compulsory, and with three governments (including local government) to vote for, Australians vote frequently.

Migrants from around the world

In the last 40 years, large numbers of migrants have settled in Australia and the population has grown rapidly to reach over 16 million. One Australian in three now comes from a family where a language other than English is spoken. Australia encourages its migrants to keep their own customs and languages. But they also enjoy the Australian life-style and take part in sports such as tennis and cricket, having barbecues and picnics and swimming at the many beaches. ■

▲ The waterfront of Sydney Harbour. The Opera House is on the left. The famous bridge is 503 m long and carries two rail tracks, eight car lanes and a footpath.

◄ The Flying Doctor service provides medical care for people living in remote parts of the country.

◄ Mining iron ore is a major industry in Western Australia.

▼ Ayers Rock, near the centre of Australia, is sacred to the Aborigines who call it Uluru. The whites have now adopted 'Uluru' as the name of the rock. It is 348 m high and over 2 km long. At sunset the sandstone glows a deep red.

Australia's history

▶ This print shows part of the harbour of Port Jackson and the country between Sydney and the Blue Mountains in New South Wales as it was in 1823.

The first inhabitants were the Aborigines, who have lived in Australia for at least 45,000 years. They lived off the land, hunting and fishing, until the arrival of European settlers destroyed their way of life. Their numbers decreased rapidly and eventually they became only a small proportion of the population.

The first European explorers

Australia was an unknown land to Europeans until about 400 years ago. Maps showed a large, shapeless landmass in the southern hemisphere called *Terra Australis Incognita*: the Unknown South Land.

Spanish and Portuguese seafarers sailed close to Australia's shores, but the first Europeans who definitely landed were Dutch sailors. Dutch ships made several voyages along the western Australian coast in the 17th century. The Dutch were not impressed with the dry, barren land and they never established any settlements.

The first British settlement

In 1768, Britain sent Captain James Cook to search for the Unknown South Land. In 1770 he reached the east coast of Australia and claimed it for Britain, calling it New South Wales.

Cook reported that the more fertile east coast seemed suitable for a settlement. The British government acted on his advice. It decided to send some convicts from Britain's overcrowded gaols to work in a new settlement in New South Wales.

A fleet of eleven ships was sent, containing convicts, soldiers, officers, and the settlement's first governor, Arthur Phillip. The fleet landed at Botany Bay on the east coast in January 1788.

Botany Bay was not a suitable site, but soon Phillip found an ideal spot for a settlement. It was far down a fine sheltered harbour. It eventually became the city of Sydney.

The spread of settlement

The small settlement of Sydney had many problems at first. The Aborigines were hostile, the convicts would not work, and there was not enough food. However, after about 1810 more free settlers arrived. They started farms, using the convicts as farm workers. The settlement gradually expanded and became more prosperous.

Explorers began to adventure into the unknown country and to chart the coastlines. They found more suitable land for farming. New settlements were started in other areas, firstly in Tasmania in 1804, then in Queensland, Western Australia, Victoria and South Australia. The worst-behaved convicts were sent to convict settlements in far-flung areas, such as in Tasmania.

Until the 1850s, these British colonies in Australia remained small, isolated settlements spread around the coasts. Farmers owned vast tracts of land where they grazed sheep. These landowners became the powerful, wealthy rulers of the colonies. In the interior, settlers and Aborigines fought over the land and large numbers of Aborigines were killed.

Gold rushes

In 1851, large amounts of gold were found in New South Wales and Victoria. These finds led to gold rushes, where people flocked to Australia to make their fortunes. The population rapidly increased. Gold made Melbourne, the capital of the colony of Victoria, into a wealthy city with fine buildings.

The gold rushes changed the colonies. They brought an influx of more educated, middle-class immigrants. These challenged the power of the wealthy landowners and made the colonies more democratic.

Australia becomes a nation

Gradually, people in the colonies realized that they were separate from Britain with their own Australian outlook and life-style. They were encouraged by Britain granting self-government to the colonies from 1855 onwards. They were then able to manage their own affairs. Between

1850 and 1905, the colonies developed into democracies where everyone, except the Aborigines, had full voting rights. Aboriginal people were not given the vote until 1966.

In 1901, Australia became one nation. The colonies became states, united together as the Commonwealth of Australia. A central Federal government managed the affairs of the whole nation, while the state governments governed the states.

Twentieth-century developments

Although Australia was a self-governing nation it continued its ties with Britain. It followed Britain's systems of law and government and the Queen of England remained the Queen of Australia.

Australia sent troops to help Britain fight in World Wars I and II, although in World War II it also had to defend itself from attack from Japan. Australia has remained a member of the Commonwealth alliance of former British territories.

Since World War II, Australia has also strengthened its ties with the United States. In the 1960s it sent troops to help the USA fight the Vietnam war. It has also increased its contact with Asian countries, particularly in trade and tourism.

The changing population

Between 1918 and 1988, Australia's population increased from 5 million to over 16 million, largely due to high levels of immigration. In the last 40 years particularly, immigrants have come from all over the world, seeking the high standard of living that Australia offers. They are rapidly changing Australia from a country of British origins to one with a varied mix of races and cultures, but which also has its own unique Australian identity. ■

Commonwealth of Australia
Formed by colonies uniting, 1901
Anzac Day
25 April, commemorates the 8,587 Australian troops killed at Gallipoli during World War I
Federal Parliament
Met for the first time in the new national capital of Canberra, 1927

▼ A photograph taken in the late 19th century of settlers outside a hut in the bush.

Austria

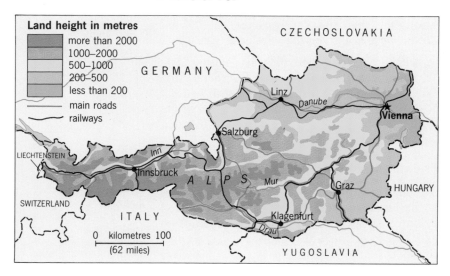

Land height in metres
- more than 2000
- 1000–2000
- 500–1000
- 200–500
- less than 200
- main roads
- railways

CZECHOSLOVAKIA

GERMANY

Linz

Danube

Vienna

Salzburg

LIECHTENSTEIN

Inn

Innsbruck

A L P S

Mur

Graz

HUNGARY

SWITZERLAND

ITALY

Klagenfurt

Drau

0   kilometres 100
(62 miles)

YUGOSLAVIA

Area
83,853 sq km
(32,375 sq miles)
Capital Vienna
Population 7,540,000
Language
German, Magyar, Slovene
Religion Christian
Government
Parliamentary republic
Currency
1 schilling = 100 groschen

◉ See also

Alps
Europe
German history
Mountains
World War I

Biography
Charles V

Scientists
Freud
Lorenz
Mendel

Composers
Mozart
Schubert
Strauss

Austria is a mountainous country in central Europe. It is dominated by Europe's largest mountain range, the Alps, which stretch from east to west across the country. To the north the River Danube flows across its flat plain from West Germany to Hungary. Austrians love to walk in the country's forests and pastures and enjoy the hundreds of lakes and rivers. In the winter skiing in the mountains is popular for both Austrians and tourists from all over Europe.

Most of the houses you see in Austrian villages are wooden chalets. You will often see the men wearing leather breeches, called *lederhosen*, and woollen jackets or capes. Austrian women often wear the *dirndl*, a dress with a fitted bodice and full skirt. Many families run farms, producing dairy products, beef and lamb. Austria's forests also support a thriving paper industry. Many of the industries are small and make very specialized things such as the high-quality optical instruments made in the city of Salzburg. Iron and steel are the main exports.

Vienna, Austria's capital, is a grand city on the River Danube. Its palaces, great churches and opera houses are visited by over 4 million tourists every year, and its pavement cafés and coffee houses are very popular meeting places for the Viennese people. The city is also an important centre for a number of international organizations, such as the United Nations and OPEC (Organization of Petroleum Exporting Countries), which have offices there.

Flashback

In 1276 the Habsburg family became rulers of Austria and in time built up an empire that included Hungary, Czechoslovakia, and northern Italy. The Habsburgs made Vienna their capital and the head of the family in each generation was elected as Holy Roman Emperor.

The most powerful of all the Habsburg emperors was Charles V who ruled from 1519 to 1556 and was also King of Spain and The Netherlands. Over the next three centuries the power of the Habsburgs gradually declined.

In 1914 the heir to the Habsburg throne was shot by a Serb in the city of Sarajevo (now in Yugoslavia). Other European countries became involved in the dispute and this was the start of World War I. After the war the Austro-Hungarian empire was broken up and a small part became today's Austria. ■

◀ **The Austrians treasure their beautiful Alpine valleys. Many villages have strict laws insisting that new buildings fit in with the traditional style of wood-faced, broad-eaved chalets.**

Authors

Authors are people who write books. Most books are written by people who have other jobs as well; they might be teachers, or gardeners, or cooks, and they might only write one book in their lives. But some authors write books for a living, and some of them write a very great number of books. The children's author Enid Blyton, for instance, wrote over 600 books.

There are as many ways of writing books as there are authors. Some like to write by hand; some use a word processor; some authors dictate their books onto cassettes and have them typed by someone else. Some people write very quickly, and others go over everything they have written many times, writing it again and again until they are satisfied.

People like to write in different places, too. Roald Dahl's books were written in a shed in his garden. Ernest Hemingway used to write at a café table. A French writer, Marcel Proust, wrote in a room which was specially lined with cork to sound-proof it.

Getting published

If authors want their books published, they have to work hard at them: not only do they have to make the story interesting (if it is a novel) or or make certain the facts are right (if it is non-fiction), but they must also present the manuscript neatly. Manuscripts have to be typed or word-processed; publishers have not got time to read through an untidy pile of handwriting.

Most authors do not make much money from writing. They might only write one book, or they might just enjoy it as a hobby. But those authors who write bestsellers can become very rich, like the romantic novelist Barbara Cartland whose books have sold over 390 million copies! ■

How to get your book published
First find a publisher. Publishers are the companies that produce, advertise and sell books. Look in a bookshop or library for the name of a publisher that sells the same sort of book as the one you have written. You will usually find the name and address of the publisher somewhere in their books (often the back of the title page). You can then either write a letter to the publisher asking if they are interested in your book, or you can just send the typescript.

The Golden Rule
Don't send your book to a publisher unless you think other people will want to pay money to read it. Be very tough with yourself and work hard to make it as good as you can before you send it. Whatever you do be ready for some criticism and disappointment. Other people might not think so much of your book as you do.

See also

Books
Poems and poetry

Biography
Blyton
Dahl
For other children's authors see: Books

Famous novelists
Austen
Brontës
Dickens
Eliot, George
Hardy
Kingsley, Charles
Kipling
Lawrence, D. H.
Orwell
Proust
Scott, Walter
Stevenson
Tolstoy
Twain

Avalanches

An avalanche is a mass of snow which comes loose from a steep mountain slope and hurtles down to the valley below. It can be huge and frightening, sweeping away trees and burying houses. Or it can be quite a small slide of snow which may block a path or move a fence. Avalanches are a danger in any mountainous area with bare slopes and heavy snow. Every year there are thousands of avalanches in the Alps, but very few cause death or destruction. They are a particular danger after a warm spell when the snow begins to thaw. Then, one snow layer can slide over another and crash down the hillside.

Avalanches are worst on bare slopes with no trees to hold back the snow. In some countries, new forests are being planted to reduce the danger. Where slopes have been cleared for skiing or farming, walls and snow fences are built to break up any avalanches that develop. Snow bridges are built over roads and railways to protect them. Trained snow patrols keep a special watch and issue forecasts of avalanches in areas popular for winter sports. At the slightest danger, warnings are broadcast and roads and ski-fields are closed. Sometimes, explosives are used to start off a small avalanche to prevent a larger one occurring. ■

The largest avalanches in the world are in the Himalayas.

The Mount St Helen's volcano in Washington, USA, erupted in 1980. It started an avalanche of 30,000 cubic m of snow which rushed down the mountain slope at a speed of 400 km/h (250 mph).

18,000 people were killed by an avalanche on the Huasoarán Mountain, Peru in 1970.

See also

Alps

▼ On steep mountain slopes like this one in the Himalayas mighty avalanches are a constant danger, especially when snow starts to melt.

Averages

Temperatures change from day to day, but a holiday brochure can give you an average temperature for each resort. Cricketers score more runs in some matches than others, but they like to keep track of their average score. Averages are useful when you have lots of numbers but need a single number to represent them all.

The chart shows you how much pocket money seven children were each given in a month. There are several types of average you can work out with these figures. One type is called the mean. You find it by adding up the total amount and dividing by the number of children:

total = 2 + 2 + 2 + 3 + 3 + 4 + 12 = 28;

mean = 28 ÷ 7 = 4.

Most of the averages you read about are means, including average temperatures, average wages, and average scores in sport.

The problem with means is that they sometimes give you results which seem unfair. For example, the mean amount of pocket money was £4, but this was hardly typical as most children got less than this. The mean was high because one child got very much more than anyone else.

For this reason, a different kind of average called the median is sometimes used. If you put the numbers in order (2, 2, 2, **3**, 3, 4, 12), the median is the one in the middle. The median for pocket money was £3.

Yet another type of average is called the mode. This is the most common number in the series. More children received £2 than any other amount, so the mode was £2. ∎

£12

— mean £4

£4

— median £3
(middle amount)

£3 £3

£2 £2 £2

— mode £2
(most common amount)

See also
Arithmetic
Statistics

Azores

Area 2,387 sq km
(922 sq miles)
Capital Ponta Delgada
Population 250,700
Language Portuguese
Religion Christian
Government Autonomous region of Portugal
Currency 1 Portuguese escudo = 100 centavos

See also
Portugal

The Azores is a group of nine volcanic islands which lie about 1,300 km (800 miles) west of Portugal in the North Atlantic Ocean. The capital is Ponta Delgada on São Miguel, the largest island. The climate is pleasant throughout the year. Much of the land is hilly and wooded, but farmers grow maize and fruit. Other occupations include fishing, although many people now work in the growing tourist industry. The islands used to be uninhabited. Portugal claimed them in the mid-15th century and they have belonged to Portugal ever since. ∎

Aztecs

The Aztecs were one of several American Indian groups who migrated into the Valley of Mexico over 1,000 years ago. Long before them another civilization, the Olmec, had spread its culture inland from the coast of the Gulf of Mexico. The Olmec people made beautiful sculpture and pottery and probably worshipped a jaguar-like god.

During a period of over 400 years from about AD 1, a huge city called Teotihuacán was very powerful in the Valley of Mexico. Further south, the Maya civilization flourished. In central Mexico in the 9th and 10th centuries the Toltecs became the most important nation.

Rise of an empire

The Toltec culture disappeared and gave way to the Aztecs. There is a legend that, after wandering for hundreds of years, they came upon an eagle on a cactus, eating a snake. Their priests had prophesied this incident, and told them to build a city there, on an island in Lake Texcoco. They called it Tenochtitlán (now Mexico City) and it became the capital of the Aztec empire. The year was about 1345. Although hunted and attacked by enemies, the Aztecs quickly adapted to new ways of life and began to conquer neighbouring nations. In time they became rulers of Mexico.

Daily life

Most Aztecs lived in small houses made of mud bricks. Men and boys worked as farmers in the fields. Women and girls looked after the home, ground corn (maize) to make pancakes and spun and wove cotton cloth. The nobles wore brightly coloured clothes, with designs which showed the rank and importance of the wearer.

Tenochtitlán was a huge city of about 350,000 inhabitants. It was intersected by canals which took the place of streets; and causeways crossed the lake. The markets of the city were filled with produce from all over the empire. Feathers, tools and cacao beans were traded and took the place of money.

Gods and government

The Aztecs worshipped many gods. One of these was Quetzalcóatl, the Plumed Serpent. He is said to have sailed away but promised to return one day. That is why, when the Spaniard Cortés later arrived in Mexico, the Aztecs mistook him for their vanished god. Prisoners of war were sacrificed by cutting their hearts out to provide offerings to the gods and keep the world from ending. The emperor had all the power. Below him were high-ranking soldiers, priests and rich merchants. The ordinary people did not have much freedom or say in government. Below them were the slaves.

Arts and technology

The Aztecs were familiar with the wheel but they did not use it for carts or other sorts of transport. They used wheels mainly in toys and ornaments. Jade, turquoise and feathers were used to make ornaments, masks and images. Goldsmiths made delicate pieces of jewellery.

Their cooking and serving vessels were made of pottery and beautifully decorated. Mirrors, knives and other sharp instruments were made of obsidian, a volcanic lava. The Aztecs are most famous of all for their superb sculptures and buildings, especially for the pyramid-shaped temples.

◄ **The Calendar Stone is not a calendar, as we know it. The face of the Sun in the centre is ringed by figures which tell the Aztec version of the history of the world.**

Conquest and destruction

In 1519, the Spanish conqueror, Hernán Cortés, arrived at Tenochtitlán. He captured the emperor, Moctezuma II, and ruled the country with Moctezuma as puppet king. The Aztecs rebelled against Cortés but they were no match for the heavily armoured Spaniards and, after fierce fighting, in which Moctezuma was killed, the Aztecs were defeated. Within two years, the Spaniards were ruling Mexico. They destroyed the temples and the city of Tenochtitlán and built a new city on the ruins. In this century archaeologists have excavated the sites of many Aztec buildings and in some places reconstructed them. ■

The Aztecs used a type of pictographic writing.

The Aztec language is Nahuatl; a modern form of the language is spoken in Mexico today.

◄ **The Pyramid of Teotihuacán near present-day Mexico City.**

See also
American Indians
Conquistadores
Hieroglyphics
Mexico
Monsters
Spanish colonial history

Biography
Cortés
Moctezuma II

Babies

See also
Birth
Children
Growth
Parenthood

All babies are different and grow at different rates, but they all need to be fed, to be kept warm and clean, to be loved and talked to, and to be protected from danger.

How a baby develops

A newborn baby can already suck and swallow milk from its mother's breasts or from a bottle. At first the baby can only see things clearly that are about 20 cm (8 in) from its face. The baby starts if he hears a sudden loud noise, and cries loudly to let us know he is hungry or uncomfortable.

Babies grow and learn very rapidly. By the time they are a year old most babies are three times their birth weight. During their first two years, babies gain more and more control over their own movement. They learn to walk and climb, to control their hands, to feed themselves, and to scribble with a pencil.

By looking and listening and touching the things around them babies learn to make sense of the world. They learn to listen and understand and to put two or three words together to make their meaning clear. They learn to recognize and depend on the people who care for them. ■

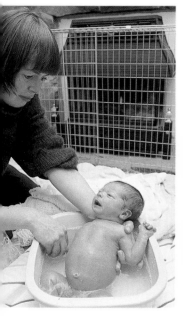

This baby is newborn. At the top of his head is a soft spot, the fontanelle, where the bones of the skull have not joined yet. He sleeps for fourteen to eighteen hours a day, waking to be fed every three to four hours night and day.

Average weight at birth is 3 kg.
Average length at birth is 50 cm.
A girl is half her adult height at 18 months.
A boy is half his adult height at 2 years old.

A baby's first tooth comes through at about 6 months old.
All 20 first (milk) teeth are through by 3 years old.

All babies are born with dark blue eyes. They gradually change colour over the first few weeks of life.

A baby's first smile is usually at about six weeks old.

320,000 babies are born in the world every day.

At four months she likes to be propped up to watch what is happening. She can hold a toy put in her hand, and stretches out to touch things. She smiles at people she recognizes.

At nine months a baby can sit securely. His hands are free to reach and grab things. He can pass toys from one hand to another, and tends to put everything in his mouth. A favourite game is to drop and throw things, and laugh out loud.

By about a year old a baby gets around fast by crawling or by shuffling on her bottom. She turns when she hears her name, and understands simple instructions like 'wave bye-bye'. She will say her first word about now.

She can pull herself up to stand, by holding onto something, and may take a few steps with the help of a favourite toy.

A few months later she starts to walk, with legs far apart and arms stretched out to help her balance. She can climb up stairs and all over the furniture! She needs to be protected from danger.

At 18 months she can say about 20 words for things she knows well, and she understands much more. She feeds herself with a spoon and drinks from a cup without much spilling. She plays happily on her own, but likes to be close to someone she knows.

Bacteria

Bacteria reproduce by splitting in two. They do this so quickly that just one could produce 4,000 million million million in 24 hours.

A row of a hundred bacteria would just reach across this full stop. Bacteria are so numerous that their total weight would be more than that of all other creatures put together. They are some of the oldest living things, and fossils have been found of bacteria that lived 3 billion years ago. Some bacteria can make their own food by using the Sun's energy (photosynthesis), but most live on decaying plants and animals, or as parasites of living things. Bacteria are found everywhere: in the ocean depths, in soil, on our skins, even floating freely in the air.

Decay and disease

Germs is a common name for bacteria.

By breaking down dead plants and animals, bacteria return vital nutrients to the soil which are used by plants for growth. But they also cause some of the deadliest diseases of humans, such as tuberculosis, pneumonia, cholera and typhoid.

Bacterial cells breed by dividing very quickly, so a new infection can cause sudden disease or rapid decay. They do not have sexes and have very simple genetics. Bacteria modify their genes by mutation and so may develop resistance to antibiotics. They can also acquire genes from other organisms, which allows them to be used commercially to make special drugs or chemicals.

Flashback

People once believed that old food went bad because it changed into moulds and microbes (bacteria). The French scientist Louis Pasteur (1822–1895) showed that it was microbes in the air that caused the decay rather than a change in the food. He placed freshly cooked food in clean glass containers, sealed one and left the other open to the air. Only food in the open container went bad. ■

Microbes are tiny living things which sometimes cause disease. Bacteria are a type of microbe.

⊙ See also
Antibiotics
Diabetes
Diseases
DNA
Genetics
Germs
Living things
Spores

Biography
Pasteur

Badgers

Distribution
Europe, Asia and North America
Largest
European badger: head and body length up to 90 cm; weight up to 16 kg
Smallest
Palawan stink badger: head and body length as little as 32 cm; weight 3 kg
Number of young 3–4
Lifespan
In the wild may be over 10 years.

Subphylum Vertebrata
Class Mammalia
Order Carnivora
Family
Mustelidae (weasel family)
Number of species 9

⊙ See also
Nocturnal animals
Otters
Skunks
Weasels

Badgers are shy, nocturnal creatures. All kinds of badgers are good diggers, using the long claws on their forelimbs to dig out food or make burrows called sets. European badgers usually live in groups of up to twelve animals in sets which may be occupied for many generations. An ancient set may contain over 100 m (300 ft) of tunnels, and a large number of entrance holes and living and sleeping chambers.

Badgers are generally peaceable creatures. In spite of their powerful teeth they feed mostly on small prey and plants. Their eyesight is poor, but they have excellent senses of hearing and smell. Badgers have special glands under their tails and with these they 'musk' familiar objects. Young

badgers even musk each other as well as their playthings, and some species with unpleasant-smelling musk use it for defence ■

▼ Badgers have striped faces as a defence. If they fluff up their fur, the black and white stripes make them look bigger and fiercer.

Badminton

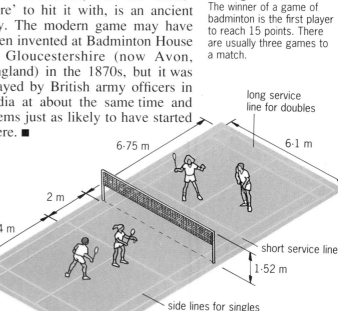

This is a game in which two players (singles) or two couples (doubles) hit a shuttlecock over a net stretched across the playing court. The aim is to hit the shuttle so that it cannot be returned by the other player. The rackets are similar to tennis rackets, but with smaller heads and thinner handles. They are also very light.

The shuttle slows down very quickly when it has been hit: its flight is different from that of a ball, and of course it does not bounce. A good badminton player is someone who can quickly judge the fall of the slowing shuttle and reach it very quickly before it hits the ground. It is a very subtle and varied game, where big hits and gentle lobs all play their part.

Many of the best players in the world come from Malaysia, Indonesia, and other Asian countries.

The shuttlecock, with the 'battledore' to hit it with, is an ancient toy. The modern game may have been invented at Badminton House in Gloucestershire (now Avon, England) in the 1870s, but it was played by British army officers in India at about the same time and seems just as likely to have started there. ■

Scoring
The winner of a game of badminton is the first player to reach 15 points. There are usually three games to a match.

long service line for doubles

6·75 m   6·1 m

2 m

4 m

75 cm

46 cm

short service line

1·52 m

side lines for singles

long service line for singles   side lines for doubles

Baha'is

Baha'u'llah was originally called Mirza Hoseyn Ali Nuri. He was banished to Acre in Palestine by the Persian authorities because of his teachings. These can be summed up in his own words:
'You are the fruit of one tree and the leaves of one branch.'

Since the 1920s Baha'is have been persecuted in some Middle East countries. Some of them have even been put to death.

The Baha'i religion began in Persia (now Iran) in the 19th century and has followers in almost every country in the world. Baha'is follow the teachings of Baha'u'llah (1817–1892), whose name means 'glory of God' in Arabic. They believe that God has helped the human race throughout history by sending prophets such as Moses, Krishna, Buddha, Zoroaster, Jesus, Muhammad and Baha'u'llah. They all teach the same basic message, which is that there is only one God, that all religions are essentially united and that all people are equal.

After Baha'u'llah's death, his son Abd ul-Baha (1844–1921) led his followers. From 1921 till his death in 1957 Shoghi Effendi established the religion in the West.

The sacred writings of the Baha'is are over a hundred works by Baha'u'llah with the interpretations by his son in Arabic and Persian. Shoghi Effendi continued to interpret in Persian and English. ■

⦿ See also
God
Prophets
Religion

Bahamas

The Bahamas are a string of hundreds of islands scattered across 900 km (550 miles) of the Atlantic Ocean. They extend from the southern tip of Florida to the south-eastern tip of Cuba.

When Christopher Columbus ended his daring voyage to the Caribbean in 1492, the first place he landed at was probably the Bahamas island of San Salvador (also called Watling Island). The capital, Nassau, stands on New Providence Island. About half the people of the Bahamas live there. The other islands are often called the 'Family Islands'.

The almost perfect climate and beautiful beaches attract tourists from all over the world.

More than 80 per cent of the people are descended from African slaves who were taken there in the 18th century. The Bahamas were a British colony until 1973. They then became an independent member of the Commonwealth. ■

Area
13,935 sq km
(5,380 sq miles)
Capital
Nassau
Population
237,000
Language
English
Religion
Christian
Government
Parliamentary monarchy
Currency
1 Bahamian dollar = 100 cents

Only about 30 of the hundreds of islands in the Bahamas chain are inhabited.

⦿ See also
Caribbean
Caribbean history
Commonwealth

Bahrain

Area
688 sq km
(266 sq miles)
Capital
Manama
Population
443,200
Language
Arabic, English
Religion
Muslim, Christian
Government
Sheikhdom
Currency
1 Bahrain dinar = 1,000 fils

See also
Arabs
Middle East

Bahrain is the smallest Arab country in the Middle East. It is a group of small islands in the Gulf close to Saudi Arabia. A 24 km (15 mile) causeway over the sea links Bahrain with the mainland. The main island is only 48 km (30 miles) long.

Bahrain has a very hot and humid climate. In contrast with the desert countries all around, it has freshwater springs which feed date-palms and other vegetation. So Bahrain has the look of an oasis.

Bahrainis used to live off pearl-diving and fishing. But in the 1930s oil production and refining took over. Between 1861 and 1971 Britain administered the islands as a constitutional monarchy under a sheikh. In 1971 Bahrain became independent. ■

Balance

You can balance on a narrow beam if you keep the centre of your weight directly above the beam. Then gravity pulls you down equally on either side of the beam, so you do not fall off. A pencil will also balance across another when half its weight is one side of the balancing point and half the other.

Some weighing instruments are called balances. A beam balance has a bar supported in the middle with a shallow pan at each end. You put the weight you want to measure in one pan and standard weights in the other until they balance exactly. Then the weights in each pan are the same. A spring balance has a hook at the bottom where you hang the thing you want to weigh. The weight stretches a spring inside, which moves a pointer either round a dial or down a vertical scale. ■

 See also
Forces
Gravity
Weight

Ballads

Famous ballads
'Sir Patrick Spens'
'Lord Randal'
'Rime of the Ancient Mariner' by Coleridge

Ballads are poems that tell stories. People have always enjoyed stories, and ballads started in the days when few people could read. Minstrels sang songs that told stories; stories of love and adventure, stories about heroes like Robin Hood. The minstrel knew his songs by heart, and the more he knew the longer people would listen.

Ballads usually had four lines in each verse. The words had a regular rhythm so that they fitted the tune. The lines had regular rhymes, which helped the minstrel to remember them.

Later, ballads were made up about exciting events such as the Spanish Armada. When Europeans emigrated to America and Australia new ballads were sung about cowboys and about folk-heroes such as Casey Jones and the Australian Ned Kelly. As more people learned to read, poets started writing ballads to be read, not sung. ■

See also
Minstrels
Poems and poetry
Robin Hood

Biography
Kelly
Pop and rock special

As I walked out in the streets of Laredo

As I walked out in the streets of Laredo,
As I walked out in Laredo one day,
I spied a poor cowboy wrapped up in white linen,
Wrapped up in white linen as cold as the clay.

'I see by your outfit that you are a cowboy,'
These words he did say as I boldly stepped by.
'Come, sit down beside me and hear my sad story;
I was shot in the breast and know I must die.

'Once in my saddle I used to look handsome,
Once in my saddle I used to look gay.
I first went to drinkin' and then to card playin',
Got shot in the breast, which ended my day.

'Let sixteen gamblers come handle my coffin,
Let sixteen girls come carry my pall;
Put bunches of roses all over my coffin,
Put roses to deaden the clods as they fall.

'And beat the drums slowly and play the fife lowly,
And play the dead march as you carry me along;
Take me to the prairie and lay the sod o'er me,
For I'm a young cowboy and I know I've done wrong.'

We beat the drums slowly and played the fife lowly,
And bitterly wept as we bore him along;
For we all loved our comrade so brave, young and handsome,
We loved the young cowboy although he'd done wrong.

Anonymous

Ballet

Ballet is a kind of dancing. Some ballets tell stories; they are like plays, with dance instead of speech. Other 'abstract' ballets are pure dance without a story and they express a mood. But whether ballets tell a story or not, the audience is mainly interested in the dancing. We enjoy the dancers' skill, the pattern of their movements, and above all the way they make each action, however difficult or energetic, seem graceful, natural and beautiful.

▲ The Dance Theatre of Harlem in *Agon*, a modern ballet by the American, Georges Balanchine. Modern ballets use a greater range of movement than older dances. In a *pas de deux* the woman plays a more equal and active role than in traditional ballet.

▶ Pupils at the Royal Ballet School taking a class. The teacher is helping one pupil to achieve a good arabesque.

▶ A scene from the ballet *Sleeping Beauty*. The prince and Sleeping Beauty are dancing a *pas de deux*, a dance for two people. In a traditional *pas de deux* the man lifts and supports his partner much of the time.

▶▶ The final Flower Waltz from *The Nutcracker*, in which the whole company dances together.

Training

To become a ballet dancer, you have to audition to enrol at one of the schools that will train you in the profession of ballet dancing. People begin at the age of 8 and have to be a certain height and build.

Ballet dancers train to make their bodies strong and supple. Even the most famous dancers have to practise every day in the dance studio. The studio has a rail running around the wall called the *barre,* and mirrors in which the dancers can see each movement as they make it.

At the start of a ballet class, the dancers hold onto the barre while doing exercises to warm up their muscles and improve their technique. Next they repeat the exercises without the barre, often with arm movements added. Then comes an *adage,* slow, sustained movements to improve balance and control. Finally, there is an *allégro* section, with turns, small and large jumps, and sequences of steps that travel across the studio.

As well as learning to control each movement of every muscle, ballet dancers have to know the music inside out, and remember each step of the ballet, both their own and everyone else's. The person who makes up the sequences of movements is the choreographer ('dance-writer'). He or she teaches the ballet movements, and the dancers learn them step by step.

For the last few rehearsals, the dancers practise on stage. Instead of the piano, an orchestra plays. By this time, scenery and costumes are ready, and the dancers start getting used to them. For the performances some dancers wear wigs and heavy make up. Ballet dancing is exhausting, so most choreographers give each dancer only a few minutes' hard work at a time, with plenty of chances to go offstage and recover. Even so, in a complete evening's performance, a ballet dancer may work three or four times as hard as an athlete in a race.

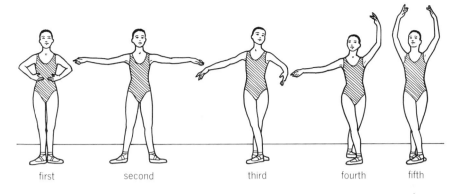

first   second   third   fourth   fifth

Dancing 'on *pointe*'

Normally, you stand on your whole foot and move your toes constantly, to help your balance. One of the challenges for ballet dancers (especially female dancers) is to forget this and dance on the toes, or 'on *pointe*'. To do this gracefully is one of a dancer's hardest challenges.

Ballerinas use special shoes with wooden blocks in the toe for *pointe* work.

Flashback

The kind of ballet we know today began about 400 years ago. Watching ballet was a favourite pastime of rich people, and some of them also took part in ballets. The 17th-century French king, Louis XIV, was a skilful dancer. He took the star part in many court ballets, including one written to celebrate his own wedding.

In the 18th century, most ballets were not stage shows on their own, but were part of the entertainment in operas. A hundred years later, the first full-length ballets were written to fill an entire evening on their own. Ballets of this kind were especially popular in Russia, and many of the most famous ballets, such as *Swan Lake* and *Sleeping Beauty*, were first produced in Russia in the 1870s and 1880s.

The Nutcracker is a Christmas ballet; the music is by the composer Tchaikovsky. He wrote it in 1892 for the Mariinsky ballet company of St Petersburg, Russia. In the ballet, a girl called Clara is given a present, a pair of nutcrackers shaped liked a doll. She falls asleep, and dreams that her nutcracker-doll comes to life as a handsome prince. He takes Clara to the Land of Sweets. There, the queen, the Sugar-plum Fairy, gives a party in Clara's honour, and orders an entertainment by dancers from Russia, Spain, Arabia and China. At the end of the ballet, Clara and her nutcracker-prince lead everyone in a swirling Flower Waltz. ■

◀ A young dancer practising. She is doing *pointe* work without the barre. In the picture she is in fifth position. Compare the position on *pointe* with the drawing of the dancer standing in fifth position.

Famous dancers
Vaslav Nijinsky 1890–1950
Anna Pavlova 1881–1931
Tamara Karsavina
          1885–1978
Margot Fonteyn 1919–
Rudolf Nureyev 1938–
Mikhail Baryshnikov 1948–

Famous ballets and their composers
Les Sylphides Chopin
Giselle Adam
Swan Lake Tchaikovsky
The Sleeping Beauty
 Tchaikovsky
Coppélia Delibes
The Three-Cornered Hat
 Falla

⊙ See also
Dance

Biography
Chopin
de Valois
Fonteyn
Nijinsky
Nureyev
Pavlova
Tchaikovsky

Balloons and airships

▶ This hot-air balloon is 16 m across. It can carry three people in the basket underneath. To make the balloon rise, the pilot heats the air by using the gas burner in short bursts.

Hot-air balloon records
Richard Branson (UK) and Per Lindstrand (Sweden) made the first transatlantic flight in 1987.

The duration record is held by Hélène Dorigny and Michel Arnould (France), who flew for over 40 hours non-stop in 1984.

In 1980, Julian Nott (UK) gained an altitude record when he reached 16·8 km (10·4 miles).

Don Cameron and Christopher Davey (UK) set a distance record in their gas and hot-air balloon, *Zanussi*. They travelled over 3,339 km (2,074 miles) in 1978.

Over 200 years ago the first person to fly did so with a hot-air balloon designed by the Montgolfier brothers in France.

How do balloons fly?

Hot air is lighter than cold air and so it rises. To make a balloon fly, the air inside it must be heated. Modern balloons carry gas burners to do this. If the burner is turned on, the balloon rises. When the air inside cools, the balloon loses height.

The toy balloons at fairs are not filled with hot air but still rise up. They are filled with helium gas, which is lighter than air. Hydrogen is the lightest gas and was used in passenger-carrying balloons and airships until the 1930s. Unfortunately it catches fire easily and after a series of bad accidents it ceased to be used. In recent years balloons are again beginning to be used for transport but they are filled with helium, which cannot burn and is more readily available than it was in the 1930s.

Nowadays the commonest balloon flights are usually for pleasure or sport. Balloon festivals are held in many countries and bring together balloonists for competitions. These include events such as 'hare and hounds'. One balloon sets off and all the others have to follow and land as close to the 'hare' as possible.

The parts of hot-air balloons

The balloon is made of nylon and can be as large as a house when it is inflated. For storing, it folds into a parcel that is small enough to fit in a car boot. There is a panel at the top which is attached by Velcro tape. This is ripped off after landing to allow the hot air to escape quickly. Hanging under the balloon from wires or ropes is the basket. This is not very large and on a long flight it can be very cold and uncomfortable, although the excitement and superb views make up for this. The basket also carries the gas cylinders and instruments, which the crew need to calculate their height, direction, and how much fuel they still have. The gas burner is fixed to the basket's frame. It is like a large camping gas stove and is used in short bursts to keep the balloon at the chosen height. Balloons go where the wind takes them and an experienced pilot will change altitude to use the winds to best advantage.

neck

gas burner

gondola

Some uses of balloons

Balloons are used to collect information about the weather. These do not carry passengers but are loaded with instruments to measure atmospheric pressure, temperatures and wind speed. The readings are either stored on board and used when the balloon returns to the ground or sent back to earth by radio signals. They help meteorologists predict what the weather is going to be like. Astronomers and other scientists also use balloons to carry out experiments and collect data from high in the atmosphere.

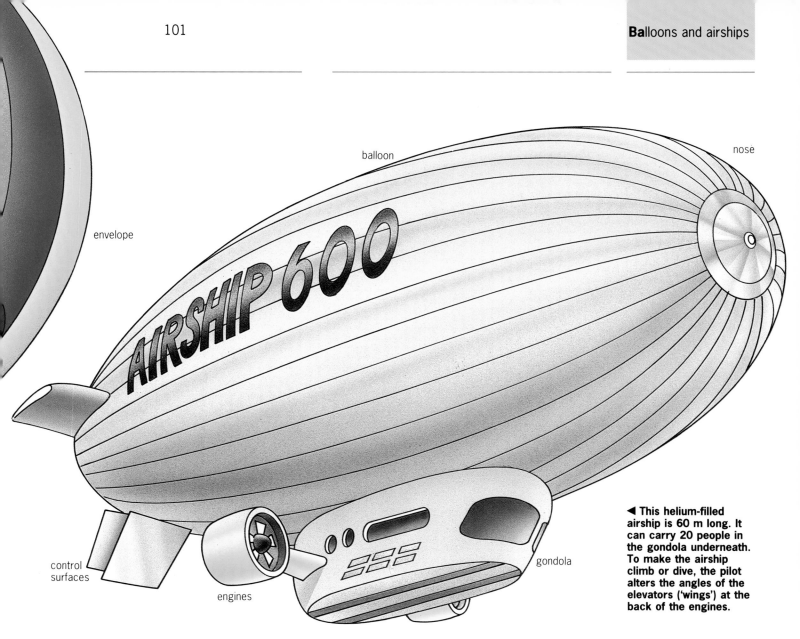

balloon

nose

envelope

control surfaces

engines

gondola

◀ **This helium-filled airship is 60 m long. It can carry 20 people in the gondola underneath. To make the airship climb or dive, the pilot alters the angles of the elevators ('wings') at the back of the engines.**

Airships

Airships, also called dirigibles, are sausage-shaped balloons powered by engines. Modern ones are filled with helium gas. They have an enclosed gondola below, which can carry as many as twenty passengers. The motors which turn the propellers to move the airship forward are attached to the gondola. Unlike other balloons, an airship is not dependent on the wind. The pilot can steer it using a large rudder. Like an aeroplane, it has elevators to make it climb or dive.

A journey in a modern airship is quiet, safe and comfortable. Its ability to remain stationary in the air means it is ideal for photographic and television work. You may well have watched pictures of a sporting event filmed from an airship. Airships also make good flying cranes and can be used to lower heavy structures accurately into position. They are not much used for commercial passenger flights.

Flashback

In 1783, the Montgolfier brothers built the first hot-air balloon which carried a person. The air was heated using a fire on the ground. The first hydrogen-filled balloon flew in the same year. These balloons were often used for military observation. In 1849 balloons were used to bomb the Italian city of Venice. The first flight of an airship, *La France*, was in 1884. Many huge hydrogen-filled airships were built to carry large numbers of passengers. In 1929 the *Graf Zeppelin* took ten days to travel completely around the world. On 6 May 1937 the *Hindenburg* burst into flames when about to moor near New York, killing 35 of the 97 people on board. After that accident hydrogen-filled airships were not used again. Two Americans set an altitude record in 1961. Their helium-filled balloon reached a height of 34·7 km (21·5 miles). They had to carry their own air supply to breathe at that height. ■

World's longest airship:
Zeppelin LZ129 *Hindenburg*
Built: Germany 1936
Length: 245 m
Crew: 61
Passengers: 36
Accommodation: 2 passenger decks (with single and twin berth cabins), dining room, reading room, writing room and lounge (with piano).
Cruising speed:
125 km/h (78 mph)
Time to cross Atlantic:
65 hours

◐ See also
Air
Atmosphere
Flight
Helium

Biography
Montgolfier brothers

Bands

Bands are groups of people who play musical instruments together. Some bands have names which tell you the kind of instruments that they play: for instance brass band, pipe band, steel band. Other names tell you what sort of music the band plays: marching band, dance band, circus band. Pop musicians sometimes call their groups bands.

Military bands

Military bands today are for show. You see them playing in parades, and the soldiers march to the beat. The instruments in a military band are mainly brass and woodwind, plus drums, cymbals and other percussion. A military band can play while marching, but it will also give concerts in halls and on bandstands in parks and at the seaside.

In the past, military bands had many different functions. Trumpet and drum bands helped legionaries in the Roman army to march in step. The Huns, a warrior people from central Asia, had musicians who played dragon-headed trumpets to encourage their side in battle. And some Celtic armies had bagpipe bands, whose playing terrified the enemy because it sounded like wailing ghosts.

Brass bands

All the instruments in a brass band are of the 'brass' family, except for some percussion. Many of these instruments were invented or developed especially for brass band use. The most common ones are cornets, flugelhorns, trombones and tubas.

In Britain, schools, factories, towns and villages often have their own brass bands. The best of them play to a very high standard, and compete in competitions to become the best brass band. The first brass bands started in Britain in the 19th century. Mill and mine owners bought brass instruments and encouraged their workers to learn to play.

▼ This is the Foden Wagon Works band practising in 1936. All the players in the band worked for the Foden Wagon Works in Cheshire. Works bands like this were common all over England, particularly in the north.

▶ The Dodcross marching band playing in a Whitsuntide parade in Saddleworth, near Manchester in north-west England.

▶▶ Benny Goodman and his Big Band were one of the most popular jazz bands of the 1930s and 1940s. They played a type of jazz known as swing, which was good for dancing to.

Steel bands

These are bands in which the players play tuned oil drums called 'pans'. The flat end of each pan is hammered into a concave shape. This is then divided up into a number of notes. On large 'bass' pans there are only a few notes to each pan, but the 'tenor' and 'guitar' pans, which play the melodies and harmonies, have as many as 30 notes on each pan.

Steel bands originated in Trinidad in the 1940s. They spread from Trinidad to other Caribbean islands, and then to Britain and Canada where many West Indians live. Today, many different kinds of people play in steel bands.

Jazz bands

Any group of instruments playing jazz can be a jazz band. A bigger group of ten or more, playing from written-out music, is often called a 'Big band'. There are many school and youth big bands. Professional bands are less common. They are difficult to keep going because of the cost of paying the musicians.

Wind bands

A wind band combines woodwind instruments including the flute, oboe, clarinet, or bassoon with military instruments like saxophones, trumpets and trombones. Wind bands play all kinds of music, from classical to pop, from hymns to jazz.

Marching bands

These are really simplified military bands. The instruments are usually easier to play and the music is less complicated. The players wear colourful uniforms and march as they play. They are mostly youth bands, which play for carnivals, processions, and in very popular marching-band contests. Some marching bands have 'majorettes' or a 'colour guard' with twirling flags. ∎

▼ A steel band playing on St Maarten, one of the small islands of the Caribbean. The player in the foreground has a bass pan. The shallow pans in the middle row are 'guitars'. The pans in the front row are the 'tenors'.

◀ A pipe band in Grampian, Scotland. Bagpipes have a chanter, on which the piper plays the tune, plus one or more drone pipes, which play only one note. The drones act as an accompaniment to the tune.

◉ See also
Carnivals
Drums
Jazz
Marches
Musical instruments
Orchestras
Pop and rock music

Bangladesh

Area
143,999 sq km
(55,598 sq miles)
Capital
Dhaka
Population
110,000,000
Language
Bengali
Religion
Muslim, Hindu
Government
Republic
Currency
1 taka = 100 poisha

Cotton was an important crop in the 18th century, and the cotton known as muslin was named after the Muslims of the capital Dhaka who wove it.

INDIA

Saidpur Rangpur

Jamuna

Mymensingh
Sylhet

Rajshahi

Brahmaputra

Ganges

Dhaka
Narayanganj

Meghna

Jessore
Comilla

Khulna Barisal

Chittagong

Mouths of the Ganges

Bay of Bengal

MYANMAR
(BURMA)

Land height in metres
more than 200
less than 200
main roads
railways

0   kilometres   100
(62 miles)

Over 110 million people live in Bangladesh, one of the most densely populated countries in Asia. Bangladesh is remarkably flat, since almost the entire country is formed by the deltas of the rivers Ganges, Brahmaputra and Meghna as they flow into the Bay of Bengal.

The climate of Bangladesh is tropical. It is hot and wet. Most of the country receives more than 2,000 mm (80 in) of rainfall every year, mainly in the monsoon season which lasts from June to September. During the monsoon Bangladesh often suffers from devastating floods which cause widespread damage to crops and loss of life. Tropical cyclones are another regular hazard to Bangladeshis. They sweep in from the Bay of Bengal between November and May and can be very destructive. A cyclone in November 1970 killed about one million people in the coastal region.

Most Bangladeshis are farmers and live in villages. They travel around by boat rather than by road, since the waterways criss-cross the flat countryside but roads are few and far between. The soils of Bangladesh are very fertile. Rice is the main crop. The low-lying land and abundant water are ideal for paddy fields. Planting, weeding and harvesting in the watery fields are all done by hand. Many farmers also grow jute, a plant whose woody stems are stripped and made into rope and sacks. Bangladeshis are mostly Muslims, and it is usually the men who work the fields while the women spend most of their day in and near the home.

The modern nation of Bangladesh was founded in 1971. It had been part of British India until 1947. Then the subcontinent was split into India and Pakistan. Pakistan itself was made up of two parts separated by Indian territory. To the west was West Pakistan (today's Pakistan) and to the east was East Pakistan. In 1971 East Pakistan became independent and was renamed Bangladesh after a bloody war in which more than a million people were killed. ■

▶ **Water buffalo and farmer in the fertile rice paddies.**

◖ See also

Asia
Ganges
Indian history
Muslims

Banks

Many of the earliest banks were started by goldsmiths. Since they had safes in which to keep their gold, customers began to deposit their own gold and valuables with the goldsmiths for safe keeping.

Most countries have a 'central bank' to keep a watch on other banks. In Britain the central bank is the Bank of England. In the United States it is the Federal Reserve System. In Germany it is the Deutsche Bundesbank.

See also
Money

Keeping a lot of cash is not very safe, so most people and businesses have a bank account. To open an account you just need some money to pay into it.

With some bank accounts you get a cheque book. You fill in a cheque with the sum of money and the name of the person to be paid. Then the money goes straight from your bank to the account of the person you want to pay.

You can also have a savings or deposit account for money you do not want to spend yet. The bank pays you interest on your savings. That means they add extra money to your account. The bank can do this because it lends your money to other people who need to borrow it. The borrowers then pay interest to the bank.

In the UK, building societies, which used to lend money only to people who wanted to buy a house, also offer the same sort of services as those offered by banks. ■

Baptism

Baptists and Eastern Orthodox Christians totally immerse the person; others sprinkle the forehead with the water.
Although there are different ways of baptizing, it is almost always done 'in the name of the Father, and of the Son, and of the Holy Spirit'.

See also
Christians
Churches
Rites and rituals

Biography
John the Baptist

Baptism and christening are both names for a service in which people are given their Christian names and become members of the Christian Church. Some Protestants think that only adults can make the decision to become full Christians and do not baptize babies. They are called Baptists. Roman Catholics, Anglicans and others who do baptize babies have confirmation services for children or adults, when they are old enough to choose for themselves.

Baptism is washing with water. It symbolizes the washing away of the past and a new beginning. The water, which is often blessed, is usually put in a font in a church. Some Christians use a river or the sea. ■

Barbados

Barbados is a small Caribbean country, 34 km (21 miles) long, and a member of the Commonwealth. Most of the island is made of coral limestone, the remains of prehistoric coral reefs. Underground rivers flowing in caves through the limestone provide the island with a pure water supply. The coral which grows in the sea around the island today provides fresh, white sand for many beautiful beaches. There is a warm and sunny climate, and over 400,000 tourists visit the island every year.

The first English settlers came to Barbados in 1627. Most Barbadians are descended from African slaves who were brought to the island to grow tobacco, cotton and sugar cane in the 17th and 18th centuries.

Much of the land is still used to grow sugar. But most people work in factories, offices, hotels and shops. Barbados is now one of the most prosperous Caribbean islands. There is a good health service and education system. There is a cultural and calypso festival called Cropover every summer, and Barbadian cricketers like Sir Garfield Sobers are internationally known. ■

Area 430 sq km (166 sq miles)
Capital Bridgetown
Population 253,000
Language English
Religion Christian
Government Parliamentary monarchy
Currency 1 Barbados dollar = 100 cents

Barbados, unlike most Caribbean islands, never changed hands. It was ruled by Britain from 1627 until independence in 1966. Its Parliament was founded in 1639.

See also
Caribbean
Caribbean history
Coral

Biography
Sports special

▼ Boats in the harbour of Bridgetown which is the capital of Barbados.

Barnacles

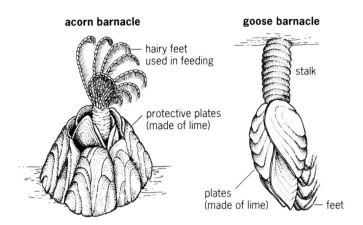

acorn barnacle
— hairy feet used in feeding
— protective plates (made of lime)

goose barnacle
stalk
plates (made of lime)
feet

▲ The small hard-shelled barnacles on the sea-shore are called acorn barnacles. Goose barnacles attach themselves to floating debris in the sea.

See also
Crustaceans
Parasites
Plankton
Seashore

Because of their hard shells, you might think that the barnacles on the beach are like the limpets and mussels which share their environment. In fact, they are more closely related to crabs. We know this because the larvae which hatch from barnacle eggs are like the young of shrimps and other crustaceans. For a while they float with the millions of other tiny sea creatures known as plankton. Then when the time comes for them to settle down, they cement themselves to a piece of rock or breakwater, where they remain for the rest of their lives. Plates made of lime grow round them to protect them. When they need to eat, they kick out large, hairy feet, to comb tiny particles of food from the water.

A second group of barnacles are called goose barnacles. These have a long, fleshy neck. Many attach themselves to floating objects in the sea, so they are part of the plankton for all of their lives. A third group are parasites of crabs. They cannot easily be seen, for they live on the underside of the crab's body. ■

◀ Goose barnacles attach themselves to floating objects, such as the bottom of a ship, by their long, fleshy stalks.

Distribution
Throughout the oceans and seashores of the world
Largest species
Some acorn barnacles of the west coast of North and South America are nearly 30 cm in circumference. They are used as food by the local Indians.
Lifespan
Up to 5 years for common seashore barnacles

Phylum
Arthropoda
Class
Crustacea
Number of species
800

Barometers

Barometers are used to measure the pressure of the air. Although we talk of things being 'as light as air' the weight of atmosphere over each square metre of the Earth's surface is about 10,000 kg (2,000 lb per square foot). We call the force on a given area the pressure. In a barometer there is a flat metal box, with a vacuum inside. The air pressure tries to squash the box flat but, because the metal is springy, it is not squashed completely. If the air pressure varies, the lid of the box rises and falls. A system of levers changes the movement of the lid into the movement of a pointer over a dial rather like a clock face.

Air pressure changes if you go up in an aeroplane, and with the weather. Barometers are used to measure the height of an aeroplane and to help in weather forecasting. Weather forecasters often measure air pressure in millibars (mb). On average air pressure at sea level is about 1,000 mb. ■

1,000 millibars are also called 1 bar. Each millibar is a force of 100 newtons per square metre. On the Earth's surface, the pull of gravity on 1 kg is about 10 newtons.

See also
Atmosphere
Pressure
Weather

Biography
Pascal

▼ Aneroid barometer. The greater the pressure of the air outside, the more the box is squashed, and the further the pointer moves round the scale.

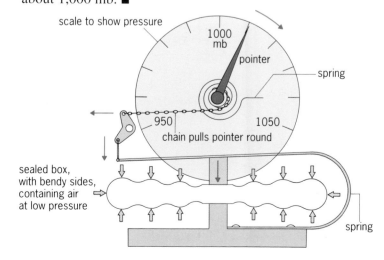

scale to show pressure
1000 mb
pointer
spring
950
1050
chain pulls pointer round
sealed box, with bendy sides, containing air at low pressure
spring

Baseball

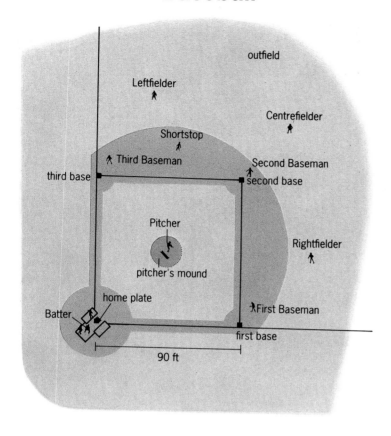

Baseball is a nine-a-side game played all over the world, but especially in the USA where the World Series is held every year. Batters aim to hit the ball thrown by a pitcher. The pitcher stands on a mound almost in the centre of the 'diamond' which is formed by the home plate and three bases. To score a run a batter must advance round all the bases without being out. One of the most exciting sights is when a batter hits the ball beyond the fielders' reach and completes a 'home run'.

Fielders, who wear a special catching mitt, can catch batters out or run them out on their way to one of the bases. Batters are also out if they miss three successive throws (or 'strikes') from the pitcher. The inning is over when three batters are out, and the fielding side takes its turn. Usually each side has nine innings.

Softball is a gentler variety of baseball; the ball is larger and softer. ■

See also
Biography
Sports special

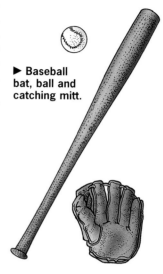

► **Baseball bat, ball and catching mitt.**

◄ **Baseball is played on a field containing four bases placed at the corners of a 90 ft (27.4 m) square (known as the 'diamond').**

Basketball

A game similar to basketball, known as 'Pok-ta-Pok', was played by the Olmec people of Mexico in the 10th century BC. A variation of this game was played by the Aztecs in the 16th century. Any player who managed to put the solid rubber ball through the fixed stone ring was allowed to claim the clothes of all the spectators!

► **The basketball court. The game begins with a 'jump-ball' at the centre circle. Two players, one from each team, stand in the centre circle and the referee throws the ball up between them. The players jump up and try to tap the ball towards a member of their own team, in order to win possession.**

In 1891 some young Americans wanted a game they could play indoors. They hung peach baskets on the walls at opposite ends of a gymnasium and two teams tried to score points by throwing a large ball into the baskets.

Basketball has now become a very popular game throughout the world. The number of players is now five on each team, and the basket has been replaced by a metal hoop and net. No physical contact is allowed, and the ball can only be passed or bounced (dribbled) around the court. The defending side wins the ball either by intercepting it or as a result of a foul by their opponents. Two points are usually scored for a basket, and the team with the most points wins the game. ■

basket 3·05 m above the floor

backboard

free throw line

1·8 m

3·6 m

1·8 m

5·8 m

26 m

14 m

6 m

See also
Biography
Sports special

Basket making

A basket is a woven container used for storing anything from grain to clothing. In the Himalayas, people carry food, firewood and their babies in baskets fixed to their backs. The craft of basket making is practised in many parts of the world today.

► Cane is soaked before use to make it soft and pliable. A thick cane is used for the uprights and a thinner cane is woven between them. This basket maker in western France has prepared the base and fixed the upright canes. He is starting to weave the softened canes in and out of the upright ones, working from the base upwards.

Baskets are usually made from natural materials that are available locally. Willow is common in England, and rushes and grasses in North America. The basket maker weaves together lengths of rushes, cane or grass. But variations in weaving stitches are used to produce more ornate baskets. Materials can be dyed to create colourful patterns. Baskets are also made by coiling plaited grasses or rushes into a shape and then stitching them together. This is a process that was popular among the American Indians.

Many other items, such as cane furniture, fences and corn dollies, are made using basket-making techniques.

▲ A woman in Rajasthan, India, is about half-way through her work, weaving the sides of a container. Behind her is the base of a basket, and a large finished one is on a step above.

▼ A pile of coiled and stitched baskets ready for sale in Nigeria.

Flashback

Examples of coiled and plaited baskets, from as early as 3000 BC, have been discovered in the sands of the Nile Delta. They are in a wonderful state of preservation and prove that the ancient Egyptians were skilled basket makers. ■

Basques

Pelota
This Basque game is the world's fastest ball game.

See also
Spain

The Basques are a people who live in the western Pyrenees Mountains of Spain and France. In the 1980s there were about 2 million of them in Spain and about a quarter of a million in France. Their language is quite unlike any other European language and nobody knows where their ancestors came from. They are noted for their folklore, games, music and acrobatic dancing. Many wish to have a separate country of their own. In 1959 some Spanish Basques formed a fighting organization called ETA (in Basque it stands for 'Basque-land and Freedom'), which has since sometimes attacked and killed Spanish representatives of authorities. ■

Bats

Bats are the only mammals that have wings and are capable of true flight. Many are grotesque-looking animals with huge ears and strange faces. They produce high-pitched sounds which bounce off nearby objects. This 'echo' is picked up by the bat's large ears and the bat uses it to locate its prey and avoid obstacles. This is called echolocation.

Almost a quarter of all mammal species alive in the world today are bats. Nearly all are nocturnal (active only at night). Most eat insects, but some feed on larger creatures such as mice, or other bats. A few catch fish, and three species take blood from large birds or mammals. Some bats feed on nectar and are important in carrying pollen from flower to flower, while others are fruit eaters.

Most bats fly more slowly than birds, but have more control. They can turn, twist and fly without hesitation, through small gaps that would defeat the majority of birds. Flight uses a lot of energy. Most bats conserve their resources by letting their temperatures drop and remaining still when they are not flying. In cool parts of the world bats hibernate, but a few species migrate to where there are better supplies of food.

There are still huge populations of many sorts of bats, but others are becoming rare, as a result of pollution and changes in the environment. ■

▲ **Mouse-eared bat. A bat's wings are made of a double membrane about 0·3 mm thick. When it is not being used for flying,** the wing contracts between the supporting bones, so that it does not impede the bat's movements.

Distribution
Throughout the world, except for the coldest areas and a few remote islands
Largest
Flying fox: head and body length over 40 cm; wingspan up to 2 m; weight up to 1·6 kg
Smallest
Kitti's hog-nosed bat: head and body length about 3 cm; wingspan 15 cm; weight about 2 g
Number of young
1, in most cases
Lifespan
Up to 20 years, even in small species

Subphylum Vertebrata
Class Mammalia
Order Chiroptera
Number of species 951

See also
Ears
Echoes
Feet and hands
Flight
Hibernation
Mammals
Migration
Nocturnal animals

Batteries

Small electric batteries are used to run torches, radios, watches and pocket calculators. Large electric batteries are used to start car engines and can even drive vehicles like milk-floats.

Small batteries are usually of a kind called primary cells. The electricity comes from chemicals sealed inside them. They can be used continuously only for a few days before the chemicals are used up. Switching torches and radios off when you do not need them makes the batteries last longer. But once a battery is 'flat' and can produce no more electricity, it has to be thrown away.

Large batteries are usually secondary cells. These also use chemicals to store electricity. But when the chemicals begin to run out, they can be renewed by feeding electricity into the battery. This is called charging. It is done by connecting

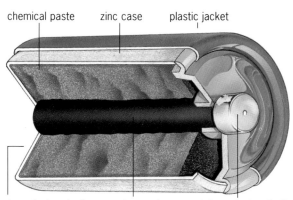

chemical paste   zinc case   plastic jacket

base (− terminal)   carbon rod   metal cap (+ terminal)

◄ A 'dry' zinc–carbon cell.

the battery to a dynamo (as in a car) or a charger which plugs into the mains. Some small batteries are marked 'rechargeable'. They can be charged, but only with a specially made charger. This must *not* be used on ordinary batteries. ■

The word battery really means two or more primary or secondary cells joined together. However, single cells are often called batteries; for example, a torch battery.

In a car battery, there are six separate cells all joined together in the same case.

See also
Dynamos
Electricity

Biography
Volta

Battles

▶ **Waterloo**
At 11.30 on 18 June 1815, the French army under Napoleon attacked the British and Dutch under Wellington. The British cavalry attacked but were repulsed. The British infantry stood firm all day under attack. At 7 pm the Prussian army advanced and attacked the French on their right flank. Wellington attacked on the left and the French retreated.

▶ **Stalingrad**
By August 1942 the German 6th Army had reached the River Volga at Stalingrad. On 19 November six Russian armies using thousands of tanks counter-attacked. By 23 November the Germans were surrounded. General Hoth tried to rescue them but was defeated. The battle ended on 2 February; 91,000 Germans were taken prisoner.

Battles were fought between tribes and villages in prehistoric times, probably about land. Since then thousands of battles have been fought all over the world, on land, at sea and in the air. Bows and arrows were used in the Stone Age and bronze weapons followed. When iron swords appeared, fighting became a lot more dangerous. Early battles in about 1000 BC might last for a day, but in the 20th century battles like the battle of Stalingrad have lasted months, involving millions of men.

Land battles

Many early battles were sieges, and cities like Troy protected themselves with walls. Greek and Roman armies fought in the open, with units of men on foot (infantry) and on horseback (cavalry). The defenders would line up and try to beat the charging enemy with swords, spears and bows. Both sides would try to surround the enemy with cavalry. Even with muskets and cannons this remained the basic battle plan for centuries; it was used for the battle of Waterloo in 1815. Cavalry regiments fought on both sides at the beginning of World War I, but by 1917 horses had been replaced by tanks.

Sea battles

Early sea battles were between trading ships and pirates, who aimed to 'grapple' the two boats together, jump on board and fight. In the Middle Ages ships had towers for archers to attack from as two ships approached each other. Cannons were added in the 16th century and these tried to destroy a ship's sails. It could then be captured, as at the battle of Lepanto in 1571 when Spanish and Venetian ships captured 117 Turkish galleys off the Greek coast. In 1805 Nelson was killed at the battle of Trafalgar by a French musketeer as his ship, HMS *Victory*, closed to grapple. The first battle between iron ships was in 1862 during the American Civil War. Later, steel replaced iron. ∎

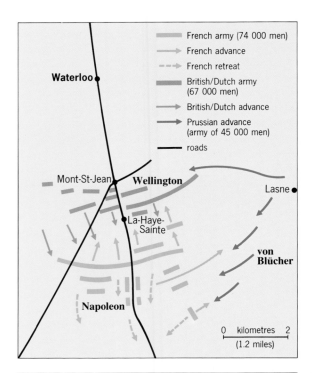

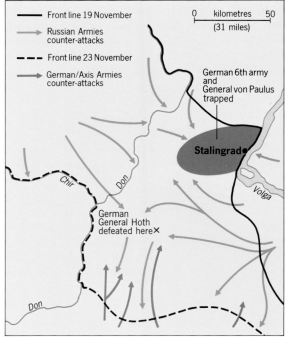

◀ An artist's painting of the fight between ironclads Merrimac and Monitor, 9 March 1862, during the American Civil War.

Bayeux Tapestry

The Bayeux Tapestry is a kind of strip cartoon which is about 900 years old. It tells the story of the Norman invasion of England in 1066. It is not really a tapestry (a design woven on a loom) but a very long strip of linen with pictures embroidered on it in eight different coloured wools, and a running commentary in Latin.

Historians think that Bishop Odo of Bayeux in Normandy ordered the tapestry to be made soon after the Norman Conquest. Bishop Odo was the half-brother of Duke William of Normandy and took part in the invasion of England. Almost certainly English women designed and embroidered the tapestry on the bishop's orders. Odo probably displayed the tapestry at feasts in his palace, and later it hung in his new cathedral in Bayeux.

The tapestry is full of colourful pictures. It shows William's great invasion fleet and the battle of Hastings itself. It gives us evidence of armour, weapons, buildings and the people in the story. It also tells us what the Normans wanted to remember about the events of 1066. It shows William's enemy Harold as a brave warrior and a worthy foe, but also as an oath-breaker who had sworn loyalty to William and then taken the crown of England himself. But even a one-sided story is very valuable, especially when it gives us so much information of different kinds about a very important event.

A long life

The Bayeux Tapestry probably spent centuries rolled up in a dusty chest. Once, in the French Revolution, the citizens of Bayeux nearly cut it up to make coverings for carts. But somehow this piece of linen cloth with its woollen embroidery has survived. Nine hundred years after it was made, the pictures are fresh and clear, and anyone can go to see them in Bayeux. ■

▼ At the height of the battle of Hastings the English desperately defend their position on a hill against repeated Norman attacks. There are so many dead and wounded that they even fill up the border.

▲ Harold becomes King of England. First, Edward the Confessor's funeral procession solemnly approaches his great new church, Westminster Abbey. His illness and death in his palace come afterwards, perhaps to show how quickly everything happened. The English nobles offer Harold the crown, and finally he sits in majesty wearing his crown. But already people are beginning to point to the comet which will appear in the next picture; most of them think it is a bad omen.

◄ This picture is the only evidence we have of how Harold died in the battle of Hastings. Many people have thought that Harold is the figure standing directly under his name, pulling an arrow from his eye. But experts now think that Harold is the figure falling to the ground under the words 'interfectus est' (he was killed). He may appear twice in the same picture: first wounded, then killed.

The tapestry includes
626 human figures
(but only 3 women)
190 horses and mules
506 other animals
37 ships
37 trees or clumps
33 buildings

◉ See also
Normans

Biography
William I

Beans

A bean-feast is the name given to a party with lots of food. It probably comes from an old custom connected with Twelfth Night festivities, when a bean was hidden in a cake and whoever got the slice of cake with the bean was made 'king' for the night.

About 17% of the world's cooking oil is made from soya beans.

Beans come in all shapes, sizes and colours. There are ruby-red kidney beans, large creamy white butter beans, pale green broad beans and pink, blotchy runner beans.

Beans are the pods and seeds of a group of plants belonging to the pea family. These plants grow as bushes or as climbing plants in areas with a temperate climate such as Europe, North America and China. They fix nitrogen taken from the air and so enrich the soil they grow in.

Shelled beans and peas are the only kinds of vegetables which contain much protein. This makes them popular with vegetarians. They are also rich in carbohydrates. Fresh bean pods and seeds contain vitamins A and B and plenty of fibre.

The pods of some beans such as French and runner beans are cooked and eaten with the seeds. Other beans, including broad beans and lima beans, are shelled first and then cooked.

The popular dish of baked beans is made from haricot beans. Some beans can be eaten raw, but others, like kidney beans, are poisonous unless they are boiled in water for at least 15 minutes. ∎

Soya beans have more protein than any other bean. They contain 30–50% protein, and have almost the same food value as meat. Soya flour extracted from the beans is used in making textured vegetable protein (TVP) which looks and tastes like meat.

Some types of beans
Broad beans
Haricot beans
Kidney beans
Lima beans
Mung beans
Runner beans
Soya beans

See also
Pulses

Bears

Bears are the heavyweights among the carnivorous (flesh-eating) mammals: the biggest bear weighs more than three times as much as a large lion. Bears will sometimes kill large animals. They are omnivores, feeding on both plants and small creatures. Only the polar bear, which hunts seals, has a diet consisting chiefly of meat. By contrast, the sloth bear eats almost nothing but termites.

▼ A female grizzly has a litter every two or three years, and the cubs may stay with her for over a year. The male plays no part in rearing his family.

Like human beings, bears can stand upright, but normally they walk on all fours. They use the whole length of their feet, as we do, rather than standing on their toes, like many other creatures. Bears can swim well and young ones can climb trees, but as they grow older, they do so less. Bears have poor eyesight and hearing, but their sense of smell is excellent.

Bears generally live alone, though groups may sometimes come together in places where there is plenty of food. In the autumn, when food is abundant, bears grow very fat. Then they find a secure den in which they snooze away the winter months. They do not go into a deep hibernation, and it is at this time that females produce their young. The cubs are very small, less than 1 per cent of their mother's weight. They emerge from the den after several months, when food is becoming plentiful.

Although some bears may become cattle killers, most pose little threat to humans. In spite of this, they have been exterminated from many areas and several species are now in need of protection. ∎

Distribution
Europe, Asia, South America, North America and the Arctic. Only the spectacled bear of the Andes is found south of the Equator.
Largest
Polar bear: head and body length up to 3 m; weight up to 800 kg
Smallest
Sun bear: head and body length up to 1·4 m; weight 27–65 kg
Number of young 1–4
Lifespan
15–30 years in the wild, much longer in captivity

Subphylum Vertebrata
Class Mammalia
Order Carnivora
Family Ursidae
Number of species 8

See also
Hibernation
Koalas
Pandas

Beavers

Distribution
North America, Europe
and Asia
Size
Head and body length
80–120 cm; tail length
25–50 cm, width up to
13 cm
Weight 12–30 kg
Number of young
2–4, suckled for about 3
months
Lifespan 10–15 years

Subphylum Vertebrata
Class Mammalia
Order Rodentia
Family Castoridae
Number of species 2

Beavers are said to be busy animals because of their dam-building activities. A young beaver looking for a place to make a home chooses a stream in wooded country. With its huge gnawing teeth it cuts down trees up to 1 m (3 ft) in diameter. Using logs, brushwood, stones and mud, it makes a dam that holds up the water and makes a still lake. From here, it can enter its burrow in the river bank or a lodge (its lair) which may be in the dam, without leaving the water.

Beavers swim well. Like many water-dwelling animals they have fine thick fur. This has resulted in them being hunted to extinction in many of the places in which they once lived. When frightened they dive, warning other members of their family by slapping the water with their big flat tails.

Beavers feed on waterside plants. They do not hibernate, but make huge stores of twigs and other food for the winter. Baby beavers are born in spring. Unlike most rodents they develop very slowly, and remain with their parents and any new offspring for at least two years. ■

◀ The beaver is well adapted for its life in the water with its torpedo-shaped body, waterproof fur, webbed feet and flattened tail.

◉ See also
Rodents

Beer

**Top beer-drinking
countries**
Litres per head per year

143 Belgium
142 Australia
132 Germany
128 Denmark
126 Irish Republic
117 United Kingdom
104 Austria
 88 Canada
 82 United States of
    America

Beer is an alcoholic drink made from barley fermented with yeast and water. The barley is soaked in water and allowed to germinate to form malt. The barley is then dried to stop further growth, and then ground to a powder.

Brewing

Brewing starts by mixing the powdered malt with hot water. The liquid, called wort, is later strained off and boiled with dried hops to give it flavour. The wort is strained again and yeast is added. Fermentation begins as sugars from the barley are converted to carbon dioxide, which gives the bubbles, and to alcohol. Ordinary beer contains about 3 per cent alcohol.

Flashback

Brewing is one of the oldest activities in the world. It was brought to Europe by tribes from the East well before the time of the Romans. The use of hops to flavour beer only became popular in the 16th century. ■

The first law about the purity of food and drink was passed in Germany in 1516. The Elector William IV of Bavaria decreed, in his famous Purity Order, that beer should contain only barley, hops, yeast and water. This still holds good today, though there is a special exception made for the traditional wheat beers of southern Germany.

◉ See also
Alcohol
Cereals
Hops
Yeasts

Bees

▶ Bumble-bee visiting flower. Her pollen baskets can be seen clearly.

Distribution
Worldwide

Phylum
Arthropoda
Class
Insecta
Order
Hymenoptera
Number of species
About 20,000

See also
Animal behaviour
Ants
Honey
Insects

▶ Worker bees change their jobs as they get older. They clean empty cells in the honeycomb ready for eggs from the queen or honey and pollen from older workers. They feed young developing bees (larvae), and then start producing wax to repair and make new honeycomb. They become guards which kill or drive away wasps, mice and other honey thieves, or beat their wings to drive fresh air into the hive. Finally they visit flowers to collect nectar and pollen.

Most people have seen honey-bees searching flowers for nectar and pollen. Honey-bees, and their close relatives, the bumble-bees, like ants and termites, live in family groups. Each hive or nest is the home of a large number of bees and their mother, the queen bee. The grubs that hatch from the eggs she lays are tended by worker bees. These are females whose sex organs are not developed and so they cannot lay eggs. A small number of the bees in a hive are males, or drones. These do not help to make stores of pollen and honey, or look after the grubs. Their job is to mate with young queen bees. After this the drones die. The queens survive to be mothers of new huge families in other nests.

workers looking after the queen while she lays eggs

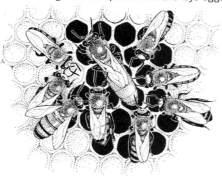

worker at hive entrance beating its wings to drive in cool air

In the summer-time a worker honey-bee has a short life and dies at about the age of six weeks. Some workers survive the winter, and these live for several months. The queen bee can survive for up to five years, so the honey-bee's nest is quite long-lived. Bumble-bee queens do not live so long, dying, with the rest of their family, at the end of the summer. Only the young bumble-bee queens, which have mated, survive. They find safe places to hide and hibernate. They wake up early next year, and it is a sure sign of spring when you see the new queen bumble-bees looking for suitable spots for their nests.

Honey

Bees make honey from nectar, which they suck from flowers. They can do this because their jaws form a tube, like a built-in drinking straw. As a bee searches for nectar, pollen from the flowers gets stuck on her hairy coat. She combs this off and presses it into her 'pollen baskets' which are on her hind legs. The pollen is used to feed the grubs for most of their lives.

If a honey-bee finds food at a time when there are not many flowers, she is able to tell her sisters about it. She does this by performing a dance on the side of the honeycomb. Her dance shows how far and in what direction food is to be found.

As well as the honey-bees and bumble-bees, there are many species of so-called 'solitary' bees, which do not lead a family life. In these species, the females lay their eggs in nests which they stock with food. They die before the grubs hatch. ■

workers constructing a honeycomb

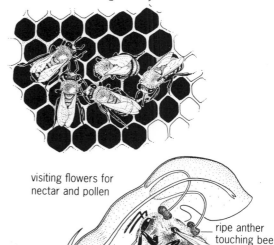

visiting flowers for nectar and pollen

ripe anther touching bee

Beetles

There are more different kinds of beetles than any other sort of animal, and new species are being discovered all the time. They are found in every environment except the sea and on snowfields, and in every continent except Antarctica. Some eat flesh, especially that of other insects; others feed on plants, both living and dead. The goliath beetle is one of the largest of all insects and weighs more than a sparrow. Yet some of the smallest of all insects are also beetles, measuring less than 1 mm in length.

It is easy to recognize beetles, for unlike most other insects they have a heavily armoured look. This is because their front pair of wings, called elytra, have become thickened and are hinged back to cover the abdomen. Their hind wings are large and papery. When the beetle is on the ground they are folded and tucked away beneath the elytra. When a beetle flies the elytra are held upwards and forwards, for only the hind wings beat. The elytra give the beetle lift, rather like the wings on an aeroplane. The hind wings are rather like the plane's engine, providing the power for flight.

Eggs and grubs

Beetles start their life as an egg, usually laid in a place where there is plenty of food. A few species, like the sexton beetles, look after their young, but many parent beetles die before their eggs hatch. The creature that comes out of the egg is very different from the adult beetle. It is a larva (grub), soft-bodied unlike its parents, but with hard biting mouth parts, to help it feed and grow. Most beetle larvae complete their growth within a year, but some, feeding in dead wood in cold places, take much longer. The record is about 30 years, making these the longest-lived

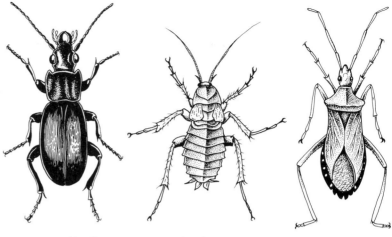

ground beetle   oriental cockroach   plant bug

of all insects. When its growth is complete, the grub finds a safe place to pupate. During pupation, the large, fat body of the larva changes to form the adult beetle. This is called metamorphosis. Some adult beetles do not feed at all, but merely drink a little dew or nectar. This is because the grub has provided them with all the energy that they need to find a mate and lay eggs.

Although there are so many beetles, on the whole they are not easy to find. This is because most of them dislike the light. They are either busy under fallen leaves, or among the roots of grasses, or simply hidden away during the daytime. Only a few, like the ladybirds, and some of the ground beetles, make themselves obvious. As these taste horrible they are safe from predators.

A few beetles are pests, feeding on crops or food stores, but many more are useful because they are recyclers, returning dead things to the soil so that plants can use them once more. Some feed off other pests, and so are useful to farmers and gardeners. ■

▲ Cockroaches and bugs look like beetles, but are different in several ways. A cockroach's head is partly hidden under the front of its body, and its front wings, if present, are not thick and hard like a beetle's. The front wings of a bug are thick and hard at the base, but are thin and papery at the tips.

The bombardier beetle protects itself by shooting jets of chemicals at attackers.

Distribution
Worldwide
Largest beetle
Goliath beetle: weight about 50 g; length about 15 cm
Smallest beetle
A feather-wing beetle: length about 1 mm

Phylum
Arthropoda
Class
Insecta
Order
Coleoptera
Number of species
Over 370,000

◖ See also
Bugs
Cockroaches
Insects
Ladybirds
Larvae
Metamorphosis
Pupae
Woodworms

▶ Sexton beetle on animal corpse. It will bury the corpse and then lay its eggs in it. Later the grubs will feed on the decaying flesh.

Belgium

Belgium is a country in western Europe. Its capital city, Brussels, is also the city where the European Community has its headquarters. People often call Belgium, The Netherlands and Luxembourg the 'Low Countries', but the Belgian countryside is not all low.

In the south-east is the Ardennes, a plateau of forests that rises to nearly 700 m (2,300 ft). The River Meuse flows through a deep valley on the northern edge of the Ardennes. To the north-west of the Meuse, the landscape slopes gently to the North Sea. This area is where most Belgians live. There are many farms on these lowland plains, mostly mixed farms where animals are reared and crops grown to feed them. But most Belgians live in the towns and cities. Antwerp is the major port where diamond cutting is an important industry. Others, such as Bruges and Gent, were rich towns 700 years ago, trading in wool and making lace. Many of their ancient buildings and winding cobbled streets have changed little since the Middle Ages.

Flashback

Before 1795 the land of Belgium was ruled by Austrians from Vienna. For a brief period it was part of the kingdom of The Netherlands. Then in 1830, after a national revolution, it became an independent kingdom. This included two main groups of people, each with their own language, and the population can still be divided along these lines. In the north people speak Flemish, a language very similar to Dutch. The southern people speak French and are known as Walloons, although very few of them now speak the Walloon dialect of French. ■

Area
30,513 sq km
(11,781 sq miles)
Capital Brussels
Population 9,860,000
Language
Flemish, French, German, Walloon
Religion Christian
Government
Parliamentary monarchy
Currency
1 Belgian franc = 100 centimes

▼ Belgian chocolates are world-famous and it is difficult to make a choice when faced with so many tempting varieties.

◄ Bilingual signs in French and Flemish show that Belgium is made up of two different groups of people each with their own language.

See also
Europe
Netherlands

Belize

Area 22,963 sq km
(8,866 sq miles)
Capital Belmopan
Population 166,000
Language
English, Spanish, Carib
Government
Parliamentary monarchy
Currency
1 Belize dollar = 100 cents

Belize is a small tropical country on the Caribbean coast of Central America. Off the coastline are many small coral islands called cays and the second longest coral barrier reef in the world. The mainland is low-lying, with the Maya Mountains in the south. The climate is warm and humid.

Cane sugar, citrus fruits and lobsters from the reef are important exports. In the interior, Belize has some splendid Mayan temples which are more than 1,000 years old. Belize is the only English-speaking country in Central America. For about 120 years it was a British colony, known as British Honduras. It became independent in 1981. ■

Bells and bell-ringing

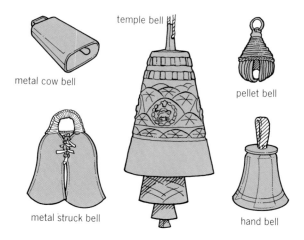

metal cow bell

temple bell

pellet bell

metal struck bell

hand bell

Bells are musical instruments. They are dome-shaped and hollow. Most are made of metal, but wood, plastic and even china bells also exist. They are all sizes, from tiny bells for sewing on clothing to the huge bells that hang in church and cathedral towers. Big bells make lower sounds than small bells, and their sound carries further. On a still day, for example, the 'bong' of Big Ben (the biggest bell in the tower of the British Houses of Parliament, which rings every hour) can be heard 15 km (about 9 miles) away.

How bells ring

Bells can be rung in different ways. Inside many bells there is a 'clapper' made of metal or wood. When you swing the bell, the clapper hits the sides and the whole bell vibrates. Big bells are hung from a frame, and you swing them by pulling ropes attached to them. To ring small bells, you simply shake them. Sometimes, instead of swinging the bell to ring it, the clapper is moved from side to side. This is called chiming.

Some bells have no clapper at all. To ring these, you hit them on the outside with a mallet or hammer.

Carillons

A carillon is a set of bells tuned to play the notes of a scale. They are found mostly in Belgium and The Netherlands. You play a keyboard below the bells, and the keys work the machinery to make them ring. Some carillons are electronic and can be programmed to play tunes without a human player. Sometimes carillons are hung in town halls and other big buildings, and are triggered to play when the building's clock shows certain times of day.

Bell-ringing

One bell is enough to give a signal: to call people in from a school playground, for example, or to sound the hours in a church or town-hall clock. But in Britain people use groups of bells, each tuned to a different note, to play tune-patterns. The ringers ring the bells in the right order to make the tune. In churches, where each player pulls a rope to play his or her bell, the actual tune-patterns are simple (just four or five notes), but the players 'change' from one pattern to another in a complicated sequence. 'Change-ringing', as it is called, can last for a few minutes or several hours, and is as exhausting to do as circuit-training in the gym. When you hear church bells pealing out at weddings or on Sunday mornings, change-ringing is going on.

Bells around the world

In Europe, groups of people sometimes ring tunes on sets of hand bells. The idea comes from China. Sets of bells were first used in Chinese music-making over 1,000 years ago, when bells were part of the court orchestra.

Much smaller bells are used by dancers in many parts of the world, to emphasize their body movements. In Britain, morris dancers tie on bells just below the knees, while Kathakali dancers from India have ankle bands with many bells on them. ∎

◄ The three bells are at different stages of ringing. The left-hand bell is 'down', and the ringer pulls on the 'sally' (the padded part of the rope) to lift it up. In the centre the bell is as high as it can be pulled. The ringer then releases the sally, letting the bell swing right round. He keeps hold of the tail of the rope so that at the top of its swing (the right-hand bell) he can pull it down again.

See also
Electronic music

Area 112,622 sq km
(43,484 sq miles)
Capital Porto Novo
Population 4,153,000
Language French, Fon,
Bariba, Yoruba, others
Religion Traditional,
Christian, Muslim
Government Republic
Currency
CFA franc = 100 centimes

See also
Africa

Benin

Benin is a country in West Africa. The southern plains are rainy. The high, grassy plains in the north are drier. Seven out of every ten people live by growing crops to feed their families. Cotton, palm oil and some other farm products are sold abroad. Some coastal families live by fishing. Their houses are built on stilts above the water.

Benin was once called Dahomey. The kings of Dahomey sold slaves to European traders, who shipped them to the Americas. France ruled Dahomey from 1892 until it became independent in 1960. The country's name was changed to Benin in 1975. ■

Beowulf

The poem of Beowulf is written in Anglo-Saxon. Modern English speakers can no longer understand Anglo-Saxon. It is like a foreign language that has to be learned.

War-wolf
Beowulf means 'War-wolf' in Anglo-Saxon.

Weapons and armour
Beowulf wore a helmet, a golden collar and a battle-harness and carried a shield made of linden wood (lime). He was armed with a sword and a keen and deadly knife. Beowulf's sword was called *Naegling*, which probably means 'Nailer'. Naegling was an ancient sword but unfortunately for Beowulf it snapped when he plunged it in the dragon's head.

Kennings
The language of the Beowulf poem is dramatic. The sea is called 'the swan's road'. The Sun is called 'the world's candle'. A harp is called 'play-wood'. These joined words are called kennings.

See also
English language

Beowulf was a legendary Scandinavian hero who belonged to a tribe called the Geats. The story of his exploits appears in an 8th-century poem, one of the earliest English writings to survive. This tells how he went to the aid of a neighbouring Danish king whose court was being terrorized by a flesh-eating monster named Grendel, who tore men apart with his talons. Scorning the use of weapons, Beowulf grappled bare-handed with Grendel and tore off his arm. The monster staggered off to die, and the arm was hung in the rafters of the hall where the warriors feasted.

Next night Grendel's monstrous mother burst into the hall, slew one of the sleeping Danes and dragged him off quickly to her underwater cave. Beowulf swam down to confront her, and killed her with a great sword picked up in the cave.

Beowulf later became king of the Geats and ruled in peace and plenty for 50 years. When he was old, he killed a fire-eating dragon which nested on a hoard of gold, but received his death-wound in the fight.■

Berbers

The Berbers are the people who were the original inhabitants of the area of North Africa that is today Libya, Tunisia, Algeria and Morocco. They lived mostly along the coast and in the mountains behind. In the 7th century AD, Muslim Arab armies conquered the whole of North Africa. At first the Berbers resisted. But in the centuries that followed, most Berbers became Muslims and there was much intermarrying. Many North African Arabs have Berber ancestors.

Arabic is the main language of North Africa, but several million people still speak the Berber language as well as Arabic. Radio stations in North Africa broadcast special programmes in Berber, and you can hear Berber music which has a distinctive African beat. The biggest Berber population, numbering more than 6 million, is in country areas of Morocco. In recent years there has been a move from country areas to towns, and this has further reduced the separate identity of the Berbers. ■

▲ This Berber man wears a traditional white headdress as protection against the desert heat.

See also
African music
Arabs
Muslims

Bermuda

Bermuda is a British colony of about 150 small coral islands located in the Atlantic Ocean about 900 km (600 miles) off the coast of the United States. Great Bermuda, the main island, is linked to some of the other islands by bridges. The islands are hilly and covered with beautiful vegetation. But there are no lakes or rivers, so the people depend on rain for fresh water. The capital, Hamilton, stands on Great Bermuda.

More than half the people are descended from Africans who worked as slaves on the plantations until 1834. Bermuda's parliament was founded in 1620. This makes it the oldest in the Commonwealth outside the British Isles. ■

Area
53 sq km
(21 sq miles)
Capital
Hamilton
Population
55,000
Language
English
Religion
Christian
Government
Self-governing British colony
Currency
1 Bermuda dollar = 100 cents

Bible

Bible comes from a Greek word *biblia* meaning 'books'. It is the title of the scriptures of the Christian religion. The Bible has two main parts, the Old and New Testaments. Testament and covenant are both words for promises or agreements made between people and God.

The Old Testament

The first Christians were Jews and used the Jewish scriptures, which were written mainly in Hebrew. Christians rearranged them into 39 books which they called the Old Testament. The books contain myths, legends, history, poetry, hymns and laws for living as God wants people to live. There are stories of Abraham and Moses and of prophets such as Amos, Hosea, Isaiah and Ezekiel who tried to encourage the people to stay close to God when times were difficult. Christians think these prophets prepared the way for the coming of Jesus.

The New Testament

Christians added 27 books called the New Testament to the Old Testament. These were written in Greek. They included the life and teaching of Jesus collected in four gospels. Gospel translates the Greek word 'good news'. The story of the early Church is told in the book called the Acts of the Apostles, and in epistles (letters) written by St Paul and others to the new churches in Corinth, Rome, Ephesus and other towns. These were all written in the century following the death of Jesus. The list of books to be included in the New Testament was agreed by Christians by the 4th century.

Translating the Bible

Later, the Bible was translated from Hebrew and Greek into Latin. Latin was the language used in church services all over western Europe for many hundreds of years. But only educated people could understand it.

At the time of the Reformation in the 16th century, Luther, Calvin and other Protestant reformers taught that Christians should read the Bible for themselves. That meant translating it into many different languages, printing lots of copies and teaching more people to read. Luther began a translation into German in 1521. At that time several people were working on translations into English; the first complete English Bible was published in the reign of Henry VIII. Today there are copies of the Bible in over 1,100 languages. It is among the best-selling books in the world.

The Bible is an important part of Christian worship and there is a copy in every church and chapel. Christians believe that when they read and study the Bible, they are in touch with God in some way. ■

◄ This is a page from the Lindisfarne gospels copied and painted by monks in the 7th century. It shows St Matthew writing his gospel. The words, *O Agios Mattheus*, mean St Matthew.

St Jerome completed a translation into Latin in AD 405. This version was called the Vulgate, from a Latin word meaning 'popular'.

The Bible was first printed by Gutenberg in Germany between 1452 and 1456.

The Bible in English
Bede translated parts of St John's Gospel into Anglo-Saxon in the 8th century.
1396 Wyclif's Bible
1526 Tyndale's New Testament printed in Antwerp
1535 Coverdale's complete Bible printed in England
1611 Authorized Version (King James Bible)
1881–1895 Revised Version
1946–1952 Revised Standard Version
1961–1970 New English Bible
1966 The Jerusalem Bible
1966–1976 Good News Bible
1989 Revised English Bible

See also

Christians
Churches
Illuminated manuscripts
Reformation

Biography
Abraham
Bede
Calvin
David, King
Gutenberg
Jacob
Jesus
John the Baptist
Joseph
Luther
Moses
Paul
Samson
Solomon

Old Testament				New Testament		
Pentateuch (first five books)	2 Samuel	Ecclesiastes	Obadiah	**Gospels**	**Epistles**	Titus
Genesis	1 Kings	Song of Solomon	Jonah	Matthew	Romans	Philemon
Exodus	2 Kings	(Song of Songs)	Micah	Mark	1 Corinthians	Hebrews
Leviticus	1 Chronicles		Nahum	Luke	2 Corinthians	James
Numbers	2 Chronicles	**Prophets**	Habakkuk	John	Galatians	1 Peter
Deuteronomy	Ezra	Isaiah	Zephaniah		Ephesians	2 Peter
	Nehemiah	Jeremiah	Haggai	The Acts of the	Philippians	1 John
Historical books	Esther	Lamentations	Zechariah	Apostles	Colossians	2 John
Joshua		Ezekiel	Malachi		1 Thessalonians	3 John
Judges	**Wisdom books**	Daniel			2 Thessalonians	Jude
Ruth	Job	Hosea			1 Timothy	
1 Samuel	Psalms	Joel			2 Timothy	Revelation
	Proverbs	Amos				

Bicycles

Bicycle comes from a Latin word *bis* meaning 'twice', and a Greek word *kuklos* meaning 'wheel'.

The tricycle has three wheels. It is more stable, and suited to younger riders.

A unicycle has one wheel. It takes acrobatic skill to ride it.

Some children learn to ride a 'two-wheeler' by using stabilizers.

The hobby horse (velocipede) invented in Germany, 1817.

Kirkpatrick Macmillan's bicycle, 1839, with pedals.

The penny-farthing (1860s): one turn of the pedal made one turn of the wheel.

The 'safety' bicycle, 1885, with pedals and chain.

Modern bicycles range from the ultra-light racer to sturdy mountain bikes built for cross-country riding. But all bicycle frames are hollow, making a light, strong structure. The frame design is based on triangular shapes. Bicycle design is always developing, making use of new materials and ideas. Some cycles have tiny wheels and can be folded for easy storage.

A bicycle makes efficient use of your body strength to get you around. When you turn the pedals, the power of your legs is transmitted to the back wheel by a chain linking two gear-wheels. On many bicycles, you can make pedalling easier by changing gear. This either moves the chain so that it fits over gearwheels of a different size, or it moves tiny cogwheels inside the hub of the back wheel. For hill climbing, you use a low gear which gives plenty of force but not much speed. On the flat, a high gear gives less force but more speed. You balance the bicycle by turning the handlebars and leaning right or left to correct each swerve and wobble. To slow down, you pull on the brake levers. This pushes rubber blocks against the wheel rims.

Flashback

The first bicycle, the hobby-horse, had no pedals, the rider pushing it along with his feet. Pedals were invented by a Scottish blacksmith who attached them to the back wheel by a lever. Then a French machine was developed with pedals attached to the front wheel. Wheels were made bigger and bigger as leg-power can turn a larger wheel fast; bikes with these huge front wheels were nicknamed penny-farthings (the names of large and small coins). Early cycles had iron wheels and later solid rubber ones which made them bumpy to ride. The safety bicycle, invented in 1885, had smaller wheels; the pedals were set on the frame and connected by a chain to the rear hub. After 1888 air-filled tyres made cycling much more comfortable, and soon after, bicycles were designed for women, with no crossbar to get in the way of skirts. ■

saddle

front brake lever

gear selectors

rear brake lever

crossbar

handlebars

rear safety reflector (red)

front safety reflector (white)

cantilever brakes grip the wheel rim like a strong hand

front forks

spokes

gear protector

pedal

crank

hub

gear rings

tyre

rim

derailleur gears have a range of gear wheels which help you to pedal easily up hills or on the flat

tyre valve

Big bang

In 1927 Georges Lemaître, a Belgian astronomer, suggested that the universe began very small. He called this state a 'cosmic egg', which violently exploded producing the expanding universe we observe. In the 1930s and 1940s the 'cosmic egg' theory developed into the 'big bang' theory.

In the 1940s and 1950s there was fierce debate among two groups: those who supported the 'big bang' theory and those, led by British astronomer Fred Hoyle, who thought the universe remains much the same throughout eternity, the 'steady-state' theory.

See also
Cosmology Radio
Energy Universe
Galaxies

Most scientists believe that the Universe started thousands of millions of years ago with an event that they call the 'big bang'. We imagine that it was some kind of explosion in which all the matter and energy in the Universe was created. At first the Universe was incredibly dense and hot. Later, as it expanded outwards, the galaxies and the stars formed. The whole Universe has gone on expanding since the big bang. We cannot tell whether it will go on growing for ever or will start to get smaller again.

Scientists are fairly sure that the theory is right since they found a faint radio signal that seems to fill all of space. The only explanation for the radio signal is that it is energy left over from the big bang. ■

Billiards

Table-top games were played in France in the 15th century with ivory balls and curved sticks. By the 18th century the straight cue was being used, and by the middle of the 19th century the game looked much as it does today.

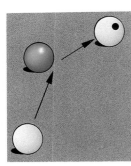

▲ A 'cannon'. A player makes a cannon and scores two points if he plays his ball so that it hits both the red ball and his opponent's ball.

See also
Snooker

This an indoor game for two played with three small, hard balls, two white and one red, on a large, flat, cloth-covered table with six pockets. The white balls are the cue-balls; one has two black spots to distinguish it.

A player strikes his own white cue-ball with the tip of a stick called a cue, and aims to score points by 'cannons', 'pots' and 'in offs'. For a cannon, which scores two points, the player has to make his ball strike both of the other balls.

Potting the red (striking it with his cue-ball and sending it into one of the pockets) scores three points. Potting his opponent's white ball scores two points.

If his own ball goes into one of the pockets off the red he scores three points; off the other white, two points. The winner is the player who reaches an agreed score first, or who has the highest score after a certain time. ■

Binoculars

People often use binoculars when they are bird-watching, to make far-away things, like the birds, seem bigger (magnified). Binoculars are just a pair of telescopes, one for each eye. They have prisms (triangular shaped pieces of glass) which reflect the light in a zigzag path. These make the binoculars much shorter than a telescope. The prisms also turn the picture the right way up. With a pair of binoculars you can use both your eyes so that you can judge distances. This is not possible with a telescope. ■

If binoculars are marked 8x30, the magnification is 8; the binoculars make things look 8 times bigger. The diameter of the objective lens is 30 mm (1·2 in). Lenses of bigger diameter collect more light and give a brighter picture.

Opera glasses look like binoculars but they do not need prisms. They use a different lens arrangement which magnifies less and gives a narrower view.

See also
Lenses
Telescopes

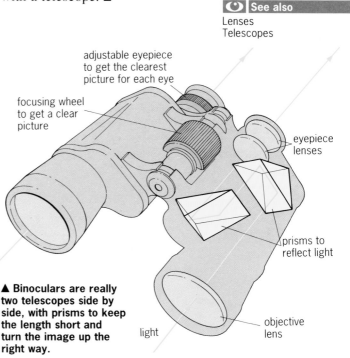

adjustable eyepiece to get the clearest picture for each eye

focusing wheel to get a clear picture

eyepiece lenses

prisms to reflect light

light

objective lens

▲ Binoculars are really two telescopes side by side, with prisms to keep the length short and turn the image up the right way.

Biologists

Biologists study living things. They include botanists who study plants, zoologists who study animals and ecologists who study the relationships between living things and their environments.

As biology itself is so varied it can lead to a vast number of careers as different as veterinary nurse, government health inspector, botanical gardener or doctor. ■

See also
Botanists
Ecology
Zoologists

Birds

Birds are warm-blooded animals which evolved from dinosaur-like reptiles millions of years ago. There are about 8,700 species of birds living in the world today.

All birds have wings and lay eggs. They are the only creatures to grow feathers. Birds have evolved a highly specialized body which enables them to fly efficiently. A few, such as the kiwi, have lost the power of flight.

World of birds

Birds live in all parts of the world. Jungles, deserts, the open oceans and even the icy wastes of Antarctica are home for some birds. Up in the sky, swans may migrate at a height of 8 km (5 miles). Under the water, penguins may swim to a depth of 265 m (870 ft).

The variety of birds is amazing. There are birds which eat only plants and others which eat only fresh meat. Most hunt by day but some hunt only after dark. Birds vary in size, too. The ostrich grows to be taller than us, while the bee hummingbird is tiny and would fit into the palm of your hand. Male birds are usually larger and often more colourful than the females; in many species they look alike. In just a few the female is larger or brighter.

Some species are great travellers. Wheatears are only a little larger than sparrows, yet each year some fly non-stop from Greenland to North Africa.

▶ **Bird record-breakers**

Largest wing-span
Wandering albatross, up to 4 m

Smallest bird
Bee hummingbird, 6 cm from bill-tip to tail

Largest bird
Ostrich, 2·5 m high and weighs 150 kg

Longest non-stop flight by small bird
Greenland wheatear, 4,100 km (2,500 miles)

Fastest bird
Peregrine, 180 km/h (112 mph)

Longest migration
Arctic tern, up to 40,000 km (25,000 miles) in a year

wandering albatross

Greenland wheatear

Arctic tern

peregrine

ostrich

bee hummingbird

Different diets

Like all animals, birds need to find food to survive. To avoid competing for the same food many species have specialized diets and different ways of feeding.

Different birds have different wing and tail shapes. But often the most noticeable difference between species is the shape of the bills and the legs and feet.

Hummingbirds have long, thin, pointed bills to reach into flowers and feed on the nectar. Many wading birds have long, strong bills for probing the mud in search of worms or shellfish. Birds of prey have hooked bills for tearing meat. Ducks have flattened bills for filtering water or mud. Sparrows have short, strong bills for cracking seeds.

Fish-eaters such as herons have long legs for wading in water. Others which feed on fish, such as cormorants, have shorter legs and webbed feet to help them swim, dive and chase fish under water.

Swifts spend most of their lives in the air. Their feet are very strong and their tiny claws allow them to cling to a rock but they are useless on the ground.

long-billed curlew

pelican's pouched bill

hawfinch cracking cherry stone

flamingo filter-feeding

eagle tearing meat

▲ Birds' bills are useful tools for feeding and some are highly specialized.

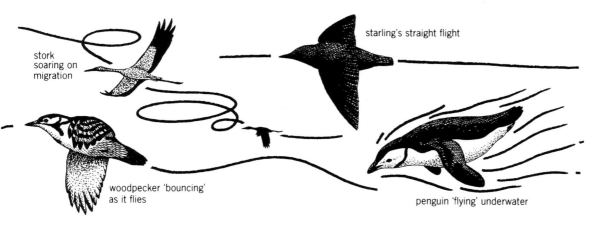

stork soaring on migration

starling's straight flight

woodpecker 'bouncing' as it flies

penguin 'flying' underwater

◄ Four very different types of flight.

Flight for survival

Most birds can fly. Even ground-living birds, such as pheasants, will fly into trees to spend the night because they are safer there from being hunted.

Not all birds fly in the same way. Starlings fly straight, moving their wings all the time and forming a star shape in the air. Woodpeckers close their wings between flaps and 'bound' along, moving up and down in the air.

Larger birds such as gulls spend much of the

time gliding, and vultures soar for hours with hardly any movement of their wings. Penguins cannot fly like other birds, but they use their wings as flippers and 'fly' under water.

In flight some species, such as kestrels, can hover in the air as they look for prey on the ground, while peregrines, which hunt other birds, can reach speeds of 180 km/h (112 mph) as they catch their prey in the air.

Hummingbirds also hover in flight while they gather nectar from flowers, their wings beating at an incredible rate of up to 80 times a second.

Cruising speeds of birds
Wandering albatross
 54 km/h (34 mph)
Grey heron
 43 km/h (27 mph)
Mallard
 65 km/h (40 mph)
Pheasant
 54 km/h (34 mph)
Dunlin
 47 km/h (29 mph)
Herring gull
 40 km/h (25 mph)
Swallow
 32 km/h (20 mph)

Wrens

Wrens usually defend territories throughout the year. Sometimes in winter they roost together. Once 63 were found to have used one nestbox. Another roost in an attic attracted 98 wrens.

Robins

Out of every 100 robins hatched in one year, only 28 are likely to survive until the following spring.

Birds should not be fed between April and October as they can find plenty of insects, seeds and other food during these months.

Remember to keep the birds' drinking water free from ice during winter.

The more berry-bearing shrubs in your garden, the more birds will visit.

▼ **Unsalted peanuts or a coconut can be suspended from the bird-table for those species which like to feed on hanging food, and for perching birds put out cheese rinds, cooked potato, seeds, berries, and bread and cake crumbs.**

Garden birds

Many people enjoy watching birds in their gardens, and if we put out the correct food in the winter months they can be attracted close to our windows.

A bird-table, on a tall post that cats cannot reach, is a safe place for birds to feed. Throughout the year, make sure that the birds have a shallow dish of water to drink from. They may even take a bath in it!

The species of birds that visit your garden will depend a lot on whereabouts you live in the world, and even within a country. In winter, in the British Isles, the most common garden birds are sparrows, starlings, blackbirds, chaffinches, blue tits, great tits, song thrushes, greenfinches, robins and dunnocks. Magpies and collared doves are becoming increasingly common.

Watching birds

Beginning bird-watching is simple. Use a bird identification book and find out the names of your garden birds. Try to discover which are males and which are females, and watch how different birds behave.

If you have a local park with a lake, arrange a visit with some friends or your parents, because water birds are generally quite easy to identify.

Always wear dull-coloured clothes and try to move slowly so that you do not frighten the birds. You will need a notebook and pencil to record what you see. If you want to look at the birds more closely you will need binoculars (those marked 8x30 or 8x40 are best).

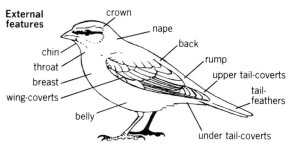

External features — crown, nape, back, rump, upper tail-coverts, tail-feathers, under tail-coverts, belly, wing-coverts, breast, throat, chin

Songs for all seasons

Some birds make noises with their bills. Others use their feathers. But most use songs and calls to communicate with other birds.

Calls are usually short and loud and they may signal danger. They may be linked with courtship or with young begging food. Some calls help to keep flocks together in thick woodland, or when migrating at night.

Song is generally given by a male to declare that he has chosen a place to nest and is prepared to defend the surrounding area, called a territory, and that he wishes to attract, or keep, a female.

great tit

blackbird

greenfinch

robin

chaffinch

dunnock

house sparrow

starling

song thrush

blue tit

Travelling around the world

Many animals, including birds, migrate: they move from one place to another and return again in a different season.

While some birds will not travel far from where they hatch, others, especially those breeding in the northern hemisphere, will fly south for hundreds or thousands of kilometres to spend the winter in warmer, food-rich places.

Sometimes only part of a population will migrate, often those living farthest north or in the most mountainous regions. Mountain birds may travel only a few kilometres to lower levels to find food and a warmer environment.

The migrations of small birds are astounding. The tiny ruby-throated hummingbird migrates from North to South America, and this journey includes an 800 km (500 mile) crossing of the Gulf of Mexico. The British swallow crosses the Equator to winter in South Africa.

Sea birds make even greater journeys. Some go out to sea and spend the winter out of the sight of land. Arctic terns fly from their Arctic breeding grounds to winter in the Southern Ocean, sometimes reaching the coasts of Antarctica. They can cover a distance of 40,000 km (25,000 miles) in one year.

Birds in a changing world

Life is tough for birds. When young they must learn to find food and shelter, to survive extreme weather and avoid enemies. Even so, most of them will die in their first year. Although nature appears cruel, if all the birds survived, many of them would not be able to find enough food, so a balance is created. Unfortunately, we have the power to upset that balance.

The dodo was a victim of our interference. It was a huge, flightless pigeon which lived on the island of Mauritius in the Indian Ocean. Visiting sailors killed many of them for food, and the cats, pigs and monkeys which the sailors brought to the island destroyed the dodos' eggs. By 1670 all the dodos were dead. They had become an extinct species. Since then the great auk, the passenger pigeon and many other birds, especially those of the tropics, have also become extinct as a result of our influence.

The rapid growth of the human population and the huge demand for natural materials have resulted in the destruction of many of the places where birds live. Marshes are drained to make farmland, forests are cleared for timber or for

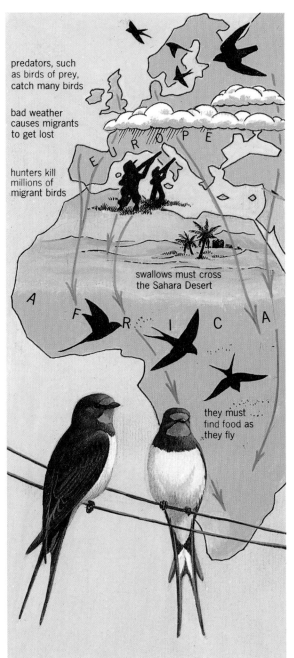

predators, such as birds of prey, catch many birds

bad weather causes migrants to get lost

hunters kill millions of migrant birds

swallows must cross the Sahara Desert

they must find food as they fly

◄ Swallows, like other birds which migrate, face many dangers on their journey.

The Arctic tern migrates further than any other bird, travelling 17,000 km (11,000 miles) between its breeding ground in the Arctic and its winter home in the Antarctic.

Oldest wild birds known
Oystercatcher 36 years
Royal albatross 35·9 years
Osprey 31·2 years
Mallard 29 years
Fulmar 23 years
Mute swan 22 years
Swift 21·1 years
Starling 20 years
Swallow 16 years
Cardinal 13·5 years
Robin 12·9 years
The lifespan of birds varies between species.

Subphylum Vertebrata
Class Aves
Number of orders 29
Number of species About 8,700

space to grow crops, and deserts increase in size because of over-grazing by domesticated animals.

Birds are also hunted as a sport by some people, but they are becoming increasingly protected by laws throughout the world. However, around the Mediterranean over 100 million migrating birds are shot or trapped by hunters each year, and unless the numbers of birds killed are controlled, even more species may become extinct. ■

◯ See also
Archaeopteryx
Birds of paradise
Birds of prey
Cuckoos
Ducks, geese and swans
Eggs
Extinct animals
Flightless birds
Game birds
Hummingbirds
Migration
Nests
Ornithologists
Parrots
Penguins
Perching birds
Pigeons
Poultry
Sea birds
Wading birds
Water birds

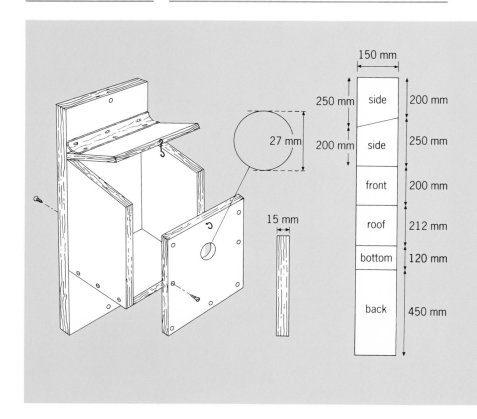

150 mm

250 mm | side | 200 mm
200 mm | side | 250 mm
27 mm
| front | 200 mm
15 mm
| roof | 212 mm
| bottom | 120 mm
| back | 450 mm

Making a nestbox

Birds which nest in holes in trees can sometimes be encouraged to nest in a home-made nestbox. The nestbox may look nothing like a tree, but if it is the right size, watertight and positioned correctly the birds will probably use it.

Use wood which is at least 15 mm thick. Cut pieces to the sizes shown in the diagram and use screws to fasten it together. The lid should be hinged using a strip of rubber or leather, and fixed with a catch. The entrance hole should be 27 mm wide for small birds, and this will stop larger birds from using the nestbox. The design shown here is for small birds like blue tits, and you can adapt it for other species.

Generally the nestbox should be put in a natural position facing away from the midday sun and away from the prevailing wind and rain. Do not look inside while birds are nesting. At the end of each summer the box should be taken down and thoroughly cleaned.

Birds of paradise

▶ **Lesser bird of paradise. All male birds of paradise have beautifully coloured plumage, very different to their closest relatives the crows.**

Subphylum Vertebrata
Class Aves
Order Passeriformes
Number of species 43
Size 12 – 100 cm

They are closely related to bowerbirds, and have strong bills and beaks.

See also

Birds
Perching birds

Birds of paradise are some of the world's most exotic birds because their feathers are brilliantly coloured and fantastically shaped.

They live mostly in the wet forests in the mountains of New Guinea or on nearby islands. But four species are found in north-east Australia.

When explorers first brought skins of these birds to Europe, people marvelled at them and thought they must have come from paradise because they were so beautiful.

Beautiful feathers

Female birds of paradise are dull coloured, it is only the males that have the magnificent plumage. They use feathers to attract the females in elaborate courtship displays which are accompanied by unusual 'songs'. Their songs may be soft or loud. Some can sound 'mechanical' and others sound loud and explosive, rather like gun-fire.

Bird of paradise feathers have been used in ceremonial costumes by local tribes in New Guinea. During the last century many of the birds were shot for a plumage trade which exported their feathers to Europe and North America for ladies' hats. ∎

Birds of prey

This name could refer to any bird which hunts and kills, even a robin catching a worm. But usually when we talk of birds of prey we mean falcons, hawks and vultures. Often owls are included, though they are not related to the others.

Birds of prey are so called because they prey on and eat other birds, mammals, fish, reptiles, insects, worms and also dead creatures. All have hooked bills, and powerful feet with talons. Their sight is better than ours and they have good hearing.

Out to kill

Hunting methods and types of prey vary enormously. Honey buzzards that eat bees have blunt talons for digging out bees' nests. Their faces are covered with stiff feathers as protection against stings. Fish eagles dive feet first into water. Vultures soar, searching for signs of a dead animal.

Lammergeyers drop bones onto rocks to get at the marrow. Harriers fly low over the ground searching for small mammals and birds. Sparrowhawks have long legs for grasping prey. They also have short, broad wings and long tails for manoeuvring in the woods which they inhabit.

Peregrines use their speed in flight to hunt other birds. Red-footed falcons use their feet to catch large insects in flight. Ospreys have water-proofed plumage, and nostrils which close as they dive into water after fish.

Hunters hunted

For years we have hunted down birds of prey. They have been shot, trapped and poisoned to protect game birds from being hunted by them. Many have been taken into captivity for falconry. The use of chemicals in the countryside between 1950 and 1980 was also harmful to birds of prey and many populations declined rapidly as a result of poisoning.

Hunters of the night

Owls are generally thought of as the nocturnal (night-time) birds of prey, but not all owls hunt at night. Short-eared owls, for instance, hunt by day, but most owls are well equipped for night hunting.

Owls have soft plumage to help them fly quietly, and a large head with forward-facing eyes to

help them judge distances. Around the eyes is a facial disc which helps to direct sound into their large efficient ears. One of the toes can be brought round so that four talons grip prey from four different directions.

Owls can see in very poor light, and their hearing is so good that they can even locate their prey in total darkness.

Falconry

This ancient sport uses trained birds of prey to hunt wild birds and other animals. It may have originated in China 4,000 years ago.

The sport was common in Europe in the Middle Ages. It almost died out in the last century, but has recently been revived. Hawks, falcons, eagles and buzzards are the most commonly kept species. Once all were taken from the wild. Now more and more are bred in captivity. ■

◀ A white-bellied sea-eagle having just caught a fish with its talons. These eagles live on tropical coasts in southern Asia and Australia. This photograph was taken in Sri Lanka.

Smallest
Black-legged falconet: length 14 cm
Largest
Andean condor: length 116 cm

Subphylum
Vertebrata
Class
Aves
Order
Falconiformes (active by day). About 287 species
Strigiformes (active by night). About 134 species

▲ A peregrine falcon is trained to sit and feed on a gloved hand. The bird is hooded to prevent it wasting strength and to keep it calm.

◀ Two white-backed vultures with a long-billed vulture in the middle. The photograph was taken at Bharatpur, a huge bird reserve in India.

 See also
Birds
Game birds

Birth

The chance of having twins is 1 in 80 in the Western world; in West Africa the chance is 1 in 33.

The chance of having triplets (3 babies at once) is 1 in 6,000.

The chance of having quads (4 babies at once) is 1 in 500,000.

Giving birth is called labour because it is very hard wo k.

When a baby is ready to be born, hormones (chemical messengers) in the mother's body send signals to her brain that start muscles in her womb contracting. Slowly the neck of the womb stretches to about 10 cm (4 in) across so that the baby's head can be pushed through. Then the womb muscles contract even harder to push the baby down the birth canal. Once the head is born, the rest of the body slides out quite easily.

The baby still has the umbilical cord that supplied it with nourishment from the placenta. This is removed, and the cord end forms the baby's navel (tummy button). Soon after the baby is born, the placenta becomes detached from the wall of the womb and is pushed out of the mother's body by more muscle contractions. The womb slowly shrinks back to its normal size.

► Most babies (in western countries) are born in hospitals but some mothers choose to have their babies at home. This woman gives birth at home in a position she finds easiest, with her husband to help.

Caesarean birth

Occasionally the baby cannot be born naturally. Then the doctor gives the mother an anaesthetic and removes the baby from the womb by making a cut in the mother's abdomen and the wall of the womb. The baby is then gently removed and the mother is stitched up. ■

See also
Babies
Midwives
Pregnancy

Bison

Bison are large cow-like animals which were once common in Europe and America. In Europe they were hunted almost to extinction in ancient times. Today, only a few survive in parks and zoos.

In America in 1850 bison herds were thought to number over 100 million animals. European settlers hunted these so heavily that by 1900 only about 1,000 bison remained. They then began to be protected, and today about 50,000 survive. ■

◄ The male bison is much larger than the female. His success in mating depends on his size, as he must compete with lots of other males.

Distribution
Grassland and woodlands, North America
Weight About 800 kg
Number of young 1
Lifespan
About 20 years in the wild, up to 40 in captivity

Subphylum Vertebrata
Class Mammalia
Order Artiodactyla (cloven-hoofed animals)
Family Bovidae (cow family)
Number of species 2, European and American bison

See also
Buffalo
Cattle

Black Death

The Black Death (1347–1351) was a dreadful disease that came from Asia. It was probably started by a 'bacillus' or germ, found in the stomach of a certain kind of flea. This flea lived on black rats, which came to Europe on trading ships or caravans from the East. A bite from one of these fleas could infect a human. Then, as the disease spread, one person could infect others just by being in contact with them. Doctors had no idea what to do. They did not understand the cause of the disease either. About one-fifth of all the people in Europe died. 'Almost everyone expected death,' wrote an Italian chronicler, 'and people said and believed, "This is the end of the world." ' Eventually the plague died down, but it came back in several smaller outbreaks over the next 300 years. ■

In China the death rate was very high. The disease was carried there by traders along the caravan routes north of the Himalayas.

In England about one-third of the population died.

See also
Epidemics
Middle Ages

Black holes

'Black hole' is the name astronomers use for a very strange kind of star. It cannot send out any light but it drags in anything that gets near enough with the incredibly strong pull of its gravity. Anything that falls in just disappears, so the name 'black hole' describes a star like this very well.

Astronomers think that there are some black holes in space but it is not easy to tell, because they cannot be seen! What you have to look for is material falling into a black hole. X-rays are given off when that happens and some of the X-ray stars astronomers have found might be black holes.

These really strange objects are probably made when a star explodes. The inside of the star, left over after the explosion, falls in on itself and keeps falling until the material is squashed out of existence. It is very hard to imagine this happening but scientists believe that it is possible. When something weighing three times as much as our Sun collapses into a black hole, its gravity is so strong that even light cannot get away. When you throw a ball up in the air, it falls back because the Earth's gravity is pulling on it. Around a black hole, the gravity can even pull the light rays back. ■

Astronomers think that there might be black holes millions of times more massive than the Sun at the centres of some galaxies. Of the stars we know about, the most likely one to be a black hole is in a double star called Cygnus X-1. The name means 'first X-ray source to be found in the constellation Cygnus'. The black hole has about eight times the mass of the Sun. A black hole with the mass of the Sun would be about 6 km (4 miles) in diameter. One with the mass of the Earth would be about 18 mm (¾ in) across.

The term 'black hole' was first used by American physicist John Wheeler in the 1960s.

It is estimated that only about one star in a 1,000 is massive enough to have any chance of ever becoming a black hole when it collapses.

See also

Astronomers
Gravity
Quasars
Stars
X-rays

Blindness

Blindness occurs in all animals including humans.

Partially sighted and totally blind people can sometimes be cured by medical treatments including surgery. For others, though, the loss of vision lasts for ever.

People who are blind develop their other senses, so that they often have, for example, far better hearing and sense of smell than people with sight. They can also use a range of practical aids such as guide dogs, 'talking books' and braille. Many blind people carry a long white cane. They move this across their path as they walk, to detect obstacles.

Why do people become blind?

Some people are born blind because of infections, or, in very rare cases, they inherit blindness from their parents. More often, people lose their sight due to disease or old age. People with diabetes sometimes suffer damage to the retinas of their eyes which can cause blindness. In Africa and South America hundreds of thousands of people are blinded by the disease 'river blindness'. This disease is caused by a parasitic worm that is spread in the bites of blackflies which breed by rivers and streams.

Cataracts are one of the commonest causes of blindness in Britain. This is a clouding of the lens of the eye that occurs in some people as they get old. Blindness caused by cataracts can be corrected by an operation, which removes the clouded lens so the person can see again. ■

About 90 per cent of people who are registered as blind have some vision. Researchers believe that they, and some totally blind people, may be able to see again using various electronic devices. One way would involve electronic stimulation of visual centres in the brain. Eventually it may be possible to implant tiny television cameras into the eye sockets with necessary electronics housed in special spectacles.

See also

Braille
Diabetes
Eyes

Biography
Keller

▲ Guide dogs are specially trained to lead their owners safely through the most crowded places.

Blindness in babies can occasionally result from the mother getting the disease rubella (German measles) during pregnancy. Girls should be vaccinated against rubella before they reach child-bearing age.

Blood

Most animals have blood inside them. Only some of the smallest and simplest animals, such as corals and flatworms, do not have any. All animals with backbones (vertebrates), and most of those without (invertebrates), have some sort of blood system. These do not all function in the same way.

The blood of vertebrates is made up of a fluid, called plasma, with blood cells floating in it. These blood cells do a number of different jobs. They may carry oxygen, help blood to clot, produce antibodies or eat invading bacteria.

The blood is pumped through tubes (blood vessels) round the body by a muscular pump, the heart. Blood acts as a transport system for carrying materials to places where they are needed. It takes dissolved foods such as glucose sugar from the intestines to all parts of the body. It also carries wastes, including urea and carbon dioxide, from all the body organs. Urea is removed from the blood in the kidneys as urine is made. The gas carbon dioxide passes out of the blood into the lungs and is breathed out. Hormones, the chemical messengers that control a number of functions, such as growth, are also transported in the blood.

The blood of vertebrates (like ourselves) is usually red. It is red because of a coloured protein called haemoglobin in red blood cells. This can carry oxygen. Blood carries oxygen from the lungs to all the cells of the body.

Blood can defend us from damage and infections in at least three quite different ways. First, it can seal up cuts or other damage to the skin because it is able to set (clot) quickly. This patching stops the escape of more blood and prevents dirt and germs from entering. Secondly, special white blood cells called lymphocytes make antibodies. Antibodies recognize germs invading the body and attach to them. The germs are then easily picked out and destroyed by other defences. Thirdly, other white blood cells, called phagocytes, destroy germs by eating them.

There are a few rare diseases that stop the proper working of the blood, such as haemophilia and leukaemia. Haemophilia is an inherited disease. The blood of a haemophiliac does not clot normally. Leukaemia is a type of blood cancer. It happens when the body makes too many of one or other type of blood cell. Choked with these extra cells, the blood cannot function as it should. ■

A drop of blood contains about 100 million red blood cells. More than 2 million red blood cells are destroyed and replaced every second.

The blood of lobsters is pale blue, as oxygen is carried by haemocyanin which contains copper.

⊙ See also

Hearts
Hormones
Human body
Kidneys
Lungs
Pulse

▶ Greatly magnified photograph of white blood cells, red blood cells and platelets. The two large rough-surfaced objects are white cells which engulf and digest foreign materials entering the body. The small spiky objects are platelets which help blood to clot.

▼ Your body has a puncture repair kit. When you bleed, tiny objects called platelets send out fibres which trap red cells. Blood then changes into a thick jelly, a blood clot, which blocks the wound.

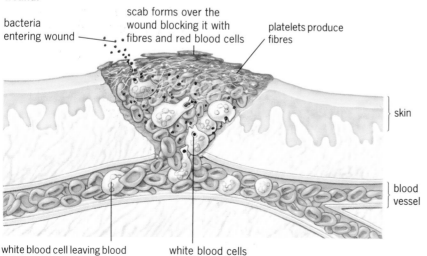

bacteria entering wound

scab forms over the wound blocking it with fibres and red blood cells

platelets produce fibres

skin

blood vessel

white blood cell leaving blood to kill germs in the wound

white blood cells destroying bacteria

Board games

The simplest board game is *Noughts and Crosses*. Most of us play it on paper, but all you need is sand or mud and a finger. The earliest board games would have started like this.

Some board games are won by luck alone, like *Snakes and Ladders*. Some are won by skill, like *Chess*. Some are a mixture, like *Monopoly*. Games of luck are usually 'race' games: who will reach square 100 first? Games of skill are usually 'war' games: who can capture the opponent's pieces?

Backgammon is one of the oldest board games that people still play, and one of the best. Its name comes from the Saxon (it means *back game* because sometimes pieces have to go back to the beginning), but the Romans played it too.

In the Middle Ages it was called *tables* and church leaders tried to stop people playing it because it is a gambling game. It is one of the games that use dice to decide how far you can move, so it is a mixture of luck and skill. It is easy to learn, but difficult to play well. ■

Mancala is a kind of game with many names (*Wari* is one of them) and many variations. Its boards have been found in the pyramids and it is still played today. All you need is 12 circles and 48 pebbles or seeds, so the game can be played anywhere. It is a game of great skill that is very simple to learn. The game starts with the seeds spread among the circles. You play by 'sowing' the seeds from a circle on your side, one by one, anticlockwise. If the last seed sown makes 2 or 3 on a circle on the other player's side, or the end of a row of 2s and 3s, you capture all those seeds (and do not use them again).

▶ **This game of Snakes and Ladders was made around 1900. It has about 100 squares. The heads of the snakes are on squares with the names of vices, such as cruelty, dishonesty and destructiveness. The snakes lead down to pictures of punishment. The ladders lead from squares with virtues such as obedience and perseverance up to the names of heroes and reformers or to moral sayings. They reflect the values and opinions of the Victorians.**

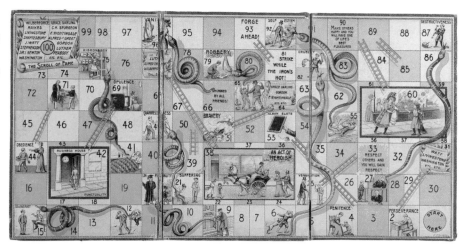

See also

Chess

Boats

Boat engines
Outboard engine: detachable engine (with propeller) usually fitted to the back of the boat.
Inboard engine: engine permanently installed inside the boat.

Rowing the Atlantic
Wayne Dickinson of the USA rowed across the Atlantic in a boat less than 3 m long. The journey took him from October 1982 until March 1983.

See also

Canoes · Sailing ships
Lifeboats · Ships
Sailing · Yachts

Many people regard boats and ships as being the same thing, but a boat is really a small craft, often with little or no deck on it. Boats can be propelled by people using oars or paddles, by small sails or by an engine. Boats are found all over the world on rivers and along the coasts.

The sides of a boat are usually only slightly above the water-level, so boats are rarely found on the oceans and they do not leave harbour if the sea is rough. In the past boats were made of wood or of reeds or rushes, but today other materials such as aluminium, plastic, rubber and fibreglass can be used. Small boats are sometimes called dinghies. ■

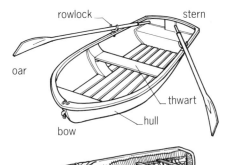

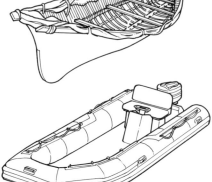

◀ **Rowing boats are often made of fibreglass or wood. They are propelled by oars which rest in special supports called rowlocks (pronounced 'rollocks').**

◀ **Inuit make boats by covering a light frame with sealskin. They use them for hunting and fishing.**

◀ **Speedboats can be used for towing water-skiers and for racing. They often have powerful outboard engines and rise out of the water at the front when going fast.**

Boer War

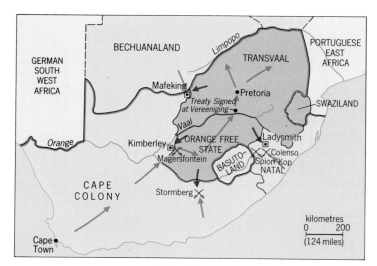

British land

Boer land

→ Boer attacks 1899

→ British attacks

— Boundary of Union of South Africa, 1910

✕ battle

⊡ besieged town

The Boers
Now called Afrikaners. Descended from Dutch settlers in the Cape. Lived mainly in the Transvaal and Orange Free State.

The British
Ruled Cape Colony, Natal, Bechuanaland and Southern Rhodesia.

1899
War began. Black Week. Boers besieged Kimberley, Ladysmith, Mafeking.

1900
British relieved Kimberley, Ladysmith and Mafeking.

1902
Treaty of Vereeniging.

Losses
Over 7,000 Boers killed. Up to 28,000 died in camps. 22,000 British died. Number of black Africans killed not known.

See also
British empire
Concentration camps
South Africa

Biography
Baden-Powell
Rhodes
Smuts

The Boers were Dutch settlers in southern Africa. They resented the growing power of the British there and this led to war between these two groups of white settlers.

The British had a big army, and their empire behind them. But the Boers were tough fighters. They were farmers who knew the land, and were good shots. The British used railways, which were easy to attack. The Boers inflicted heavy losses. There were three British defeats in 'Black Week', 10–15 December 1899.

Next year the British sent out more troops and two new generals, Lord Roberts and Lord Kitchener, who swept into Boer lands. But the Boers hid in their farms and ambushed British troops. So the British burned farms, and put the women and children in concentration camps where disease killed thousands. Both sides used black Africans as scouts and servants. Many Africans died, and their families suffered in the fighting. The war dragged on for two more years.

Peace was made in 1902 and the British and Boers agreed to live together in a new country, South Africa. But many Boers did not forget the war; and these two white races did not work out how to live fairly with the black peoples of South Africa. ■

Bolivia

About three-quarters of all Bolivians live 3·2 km (2 miles) above sea-level. Their capital, La Paz, is the world's highest capital city, and Lake Titicaca, on the Peruvian border, is the highest navigable lake in the world. Bolivia has no sea coast.

Between two ranges of the high Andes Mountains, in the south-west corner of the country, lies a high, bleak, cold plain called the *altiplano*. It is where most of the towns are. To the east lie steaming rainforests, scrub forests, and grasslands. The coca plant, from which cocaine is made, is grown in the fertile, deep valleys that cut into the slopes of the eastern range. Many poor families rely on this illegal drug trade to make a living. Most of Bolivia's income comes from minerals, especially tin.

Bolivia formed part of the ancient Inca empire. It was conquered by the Spaniards in the 16th century and liberated in 1825 by Simón Bolívar, after whom it was named. More than half of all Bolivians are Indians; one of the languages they speak, Quechua, was spoken by the Inca people. ■

Area
1,098,600 sq km
(424,170 sq miles)
Capital
La Paz
Population
6,310,000
Language
Spanish, Quechua, Aymará
Religion
Christian
Government
Parliamentary republic
Currency
1 Bolivian peso = 100 centavos

See also
American Indians
Andes
Incas
South America
Spanish colonial history

Biography
Bolívar

▼ On Lake Titicaca, the largest lake in South America, the Uru Indians use boats made from totora reeds to travel to and from their floating island homes.

Bombs

Bombs consist of a container, usually a metal case, filled with explosive material and a device called a fuse or detonator to set it on fire or make it explode. Aerial bombs, which were widely used in World War II, are dropped from aeroplanes and are filled with thousands of pounds of high explosives like TNT. During World War II, the Germans developed 'flying bombs'. The V1 was a pilotless aircraft with explosives in its nose, and the V2 was rocket-propelled.

Nuclear bombs release the enormous energy produced during the processes of fission (the atom or A-bomb) or fusion (the hydrogen or H-bomb).

The first aerial bombs were dropped from unmanned balloons on Venice by the Austrians in 1849. ■

See also

Atoms
Explosives
Hiroshima
Missiles
Nuclear power
Rockets
Weapons

Bones

Bones are alive. This is why they can mend and regrow after they break. They are as strong as some kinds of steel, but only one-fifth as heavy. So they form a firm, light skeleton on which are attached the soft parts of the body. Bones are made out of a mixture of a tough protein, called collagen, and very tiny hard mineral crystals which contain calcium and phosphorus. This mixture gives the bones their strength.

At the centre of many bones is a soft tissue called bone marrow. This contains blood vessels that supply the bone with food and oxygen. The marrow is also the place where new red and white blood cells are continually made. Embedded in the hard part of bone are the cells that make the actual bone material.

As a baby grows in its mother's womb, its bones slowly develop. To begin with they are made of the softer, gristly substance called cartilage. During growth the cartilage is mainly turned into bone, apart from those parts that remain bendy like the tip of the nose and the ears. Wiggle them and feel the texture of cartilage.

Cartilage is still found in an adult's bones. It forms the smooth surfaces where bones slide against one another at joints. Different-shaped joints let bones move in particular ways. You can only curl or uncurl the tip of a finger, because of the restricted shape of the joint there, but your shoulder joint enables the arm to be moved in any direction.

Animal bones are constructed in the same way as human bones. Some animals have unusual bones, such as the antlers of deer. These are bones which grow from the skull and are shed each year. They are used by rival males in fights over females. ■

See also

Deer
Fractures
Human body
Skeletons

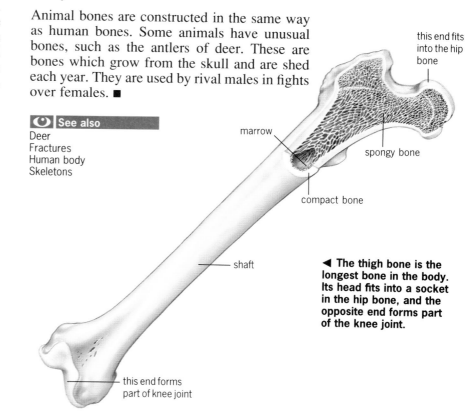

this end fits into the hip bone

marrow

spongy bone

compact bone

shaft

◄ The thigh bone is the longest bone in the body. Its head fits into a socket in the hip bone, and the opposite end forms part of the knee joint.

this end forms part of knee joint

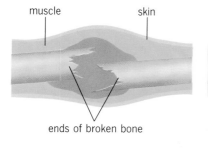

muscle   skin

ends of broken bone

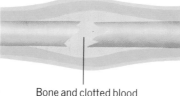

Bone and clotted blood and cartilage form around the two broken ends.

The two ends joined together. There is a slight swelling where the new bone has formed.

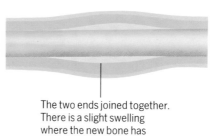

◄ If you break a bone it is called a fracture. A bone should be set back in its proper position as soon as possible. A plaster cast may be needed to keep it in place.

Books

You are looking at a book at this moment: a large one which has taken a team of people over four years to plan, write, illustrate and print. An encyclopedia is an unusual kind of book because it needs the skills of so many different people: artists and scientists, mapmakers and historians, photographers and designers, and writers with all sorts of specialist knowledge. Most books are written by just one author, but sometimes two or more may collaborate.

Authors

Authors must first have an idea of what they want to write about, of course. Books may be either fiction, made up out of the author's imagination like a novel or a poem, or non-fiction. Non-fiction books may be about sport, science, astronomy, dinosaurs, history, computing, engineering or a host of other subjects. When the work is completed it must be typed neatly or prepared on a word processor, before it is sent off to a publisher.

Publishers and editors

Publishers are in business to select, produce and sell books. If the publisher's editor does not like the work submitted it may simply be returned, or the author may be asked to revise it somehow. Sometimes an editor may like it so much that plans to produce it begin straight away. One of the youngest authors to get a book accepted at once was Janet Aitchison, who wrote *The Pirate's Tale*, published by Puffin Books, when she was only 6½.

Sometimes publishers themselves decide that they want a certain kind of book and try to find the best person to write it or to act as the editor. This is what happened with this encyclopedia. Oxford University Press, the publisher named on the title-page, thought of the idea and chose editors who asked over 100 authors to write articles. As typed pages of these arrived in the publishing office, they were checked by experts to get rid of mistakes, and to see that the articles and illustrations fitted into the space allowed.

Designers

A designer is given the task of deciding what kind of print to use and how large it should be, and, in books such as this encyclopedia, how the pictures are to be arranged on the pages. Artists have also to be found to draw or paint illustrations.

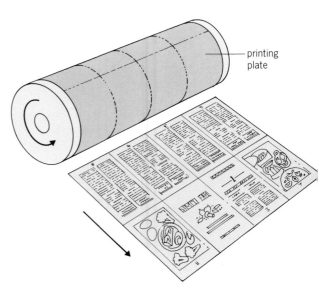

Eight pages are printed on each side of a large sheet of paper.

Production and selling

When all is complete, the publisher's production manager sends the typescript or word-processed disc to a typesetter. After it has been set, proofed and checked, it is printed, and finally the printed sheets are folded, gathered together and bound.

Efforts to sell the book begin long before bound copies are ready. There may be advertisements in newspapers, and sales representatives will be sent out to persuade booksellers to order copies.

From every copy sold, the publisher, the bookseller and the author will each receive a share of the money received. A few writers become quite rich and famous by writing several books that all sell well. Far fewer copies of some other books may be sold. It is very hard to tell in advance which books are going to become bestsellers. Publishers are always hoping they may find one!

Flashback

The first attempts at anything like a book were made by the Egyptians about 5,000 years ago. They used papyrus, the dried pith from a reedy plant growing by the River Nile. Scribes wrote on this with a reed pen, then rolled it all up into a scroll. The Romans too made rolls out of papyrus, some of which were about 9 m (30 ft) long. But it is not easy to find your place in a large roll, so it must have been a relief when parchment was invented. This was made from animal skins and it was tougher and easier to cut than papyrus. By the 4th century AD there were books with proper pages you could turn. Early in the Middle Ages, the secret of making

---

Illuminated manuscripts
Before the 15th century there were no printed books. The first books all had to be written by hand. They were copied out and illuminated (illustrated) by monks in the *scriptorium* (writing room) of a monastery. Copying was hard work. Candles and lamps were forbidden in case of fire. To avoid mistakes the monks were forbidden to speak. All communication was by signs. If a monk wanted a book fetched he held out his hands and pretended to turn the pages. It might take months or even years for a book to be finished. Because of all this work, books before printing were very rare and valuable.

Why do you sometimes get blank pages at the end of a book?
This is because of the way the pages are printed on large sheets of paper. Modern printing machines usually print 16, 32 or 64 pages of a book on both sides of one giant sheet of paper. The large printed sheets are then folded and cut to form sections of 16, 32 or 64 pages. The sections are then put together in a binding to make the book. Of course, sometimes there is not enough writing to fill up all the pages of the last section, but because a section is really all one large piece of paper the blank pages (sometimes used for advertisements) are still included.

Parchment
The very best parchment was called 'vellum'. Vellum is smooth, white, tough and long lasting.

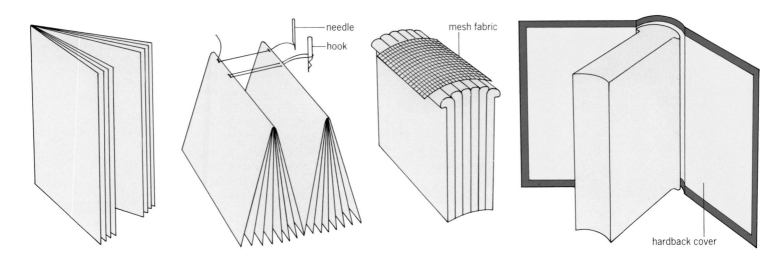

A printed sheet is folded to make a sixteen-page signature.

The signatures are sorted into the correct order and sewn together at the spine.

The spine is rounded and a mesh fabric glued on for extra strength.

The bound pages are trimmed on three sides by a guillotine and then the hardback cover is glued on.

paper found its way from China to Europe. Paper was cheaper and not so heavy as parchment. But the only way to make a book was for scribes to copy it out, page after page, by hand. Monks were the most expert writers and copyists, sometimes decorating the words with detailed pictures and intricate designs.

In the 15th century, at the end of the Middle Ages, Johann Gutenberg in Germany found a way to produce copies of books on a printing press, using movable metal type. It still took some time to complete a whole book because his press was small and he had only a limited amount of type, which had to be used over and over again. But he could make exact copies quickly, and so produce editions in large numbers. By 1500, printing was being carried out all over Europe. William Caxton learned how to print, and produced the first book in English on his press in Bruges in 1474. Two years later he moved to Westminster in London, and there he printed many other works, including Chaucer's *Canterbury Tales*, putting this marvellous collection of stories within the reach of a much wider audience.

In England, in Tudor times, there was a great demand for printed books. Students in the new Grammar Schools needed textbooks and, after the Reformation, every church was ordered to have a copy of the Bible in English. There were little books, too, called 'chapbooks': pamphlets of sixteen pages with ballads, nursery rhymes, stories and political news. These were sold for a penny or sixpence by travelling salesmen.

Children's books

Before the 18th century, hardly anyone thought children needed any books other than dry little volumes used for teaching. Young readers looking for something more entertaining had to manage with fairly difficult books written for adults, such as *Robinson Crusoe* or *Gulliver's Travels*. But things improved as nursery rhymes and fairy stories got into print, followed by some books of verse.

In 1865, in the reign of Queen Victoria, the first great fantasy for children was published, *Alice's Adventures in Wonderland*, by Lewis Carroll. After this, other authors began writing books aimed at pleasing children rather than just teaching them. Older children could have a laugh and a good cry with Louisa May Alcott's *Little Women*, or else thrill to Robert Louis Stevenson's story *Treasure Island*. Smaller children could turn to brilliant picture books based on ABC rhymes, nursery rhymes and traditional fairy tales. Beatrix Potter's *The Tale of Peter Rabbit*, published in 1902, was the first of a long and popular series of stories for parents to read to young children. Lively comics began to appear in newsagents' shops, and although parents did not always approve, most children liked to read them.

Today over 3,000 new children's books are published in Britain alone every year, and thousands more in Europe, America, Australia and other parts of the world. You can choose from adventure stories, animal stories, family sagas, fantasies, historical novels, picture books, and of course from non-fiction books too. ■

▲ This diagram shows the main stages involved in making a hardback book.

The first known printed book in the world was made in China in AD 868.

The first European printed book was the Bible, printed in Germany between 1452 and 1456.

👁 **See also**

Authors'
Bible
Canterbury Tales
Comics
Folk tales and fairy tales
Gulliver's Travels
Illuminated manuscripts
Paper
Poems and poetry
Printing
Robinson Crusoe

Biography
Alcott
Andersen
Blume
Blyton
Carroll
Dahl
Grimm brothers
Kipling
Lewis
Potter
Stevenson
Tolkien

Boomerangs

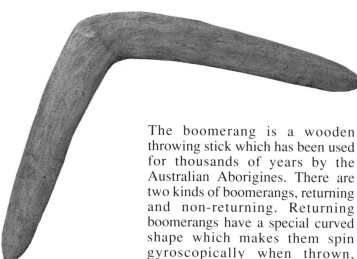

The boomerang is a wooden throwing stick which has been used for thousands of years by the Australian Aborigines. There are two kinds of boomerangs, returning and non-returning. Returning boomerangs have a special curved shape which makes them spin gyroscopically when thrown, banking like an aircraft and then coming back to the thrower. Non-returning boomerangs make effective weapons for hunting and fighting. A spinning boomerang hits a target with far greater force than a thrown rock or stick. ■

See also
Aborigines of Australia
Gyroscopes

Borneo

Borneo is one of the world's largest islands: 751,900 sq km (290,300 sq miles)

Borneo is a large island in southeast Asia. It is divided between three countries. The largest part of the island is the Indonesian province called Kalimantan. Sarawak and Sabah, in the north, are part of Malaysia. Brunei, on the north coast, is an independent country, ruled by a sultan. The Equator crosses Borneo, so you can expect the weather to be hot and wet all through the year. The forested hills shelter people who rely on hunting and gathering for their food, but their way of life is threatened by forestry. The forests are also the home of the orang-utan and other animals which are becoming very rare because the trees in which they live are being cut down. Borneo's timber is very valuable, and the best trees are used for plywood.

Borneo has some amazing caves. The Sarawak Chamber is the world's largest cavern. The area around it is now a national park. ■

See also
Asia
Brunei
Indonesia
Malaysia

Botanists

Botanists are scientists who specialize in studying plants. From the earliest times people have studied plants, because they provide food, fuel, medicines and material for clothes. An ancient Greek called Theophrastus was the first to classify plants; that is, to organize them into groups and name them. In the 18th century Carolus Linnaeus developed our present system of naming plants. Sir Joseph Hooker (1817–1911) collected and named many plants from around the world for the collection at Kew Gardens in London. ■

At universities the botany departments are now often called Plant Science departments.

See also
Classification
Ecology
Plants

Biography
Linnaeus

Botswana

Botswana is a big country in southern Africa. The dry Kalahari Desert, a region of sands with some grass and thorny shrubs, covers much of the land, but the marshy Okavango Swamp in the north is a haven for wildlife. Most of the people, who are called Tswana, live in the east, where many of them are cattle farmers. Some people work in mines, digging up diamonds, coal and various metals. A few thousand Bushmen live in the Kalahari.

Britain ruled the country, which used to be called Bechuanaland, from 1885 until 1966, when it became an independent republic. ■

Area
581,730 sq km
(224,607 sq miles)
Capital
Gaborone
Population
1,127,880
Language
English, Setswana
Religion
Christian, Baha'i, Muslim, Hindu, Traditional
Government
Republic
Currency
1 pula = 100 thebe

◀ The Okavango River in Botswana becomes a swampy inland delta providing a dramatic contrast with its desert-like surroundings. The swamp attracts a wide variety of wildlife.

See also
Africa
Bushmen
Deserts
Wetlands

Bowling

Bowls

In this game heavy wooden or hardened rubber balls, called 'bowls' or 'woods', are bowled along a grass 'green'. The aim is to get your woods near to a smaller white bowl called the 'jack'. To make the game more interesting, the woods are flattened slightly on one side so that they run in a curved line instead of a straight one. This is called the 'bias'. In crown green bowls, another complication is added by making the green slightly higher in the middle than at the sides.

Boules is a French version of bowls. It is played on rougher ground, with smaller, heavy balls which are thrown underarm rather than just bowled along.

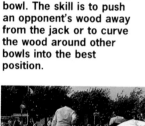

▼ The bowler stands on a small mat to deliver his bowl. The skill is to push an opponent's wood away from the jack or to curve the wood around other bowls into the best position.

Tenpin bowling

In this game, heavy balls with finger holes for gripping are bowled along a polished wooden 'lane'. At the far end of the lane there are ten skittles, or 'pins', set up in a triangle. Each player tries to knock as many down as possible with each shot.

Flashback

Bowling games are all very old. Sir Francis Drake is supposed to have been playing bowls when the Spanish Armada was sighted in 1588. Modern bowls, though, with a rule book, dates from 1849. Tenpin was developed in America from the various skittles games which are still played in pubs in Britain. ■

See also
France (photo)

Boxing

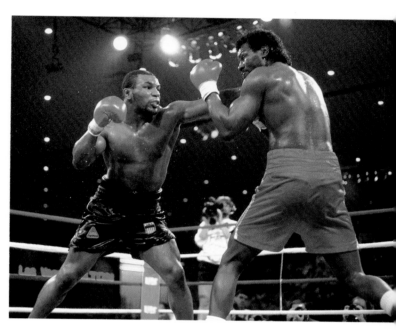

▲ In 1986, at the age of 20, Mike Tyson became the youngest ever world heavyweight champion. Here he fights Tony Tucker (USA), who was champion for only 64 days in 1987.

Boxing is the sport of fist-fighting between two men or boys wearing padded gloves. The boxers are of similar weight, and they fight in a roped-off square called a 'ring' for periods of three minutes at a time. Each period is called a 'round'. At the end of each round the boxers retire to their corners for a minute's rest. There they are attended by their helpers, called 'seconds'. Amateur boxers usually fight for only three rounds. Professionals may fight for up to fifteen rounds.

The object of the fight is to score points by hitting your opponent while trying to avoid being hit yourself. You can also win by a 'knock-out'. This happens when you have knocked your opponent to the floor and he cannot get up again within ten seconds.

In 1867, the Marquess of Queensberry helped to establish the modern rules of boxing. They are called the Queensberry Rules, after him. Even with these rules, many boxers have been badly injured over the years, and some have suffered brain damage later in life. A few have died in the ring. As a result, many doctors do not approve of the sport. ■

See also
Biography
Sports special

Braille

You are reading the words on this page with your eyes, of course, but some blind people would not be able to see the words, so they could not read them. Some blind people read special books, written or printed in the 'braille' system of writing. In braille, the letters of each word are printed in patterns of small dots. The dots for each letter stick up from the surface of the paper for the blind reader to feel. You can read braille by brushing the tips of your fingers lightly across the dots on the page.

There are 63 possible letter shapes in modern braille.

Braille letters are made from combinations of any of six dots in two columns of three, like the dots on a dice:

$$1 \quad \bullet \quad \bullet \quad 4$$
$$2 \quad \bullet \quad \bullet \quad 5$$
$$3 \quad \bullet \quad \bullet \quad 6$$

So in braille writing, the word 'braille' looks like this:

For **b** you feel dots 1 and 2 only, for **r** you feel 1, 2, 3, and 5 only, and so on. Blind people learn to feel these letters and to read in this way almost as fast as you are reading now.

Writing in braille

There are now special machines which blind people can use to write in braille, for other blind people to read. These machines look rather like an electric typewriter, and they punch the dots for each letter into the paper as the words are written.

Flashback

Louis Braille invented this clever system of writing in 1824 when he was only 15. When he was 4 years old he had an accident in his father's workshop and went blind. Later, he went to a special school for blind people in Paris. ∎

⟟ See also
Blindness

Brain

Many animals have a brain that controls their actions. The brain consists of many nerve cells. Each cell is connected to many other nerve cells, some of which pass information from sense organs, such as ears or eyes, into the brain, while others are connected to nerves that lead from the brain to muscles.

Most of the brain cells in mammals connect to other brain cells and process incoming information, carry out thought processes and make elaborate decisions. Even smaller and less intelligent animals, such as bees, can remember where their hive is and calculate the time of day.

Information from the senses

The sense organs pass information to different parts of the brain as a series of nerve impulses which act as signals. These may be simple signals, giving information about what part of the body has been touched, or a very complex series of signals using thousands of nerve cells to allow you to see the shape of the letters and read the words on this page.

There are about 100 billion cells in a human brain but only about 10,000 in that of an ant.

Using information from different parts of the brain, an animal can send signals to its muscles so that it can move in a controlled way. Some types of movement, such as a single kick, do not require much control, but walking and flying require exact control of the muscles. You would fall over and bump into things if you could not adjust your muscles continually.

In humans, each of the 100 billion brain cells probably makes 1,000 connections to other nerve cells, so the total number of nerve connections is about 100 trillion.

The brain receives and processes signals from the sense organs to make these adjustments. It connects with nerves in the spinal cord which runs down from the head, inside the backbone. Nerves from the spinal cord connect with muscles, while other nerves from sense cells in the skin and muscles connect back into the spinal cord. Other nerves connect the spinal cord back to the brain.

The human brain weighs about 1.5 kg (3 lb) and, for our body size, is far bigger than that of any other animal.

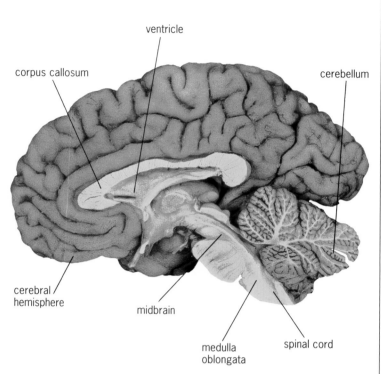

▲ The human brain has enormous cerebral hemispheres. These are involved in thought and memory; some parts respond to signals from the sense organs to allow sight, hearing, feeling, speech and movement. The cerebellum is involved in balance and muscle co-ordination and the medulla oblongata controls breathing and blood pressure.

Thinking and brain damage

Our brain allows us to think. We do not know exactly how this happens, but in humans the cerebral hemispheres are very large and are involved in consciousness, thought, recognition, memory and personality. If parts of the human brain are damaged, there is usually some loss of function or of mental ability. Damage to the cerebellar region of the brain may cause partial paralysis, as this part of the brain is involved in the control of the body's muscles. If your head is hit hard, parts of your brain may stop working for a while, causing unconsciousness and loss of memory.

Learning

Many animals with brains are able to learn. Animals with big, complicated brains are usually able to learn more than those with small brains. Having a large memory, based on life's experiences, allows an animal to make more complex decisions and generally to respond in a more intelligent manner. Humans, with their large brains and prodigious memories, are probably the most intelligent animals. ■

See also

Animal behaviour
Human body
Instinct
Memory
Nervous systems
Senses

Brakes

Brakes are used to slow vehicles down and stop them moving. On a bicycle, the brakes are rubber blocks which press against the rims of the wheels when you pull on the brake levers. Friction slows the wheels.

Most cars have two types of brakes: disc brakes on the front wheels and drum brakes on the back. In both types, hydraulic pressure is used to push a special friction material against a metal surface which rotates with the wheel. ■

Power-assisted brakes: air pressure is used to put extra force on the brakes.

Train brakes are failsafe. Air pressure holds them off against a spring. If the pressure fails, the spring automatically puts the brakes on.

Many cars have ABS (Advanced Braking System) to stop skidding. This senses when the wheels are about to skid and releases the brakes for an instant. It can do this up to 100 times a second.

Drum brakes

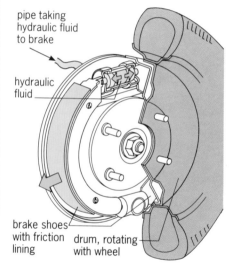

◄ Drum brake on a car wheel. When the driver presses the brake pedal, hydraulic fluid pushes two curved pieces, called shoes, against a metal drum which rotates with the wheel.

Disc brakes

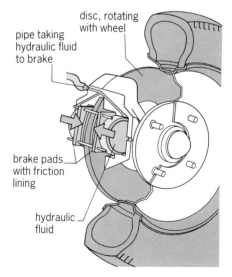

◄ Disc brake on a car wheel. When the driver presses the brake pedal, hydraulic fluid pushes two pads against a metal disc which rotates with the wheel.

See also

Hydraulics
Motor cars
Motor cycles

Brazil

Brazil is the biggest country in South America and covers nearly half the continent. It is almost as big as the USA. It stretches from the foothills of the Andes Mountains in the west to the Atlantic Ocean in the east. Brazil borders every country in South America except Ecuador and Chile.

Land height in metres
- more than 2000
- 1000–2000
- 500–1000
- 200–500
- less than 200

main roads
railways

0   kilometres   1000
(621 miles)

Area
8,511,965 sq km
(3,286,500 sq miles)
Capital
Brasília
Population
135,564,000
Language
Portuguese
Religion
Christian
Government
Federal republic
Currency
1 cruzado =
1,000 cruzeiros

See also

Amazon River
American Indians
Carnivals
Coffee
Portugal
South America
Biography
Sports special

▲ Brazil is a country of contrasts. Some Brazilians live in luxury, others live in shanty towns called favelas, like this one. Poverty is so great that 13 million children live on the streets.

The Amazon rainforest

The River Amazon flows across the northern part of Brazil. The huge area that is drained by the Amazon and smaller rivers that feed it contains the world's largest rainforest. It has a richer plant life than anywhere else on earth. Jaguars, monkeys, snakes, and thousands of species of birds and butterflies and other insects live in this hot region. But long, dusty roads are beginning to slice through the greenery as more and more of the forest is cleared to make cattle ranches. Fewer and fewer Indians now live here, as bulldozers destroy their forest homes.

Contrasts

The north-eastern corner of Brazil is a vast, harsh, very dry region made up mostly of thorny scrub. The most pleasant part of the country lies to the south-east. There you will find beautiful Rio de Janeiro with its famous annual carnival; busy, hard-working São Paulo (the largest city in South America); and the new capital, Brasília, with its spectacular modern buildings.

Crops and industry

In the south the climate is almost perfect for many crops. Brazil is one of the biggest producers of coffee in the world and also grows sugar cane, tobacco, rice, maize, oranges, bananas and other fruits. Nuts are gathered from the forests.

There are deposits of iron ore and other minerals. Much of the ore is used for steel-making, and the steel is manufactured into motor cars, locomotives, railway lines, ships and other goods. Brazil is one of the ten biggest industrial nations in the world. But her wealth does not benefit all the people. There is a great gap between the few very wealthy people and the millions who are poor.

Flashback

Brazil was discovered in 1500 by the Portuguese and later became a Portuguese colony. That is why Brazilians are the only South Americans whose language is Portuguese. When Napoleon invaded Portugal in 1807, the Portuguese royal family fled to Brazil. In 1825 Portugal recognized Brazil's independence under Emperor Pedro I. Brazil became a republic in 1889. As well as the original Indians, the Portuguese colonists, and the African slaves, many other nationalities have emigrated over the centuries to Brazil from Europe, the Middle East and the Far East. ■

Bread

Bread comes in many shapes and sizes. As well as tin-shaped and cottage loaves, there are flat pitta breads from the Middle East, puffed-up puris from India, black ryebread from Poland, corn bread from America, millet cakes from Africa, and many other varieties.

Whatever the shape, the basic ingredients are flour and water. The bread you eat is probably made from wheat flour, but flour can be made from rye, oats, corn and other cereals, too.

Flat bread and risen bread

Bread which stays completely flat when cooked is made by mixing flour with water and salt into a soft dough. The dough is rolled out and cooked straight away on a metal plate over a fire or on a stove. Indian chapatis and Mexican tortillas are made like this. The bread does not rise and is called unleavened bread.

Leavened bread uses yeast as well as flour and water and salt and the mixture is left to stand for a while before cooking. The yeast reacts with the sugars in the flour and causes the dough to ferment. This produces carbon dioxide gas which helps the dough to rise and swell. The bread is then baked in a hot oven. You can see the tiny holes of air in the bread.

Factory-baked bread

The bread sold in supermarkets and other big shops is probably made at a very large bakery. Some bakeries produce 16,000 loaves a day or more. In the 1960s the bakers developed a process which cut out the raising stage and replaced it with a few minutes high-speed mixing.

Some bread is still made in small bakeries or is baked at specialist bread shops. In a small number of these, the bread is made in much the same way as the recipe below, but with machinery for mixing.

pumpernickel

wholemeal loaf

black ryebread

French bread

pitta bread

white split-tin loaf

Nutritional value

Bread has been called the Staff of Life and is such an important part of what we eat that it is known as a staple food. As well as protein, bread contains plenty of starch (a carbohydrate) and is a good source of dietary fibre, calcium and some of the B vitamins.

Wholemeal bread is made from flour which is milled from the whole grain. Brown flour has 15 per cent of the outer coating and germ of the wheat sieved out and white bread has 30 per cent removed. This process removes some of the nutrients which are good for you, so in some countries the millers have to replace them by law.

Flashback

The ancient Egyptians were known as the 'bread eaters' and were among the earliest people to make leavened bread.

In Europe in the Middle Ages bread was made with whatever grains there were to hand. Wheat was scarce and expensive and poor people had to eat a coarse bread made from rye, barley and even beans and peas. A very thick four-day-old slice of bread was used as a plate, and called a trencher. People ate it up at the end of the meal.

Until the introduction of roller mills in the 19th century, the best 'white' bread was almost as dark as our wholemeal. ■

Sandwiches were invented by the Earl of Sandwich, who wanted a quick meal to save time away from the gaming (card) table.

Homemade wholemeal bread

Here is an easy loaf to make at home.

450 g (1 lb) wholemeal flour

14 g (½ oz) fast-acting dried yeast

1 teaspoon salt

350 ml (12 fluid oz) warm water

Mix flour, yeast and salt in a bowl. Make a well in the centre of the flour and mix in the water with your hands. Turn the dough onto a floured surface and knead for 8–9 minutes. Place in a 450 g (1 lb) loaf tin and leave in a warm place to rise for about one hour. Set the oven to 230°C/450°F/Gas 8 and bake for 30–35 minutes. Test if the bread is ready by rapping the base with your finger-nails. It should sound hollow.

See also
Cereals
Food
Vitamins
Yeasts

Breathing

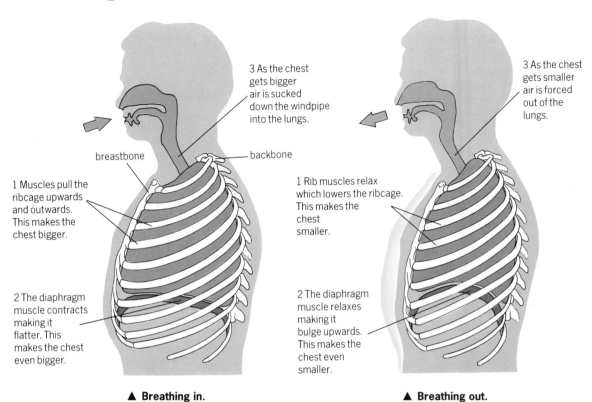

1 Muscles pull the ribcage upwards and outwards. This makes the chest bigger.

2 The diaphragm muscle contracts making it flatter. This makes the chest even bigger.

3 As the chest gets bigger air is sucked down the windpipe into the lungs.

breastbone

backbone

1 Rib muscles relax which lowers the ribcage. This makes the chest smaller.

2 The diaphragm muscle relaxes making it bulge upwards. This makes the chest even smaller.

3 As the chest gets smaller air is forced out of the lungs.

▲ Breathing in.

▲ Breathing out.

See also

Blood
Lungs
Oxygen
Respiration

Adult human lungs can hold a total of 5 litres of air. But in normal breathing only half a litre of air is breathed in and out.

▶ During exercise you need more energy to work your muscles. So you breathe faster to get more oxygen, which is needed to release extra energy from food stored in your body.

Like most land animals, people breathe air. Breathing has to go on all the time for you to stay alive. Every minute you breathe in about twelve times and breathe out about twelve times.

Breathing is the forcing of air in and out of the lungs. Your lungs are in your chest and are connected to the back of your throat by a tube called the windpipe. Air moves in and out of the windpipe through your mouth or nose.

You breathe in by making your chest bigger so that air is sucked into your lungs. This happens when muscles pull your ribs upwards and outwards, and a sheet of muscle below the lungs, called the diaphragm, is pulled downwards. You breathe out by lowering your ribs and raising your diaphragm.

We breathe all the time because our bodies need a constant supply of the gas called oxygen. We use oxygen to gain energy from our food. We, and other land animals, get oxygen from the air. Fish use their gills to extract the oxygen which is dissolved in water. Oxygen in the air you breathe passes into the red blood cells in the blood vessels of your lungs. At the same time the waste gas carbon dioxide passes from your blood into your lungs and is breathed out.

Our brains control the speed of our breathing. This is to provide enough oxygen at all times for the body's needs. When you are quiet and still, perhaps asleep, your energy needs are low; you require little oxygen and your breathing is slow and shallow.

If you start exercising hard, say running 200 m (650 ft) as fast as you can, you need much more energy. Without thinking about it you automatically find yourself breathing faster and more deeply. ■

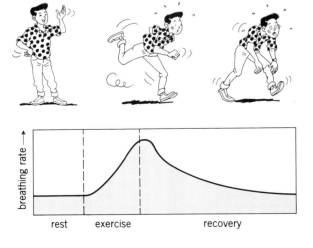

rest   exercise   recovery

Brer Rabbit

Brer Rabbit is the hero of many stories told by Uncle Remus, an African American, to the young son of a plantation owner in the deep South of the United States. The stories were written in the dialect language that was spoken by black people on the cotton plantations over 100 years ago.

Most of the Brer Rabbit stories are about the attempts of Brer Fox to catch him. In one of the best-known stories Brer Fox makes a model baby out of tar. Brer Rabbit comes down the road ('lippity-clippity, clippity-lippity') and talks to the Tar-Baby. But of course, the Tar-Baby doesn't reply. 'Tar-Baby ain't sayin' nothin', en Brer Fox, he lay low.' Eventually Brer Rabbit becomes so cross that he hits the Tar-Baby, and sticks to it. He sticks so tight that he can't get away. The boy asks Uncle Remus if this means that Brer Fox caught Brer Rabbit and ate him. 'That's as far as the story goes,' says the old man. 'He might, and there again, he might not.' ■

Uncle Remus: His Songs and His Sayings was published in 1880, fifteen years after the abolition of slavery in the USA.

The Uncle Remus stories were written down by Joel Chandler Harris who collected stories from slaves on a plantation where he worked.

See also
Anansi

Bricks

Bricks are long-lasting building materials. They are strong and also safe, because they help to stop a fire spreading if one breaks out. A normal brick is 22 cm (8⅔ in) wide, 5½ cm (2⅙ in) high and 11 cm (4⅓ in) deep. This is a convenient size for a man's hand to hold.

Making brick

Bricks are made from baked clay. Originally all bricks were made by hand, as some still are today. But now bricks can be made by machines quickly and cheaply. Some machines shape the clay by pressing it into rectangular moulds. Other machines squeeze out a rectangular ribbon of wet clay which is cut by wires into the right widths.

After this moulding or shaping process, the bricks are dried for a short time and then baked or fired in large ovens known as kilns. Many modern kilns have between 16 and 36 compartments. The air to make the fire burn is first warmed by passing it through compartments where bricks are cooling down. The heated air is then taken into other compartments in which the bricks are being warmed up.

The colour of bricks varies due to the type of clay used and to the way the bricks are fired. Dyes are often used to colour the clay. Sometimes the surfaces of the bricks are glazed with a glossy white or coloured finish.

Flashback

Bricks made from clay have been used for at least 5,000 years. They were probably first used to build the ancient cities in Mesopotamia and in the Indus Valley in Pakistan. Originally people made bricks by using their feet to mix together wet clay and straw. The mixture was then shaped in rectangular moulds and baked in the sun. Without straw these sun-baked bricks would not hold together. Eventually the Babylonians, Assyrians and ancient Egyptians discovered that burning the clay on its own with fire produced bricks that were much harder and more weatherproof. ■

See also
Buildings

▼ Bricks are made where a suitable layer of clay lies near the ground. There are a number of different ways of making bricks. Most use intense heat to turn the clay hard.

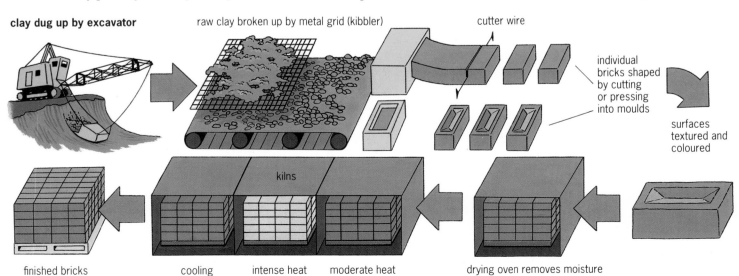

clay dug up by excavator   raw clay broken up by metal grid (kibbler)   cutter wire   individual bricks shaped by cutting or pressing into moulds   surfaces textured and coloured

finished bricks   cooling   intense heat   moderate heat   drying oven removes moisture   kilns

Bridges

Bridges can carry roads, railways or footways. Most are fixed but some can be raised or swung round. With all bridges, the problem for engineers is to design and build structures which will not sag or crack under the weight they have to carry. There are several ways of solving this problem.

▼ The Europa bridge on the Brenner autobahn between Austria and Italy. It is a box girder bridge, which is a modern development of the simple beam bridge.

Beam bridges have rigid beams which are supported at each end. The earliest bridges used this idea. They were just tree trunks or slabs of stone resting between the banks of a stream. In modern beam bridges, the beams are often long, hollow boxes made of steel or concrete. This makes them light but very strong. Bridges constructed like this are called **box girder** bridges.

Cantilever bridges have long, rigid sections like beam bridges. However, each section is supported in the middle rather than at its end.

Arch bridges take the strain of the main span with an arch that pushes on the ground at each end. Modern arch bridges often have a light, open structure.

Suspension bridges are best for very large spans. The span is suspended from steel cables which hang between towers. To take the strain, the ends of these cables are anchored in the banks. Older suspension bridges sometimes have chains rather than cables.

▼ **Truss girder bridge**
A type of beam bridge which uses a rigid steel framework as a beam.

Caesar's army built a pontoon bridge in ten days when invading Gaul.

The famous Bridge of Sighs is one of 400 bridges across Venice's 150 canals. Condemned prisoners sighed as they crossed it from the Doge's palace to the prison.

In the three years it takes to paint the Forth Bridge in Scotland, the paint weathers so much that as soon as it is finished, it is time to start all over again.

▼ **Arch bridge**
The weight is supported by one or more curved arches. The biggest steel arch bridge in the world is across the New River Gorge in West Virginia, USA. It is 518 m long.

▼ **Clapper bridge**
A type of beam bridge in which two or more beams are supported by piers.

▼ **Simple beam bridge**
A single beam rests across the river.

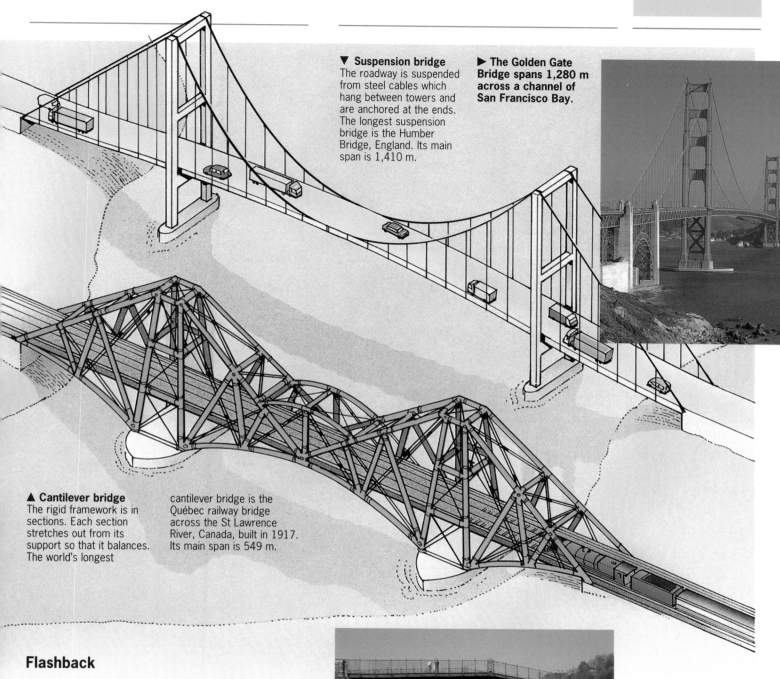

▼ Suspension bridge
The roadway is suspended from steel cables which hang between towers and are anchored at the ends. The longest suspension bridge is the Humber Bridge, England. Its main span is 1,410 m.

► The Golden Gate Bridge spans 1,280 m across a channel of San Francisco Bay.

▲ Cantilever bridge
The rigid framework is in sections. Each section stretches out from its support so that it balances. The world's longest cantilever bridge is the Québec railway bridge across the St Lawrence River, Canada, built in 1917. Its main span is 549 m.

Flashback

One of the world's oldest bridges is the prehistoric stone clapper bridge called the Post Bridge, on Dartmoor in Britain. The Romans built bridges using concrete made by mixing volcanic soil, lime and water. The concrete was so good that six out of the original eight bridges across the River Tiber near Rome are still standing. About 1,800 years later, when methods of making large cast iron girders developed, iron bridges were built. The first was at Coalbrookdale, England, in 1779. The Menai Suspension Bridge, built of iron by Thomas Telford between 1820 and 1826, lasted for over 100 years before the iron chains were replaced. By the 1880s bridges were being built of steel, which is stronger and less brittle than cast iron.

◄ The Iron Bridge at Coalbrookdale, England, crossing the River Severn. It was the first cast iron bridge in the world, built by Abraham Darby and completed in 1779.

Reinforced concrete has been used for many bridges in the last hundred years. The concrete is strengthened by burying steel bars inside it. Nowadays the concrete is 'pre-stressed' by tensioning (stretching) the steel bars as they are put in. This doubles the strength of the concrete. ■

See also
Aqueducts
Arches
Concrete
Viaducts

Biography
Telford

British empire

At its height in about 1900 the British empire included one quarter of the world's population and land area.

In 1900, people in Britain would talk of their empire as 'the empire on which the Sun never sets'. The British had settled in more lands and taken over more peoples than any nation in history: countries in every continent and islands in every ocean. We have to go back 300 years to understand how this happened. In about 1600, at the end of the reign of Elizabeth I, the English were great seafarers and their trading ships sailed as far as North America and India. Here they discovered useful goods: tobacco and potatoes in America; furs in Canada; silk and spices from Asia. Some English and Scots people then decided to make their homes in these foreign lands, at first in North America and the Caribbean.

North America

One of the earliest English colonies was Virginia, named in honour of Queen Elizabeth I, the 'Virgin Queen'. Gradually, more people crossed the ocean until there were colonies all along the Atlantic shores of America. But the British were not the only European people to have colonies. The Spanish, Portuguese, Dutch and French did so too. French people settled in Canada and also traded in India. Britain and France were great rivals and fought each other throughout the 18th century. In the Seven Years War, General Wolfe defeated the French in Canada, and Robert Clive was victorious in India. And so Britain controlled even larger parts of these lands. However, soon afterwards, thirteen of the American colonies rebelled and became independent as the United States of America.

India

Many Indians objected very strongly to being ruled by Britain. But the British army was too strong and the Indians were defeated in the Indian 'Mutiny' of 1857. After this many more of India's princes were brought under British control, while Britain also occupied Burma and the Malay peninsula.

First colonies

Virginia	1607
Bermuda	1609
New Plymouth (Pilgrim Fathers)	1620
St Kitts	1624
Barbados	1627
Antigua	1632

Seven Years War
1756–1763
Clive won battle of Plassey 1757
Wolfe captured Québec 1759

◀ Queen Victoria was proclaimed Empress of India in 1877 following an Act of Parliament passed the previous year.

The Dominions

From 1815 onwards an increasing number of British people emigrated to lands with climates similar to Britain's: Canada, Cape Colony in South Africa, Australia and New Zealand. The people already living there (North American Indians, Xhosa and Zulu Africans, Australian Aborigines and the Maori of New Zealand) resisted but they lost much of their lands to the white settlers. Britain gave these settlers a great deal of freedom to govern themselves and gradually the lands came to be called 'dominions' instead of 'colonies'.

Africa

Until the late 19th century very few Europeans were living in Africa, except in Cape Colony at the southern tip and on the coasts. But from about 1880 there was a great 'scramble for Africa', as several European countries divided up and ruled almost the whole of the continent.

In 1882 the British conquered Egypt, after a battle in which British soldiers for the last time fought in their red tunics. The Suez Canal had been opened thirteen years before and the occupation of Egypt gave Britain control of the vital waterway for the next 70 years.

Soon the British had occupied so much of East Africa that the prime minister of Cape Colony, Cecil Rhodes, wanted Britain to control the whole stretch of the continent from 'the Cape to Cairo'. Other whites in South Africa, the Boers, objected to British rule and fought the British in the Boer War. Although they were defeated, the Union of South Africa was created as a dominion in 1910.

In the meantime, Britain developed a series of colonies in West Africa: the Gambia, Sierra Leone, the Gold Coast (now Ghana), and Nigeria, by far the largest. In East Africa, Kenya and Uganda became colonies.

Islands

As a great trading nation with a powerful navy, it was very important for Britain to have control of islands in various seas and oceans. West Indian islands were especially valuable for growing sugar, and from the mid 17th century Britain began to capture islands from her Spanish and French rivals. Slaves from Africa were imported to work the sugar plantations.

But trade with India became the most profitable. So Britain occupied Gibraltar in 1704

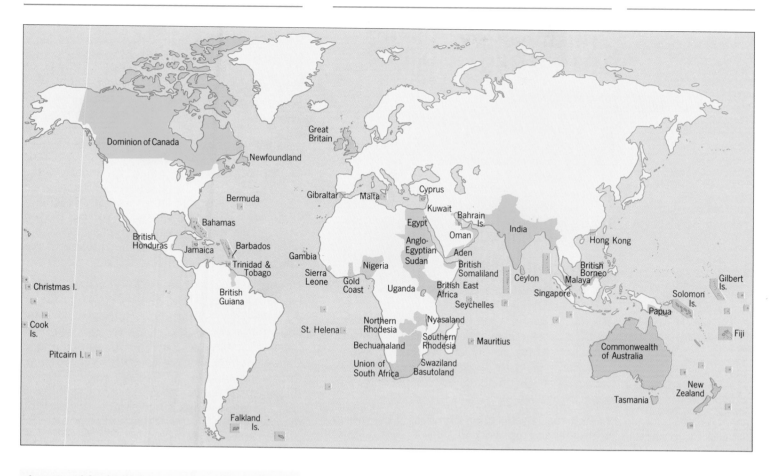

▲ The British empire in 1914.

Important island colonies

Jamaica
captured from Spain 1655
Trinidad
captured from Spain 1797
Malta
captured, 1800, from French who had taken it from Knights of St John
Cyprus
taken from Turks 1878
St Helena
British-ruled from 1673; formerly Portuguese

Falklands
British-ruled from 1833
Mauritius
captured from French 1810
Hong Kong
Island occupied 1841, Kowloon peninsula 1860, New Territories 1898
Fiji
Chief Cakobau asked British to take over as Crown Colony 1874

and later the islands of Malta and Cyprus to guard the route through the Mediterranean.

Hong Kong island was seized from China in 1841 and territories on the Chinese mainland added later. A 99 year lease was agreed in 1898 which meant that Hong Kong would be returned to China when the lease expired in 1997. Other British islands were scattered over many oceans.

The effects of the empire

Britain imported food and raw materials for her factories from all over the empire, while selling back manufactured goods. Many British were employed in these lands, as soldiers, civil servants, tax-collectors and traders.

English is spoken today by hundreds of millions of people not only in North America and Australasia, but in India, South Asia and many areas of Africa because they were once part of the British empire. The British also introduced their own styles of clothes, the English system of law, railways, cricket, football, and Christianity.

Schools used to celebrate 'Empire Day' on 24 May each year. At first, few people in Britain thought very much about whether it was right to rule over people with different traditions, customs and religious beliefs.

But many original inhabitants of the colonies strongly objected to foreign rule and began to demand the right to govern themselves.

In the first half of the 20th century there were many campaigns for independence. In India, for example, Gandhi and his followers peacefully broke laws to make the British leave India. There were also strikes and, in some colonies, riots and wars to win independence.

Even so, as India and former colonies became independent, from 1947 onwards, most of them kept their connection with Britain through the organization called the Commonwealth. ■

See also
African history
American colonial history
American Revolution
Australia's history
Canada's history
Caribbean history
Commonwealth
Indian history
Slave trade
South Africa
Spanish colonial history

Biography
Clive
Gandhi, Mahatma
Rhodes
Wolfe

British history 1919–1989

When World War I, 'the war to end all wars', came to a close in 1918, people hoped that their problems would be over. One problem that did seem to be at an end was the Irish question. The Irish republicans had been fighting for years to free Ireland from British rule. In 1921 a truce was called and, after talks, the Irish Free State was born. Six counties in Ulster remained in the United Kingdom because a majority of people there wanted to remain British subjects.

The twenties and thirties

By 1921 the number of people without work had reached one million. It was hard to sell British goods to countries which had been fighting an expensive war, and business profits were low. Many people said the answer was to cut wages in order to lower prices and raise sales. The trade unions did not agree and there were many disputes.

In 1926 the Trades Union Congress (TUC) asked all unions to stop work in support of a miners' strike. This General Strike lasted only nine days before the TUC called it off. The unions remained weak as unemployment rose to more than 2 million in the 1930s. Some towns suffered more than others. When 68 per cent of the workers in Jarrow found themselves out of work in 1936, marchers set out for London to show people their plight.

In the same year, George V died and was succeeded by his son, Edward VIII. In December Edward abdicated because he wanted to marry Mrs Simpson, an American who was divorced. The government and public opinion would not accept the idea of a divorced woman as Queen, so Edward's brother became King George VI.

People's attention then switched to Germany where Hitler had become leader. Some feared that he would cause war in Europe. Others believed that war could be avoided by talks. Many people were very happy when Prime Minister Chamberlain came back from meeting Hitler in 1938 with the Munich Agreement promising 'peace in our time'.

World War II: the home front

This 'peace' lasted just one year. In September 1939, after Hitler's invasion of Poland, Britain declared war on Germany. Air raid shelters were built, gas masks were issued, and children were evacuated from cities likely to be bombed.

German aeroplanes bombed London daily during the 'Blitz' in the winter of 1940–1941, and later bombed other cities too. Shortages of food and other necessities, like soap and clothing, led to rationing, so that limited supplies were shared out fairly between people. Even so, some things were almost impossible to get. It was illegal, for instance, to use sugar to decorate a cake, so many people hired cardboard cakes for their weddings.

Men between 18 and 50 years old could be called up into the armed forces or to work down coalmines. Women were ordered to replace men in their normal jobs. Under the Emergency Powers Act, the government could order all women between 18 and 45 years old to do part-time work.

Timeline

1918 World War I ended; Lloyd George PM (Coalition); votes for women aged 30 and over
1921 Irish Free State
1922 Bonar Law PM; BBC created
1923 Baldwin PM
1924 MacDonald PM, Baldwin PM
1926 General Strike
1928 Votes for women aged 21, same as for men
1929 MacDonald PM
1931 National government; unemployment over 2,700,000
1935 Baldwin PM
1936 George V died; Edward VIII abdicated
1937 George VI crowned; Chamberlain PM
1939 World War II
1940 Churchill PM (Coalition)
1944 Education Act: free secondary education for all
1945 War ended; Attlee PM
1948 National Health Service
1951 Churchill PM
1952 George VI died
1953 Elizabeth II crowned
1955 Eden PM; ITV started
1957 Macmillan PM
1959 M1 motorway opened
1964 Wilson PM
1969 Civil rights marches in Northern Ireland; troops sent to Northern Ireland
1970 Heath PM
1972 'Bloody Sunday' in Londonderry: 13 killed when British troops fire
1973 Britain joined EC
1974 Wilson PM
1976 Callaghan PM
1979 Thatcher PM
1982 Falklands War; unemployment over 3,000,000
1990 Major PM

Conservative
Labour
Liberal

▶ During the nine-day General Strike in 1926 buses and trains were driven by volunteers, including some students. Many young people enjoyed the experience.

▶ Women workers making munitions in a Coventry factory during World War I. Both of the world wars created more opportunities for women to work outside domestic service.

Post-war Britain

In 1945 a Labour government was elected with a large majority, and Parliament passed a series of Acts which made great changes, especially to the lives of families who had been poor. Child allowances and maternity benefit started. Unemployment pay and Old Age Pensions were increased. A National Health Service was organized so that for the first time medical care was free for all. These changes were described as 'the Welfare State'.

The government made other big changes too. The mines, railways, gas, electricity and other industries which had been privately owned were taken over by the state.

The fifties

In the 1950s jobs remained plentiful. In fact there were so many jobs to be done that people from the Caribbean and South Asia were encouraged to move to Britain. People began to enjoy the benefits of higher incomes. Television spread throughout the country, and in 1955 ITV companies joined the BBC in transmitting programmes, giving viewers a choice between channels.

More and more families bought their own cars, and the government had to improve the road system. The first motorway, the M1, opened in 1959. That was the year that Harold Macmillan led the Conservatives to election victory with a slogan: 'You've never had it so good.'

The sixties and after

In the 1960s designers such as Mary Quant led a fashion revolution in 'Swinging Britain', and groups like the Beatles made British music popular all over the world. Increased spending by consumers, often with borrowed money, led to more rapidly rising prices.

This led in turn to demands by unions for higher pay, and strikes were frequent. Successive governments, both Conservative and Labour, tried to stop this spiral of rising wages and prices, but with little success. When oil-producing countries pushed up the price of oil in 1973 and 1979, unemployment began to climb. By 1982 it had reached over 3 million, but by then inflation was being gradually reduced.

That year Britain went to war in the South Atlantic. Argentina invaded the Falklands, a group of islands under British control. The Conservative Prime Minister, Mrs Thatcher, responded by sending a task force to free the islands. This was successful, but nearly 1,000 people, both British and Argentinian, lost their lives.

In Northern Ireland, too, 'the troubles' returned once more. After protests by Catholics in the 1960s, violence flared and the IRA began a military campaign against the security forces. Their bombing campaign led to many civilian deaths too, and there have been many revenge killings by opposing terrorist groups.

In spite of problems like these, most people in Britain found themselves by the end of the 1980s much better off than people had been at the start of the century. There is a feeling that Britain's power in the world has declined, but there are also new opportunities as part of the European Community. ■

◄ In the first half of the century it was very common for cooking to be done on a range. This photograph was taken in the home of a Welsh shepherd in 1951. By that time most households used gas cookers.

▲ One of the changes this century that affected everyday life was the increase in kitchen equipment. Design of cookers, both gas and electric, improved in the 1960s. Electric toasters and food mixers made preparation of meals quicker and easier. The photograph shows an ideal kitchen of the 1960s.

👁 See also

British empire
Commonwealth
European Community
Household equipment
Ireland's history
Northern Ireland
Political parties
Trade unions
Twentieth-century history
Welfare State
Women's movement
World War I
World War II

Biography
Attlee
Churchill
Edward VIII
Elizabeth II
George VI
Lloyd George
Mountbatten
Thatcher
Pop and rock special:
 Beatles

British Isles

Area
314,329 sq km
(121,363 sq miles)
Population
59,118,000
Highest peak
Ben Nevis (Scotland)
1,344 m
Largest lake
Lough Neagh (Northern
Ireland) 388·5 sq km
(150 sq miles)
Longest river
Shannon (Irish Republic)
386 km
(240 miles)

See also

Depressions
England
England's history
Europe
Ireland's history
Irish Republic
Northern Ireland
Scotland
Scotland's history
United Kingdom
Wales
Welsh history

Land height in metres

more than 1000
500–1000
200–500
100–200
less than 100

land below sea level
▲ highest peaks with
heights given in metres
roads
railways

Shetland
Islands
Lerwick

Orkney
Islands
Kirkwall

Cape
Wrath
Thurso
Duncansby Head

The Minch

Outer Hebrides

NORTHWEST HIGHLANDS

Ullapool

Moray Firth

Inverness
Spey

Kyle of
Lochalsh
Skye
Loch
Ness
CAIRNGORMS
Dee
Aberdeen

Mallaig
Ben
Nevis
▲
1344
GRAMPIAN MOUNTAINS
Tay
Dundee

Inner Hebrides

Mull
Oban
Perth
SCOTLAND

Loch
Lomond

Atlantic Ocean

Edinburgh
Glasgow
Clyde
Firth of Forth

Ayr
SOUTHERN UPLANDS
Tweed

Firth of Clyde

CHEVIOT
HILLS

Malin Head

Newcastle
upon Tyne

Lough
Foyle
Coleraine
Londonderry
ANTRIM
MTNS.
Larne
Belfast
Stranraer
Tyne
Sunderland

Carlisle
Middlesbrough

Donegal Bay

NORTHERN
IRELAND
Lough
Neagh
Erne

Sligo

MOURNE
MTNS.
Slieve
Donard
852

Dundalk

Scafell Pike ▲
978
CUMBRIAN
MTNS.
NORTH
YORK
MOORS

PENNINES

Douglas
Isle of
Man
York

Irish Sea
Blackpool
Kingston-upon-Hull

Lough
Ree
IRISH

Galway
Lough
Corrib
Athlone
Boyne
Drogheda
Dublin

Galway Bay

REPUBLIC

Lough
Derg
Portlaoise
WICKLOW
MTNS.

Preston
Bradford
Leeds
Huddersfield
Grimsby

Bolton
Aire

Anglesey
Liverpool
Manchester
Sheffield
Humber

Holyhead
Mersey
Stoke-
on-Trent

Snowdon ▲
1085
Chester
Dee
Derby
Nottingham
Trent

The Wash

Limerick
SILVERMINE
MTNS.

Barrow

Suir
Blackwater
Killarney

▲
1041
Carrauntoohill

Cork

Wexford
Rosslare
Waterford

Shannon

St George's Channel

Fishguard

CAMBRIAN MOUNTAINS

WALES
Severn
Birmingham
Wye
Worcester
ENGLAND
Gloucester

BRECON
BEACONS
Newport
Swansea
Cardiff ★
Usk
COTSWOLD
HILLS
Thames

Bristol Channel
Bristol
SALISBURY
PLAIN

Wolverhampton
Coventry
Northampton

Leicester
Peterborough
THE
FENS
King's
Lynn
Norwich

Great Ouse
Cambridge
Ipswich

Milton Keynes
Oxford
Luton
Harwich

CHILTERN
HILLS
London
Reading
Southend-on-Sea

NORTH
DOWNS
Dover

THE
WEALD
Strait of Dover

EXMOOR
Southampton
SOUTH DOWNS
Brighton

DARTMOOR
Exe
Bournemouth
Portsmouth

Torbay
Isle of Wight

Exeter

Penzance
Plymouth

English Channel

Land's
End
Isles of Scilly
Lizard Point

**North
Sea**

0 kilometres 100

(62 miles)

The British Isles consist of the two large islands of Great Britain (which is sometimes called simply Britain) and Ireland, and a number of smaller islands. They are separated from the rest of Europe by the English Channel and the North Sea and extend from latitude 60°51′ N at the northernmost tip of the Shetland Islands to latitude 49° 57′ N at the Lizard Point in Cornwall. Great Britain is about 1,000 km (600 miles) from John o' Groats in the far north of Scotland to Land's End at the tip of Cornwall. It is quite small compared with other parts of the world. Even so, it would take about 30 or 40 days to walk the length of the island.

Landscapes

The north and west of Great Britain is highland. Northern Scotland, Wales and the English Lake District have mountains made from the oldest rocks in Britain. These are rocks such as slate, gneiss and schist as well as granite. Western coasts are rugged with jagged rocks and small bays. Much high moorland is found in the south-west peninsula of Cornwall and Devon. To the east and south of Great Britain the coastline is smoother, with long sandy beaches. The North Sea coast of Britain between the Thames and the Humber is mostly shingle and in parts is being rapidly worn away by the sea. Much of lowland Britain has long ridges of low hills including the Cotswolds, Chilterns and North and South Downs.

Many southern hills are made of chalk. The soil is thin and the chalk rock shows through the grass. East Anglia is low and very flat. The rocks here are soft clay and peat. Parts of the East Anglian Fens are as much as a metre below the level of the sea.

The middle part of Ireland also is flat and low. Slow rivers wind through moors and pasture. The River Shannon flows through a series of lakes to reach its estuary on the Atlantic coast. Near the south coast, wooded valleys separate sandstone mountains and hills, while in the north, features such as the Giant's Causeway are formed from black basalt rock.

Flashback

The British Isles became separated from the European mainland about 12,000 years ago when the sea-level rose after the last ice age. Many mainland plants and animals were prevented by the rising sea from reaching the British Isles. Some, like snakes, reached as far as Great Britain but not as far as Ireland.

Climate

The British Isles are cool and moist. The surrounding sea stops the land from becoming too hot or cold. The highlands are wet with about 2,000 mm (80 in) of rain a year in places. Further east it is much drier, with only about 750 mm (30 in) of rain a year. The weather from day to day is very variable. It is mostly affected by depressions which move eastwards across the Atlantic Ocean. In summer it is rarely warmer than 18°C (64°F). Winter temperatures rarely fall below about 2°C (36°F).

▲ Haystacks and stone walls make a peaceful picture in the 'Emerald Isle', Ireland.

◄ In Wales Llyn Mymbyr and Snowdon dominate the winter scene.

▼ A crofter's cottage on the edge of Staffin Bay on the island of Skye, in Scotland.

Countries and people

The British Isles are made up of Great Britain (England, Scotland and Wales) which, together with Northern Ireland, forms the United Kingdom; the Isle of Man and the Channel Islands (which are not part of the United Kingdom and have their own laws and taxes); and the southern part of Ireland (which forms the Irish Republic). ∎

▼ The vale of Severn in summer from Standish Wood, Gloucestershire, England.

Bronchitis

Smokers are more likely to get bronchitis than non-smokers.

Bronchitis is a disease of the tubes called bronchi inside the lungs. The lining of these tubes becomes red, sore and swollen (inflamed).

Bronchitis is caused by viruses and bacteria. It may start in the chest or follow a cold which spreads to the chest.

At first there is a feeling of soreness in the chest with an irritating cough and sometimes a high temperature (fever). A day or two later the patient coughs up sticky slime, called sputum.

Most people recover in a week or two. If not, doctors can prescribe medicines called antibiotics. ■

See also
Antibiotics
Bacteria
Lungs
Viruses

Bruises

A bruise is caused by bleeding under the skin. It is purple because the oxygen in the blood has been used up. If the bruise is due to something striking the skin, such as a blow from a cricket ball, then the blood is shed from small vessels under the skin, and it usually appears after a few minutes.

Sometimes the bleeding comes from deeper inside, for example from a fractured bone in the arm or leg. Then the bruise may not appear until several days later.

After a few days the bruise becomes brownish yellow, and it finally fades completely. ■

The pain of a bruise can be reduced by applying something cold, like an ice pack.

See also
Fractures
Skin

Brownies

Brownies are the younger members of the Girl Guide movement. In Britain they are between 6 and 10 years old. The name 'Brownie' comes from a fairy story about a wise owl who encourages two lazy children to help others. Adults who run Brownie packs are named after owls, and the Brownie motto is 'Lend a Hand'.

The leader is called Brown Owl and her assistants are Tawny Owl and Snowy Owl.

There are Brownies in many other countries, though they may have another name. They are 'Little Bees' in Switzerland, 'Ladybirds' in Italy, and in Ghana an Anansi Guide has a spider on her badge.

Flashback

When the Girl Guide movement started in 1910, younger girls wanted to share the fun. In 1914 they were allowed to become 'Rose-buds'. Lots of girls wanted to join but they did not like the name. Lord Baden-Powell suggested the name 'Brownie' after he read the fairy story, so the new name, badge and uniform became official in 1916. ■

See also
Cub Scouts
Guides
Scouts

Biography
Baden-Powell

▶ A group of Brownies in the uniform which was designed by Jeff Banks and first worn in 1990.

Brunei

Brunei is a tiny country on the island of Borneo in south-east Asia next to the Malaysian state of Sarawak. The people of Brunei are among the wealthiest people in the world, because Brunei's offshore wells produce oil worth billions of pounds.

Brunei is ruled by a sultan who has total power. His huge palace in the capital reflects Brunei's wealth. The people pay no taxes, receive free services and drive air-conditioned cars. Most live in traditional villages called 'kampongs' along canals. For almost a hundred years Brunei was a British protectorate. It gained full independence in 1984. ■

Brunei's government bought a cattle station in Australia which is bigger than the whole of Brunei. It flies fresh beef daily to the capital.

Area 5,765 sq km (2,226 sq miles)
Capital Bandar Seri Begawan
Population 221,900
Language Malay, Chinese, English
Religion Muslim, Buddhist, Christian
Government Sultanate
Currency 1 Brunei dollar = 100 cents

◄ **Waterways in Brunei are always busy. Boats ferry children to school and people to work.**

See also
Borneo

Bubbles

The word bubble is used to describe pockets of gas trapped inside a liquid. In fizzy drinks, such as lemonade or Coke, the bubbles contain the gas carbon dioxide. But most of the bubbles you see are made of a thin layer of soapy bubble solution with air inside. Plain water cannot be spread out into a very thin layer. Put a drop of water on a clean surface and see what a tight little blob it forms. The molecules of water pull each other close together with a force called cohesion. Add a detergent, such as washing-up liquid, and the cohesion between the molecules is weakened.

In a bubble, the detergent molecules form two stretchy surfaces either side of a thin layer of water. ■

Something to do

To make super bubbles, mix the following: 1 cup of water, ¼ cup of baby bubble bath, ⅛ cup of glycerine, ½ cup of warm vegetable gelatine substitute (buy this in a health food shop). Take a straw and cut four slits at one end, each about three centimetres (about an inch) long. Bend back the cut strips, dip into the bubble solution, take out and blow gently. Or make a frame out of wire, dip it in your bubble mix, then wave it through the air.

▼ It takes a special bubble mix and a huge frame to make bubbles as big as this.

▼ In a bubble, the water molecules are sandwiched between layers of detergent molecules.

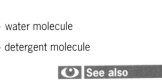

water molecule
detergent molecule

See also
Detergents
Liquids
Molecules
Water

Buddhists

The religion that Buddhists follow began between the 6th and 5th centuries BC. An Indian prince called Siddhartha Gautama tried to find a way of life that could make all beings peaceful and happy. When he succeeded in finding a pathway to peace and contentment he was called Buddha, meaning the Enlightened One. Today he has followers all over the world.

Buddhists live in Burma, Sri Lanka, Thailand, Cambodia, Vietnam, China, Japan, Korea, Mongolia, Tibet, USSR and in Europe and North America.

▲ Buddhists have statues of Gautama Buddha in their homes and their temples. These images inspire them to try to follow his teachings and become enlightened. This kind of statue is common in Burma and Thailand.

The experience of the Buddha

Siddhartha was the son of a Hindu prince and lived a very comfortable life. He married and had a baby son, but became restless to know more about life outside the palace.

There is a legend that one day his chariot driver took him out of the palace grounds. There he saw an old man, someone who was very sick, and a corpse.

Siddhartha felt that he had to leave his home in the palace in order to discover the cause of such suffering and the meaning of life. He spent six years studying with different religious teachers and, although he learned a lot from them, he was still not satisfied.

One night he sat alone under a sacred tree and put all his energy into meditating. That night he realized the truth about the way things are. Buddhists call this being enlightened.

What he realized was that all living things are linked together in a chain of cause and effect. Problems arise when we think of ourselves as somehow separate.

The Buddha spent the next 45 years teaching others what he had discovered. He died at the age of 80.

Teachings

The Buddha taught through his own example and through stories and parables. He understood that everything in the universe, from the tiniest particle of matter, is changing constantly. We ourselves are changing all the time. We grow and in the end the body must die. This is the nature of things, the truth about the way things are. Those who understand and accept this truth are wise. If we ignore the truth and try to cling onto things as if they are permanent, then we suffer.

True happiness and contentment arise when we accept the fact that everything changes, when we respect the life of every living thing, and when we are generous, kind and compassionate. All beings are connected, so if we damage anything we hurt ourselves too.

The Buddha taught four truths, which Buddhists call 'noble truths'.

The first of these is that life, as we know it, is unsatisfactory and full of suffering.

The second truth is that suffering has a cause and that cause is attachment to greed or desire.

Thirdly, he said that suffering can end when we stop clinging to impermanent things.

Fourthly, he taught a path or way of life that can lead to peace and contentment. This state of peacefulness is called nirvana. The path lists eight things which people can do. The path is not extreme; it is a middle way.

The eightfold noble path

Right understanding
seeing the world as it really is

Right intentions
those of kindness and compassion

Right speech
not lying or gossiping

Right action
not harming living things, not stealing, not having wrong sexual relationships and avoiding alcohol and drugs

Right livelihood
earning a living in a fair and honest way and not by harming others

Right effort
knowing what you can do and using just the right amount of effort

Right mindfulness
being alert to what is going on within and around you

Right concentration
applying the mind to meditation and to everything that you do

Way of life

Buddhists follow a way of life which, though ancient, can be applied in the modern world. The essence of Buddhism is compassion for all living things and making the effort to help them all to obtain true happiness. Buddhists try to develop the virtues of sympathetic joy, generosity, equanimity, and loving-kindness. Children are taught a passage about loving-kindness from the scriptures. It says: 'Just as a mother would protect her only child even at the risk of her own life, even so let us cultivate a boundless heart towards all beings. Let one's thoughts of boundless love pervade the whole world above, below and across – without any obstruction, without any hatred, without any enmity.'

Buddhists know that these attitudes come from freeing the heart and mind from greed, hatred and ignorance. Meditation is the way of doing this. It calms the mind so that one can see the truth. Showing respect for the Buddha by putting flowers, incense and candles before his statue can also help to calm the mind and bring about a change of heart. Pilgrimage to sites where the Buddha lived is a way of learning about the religion and meeting other Buddhists. Festivals are usually occasions for giving and sharing.

◄ A Buddhist couple showing generosity by offering food to monks. Monk are only allowed to take what is given, so they depend on lay people offering food every day.

Nirvana means the blowing out (extinction) of desire and attachment.

▼ This stupa at Sanchi, north India, is over 2,000 years old. It is a burial mound containing relics of the Buddha, and it is a holy place for pilgrims.

Buddhists say that they 'take refuge', that is, they depend on three precious things: the Buddha, his teachings (dharma), and the community (sangha). Buddhists call them the three jewels or 'triple gem'.

The community

The Buddhist community is called the sangha. It is made up of monks and nuns and of house-holders and their families, the lay people. The lay people try to follow five guidelines, called precepts:

1 not to harm living things
2 not to take anything which is not given
3 not to lie and gossip
4 not to have wrong sexual relationships
5 not to take drugs or alcohol, which confuse the mind.

Monks and nuns follow many more rules, which give them a very simple way of life. They own little except their robes and alms-bowl, and spend their time looking after these things and in meditation and study. They also teach.

Both parts of the community give a lot to each other. Householders give monks and nuns their food, clothing and somewhere to live. The monks and nuns give the householders and their families what is called 'the greater gift', the gift of the dharma (teachings).

They may also give advice if people ask for it. Families visit temples and monasteries to worship and meditate, for festivals, and to talk to the monks and nuns.

The spread of Buddhism

The Buddha sent monks out to teach people in their own languages. One of the rules they had to keep was never to ask for food and never to teach unless the lay people asked them to do so. This was to ensure that they were not a burden to them or a nuisance.

▶ **Pilgrims outside a temple in Lhasa, Tibet. Those nearest the temple are bowing down to the ground (prostrating themselves) as a symbol of respect to the Buddha and his teachings. On the roof is a wheel, symbol of the teaching which is set in motion by the Buddha, and two deer. The Buddha taught his first sermon in a deer park.**

In the 20th century Buddhism has started to grow in Western countries.

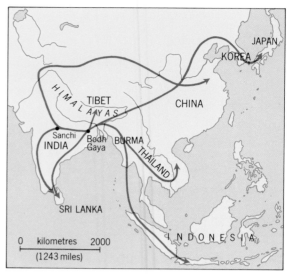

Buddhism spread all over India. It also went with traders on the silk road to China and then through Korea to Japan. In the 3rd century BC, the Indian emperor Ashoka supported the monks and set up pillars all over India. On them were written teachings about being kind to animals and fellow human beings. These were read to the people by special dharma officers.

Buddhism almost died out in India, but it established itself in Sri Lanka, Tibet and south-east Asia.

There are two main branches of the Buddhist religion: Theravada and Mahayana. Theravada means doctrine (*vada*) of the elders (*thera*). This is the kind of Buddhism practised in Sri Lanka, Burma and Thailand. Theravada Buddhists believe that theirs is the original form of Buddhism. They have only very few simple rituals, which focus on the memory of the Buddha.

Mahayana means 'the great way'. It is called great because it claims to provide many ways to enlightenment for a variety of people. There are Mahayana Buddhists in Tibet, Nepal, China, Korea, Japan and elsewhere. They rely for help on those enlightened beings (bodhisattvas) who are prepared to be reborn in the world in order to help others to reach enlightenment. Mahayana Buddhists have elaborate rituals and worship the bodhisattvas as well as the Buddha.

Zen Buddhists (a Japanese branch of Mahayana) use riddles, calligraphy, flower arranging, the tea ceremony, as well as sitting and walking, as ways of meditation, which is what the word 'zen' means. And like all Buddhists they believe it is important to be mindful every moment of the day, whether cleaning your teeth, washing up, or doing any other ordinary thing. ∎

Buffalo

Distribution
Africa, India, south-east Asia, Philippines and Indonesia
Weight
African buffalo up to 900 kg; wild water buffalo 1,200 kg
Horn span
Water buffalo up to 2·4 m
Number of young
1 per year
Lifespan of both species
About 29 years in captivity

Subphylum Vertebrata
Class Mammalia
Order Artiodactyla (cloven-hoofed animals)
Family
Bovidae (cow family)
Number of species 4

American bison are also sometimes called buffalo.

The African buffalo and the water buffalo are both large, dark-coloured, cow-like animals, which live in herds. It is easy to tell them apart, for their horns are very different shapes.

The African buffalo is less common than it used to be, for it feeds mainly on grass and its habitat is suitable for farming. It needs water for drinking and likes to wallow in mud, so it cannot occupy very dry places. In protected areas, such as the Serengeti National Park, Tanzania, herds of several hundred buffalo may still be seen. They are often said to be the most dangerous of game animals.

The horns of water buffalo are bigger than those of any other animal. These creatures are rare in the wild, but they have been domesticated and are common as farm animals in wet places from

southern Europe to south-east Asia. They have been released in Australia, where over 100,000 are said to run wild in part of the Northern Territory.

The tamaraw of the Philippines and the anoa of Celebes are relatives of the water buffalo. Both of these small, shy animals live in wet forests and are extremely rare. ■

▲ Water buffalo were first tamed about 3,000 years ago. They are used today to pull loads or ploughs, and for their meat, hides and milk.

See also
Bison
Cattle
Domestication
Milk

Bugs

Phylum
Arthropoda
Class
Insecta
Order
Hemiptera
Number of species
About 55,000

▶ Bugs do not have a complete metamorphosis as butterflies do, but develop gradually, although colour change can be dramatic. These are the young of the harlequin bug, and already look similar to the adult.

'Bugs' is a word used by many people when they want to talk about insects. But not all insects are bugs. True bugs all have one thing in common, despite varying greatly in size, shape and way of life. This common characteristic is their inability to eat solid food. All bugs have mouth parts which are like long, thin, sharp-tipped drinking straws. With these, bugs pierce the stems of plants to suck up the sap, or the skin of animals to drink blood.

Pond skaters and water boatmen are bugs that hunt other small animals. They are easy to see in ponds or slow-flowing streams. They are protected by having partly toughened wings. So are the shield bugs, which are common on plants in the summer-time. Some shield bugs are brightly coloured, which is a warning that they taste nasty. Some of them smell very nasty too.

Bugs can be pests. Many are agricultural pests. Greenfly and other aphids are probably the best known of these. But some, like the bed bug, attack humans, and can sometimes spread diseases. ■

See also
Aphids
Beetles
Insects
Metamorphosis
Ponds

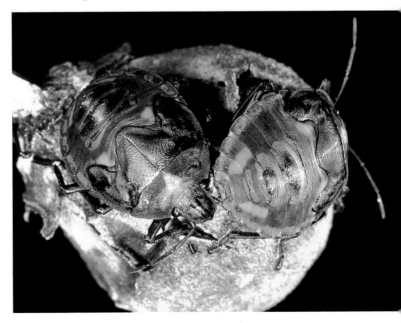

Buildings

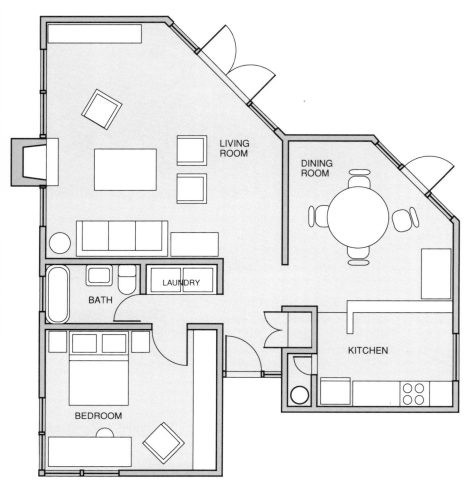

▲ An architect's plan of a bungalow with one bedroom.

▶ A bricklayer at work. He is building the base of the wall on top of the concrete foundations.

Before work can begin on any building, a surveyor studies the chosen plot of land. He examines the soil and underlying rocks on the site, because these affect the type of foundations the building will have. The surveyor makes a plan of the building plot; this shows the size and shape of the plot, the nearest roads and the nearest supplies of water, gas and electricity.

The plan is then sent to the Building Control Officer who works for the local council and has to give approval before any structure is built. Next an architect draws a detailed plan showing every wall, door and window with exact measurements and information about materials. Builders have to estimate the costs and the final plans have to be sent to the local council. If the planning committee gives permission, the builders can get to work.

Foundations

For a garden shed the only foundations necessary may be a firm, level surface. The foundations for a house have to be much stronger; otherwise it might sink into the ground or tilt over.

The builder digs trenches along lines where the walls are to be built. Concrete is then poured into the trenches and allowed to set. This makes a firm wide base, a foundation for the walls. The foundations are wider than the walls so they spread the weight over a bigger area. On soft ground, the house may have to be built on a big slab of concrete.

Bricklayers build the walls on top of the concrete foundation below the ground floor level. These are the 'footing' walls. They have to be extra strong because they support the ground floor concrete slab and all the structures above. Hardcore (broken bits of material) is put around the walls, and concrete is poured on top to make a level surface. A waterproof membrane (plastic sheet) goes on next, and the layer of concrete for the floor is poured on top of that.

The footing walls finish level with the ground floor concrete, which has to be at least 15 cm (6 in) above the earth. A layer of waterproof material separates the foundation brickwork from the walls above. This is the damp-proof course and, together with the plastic membrane below the floor, makes the building waterproof from rising damp.

The bricklayers then continue to build the walls. The mortar which joins the bricks together is made from cement mixed with sand and water.

Like the concrete, it soon sets hard. As the bricklayer makes the wall he 'bonds' the bricks. This means the bricks are overlapped so that there are no straight joints up the face of the wall.

The wall of a house is really two walls. Sometimes the inner wall is made of cheaper quality bricks; sometimes it is made of concrete blocks that are cheaper and quicker to lay than bricks. At intervals between the inner and outer walls the builder puts wire or metal 'ties' in the mortar to help to hold the two walls together.

The space between the walls, the wall cavity, prevents driving rain soaking through to the inside. It also helps to keep the house warm in winter and cool in summer. Often the wall cavity is filled with a special insulating material to help keep the house warm.

The roof

Most houses in wetter climates have a pitched (sloping) roof, so that rain-water runs off easily. The roof is built on a timber frame. First the ridge is built between the two end walls. Rafters are then fixed between the ridge and the eaves. This timber frame is covered with waterproof felt. Thin strips of timber (battens) are put across the rafters to take the tiles or slates. To stop heat escaping through the roof, the loft is lined with fibreglass or some other insulating material. As soon as the roof is on, the carpenters, plumbers and electricians start work inside the house.

Large buildings

Unless there is solid rock just below the surface of the ground, a tall building will need deep foundations to stop it sinking, slipping sideways or being blown over in a gale. Most tall buildings are supported by piles. Sometimes these are huge steel girders that are hammered deep into the ground until a firm layer of rock is reached. Sometimes deep holes are drilled into the ground. Steel rods are put into the holes, then wet concrete is poured in. The building is put on top.

Tall buildings used to need thick walls. The walls had to be thick to carry the great weight above them. If a skyscraper were built like this, the walls would have to be so thick that there would be no room inside on the lower floors. Modern tall buildings are often built around a steel framework. This is strong but light, and supports the building, just as the human skeleton supports the body. Other tall buildings have a framework of reinforced concrete.

The material used for filling the spaces between the steel or concrete framework is called cladding. This cladding may be brick, steel or aluminium sheet, or glass or concrete panels. ■

▲ Four different ways of bonding bricks.

◄ On the roof of a house, the tiles are nailed to wooden battens fixed to the rafters. There is a layer of waterproof felt between the battens and the rafters.

See also

Arches
Architects
Bricks
Cement
Concrete
Houses
Plumbing
Surveyors

Bulbs and corms

See also
Flowering plants
Tubers

A bulb is an underground bud in which food is stored. During the growing season food made by the leaves is passed down into a new bud. As the food accumulates the bud swells, until the leaves die and no more food is produced. Tulip bulbs are like this. The plant is able to use the stored food to survive winter and produce a flower in early spring.

In some bulbs food is stored in the leaf bases. You can recognize these because the bulbs still have the shaggy remains of the dead leaves around their pointed tops. Hyacinth, daffodil and onion bulbs are like this.

► Tulip bulbs are large underground buds that have leaves full of stored food and water.

► Corms are short stems, swollen with stored food and water, and enclosed in the dead remains of last year's leaves.

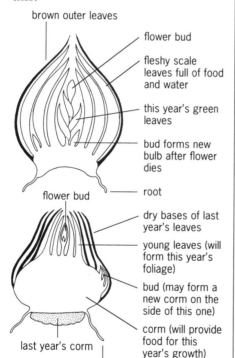

brown outer leaves

flower bud

fleshy scale leaves full of food and water

this year's green leaves

bud forms new bulb after flower dies

flower bud

root

dry bases of last year's leaves

young leaves (will form this year's foliage)

bud (may form a new corm on the side of this one)

corm (will provide food for this year's growth)

last year's corm

root

In a corm the food is stored in the base of the stem. You can find this in crocuses and gladioli.

Because plants store food in this way, many animals including humans eat bulbs and corms. In onions the food stored in the leaf bases is sugar, which is why cooked onions have a sweet taste. The food stored in the crocus corm is starch. ■

▲ **Gladiolus corms**

Bulgaria

Bulgaria is a country in south-eastern Europe. The River Danube marks most of its northern border with Romania. The Balkan Mountains rise near the coast and stretch west, towards the capital, Sofia.

More than half of all Bulgarians are peasant farmers. They grow cereals, fruit, cotton and fine tobacco. Among the country's most important exports are wine and attar of roses (rose oil) for perfume-making. There are also a number of important industries, including steel, coal, chemicals and engineering, which account for two thirds of Bulgaria's exports. Most Bulgarians live in neat, tiled houses built of wood or brick. They grow their own food and live mostly on bread, beans, vegetables and delicious home-made yoghurt.

For nearly 500 years Bulgaria was part of the Turkish Ottoman empire. It became an independent monarchy in 1908 after rebellions and war against the Muslim Turks. After World War II the monarchy was abolished and a republic formed under a communist government. ■

Area
110,911 sq km
(42,823 sq miles)
Capital
Sofia
Population
8,948,390
Language
Bulgarian
Religion
Christian
Government
Republic
Currency
1 lev = 100 stotinki

See also
Europe
Ottoman empire

▼ **Many Bulgarians and foreign tourists enjoy holidays at beach resorts on the Black Sea. This one is in Sonnenstrand.**

Bulldozers

These are tractors with a large blade in front which is used to level rough ground or to give it the right slope for building work. The tractor has caterpillar tracks so that it can travel over uneven or soft ground. The blade is usually square across the tractor so that the earth is pushed in front. Sometimes one end of the blade is slightly in front of the other so that the earth is pushed to one side. The blade can be raised or lowered hydraulically according to the amount of earth to be moved. Very small bulldozers are called calfdozers. ■

◄ This bulldozer weighs 93 tonnes and has a 770 horsepower engine. It is one of the largest tracked vehicles of its type in the world.

See also
Hydraulics

Bullfighting

► The matador makes passes at the bull with his *muleta*, a red cloth or cloak draped skilfully across a stick.

Bullfighting is the overcoming and killing of special fighting bulls in a public ring. In Spain, and parts of France and Central and South America, it is a popular sport. In Portuguese bullfights the animal is not killed.

The 'matador' (bullfighter) fights on foot. He has an assistant on horseback who stabs the bull in the neck with a spear. This weakens the bull and makes it lower its head. After other assistants have stuck coloured darts in the bull's neck, the matador makes a series of moves with his cape to encourage the bull to charge. Once he has shown he has mastery of the bull he kills it with his sword. ■

See also
Spain

Burial mounds

▲ **This prehistoric cemetery at Winterbourne Stoke in Wiltshire, England has a long mound (barrow) near the road and a number of round barrows. Notice the different types: some big, some small, some with a circular ditch all round.**

People honour their dead in a number of different ways. The body can be buried (called inhumation) or burnt (cremation) or left to rot (exposure) until the clean bones can be collected together. Some ancient peoples put up buildings or mounds over their dead.

Prehistoric mounds

The most common form of monument which covered the dead was the mound, which is often called a barrow. This was usually made of earth, but there may have been a stone or wooden structure over the burial itself. In Britain in the first farming period (called the neolithic), from about 4500 BC, important people had long mounds of earth as burials.

The most common type of mound, in Europe and in America, is round. In Britain these often have the cremated remains of a person in a pottery jar buried in the ground before the mound was built.

Roman, Saxon and Viking mounds

The idea of burial mounds lasted and in later periods in Britain and Europe remains were sometimes put into mounds built by earlier peoples. Some Roman burial mounds still exist. There is an Anglo-Saxon burial mound at Sutton Hoo in Suffolk, and Vikings were buried in a similar way. ■

There are some burial mounds in North America which have been built in the shape of animals. One of the largest is Grave Creek Mound in West Virginia, USA. It is 20 m high and 100 m in diameter at the base.

See also
Anglo-Saxons
Archaeologists
Prehistoric people
Pyramids

Burkina Faso

The country was called Upper Volta when it became independent from France in 1960, but the name was changed to Burkina Faso in 1984.

Burkina is a country on the southern edge of the Sahara Desert in West Africa. Three rivers flow southwards from a central plateau. They are the Black, Red and White Voltas, which join to form the main Volta River in Ghana. In the south-west, elephants and hippos are among the animals living in this savannah region. In the dry north farming is difficult, but cotton is grown for export in the south, and sorghum and millet are the main food crops. Burkina's infertile soils have been made worse by over-grazing and over-cultivation. This has led to unemployment, poverty and famine.

More than half the population is of the Mossi tribe. Ouagadougou has been their capital since the 15th century. ■

Area
274,200 sq km
(105,870 sq miles)
Capital Ouagadougou
Population 7,080,000
Language
French, Mossi, Gurma, Fulani, others
Religion
Traditional, Muslim, Christian
Government Republic
Currency
1 franc = 100 centimes

▶ **A Mossi-style mosque in Ouagadougou.**

See also
Africa
Famine
Sahara
Sahel

Burma (Myanmar)

Burma is a country in south-east Asia. The River Irrawaddy runs through it from north to south. This river valley is where most of the Burmans live and they make up the biggest of the ethnic groups. In the mountains which surround the valley on three sides live over 50 different ethnic groups, some of whom are known as tribal people. The climate is tropical; from May to September is the season of the monsoon rains. About half the country is covered by trees, including teak trees. Teak wood is a valuable hardwood and used to be a major export, as did rice, the staple crop. The country is rich in oil and natural gas as well as timber.

Area
676,552 sq km
(261,218 sq miles)
Capital
Rangoon (Yangon)
Population
37,153,000
Language
Burmese, Karen, Shan, Chin, others
Religion
Buddhist
Government
Republic
Currency
1 kyat = 100 pyas

Flashback

For over 900 years the country has been the land of the Burman people. In the ancient capital of Pagan in the north there are Buddhist temples built in the 11th century. The Shwe Dagon Pagoda in Rangoon, an immense golden spire surrounded by hundreds of temples, was started more than 2,000 years ago.

British troops invaded Burma three times in the 19th century and finally deposed the king. For over 60 years it was a British colony. In 1948 it became independent. There has been fighting between government troops and some of the ethnic minorities since then. ■

The official name was changed from Burma to The Union of Myanmar in 1989.

◄ **Water buffalo moving logs in Mandalay, Burma.**

See also
Asia
British empire
Buddhists
Monsoon

Burundi

Area
27,834 sq km
(10,747 sq miles)
Capital Bujumbura
Population 4,718,000
Language
Kirundi, French, Swahili
Religion
Christian, Muslim, Traditional
Government Republic
Currency
1 Burundi franc = 100 centimes

Burundi is a small country in central Africa. Near Lake Tanganyika in the west the land is hot and dry. But high grasslands with a pleasant climate cover most of Burundi.

Some of the tallest and shortest people in the world live in Burundi. The Tutsis can be 2·1 m (7 ft) tall, and the Twa people (Pygmies) are only about 1·2 m (4 ft) high. But most of the people are

Hutu and they are of medium height. The Tutsis, who are fine dancers famed for their high leaps into the air, are cattle owners, while the Hutu grow crops, including such foods as beans and maize. Coffee is grown for export.

Burundi was part of German East Africa from 1890 onwards, and was administered by Belgium from 1919 until 1962 when it became independent. ■

See also
Africa
Pygmies

Bushmen

▼ Two Bushmen in Botswana look at the rock paintings of rhinoceroses painted many years previously by their ancestors.

Bushmen, who are also called San, are a group of people in southern Africa. Most of them live in or near the Kalahari Desert in Botswana and Namibia.

Some San people work on farms, while others are nomads (wanderers). There are probably about 50,000 Bushmen altogether. The nomads live in bands of 25 to 30 people. Each band has its own special area. These nomadic groups are hunter-gatherers. They have learned how to survive in harsh desert conditions and can find food and water where there appears to be nothing but sand or scrub.

The hunters use bows and poison-tipped arrows to kill wild animals. Boys are taught to hunt,

▲ This woman is making holes in ostrich-shell beads with a sharp, pointed stick.

and they are not allowed to marry until they have killed one large animal. Other members of the band gather roots, berries, nuts and seeds. The band often needs to move to find food and water, walking about 30 km (18 miles) a day. They carry their babies on their backs in leather pouches and water in ostrich eggshells. Sometimes they build shelters with branches and grass and live in them for several weeks. At night, they often listen to stories told by the older people.

The Bushmen were probably the first people in southern Africa. Their ancestors' rock paintings are found in many places. ■

Businesses

Businesses can be of three main sorts. **Primary** businesses, like mines or quarries, take raw materials from the earth and sea. **Secondary** businesses, like factories, make products or construct buildings. **Tertiary** businesses offer people services rather than goods.

Many people earn their living by running businesses or working for them. In any town there are shops, offices and factories. These are the places where different kinds of businesses are run.

Manufacturing businesses start with raw materials and use them to make things to sell. They might buy cocoa beans and turn them into chocolate, or make television sets from lots of different electrical parts. The finished products often go to shops.

Shops make their money from trading. They buy goods in large quantities, then sell them at a higher price to make a profit. Other sorts of businesses provide services that people want. Hairdressers, hotels and entertainers all make their money from giving a service.

Most businesses are small. Often they start with a person working alone. A group of people who work together sometimes become partners in a business. If you have a good idea for a business, you might be able to borrow the money to get started.

Larger businesses are usually limited companies. The people who own a company have shares in it, and those in charge of it are called the directors. Shareholders are allowed to vote at an Annual General Meeting.

A big successful company can become a public limited company (PLC). That means that anyone can buy the shares. A company can get money to expand its business by selling new shares to people who have money to invest. The biggest companies have thousands of shareholders. Each shareholder gets a share of any profits the company makes. ■

Butterflies

Butterflies are mostly brightly coloured, day-flying insects. Their colours come from thousands of tiny scales, which are set on their wings like tiles on a roof. Sometimes these are actually coloured, but in some cases the surface of the scales causes light to be broken, so the wings are iridescent with rainbow colours which change as the insect moves. Often the undersides of the wings are grey and brown, in contrast to the brilliance of the upper surface. The dull colours camouflage the butterfly when its wings are folded. This protects it from birds and other creatures that might eat it if they saw it.

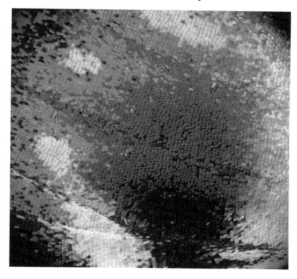

Mating, eggs and caterpillars

Bright colours are very important to butterflies. They find and court their mates with a show of colour. Some butterflies also use scent in their courtship; some of the scales on the wings of the males have a perfume which attracts the females. After mating, female butterflies lay batches of eggs on suitable food plants, but die soon after and never see the caterpillars which hatch from the eggs. The caterpillars feed and grow, then they pupate. In the pupa (chrysalis) the butterfly develops and then emerges.

The longest-lived butterflies are those which hibernate through the winter and appear on sunny days early in the springtime. It is one of these, the brimstone butterfly, with its pale yellow, butter-coloured wings, that has given the whole group of insects their name.

Brightly-coloured flowers can attract butterflies to feed. The butterfly unrolls its long, tubular tongue and sucks up the nectar which is hidden deep inside the cup of a flower. Some butterflies

are not only attracted to beautiful things but to decaying corpses, or the droppings of animals, from which they suck the liquid.

Long-distance flights

All butterflies have four wings, but these work together like a single pair. A butterfly beats its wings fairly slowly: about twenty times a second for a cabbage white. Yet many butterflies can fly fast and powerfully. Even some of the smaller species travel long distances on migration. Comma butterflies, for instance, can fly from the central Sahara to Britain, a distance of about 2,000 miles, in fourteen days. Monarch butterflies make yearly migrations from California to Canada and sometimes, accidentally, cross the Atlantic.

Endangered species

The beauty of butterflies has often been their downfall, as they have been collected on a vast scale. Some of the big tropical butterflies, such as the morphos from Brazil and the birdwing butterflies from south-east Asia and north Australia, have been used as decoration and in jewellery, and are now in danger of extinction. Some of them are protected in the wild by law, and a few species are now bred in butterfly farms. Even some of the small butterflies from Britain and Europe are now in danger of extinction, largely because of the destruction of the plants on which their caterpillars feed. Official protection may well have arrived too late for some of them. ■

▲ The brightly coloured Cairn's birdwing butterfly with a chrysalis.

◄ Close-up of a butterfly wing showing the thousands of tiny scales.

Distribution
In all but the coldest parts of the world
Largest butterflies
The females of some of the birdwing butterflies have a wingspan of about 28 cm.

Phylum Arthropoda
Class Insecta
Order Lepidoptera
Number of species
About 20,000

See also
Caterpillars
Insects
Metamorphosis
Migration
Moths

Byzantine empire

▶ This huge mosaic is high overhead in the curved dome of Saint Sophia (*Hagia Sophia* in Greek). Mary, the mother of Jesus, is enthroned with the child Jesus. The emperors Constantine (on the right), who chose the city, and Justinian, who built the church, offer models of them to Jesus. When the Muslim Turks captured Constantinople (Istanbul) Saint Sophia was turned into a mosque. It is now a museum.

Byzantium is now the city of Istanbul in Turkey.

For over a thousand years, the city of Byzantium was the centre of an empire. During this long period, the boundaries and shape of the empire changed many times. There were times of peace and prosperity and times of great danger. The city itself became one of the largest and richest in the world. In its bustling bazaars, traders did business with merchants from as far away as China and India.

Byzantium was an ancient Greek town built on a narrow strip of land called the Golden Horn, on the shores of the Bosporus strait. It was easy to defend because there was sea on three sides. Constantine, the Roman emperor who made Christianity legal, decided to make Byzantium the capital of the whole empire instead of Rome and in AD 330 he changed its name to Constantinople. The city soon became famous for its splendid palaces, houses and gardens and for its churches, mosaics and icons.

The greatest of all the churches was the cathedral of Saint Sophia, built in the reign of the emperor Justinian. There are hundreds of churches and cathedrals in Greece, Italy and Yugoslavia, built in this Byzantine style. The walls were covered in glowing mosaic pictures of stories from the Bible, and with holy paintings, called icons, of Jesus and the saints.

Gains and losses

While the Roman empire in Italy, France and Britain was crumbling under the attacks of barbarians, the eastern empire stayed prosperous and strong. In the 6th century, when western Europe was in the so-called Dark Ages, the Byzantine emperor Justinian succeeded in winning back parts of Italy, Spain and North Africa. Justinian's most lasting achievement, however, was a Code of Law. He had all the laws that had been made over a thousand years put into a single legal system. This code of Roman law is still the basis of the legal system in France, Italy, Germany, Scotland and many other countries. Justinian died in 565. Less than a hundred years later, the Arab followers of the prophet Muhammad conquered much of Spain, Sicily and North Africa. The Byzantine empire shrank again.

Under attack

From now on the empire was continually being attacked. Slavonic tribes came down from the north. They were defeated, became Christians, and settled down in what is known as Bulgaria. Muslim Arabs tried to reach Constantinople but they too were beaten back. At about the time when the Normans were conquering Saxon England, Turks from the east invaded the Byzantine empire, won a great battle at Manzikert in 1071 and occupied Palestine.

The emperor sent an appeal to the Christians of western Europe for military help. The result was the Crusades. When the crusaders reached Constantinople, they were amazed at the wealth and splendours of the city. In 1204, on the fourth Crusade, instead of fighting the Turks, they turned aside and attacked Constantinople, looting and wreaking terrible damage. The emperor recaptured it and the Byzantine empire survived for another 250 years. Finally, the Turks captured the city in 1453. Constantinople then became the capital of the Ottoman empire. ■

◉ **See also**
Christians
Churches
Crusades
Icons
Mosaics
Ottoman empire
Roman ancient history
Turkey

Biography
Constantine

A 'coalition cabinet' is a group of ministers from different political parties.

Cabinets

A cabinet is a group of the most important ministers in the government of a country, headed by the prime minister or president. The word originally meant a small room. It was first used to refer to the ministers who met in such a room in London in the late 17th century.

Some prime ministers have an inner cabinet or 'kitchen cabinet' of their most trusted ministers and advisers.

In Britain and other countries who follow the British system, the members of a cabinet are also members of Parliament. In the United States members of the cabinet are appointed directly by the president, and are not members of Congress. ■

See also
Prime ministers

Cables

Cables are bundles of wires for carrying electricity. The electricity flows in the metal cable 'cores', and the plastic or rubber insulation around the cores keeps them apart and prevents us from getting an electric shock. Large cables, such as those that bring electricity into our houses, also have an outer sheath of metal or tough plastic, for further protection.

Small cables, like those that connect domestic appliances to the plug, have cores made up of many fine strands of metal so that they can bend easily.

The cables connecting television aerials are 'concentric', that is, one wire is inside the other. This prevents radio interference getting to the inner core, which is carrying the television signal from the aerial.

The word 'cable' is also used by sailors for the ropes that tie up a ship to the dockside. A 'cable's length' is a distance of 100 fathoms (about 180 m/600 ft).

Electric cables were first called cables because they looked like the ropes used on ships. ■

See also
Electricity
Fibre optics
Rope

Cacti

Cacti are plants adapted to live in dry desert conditions. Deserts can have up to 250 mm (10 in) of rain in a year, but it may all fall in one day (a flash flood) followed by a long period of drought. So cacti have evolved ways to store water and reduce water loss.

When it rains, a cactus must absorb as much rain as possible. It has one root going deep into the ground and a spreading net of side roots to collect every available drop of water before it evaporates.

The water is stored in the fleshy stem, which is surrounded by a thick skin to reduce water loss by evaporation. After rain, the cactus swells and then gets slowly thinner as it uses the water, which may last it for up to two years of drought.

Cactus leaves have evolved into spines. These protect the cactus from being eaten by hungry animals and they also reduce water loss. Leafy plants lose water continuously by evaporation through stomata (pores) on their leaves. ■

▼ **Cactus plants flowering in the Andes Mountains.**

flowers

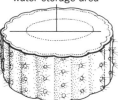
water storage area

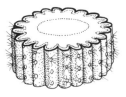
stem swollen after rain

stem shrivelled after drought

▲ **During a drought the stem of a giant saguaro cactus shrinks and develops deep pleats. But after heavy rains it swells, the stem expands, and the pleats almost disappear.**

See also
Deserts
Leaves
Plants

Calculators

Calculators are machines that add, subtract, multiply and divide. Many can do more complicated calculations. They are used by students, engineers, accountants and anyone who works with figures.

At one time, calculators were mechanical. They used rods, levers and gearwheels to do their working out. Nowadays, most calculators are electronic. They work using tiny electric currents. They are very fast, and they do not make mistakes unless you feed the numbers in wrongly.

How they calculate

You can subtract 3 from 5 by finding the number you must *add* to 3 to make 5. And you can multiply 5 by 3 by *adding* three fives: 5 + 5 + 5. Electronic calculators work in a similar way. They use very fast addition to add, subtract, multiply and divide.

When you press the buttons on a calculator, you use ordinary numbers like 0, 1, 2, 3, 4, 5, 6, 7, 8 and 9. The first thing the calculator does is to change these into binary.

Binary is a method of counting which uses just two numbers, 0 and 1. These are easy for the calculator to handle, because its tiny circuits can be OFF for 0 and ON for 1. The calculator does all its working out in binary. Then it changes back to ordinary numbers to display the answer.

◄ Looking inside a pocket calculator. The logic circuits are underneath the middle layer. The bottom layer holds the battery.

◄ Storing numbers in binary. The binary system is explained in the article on Numbers.

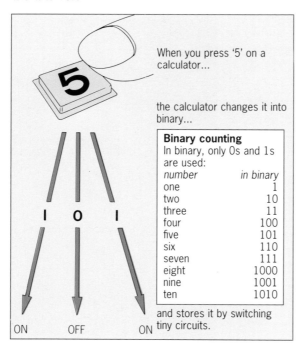

When you press '5' on a calculator...

the calculator changes it into binary...

I   O   I

ON   OFF   ON

Binary counting	
In binary, only 0s and 1s are used:	
number	*in binary*
one	1
two	10
three	11
four	100
five	101
six	110
seven	111
eight	1000
nine	1001
ten	1010

and stores it by switching tiny circuits.

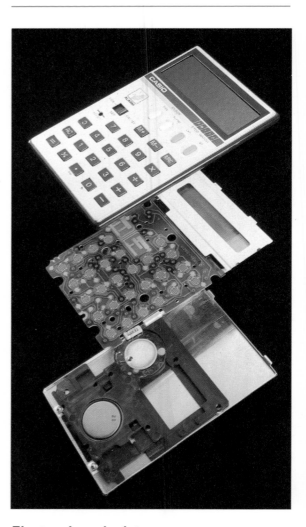

Electronic calculators

Electronic calculators have a tiny logic circuit inside them. These are the 'brains' of the calculator. They run on electricity. They do all the working out, then display the answer on a small screen. Most electronic calculators have a memory so that you can store your answer and use it again later. Some electronic calculators are rather like computers. You can give them a list of instructions, called a **program**. The program can make the calculator do a series of complicated calculations one after another.

There are two types of electronic calculator. **Desktop calculators** can usually be plugged into the mains. Some have a printer in them so that you can print out the answers on paper. **Portable calculators** are small enough to fit in your pocket. Some are as small as a credit card, and some are so small that you can wear them on your wrist in a digital watch. Portable calculators need very little power. Their tiny batteries last for years. Some do not need batteries at all. They use solar cells which turn light into electricity.

Electronic calculators in use

A simple calculator is useful for checking bills or helping with your mathematics at school. But for some jobs, more advanced calculators are needed. Often, these are specially designed to suit particular jobs. Scientists and engineers use specially designed calculators; so do accountants. The electronic checkouts in supermarkets are calculators specially designed to work out customers' bills. On some, you do not even have to press the buttons. The price labels are read automatically by a laser light beam.

Flashback

The **abacus** (counting frame) was probably the first calculating machine. It is an oblong frame holding wires on which beads are strung. On a Chinese abacus there are seven beads on each wire: two above and five below a crossbar. Each bead above the crossbar represents five. Each bead below represents one. The first wire on the right is the units column; the next wire is the tens column, and so on. The thirteenth wire represents trillions. To add you move the beads to the bar, and to subtract you move them away. When you run out of beads, you swap five ones for a five, or two fives for a one in the next column. The abacus is still used in China and Japan today. Skilled operators can work it almost as fast as an electronic calculator.

Mechanical calculators

Before electronic calculators were invented, shops, offices and laboratories used mechanical calculators. These had gearwheels inside them to do the calculating. Mechanical calculators were too large and heavy to be really portable. They were difficult to use and very slow. With

▲ On an abacus, calculating is done by sliding beads along wires. It was probably the first calculating machine but, in skilled hands, can be almost as fast as an electronic calculator.

some, if you wanted to multiply by five, you had to turn a handle five times. Later versions had electric motors to speed things up, but they were still not as fast as electronic calculators.

The first mechanical calculator was built by Wilhelm Schickard in Germany in 1623. A more famous one was made by the Frenchman Blaise Pascal in 1642. The first calculator to go on sale was the 'Arithmometer' invented by Charles Thomas from France in 1820. By the late 19th century many types of mechanical calculator were being produced. The first electronic calculator was made in 1963 by the British Bell Punch Company. It was as large as a cash register. Four years later, Texas Instruments produced a smaller version. This soon led to the cheap, portable electronic calculators we use today. ■

See also
Electronics
Lasers
Numbers

Biography
Babbage
Napier
Pascal

▼ Mechanical calculators were common in laboratories and offices before electronic calculators were developed. To do calculations, the handle had to be wound many times.

▶ Slide rules were once used for doing multiplications and divisions, but have been replaced by electronic calculators which are faster and more accurate.

Calendars

A calendar is a way of grouping days so as to help people organize their lives. It is needed for planning farming, business, religion and domestic life. The calendar used now by Western countries is based on one started by the Roman dictator Julius Caesar in 45 BC.

Days and years

A day is the time it takes the Earth to rotate once on its axis. A year is the time it takes for the Earth to travel around the Sun. It is not a whole number of days. That has always made it hard for communities to make calendars that keep in step with the seasons, something that is very important for farming. The year is actually 365 days, 5 hours, 48 minutes and 46 seconds long. Putting in an extra day, 29 February, every four years helps, but there is still a small difference that adds up over many years.

In 1582, Pope Gregory XIII proposed that century years should not be leap years unless 400 divides into the year exactly, so that 2000 is a leap year, but 1900, 1800 and 1700 were not. The Gregorian calendar was adopted in England in 1752.

Months

The word 'month' comes from the name Moon. As the Moon travels round the Earth, it takes about 29½ days to go through its phases. It does this just over twelve times in a year. In the Gregorian calendar the months have 30 or 31 days (28 or 29 in February). There are exactly twelve months in a year so the months do not quite keep in step with the Moon's phases. Some communities have calendars based on the Moon. An example is the Jewish calendar, which has twelve months of 29 or 30 days. An extra month is put in seven times in a 19-year period. The Muslim calendar has twelve lunar months of 30 or 29 days and does not keep in step with the seasons.

Other calendars

Different societies have used a wide variety of different calendars. At one point, the ancient Egyptians used three calendars at the same time: a civil calendar of 365 days, a natural calendar based on the seasons and a religious calendar. The Hindu calendar uses the idea of 'lunar days', which are exact thirtieths of a lunar month and so do not coincide with natural solar days. ■

Thirty days hath September, April, June and November. All the rest have thirty-one Excepting February alone Which hath but twenty-eight days clear And twenty-nine in each leap year.

Different calendars begin the new year on different days. The Egyptians and the Persians chose the autumn equinox (23 September), when day and night are the same length. The Greeks chose the winter solstice, 21 December (the shortest day of the year). In Anglo-Saxon England the Church chose 25 December as New Year's Day, but the state kept 1 January. In 1752 it was finally settled to be 1 January for everyone.

Seasons
Vernal or spring Equinox
21 March
Summer Solstice
21 June
Autumn Equinox
23 September
Winter Solstice
21 December

See also
Days of the week
Equinoxes
Festivals
Seasons
Time

▼ A calendar for the month of October painted in the 15th century for an illuminated manuscript called Les Très Riches Heures du Duc de Berry. In the centre the Sun is driving his chariot across the sky. In the third circle are the phases of the moon. In the fifth circle you can see the signs of the zodiac for Libra and Scorpio with the stars as they appear in the October sky.

Calligraphy

Calligraphy means beautiful writing. You do it with a broad lettering nib. These can be bought as dip pens or special Calligraphy Fountain Pen sets.

You can find hundreds of different styles of calligraphy, including the special brush calligraphy used in China and Japan. But to start you off, here is an illustration of the alphabet which Western calligraphers learn as a basis for their other styles. You will need a good black (non-waterproof) ink and a broad nib.

Modern calligraphy dates from the studies of Edward Johnstone in 1898 in London. Before the invention of printing, calligraphers (then called scribes) would sit writing books out by hand on parchment pages made of sheepskin and calfskin. ■

Something to do

Practise the simple patterns and movements first. Hold the pen at 45 degrees to the horizontal writing line as shown. The small letters should be the height of four nib widths. Capital letters are six nib widths high.

The distance between letters is judged by making the areas of white space equal to each other. This means that two o's will be closer than two n's.

See also

Illuminated manuscripts
Writing systems

Cambodia

Cambodia is a country in south-east Asia. If you fly into Phnom Penh, the capital, you see a lot of water. The great Mekong River flows south from Laos through Cambodia to Vietnam. It is joined by the Tonle Sap River, which comes from a huge fish-laden lake. For about 100 days each year this river flows backwards with a tidal bore from the sea. Cambodia is an agricultural plain, with forested hills near Thailand, so rivers and canals are vital for irrigation and transport.

▼ Weaving cloth at a loom.

Climate and crops

Rice is the main crop and food in this tropical monsoon country. Travelling by boat among the bright green paddy fields you see farmers pedalling their *rohats*, giant wheels which scoop water up into the crops. Other crops include maize, sweet potatoes, bananas, coconuts, jute, rubber, cotton for the textile industry, and timber.

Flashback

The magnificent 12th-century temples of Angkor Wat were built by the Khmer people. In the late 19th and early 20th century, Cambodia was part of French Indo-China. In 1975 the communist Khmer Rouge forces led by Pol Pot took over the Khmer Republic. A terrible massacre of educated people and destruction of the country followed. The Khmer Rouge were overthrown by the Vietnamese in 1979 and a People's Republic of Kampuchea was established. In 1989 the Vietnamese troops withdrew. ■

Area
181,035 sq km
69,898 sq miles
Capital
Phnom Penh
Population
7,284,000
Language
Khmer, French
Religion
Buddhist, Muslim, Christian
Government
Republic
Currency
1 riel = 100 sen

Between 1979 and 1989 the official name of the country was Kampuchea. In 1989 it reverted to its old name of Cambodia.

See also
Asia
Buddhists
Vietnam

Camels

Camels are the largest animals found in deserts. They are well suited to this harsh, waterless environment. They have thick fur which protects them against the hot days and cold nights of the desert. Their two-toed, broad feet are ideal for walking on loose sand or gravel, and their bodies are adapted to save water.

Camels do not sweat, and lose very little moisture when they excrete. Even liquid lost from their nostrils is collected in a groove which runs down into their mouths. But most importantly, a camel can go without drinking for long periods, losing up to 40 per cent of its body weight. Their humps do not contain water, but fat. This is used up in times of hardship and the hump becomes

shrivelled and floppy. When a camel reaches water it will replace the liquid that it has lost. It can drink up to 57 litres (12½ gallons) without a pause.

The Arabian camel and the Bactrian camel have both been domesticated. Camels are now very rare in the wild, but both these species have been released in the drier parts of North America and Australia, where they now flourish in large numbers. ■

Distribution
Arabian camel, originally in Middle Eastern deserts; Bactrian camel originally from the dry steppes of Asia
Size
Head and body length 225–345 cm; height at shoulder 180–210 cm
Weight 450–690 kg
Number of young
1 young every other year. Young fully independent at 4 years
Lifespan Up to 50 years

Subphylum Vertebrata
Class Mammalia
Order Artiodactyla (cloven-hoofed animals)
Family Camelidae
Number of species 6

Alpacas, llamas, guanacos and vicuñas are all members of the camel family.

See also
Deserts
Domestication
Llamas
Milk

▼ The Arabian camel has longer legs and is not as heavily built as the Bactrian camel. These are Arabian camels.

Cameras

A camera will make a picture of a person or a scene that you can keep, called a photograph. Its lens takes in the light from the person or scene and makes a small picture on the film inside the camera. The film stores the picture because it is covered with chemicals which are sensitive to light. If too much light falls on the film it will spoil the picture, so the film is kept in the dark until it is processed to produce the finished photographs.

Using a camera

A camera may need setting before you take a picture, though automatic cameras do the adjustments for you and simple cameras have nothing to adjust. The lens is set to take a clear picture of something close up or far away. The shutter is a door that opens for a fraction of a second to let in the light. The aperture is a hole that lets in the right amount of light. Both are set to let in more light on a dull day or less light on a bright sunny day. If there is not enough light, a flash will give extra light while you take the picture. When you take a photograph, you look through the viewfinder to see what the picture will look like. Then you press the button to open the shutter and take the picture. The film must then be wound on to get a fresh part in position.

Different kinds of cameras

Instant cameras can produce finished photographs a few minutes after they are taken. The film is in a flat package with everything needed to produce a picture. The package comes out of the camera and you can see the picture appear as you hold it in the light. Some special cameras, like TV and video cameras, do not use film at all; the pictures are made electrically. Others do not use light; X-ray cameras make pictures by sending X-rays through the body.

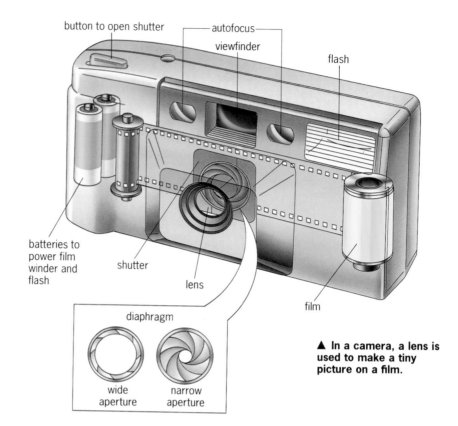

▲ In a camera, a lens is used to make a tiny picture on a film.

Flashback

In the 16th century the 'camera obscura' was invented in Italy. It was just a dark box with no windows and a small hole in one wall. It made a picture of the scene outside, just like your pin-hole viewer, but it did not make a picture that lasted. In 1826 Joseph Niepce, a Frenchman, made the first real camera. It was a wooden box with a lens at the front and it made the first permanent picture on a metal plate. The French inventor, Daguerre, and the British, Fox Talbot, made improvements in photography. Then in 1888 an American, George Eastman, produced the first popular camera. This had a roll of film that took 100 pictures. Edwin Land (also American) invented a camera that could produce instant photographs in 1947. ■

Making a pin-hole viewer

You can see an image like the one in a camera without using a lens. Cover one end of a cardboard tube with foil and the other with white tissue paper, shading it with an extra tube. Make a large pin-hole in the middle of the foil and point this at a bright light or window. The pin-hole acts like a lens and makes an upside-down picture on the tissue paper.

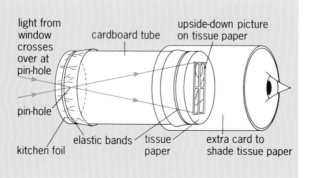

Cameroon

See also
Africa

Cameroon is a hot and mostly rainy country in west-central Africa. Behind the swampy coastal plain lie highlands covered by forests, with grasslands in the north. Mount Cameroon, West Africa's highest peak and one of Africa's highest mountains, is an active volcano.

Over a hundred languages are spoken in Cameroon. Most people live by farming, and cocoa and coffee are the chief crops. Many northerners rear cattle. Earth walls around their villages keep out wild animals.

Cameroon was conquered by Germany in 1884 and later divided into two parts, one ruled by France and the other by Britain. French Cameroon won its independence in 1960, and in 1961 it united with part of the former British Cameroon. ■

Area
465,054 sq km
(179,558 sq miles)
Capital Yaoundé
Population 9,880,000
Language
French, English, Fang, Bulu, others
Religion
Christian, Muslim, Traditional
Government Republic
Currency
1 African Financial Community (CFA) franc = 100 centimes

Camouflage

▶ This turbot is camouflaged from predators, as its speckled brown colouring and flattened body enable it to blend in on the sea-bed.

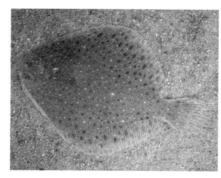

▼ The military have adopted many of the camouflage strategies that are used in nature. These soldiers are wearing dark green and have covered themselves with branches so that they are harder to see against their woodland background.

Most kinds of wild animals are hard to see, because they are camouflaged (coloured to match the places in which they live). Defenceless creatures need camouflage to hide from predators. Hunters need camouflage to be invisible to their prey until the moment before they attack.

Countershading is a form of camouflage shared by almost all active animals. The colour of their backs is darker than that of their undersides. The darker upper parts are lit more brightly by light from above and the paler under-parts are less brightly lit. This makes the animal's rounded body appear evenly coloured and flat, so it is less easy to see.

A few kinds of animals, including some large caterpillars and a fish from the River Nile, are paler on their backs than on their undersides, but they always live and move upside-down.

Disruption Spines, flaps of skin or a coat patterned with spots or stripes will break up an animal's outline against its background.

Mimicry A few defenceless animals have the same patterns and colours as animals which taste unpleasant or are protected by stings. Many hoverflies look like wasps, and so are less likely to be eaten.

More obvious methods of camouflage include changing colour and impersonating part of the habitat. Chameleons and octopuses are both able to change colour quickly to avoid predators. Stick insects look like twigs, and leaf fish like dead leaves. For their camouflage to be successful these animals must remain very still and only move slowly. ■

Being transparent is another form of camouflage. Jellyfish, fish larvae and other aquatic animals are transparent and so not visible in water.

Some beetles that live in ant colonies produce secretions that are so similar to ants that they are accepted as ants themselves. Smells can act as a sort of camouflage as well as visual markings.

See also
Chameleons
Stick insects

Camping

Many children's first experience of camping is in their own back garden in a small waterproof tent, a shed, or a caravan. Some school and youth organizations, such as the Guides and Scouts, hold camps for young people. Here, tents are likely to be large, sleeping six or even more people under one canvas roof. Some campsites accommodate young people in chalets or huts where they sleep on the floor or in bunks. All such camps include outdoor activities such as cooking, walking, and sports and games.

Family camping

Many families go on holidays where they camp instead of sleeping in a permanent building such as a hotel or house. Camping families generally buy and cook their own food, organize their own washing, and clean and look after their own accommodation. Also, they need to plan clothing for outdoor life, and choose personal luggage more carefully than on a hotel holiday. It is easy to take unnecessary items or to forget essential pieces of equipment.

A camping family may own or hire a large frame tent, like the one in the photograph below, which has almost as much space as a small house. A frame tent can be packed and moved in the boot of a large car, on a roof rack, or in a special small trailer.

Some families go camping in a caravan, which may be towed behind their car, or hired when the family reaches a campsite. Caravans have all the features of home, including a toilet, carefully fitted into a small vehicle generally on two wheels. They are popular in the UK and European countries, and in North America, where they are called trailers. A camper is another popular North American vehicle, and is in essence a caravan with four or more wheels, an engine and a driving cab.

In most parts of the world, people camping must have permission from the owner of the land on which they camp. Most camping holidays are based on organized campsites which hire land for camping and provide shopping, washing and toilet facilities.

Holiday camps may have sites for tents and caravans, and also have some chalets built of wood or brick. Some accommodate all their visitors in chalets, and provide central facilities for eating or entertainment.

Backpacking and cycling

Camping in which people tour on foot, carrying their accommodation and food with them, is backpacking. It is especially popular with young people, as is camping in which the equipment is carried round on a bicycle. This type of camping usually involves moving every day to a new location which may be a small or unorganized campsite.

Light, compact equipment is needed, such as a small tent that will sleep only one or two people, a sleeping bag and groundsheet, personal cooking and eating utensils, and a container of water.

Backpacking is particularly popular in remote regions, with difficult terrain, where there are significant risks of injury or getting lost. Safety precautions are important, such as carrying a good map and compass, and telling someone the planned route before starting. ■

▲ This ridge tent is made in two main parts. The tent itself, made of brown canvas, is covered with a green flysheet. The rainwater runs off well outside the main tent walls. This type of tent can be rolled up into a compact bundle and carried by backpackers. It will withstand high winds and rough weather.

◀ The large frame tent has two compartments and an awning to make a covered area. This type of tent provides much more space, but it is bulky and not designed to withstand high winds.

See also
Guides
Scouts

Canada

Canada is the world's second largest country. It stretches over 5,000 km (3,000 miles) from the Pacific Ocean to the Atlantic Ocean and almost as far from near the North Pole half-way to the Equator.

St John's, Newfoundland, is closer to the United Kingdom than to Vancouver. Flying from St John's to Vancouver takes around eight hours, while driving takes about eight days with stops for sleeping and eating. Canadians have overcome these great distances by building excellent transportation and communication systems.

Climate

Snow covers most of Canada from November until April. Sometimes a midwinter warm spell melts the snow, but then more replaces it. Ploughs push snow off city streets and salt melts ice on sidewalks (pavements). Winter can be difficult in the cities but fun in the country. People ski and skate and travel over frozen lakes on snowmobiles, a Canadian invention similar to a motor cycle. Summers are warm enough for gardening and swimming in the lakes. With the first freezing weather in October, the maple leaf, Canada's symbol, turns red and the forests appear to be on fire.

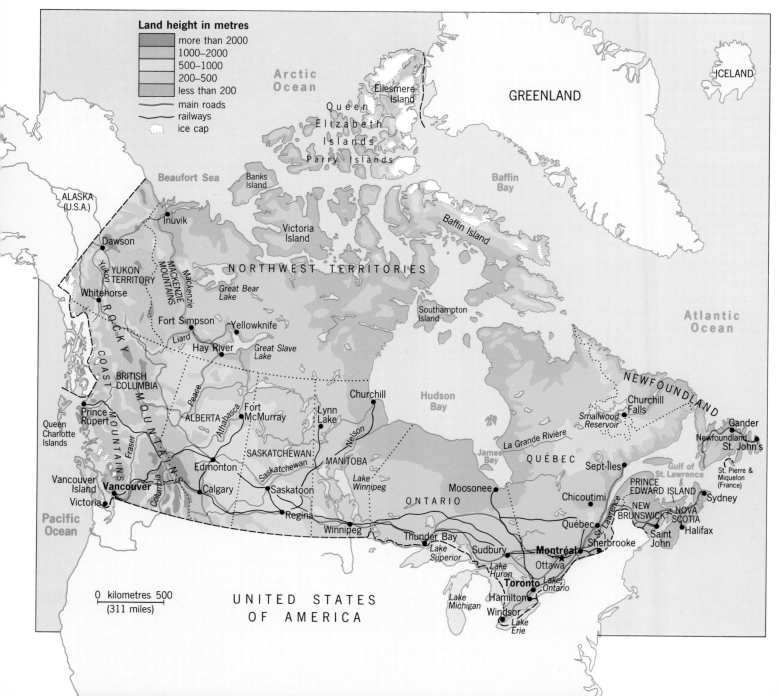

Land height in metres
- more than 2000
- 1000–2000
- 500–1000
- 200–500
- less than 200
- main roads
- railways
- ice cap

▲ A fishing village on the Atlantic coast of Nova Scotia, near Halifax.

Settlement

Three out of every four Canadians live in cities. Along the Atlantic and Pacific coasts, cities with safe harbours flourish. The largest city on the Atlantic, Halifax, began as a British naval base built to defend the American colonies from the French. Vancouver on the Pacific grew as the port at the western end of Canada's first continental railroad.

Between the coasts, cities are strung along railroads, highways and the Great Lakes–St Lawrence Seaway. Half of Canada's population and most of its large cities are found along this water system.

Canada's two largest cities, Toronto and Montréal, have a combined population of over 5 million. Montréal, founded by the French, was Canada's commercial centre until many companies moved their head offices to Toronto. Now high office buildings crowd the sky of the city that was first named 'the meeting place' by the Indians.

Resources

Canada exports large amounts of natural resources to other countries. Canadian wheat feeds many millions. Some Canadians work cutting trees and driving them to mills where they are sawn into lumber, formed into plywood and made into paper. Many others work to transport, warehouse and market the wood products. Gold, nickel, asbestos and platinum from Canada's mines are exported all over the world. North Americans buy the more common materials such as iron, salt and potash. Mining, forestry, fishing and farming in Canada are very mechanized. With modern equipment one person

▲ The Yukon Territory, in north-west Canada, is a vast area of mountain ranges, plateaux and forests. It contains Canada's highest peak, Mount Logan (5,951 m).

◄ Roof tops in the city of Québec. You can see the St Lawrence River in the background.

can do the work of 20 in the forests, fields and farms. Many people keep the machines running and develop new ones and increasing numbers of people find work doing research and providing information.

People and culture

Most Canadians speak one of Canada's official languages, French or English. One in five Canadians speaks French as a first language and learns English in school. Similarly, schools teach French as a second language to English-speaking students. Most of Canada's 500,000 native people (Indians and Inuit) speak one of eleven native languages and English or French, which they learn in school. Labels on goods in stores also have both languages. A high level of immigration from non-European countries, however, has greatly increased the ethnic diversity of Canada. ■

Area
9,970,610 sq km
(3,849,674 sq miles)
Capital
Ottawa
Population
25,309,330
Language
English, French, Inuktitot, Indian languages, others
Religion
Christian
Government
Federal parliamentary monarchy
Currency
1 Canadian dollar
= 100 cents

⊙ See also
American Indians
Canada's history
Inuit
North America

Canada's history

▶ Painting of an Indian settlement on Lake Huron in about 1850. The artist is the Canadian, Paul Kane.

The first colonies
Newfoundland
Nova Scotia
Prince Edward Island
Québec (called Canada by the French)
British Columbia

▼ British soldiers under the command of James Wolfe climbed a path up the cliffs at night and formed up in ranks on the Plains of Abraham, outside Québec. The French attacked next morning, 13 September 1759, but were defeated. Wolfe was killed and the French General Montcalm died of wounds next day.

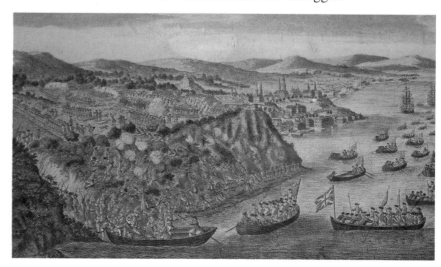

The original Canadians emigrated from Asia during the Ice Age at least 25,000 years ago. Many bands of people crossed what is now the Bering Sea, when sea levels were lower. The Inuit of Canada, whom Europeans called Eskimos, arrived 4,000 years ago. They came in their sealskin boats along the Arctic coast. The North American Indians have many distinct language and cultural groups. The Haida of the west coast are known for their totem poles; the Ojibway perfected the birch-bark canoe; and the Cree invented the toboggan.

European settlement

In 1497, five years after Columbus discovered America, John Cabot landed in Nova Scotia, explored the St Lawrence estuary and claimed the area for the King of England. English, French, Spanish, Basque and Portuguese fishermen came each summer to fish along Newfoundland's coast, but English colonists preferred to settle in the warmer lands to the south. In the 17th century the French explored much of Canada and sent 10,000 settlers to the St Lawrence River to farm and trade for fur. The Indians became partners with the French fur traders and taught them how to dress for the harsh climate.

In the next century the French and British fought for control of these valuable lands. The British captured the town of Québec in 1759 and Canada became the Province of Québec, which is now English-speaking Ontario and French-speaking Québec. Britain also owned Nova Scotia. When the United States of America became independent of Britain, thousands of Loyalists, who had supported the British, fled to Canada, including Afro-Americans, some free and some slaves. Canada outlawed slavery in 1834 and runaway slaves continued to escape to Canada from the USA for almost 30 years.

Nation building

Canadians were afraid that their powerful southern neighbour, the USA, might try to invade and take them over. As a result, several of the biggest colonies joined to form the Dominion of Canada in 1867. Each colony became a province. The new country purchased the vast lands of the Hudson's Bay Company and planned a cross-continental railroad, the Canadian Pacific. As the number of settlers increased and moved westwards, new provinces were founded: Manitoba, British Columbia, Alberta, and Saskatchewan. Newfoundland joined in 1949. At first most immigrants to Canada came from Britain but settlers from eastern and northern Europe followed. They found jobs on the wheat farms of the prairies and in the timber industries of the forests.

New Canadians

Immigration slowed down during the two world wars and the economic depression of the 1930s, but after 1945 Canada welcomed an average of 150,000 people every year. Displaced persons (people who had lost their homes in World War II) from the Ukraine, Poland, Estonia, Latvia, and Lithuania were recruited to take low-paying jobs on farms. Soon they sought better jobs in the cities. During the 1960s immigrants from Italy, Greece and Portugal arrived to do construction work but many soon started their own businesses. Today most immigrants are from Asia and the Caribbean. Canada's system for selecting immigrants does not discriminate over race or religion.

Making war

Canada, as a member of the British empire, was automatically at war when Britain entered World War I. Canadians enlisted enthusiastically to help the motherland. Canada, with a population of 8 million put 600,000 in uniform: that is, 1 in 13. Many joined the Royal Flying Corps and four of the top aces were Canadian. Billy Bishop alone shot down 72 enemy planes. Women and teenagers helped farms increase food production fourfold. 350,000 people worked in 1,500 factories to manufacture guns and shells.

When Britain declared war on Germany in 1939, Canada was an independent nation. It declared war immediately. Once again, both French and English Canadians wanted to assist. Over 1 million enlisted: that is, 1 in 11. Canadian factories produced ships, tanks, aircraft, motor vehicles, guns, shells, clothing and food. Most of the war effort was financed with people's

◄ Poster encouraging British people to migrate to Canada in 1914.

The first provinces of the Dominion
Québec (formerly Lower Canada)
Ontario (formerly Upper Canada)
New Brunswick
Nova Scotia

savings, while prices, rents and earnings were controlled by government. By the end of the war, Canada was an industrialized country and was recognized internationally as a 'middle power'.

Making peace

Canada helped to create the United Nations in 1945 and the defence alliance called the North Atlantic Treaty Organization (NATO). Canadians have served with the UN peace-keeping forces in the Middle East, Cyprus and Zaïre. Canada has also strongly supported UN organizations such as UNESCO. She has played an important part in keeping the Commonwealth together, and often supports the aspirations of developing nations. Canada opposes the increased use of nuclear weapons and wishes to play a role in the supervision of disarmament. ∎

▲ A road-painting caution sign in French and English.

◉ See also
American colonial history
American Indians
British empire
Commonwealth
Inuit
USA: history

Biography
Cabot
Cartier
Frobisher
Hudson
King Mackenzie
Laurier
Macdonald, John
Pearson
Trudeau
Tubman
Wolfe

Famous Prime ministers	
John A. Macdonald	1867–1873
	1878–1891
Wilfrid Laurier	1896–1911
W. L. Mackenzie King	1921–1926
	1926–1930
	1935–1948
Lester B. Pearson	1963–1968
Pierre Elliott Trudeau	1968–1979
	1980–1984
Brian Mulroney	1984–

Canals

▼ **This boat is in a lock on an aqueduct which crosses over the valley of the River Garonne in France.**

A canal is an artificial river. Most have been built for boats, although others are used for irrigation or drainage. People have always used rivers as a cheap and easy way of moving heavy loads. Where there was no river, or where rivers flow too fast or are too narrow and winding for boats, canals were built. The first canals were built in Mesopotamia in about 4,000 BC. Since then canals have been built in many countries. Nowadays barges transport enormous loads over great distances, and boats take people for peaceful, relaxing holidays.

▶ **The Corinth canal cuts a passage through Greece 6.3 km (3.9 miles) long from the Gulf of Corinth to the Aegean Sea. A passenger ship is pulled by two tugs.**

The Chinese built a Grand Canal, linking stretches of rivers. This was begun in the 6th century BC and construction continued over hundreds of years. By the 14th century it stretched from Beijing to Hangzhou and was 1,780 km (1,106 miles) long.

The canal boom

In Britain during the Industrial Revolution people needed to transport heavy loads of coal and other materials between mines and factories. From the 1780s onwards a whole network of canals was built. These linked the industrial areas of the Midlands and North with London. Talented engineers, including James Brindley, William Jessop and Thomas Telford, designed them, and Irish labourers, known as navvies, did much of the constructional work. During the 19th century a canal network was built in North America linking the main industrial centres. Over a hundred years ago ship canals were built to join seas and oceans. These waterways dramatically reduced the time taken by ships to travel around the world.

Constructional problems

Canals cannot go up or down slopes. Canal builders had to find ways of changing the water-level. One solution was to build a series of locks. A lock is a section of canal with watertight gates. The water-level is different in each section.

Often tunnels had to be constructed to avoid high points on a route. Cuttings and embankments were built to avoid unnecessary gradients. To cross a valley the only solution was to build an aqueduct that carried the canal high above the ground.

Canals need a constant supply of water. This is usually provided directly by rivers and streams. In some places it was necessary to build reservoirs at the highest points on the route to keep the canal filled.

Travelling on canals

The long, thin boats that were used to carry large loads on the canals were called narrow boats. At first they were pulled by a horse that was led along a tow-path on the canal bank. The horse could not go through the small tunnels. Members of the crew had to lie on their backs on the top of the boat and 'leg' their way through by pushing with their feet on the tunnel roof. Sometimes this was done by children. The horse had to be led over the tunnel and then harnessed up again at the other side. Later the narrow boats were motorized.

Nowadays, most British ones are used by people holidaying on the inland waterways. On wider waterways, large barges are used, some of them pushed or pulled by tugs. They are often strung together so several can be pulled by a single tug.

Canals that link seas and oceans

The Suez Canal links the Red Sea and the Mediterranean. It was designed by the Frenchman, Ferdinand de Lesseps, and has no locks. It was completed in 1869, and then ships travelling from Europe to India and the East no longer had to sail around Africa. From 1967 to 1975 the Suez Canal was blockaded because of the Arab–Israeli Wars and could not be used.

In 1895 the Kiel Canal opened, making the journey from the Baltic to the North Sea much quicker and safer. Centuries before that, the Vikings had avoided this dangerous sea journey by dragging their ships overland on huge wooden rollers.

The Panama Canal was built to allow ships to go from the Atlantic and Caribbean to the Pacific without travelling around the continent of South America. It was finished in 1914, and its 82 km (51 miles) and six enormous locks contain more material than any other man-made structure in existence. At one point the canal rises 22 m (72 ft) above sea-level. During the many years of its construction, over 25,000 workers died from disease or accidents.

Canals linking rivers and lakes

The St Lawrence Seaway, opened in 1959, allows large ships to reach Lake Ontario from Lake Erie and so opens up 3,830 km (2,380 miles) of waterway, from the west of Lake Superior to the Atlantic. The New York State Barge Canal joins Lake Erie with the Hudson River.

The Illinois Waterway was built to connect with the Mississippi River, providing a north–south route from Chicago to Mexico. The Gulf Intracoastal Waterway links Mexico with Florida by a safe inland route.

In Europe there is an extensive network of canals that connect the Rhine and the Rhône and other main rivers. This means that large loads can be transported across national borders throughout the continent. New canals are being constructed in France and Germany.

Tow boats can now be used that will pull up to 50 barges at a time carrying very heavy loads. This is such an economical form of transport that canals and waterways are likely to be used extensively in the 21st century. ■

▲ A fully loaded container ship passes through the Miraflores lock of the Panama Canal.

Ferdinand de Lesseps started to build a canal at Panama in 1879 but abandoned the work ten years later.
The country of Panama will take full control of the canal from the USA on 31 December 1999.

🕐 See also
Georgian Britain
Locks
Panama

Biography
Telford

Area
7,273 sq km
(2,808 sq miles)
Capital
Las Palmas of Gran Canaria
and Santa Cruz of Tenerife
Population 1,444,600
Language Spanish
Religion Christian
Government
Spanish provinces
Currency Spanish peseta

See also
Spain

Canary Islands

The Canary Islands are a group of volcanic islands in the Atlantic Ocean, about 100 km (60 miles) off the north-west coast of Africa. There are two main groups of islands, each forming a province of Spain. One province is called Las Palmas and the other Santa Cruz de Tenerife. Fishing and farming are major industries, though droughts often occur. The mild, sunny weather, especially in winter, attracts many tourists to the Canary Islands.

The people are descended from the Guanches, the earliest inhabitants, and Spaniards who settled there after the islands became Spanish in 1479. ∎

Cancer

Cancers are serious diseases caused by the uncontrolled growth of abnormal cells in the body. Groups of these cells are called tumours. Malignant tumours are damaging ones that can grow fast or spread rapidly through the body, damaging vital organs.

Cancers appear to start when normal cell division goes out of control to make a mass of abnormal cells, which is the cancer. Sometimes we do not know why this happens, but virus infections, radiation, and some dangerous chemicals like those in tobacco smoke can all start cancers in body cells.

There is no doubt that tobacco smoke is almost always the cause of lung cancer. Non-smokers are very much less likely to get this disease than smokers.

Each year 60,000 people in Britain receive treatment for their cancer which lets them return to a normal, active life.

See also
Cells
Smoking

Cancers can be cured if they are found and treated at an early stage of development. Some types of cancer, such as skin cancers and the blood cancer called leukaemia, can often be successfully treated with surgery or anti-cancer drugs. ∎

Candles

No one knows who invented candles, or when. We do know that the Romans, and other people in ancient times, used them. Candles have always consisted of a thick coating of wax or some other fatty material around a wick made of cotton yarn or another fibrous material. This, when lighted, burns fairly slowly and gives a reasonable amount of light.

Some modern candles are made by repeatedly dipping and cooling the wick in wax. But this is largely to make tapered altar candles for churches, and other special candles. Paraffin wax is now used to make most candles, because it gives a good light and it is not as smoky as animal fat, but beeswax is sometimes used.

Mass production

Most candles are made by one of two methods. Either a machine is used which contains several hundred tubular moulds. The wicks are suspended in these and then the molten wax is added. When the wax has hardened, the candles are pushed out of the moulds by pistons. Alternatively, wax powder or flakes is pushed under high pressure through an opening which is the width of the finished candles. The wick is fed continuously into the centre of the candles as they form. By this process, large numbers of candles can be produced quickly and cheaply. ∎

Candlesticks have been found in Egypt and in Crete that are at least 5,000 years old.

In Britain hundreds of years ago candles were used at auctions. Bidding was allowed to continue for as long as a 1 inch (2·5 cm) candle was alight. When the flame burnt out, the bidding had to stop.

Candle clocks
If you have two candles of the same kind you can make a candle clock. Light one candle and time how long it takes to burn. If it burns 1 cm in an hour you can then mark off your second candle in centimetres. When you light this second candle you will know how much time passes.

See also
Light
Time
Wax

▼ **Candles in the Cathedral of St Stephen in Vienna, Austria.**

Canoes

A canoe is a small boat without a keel which is propelled by a paddle or sail. The canoeist faces forward, often kneeling to paddle. A canoe is long and narrow and usually pointed at both ends. ∎

► This dugout canoe is hollowed out from a single, solid tree trunk. Such canoes are used for inshore fishing in West Africa.

► The Inuit kayak has a wooden frame covered with sealskin. The paddler is well protected from the cold. The double paddle has a blade at each end.

► American Indians developed the graceful birchbark canoe. It has a wooden frame covered with sheets of bark sewn together.

◄ The Sri Lankan double canoe has two hulls linked by a deck, part of which is covered over with a thatched cabin.

◄ Outrigger canoes are used in the Indian Ocean. The light hull with its large sail is balanced with a shaped log. The canoe is sailed with the outrigger to windward.

See also

Boats
Coracles

Canterbury Tales

Chaucer's pilgrims

The Knight
The Miller
The Reeve (chief magistrate)
The Cook
The Man of Law
The Shipman
The Monk
The Priest
The Physician
The Pardoner (who sold pardons – the forgiveness of sins – in exchange for money)
The Wife of Bath
The Friar
The Summoner (who called people to appear before a judge or magistrate)
The Clerk
The Merchant
The Squire (knight's attendant)
The Franklin (landowner)
The Prioress
The Second Nun
The Canon's Yeoman (cathedral clergyman's attendant)
The Manciple (buyer of provisions for colleges)
The Parson

The man whom some people call 'The Father of English Literature' lived about 600 years ago. His name was Geoffrey Chaucer and his most famous book is called *The Canterbury Tales*. It begins in spring at the Tabard Inn, Southwark, London, where a group of about 30 travellers are preparing to go on a pilgrimage to Canterbury. They are a lively assortment of people and agree to pass the time by telling stories.

Chaucer is a part of the group and he begins by describing the pilgrims to us one by one. They turn out to be an amazingly mixed bunch! There is a battle-stained knight with his trendy son, a prioress (head nun) with her pet dogs, an assortment of crooks, a widow called the Wife of Bath looking for a fifth husband, and a drunken miller, forever deafening the company with his bagpipes!

When we read *The Canterbury Tales* today, we notice two things. First, it is written almost entirely in rhyming verse. Second, it is in a much older form of our language, now called Middle English. There are many modern versions, but it is fun to read *The Canterbury Tales* as Chaucer wrote it.

You might have heard one or two of the pilgrims' stories. The Pardoner tells of three villains who go in search of Death and come to a sticky end themselves. The Priest relates the fable of the Cock, the Hen and the cunning Fox.

Sadly Chaucer never enabled his pilgrims to tell all their tales. When he died in 1400, he had written only 24, and not all of those were finished. Fortunately he had completed the wonderful opening 'General Prologue', in which he describes the pilgrims:

'Wel nyn and twenty in a companye Of sondry folk . . .' ∎

The Canterbury Tales was one of the first books printed in English by William Caxton.

See also

English language
Pilgrimages

Biography
Chaucer

Capitalists

Capitalists are people who own property and make profits. The word 'capital' is here used to mean a stock of anything that has been made. It can mean, for example, all the items made in a factory, and also the factory buildings themselves and the machinery in them.

Capital is often used to mean money that has been saved. So capitalists can be people who own a lot of money, which they can lend to others or put into a business to earn more money. Even money in a bank account is capital lent to the bank. Western countries depend on capitalists to fund their industries. ■

See also
Banks
Businesses
Money

Carbon

Carbon is the black material you see on burnt wood or toast. Carbon can also form two very different types of crystal. One is graphite, the black material used as the 'lead' in pencils. The other is diamond, the hardest substance known.

When carbon combines with hydrogen, it forms a whole family of new materials called hydrocarbons. These include fuels such as natural gas, petrol, paraffin and diesel oil. Carbon also combines with hydrogen and oxygen to form foods like sugar and starch. These are called carbohydrates. When foods and fuels are burned, the carbon in them combines with oxygen to form carbon dioxide gas. Other things with carbon in them include vinegar, alcohol, perfumes, plastics and disinfectants.

The carbon cycle

Plants and animals are mainly made from materials containing carbon. So carbon is essential for life.

The air around us contains tiny amounts of carbon dioxide gas. Plants take in carbon dioxide through their leaves and water through their roots. Using the Sun's energy, they turn the gas and water into new plant material. So, plants are partly carbon. Animals like us eat plants for food, so our bodies are also partly carbon. When we 'burn up' our food, carbon is used in making carbon dioxide gas. In this way, carbon goes round and round from air to plants to animals and back into the air again. Scientists call this the carbon cycle.

Fuels also take part in the carbon cycle. Fuels like petrol were formed from the decayed remains of plants and animals which lived millions of years ago. When fuels burn, their carbon is used in making carbon dioxide gas. This goes into the air with the other exhaust gases.

Carbon dating

Like all materials, carbon is made up of atoms. A tiny fraction of all carbon atoms are different from the rest. They are unstable. In time, they break up and give off a burst of nuclear radiation. We call atoms radioactive if they behave like this. Some of the carbon atoms in you are radioactive, though the radiation from them is far too weak to do you any harm.

Living things are always taking in fresh supplies of carbon. They get rid of some carbon every time they breathe out. But when they die, the carbon is trapped. And some of this trapped carbon is radioactive. Over thousands of years, the radiation from the trapped carbon gets weaker and weaker. By measuring the radiation, scientists can work out the proportion of radioactive carbon. From this they can work out how long ago death occurred. Scientists call this carbon dating. They can use it to work out the age of old bones, wood, mummies, and even old cloth, because the fibres come from dead plants. ■

See also
Crystals
Diamonds
Elements
Fossils
Fuel
Greenhouse effect
Photosynthesis

Grass is about 4% carbon (by weight).

Human beings are about 20% carbon.

Coal can be over 90% carbon, depending on the type.

Charcoal is almost 100% carbon.

▶ The carbon cycle. How carbon is used over and over again.

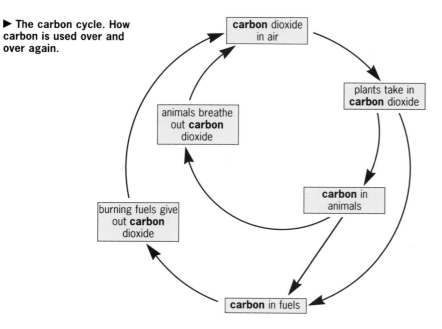

Card games

There are hundreds of games which can be played with a pack of playing cards. Some depend on luck, but many need a lot of skill and speedy decisions.

Pairing games include pelmanism. The cards are spread on a table, face down. The players turn up two at a time, trying to make pairs. Cards which do not make pairs are turned face down again. The skilful player remembers where the cards are.

Set-collecting games include rummy and canasta. The aim is to collect a set of cards with the same number, or a sequence of the same suit.

Trump and trick games include nap, whist and bridge. The whole pack is dealt to the four players (any number in nap). The aim is to win the greatest number of tricks. One suit is chosen as trumps. A trump card can beat any card of another suit.

▼ How to sort by suit.

▲ How to sort by numbers.

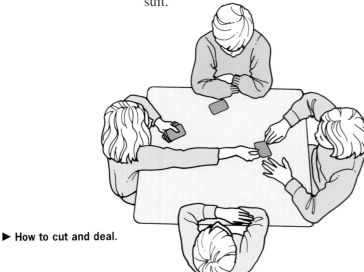

▶ How to cut and deal.

Card manners

1 Do not touch your cards until the dealer has finished.

2 Hold your cards so that no one else can see them.

3 Never look at anyone else's cards.

4 Do not talk about the cards in your hand.

5 Be a good loser.

Klondike, a game of patience for one

Deal a row of seven cards starting from the left. The first one is face up and the others face down. Then start on the second pile and put one card face up on it and one card face down on each of the others. Go on doing this until you have a pattern that looks like the one here.

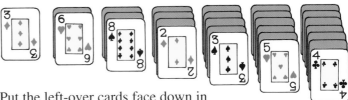

Put the left-over cards face down in a stock pile. Now you can move cards and put them on top of each other.

Rules

1 Only move cards that are face up.

2 A red card must go on a black card, and a black card on a red card.

3 Each card must go on the next above it: a 6 on a 7, a queen on a king.

4 You can pick up a complete group of cards if they obey rules 1 to 3.

5 When you uncover an ace, move it to a new row above your other cards. Each pile in this row must only have one suit. Go up in order, starting from the ace as 1 and ending with the king.

6 If you have moved all the face-up cards from one pile, then you turn over the next card that was face down. If one of the seven places becomes empty a king can go there.

When you have moved all the cards you can, take the top card off the stock and turn it over. If you can place it anywhere, move as many cards as possible. If you cannot, leave the card face up next to the stock. You can use the top face-up card on this pile whenever you get the chance. When you are stuck again, turn over the next card. You are allowed to go through the stock pile only once.

You win if you can get all the cards piled up on their right aces. It won't happen very often. ■

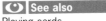
See also

Playing cards

Caribbean

Area
1,943,000 sq km
(750,200 sq miles)
Greatest depth
7,680 m
Highest mountain
Pico Duarte, Dominican
Republic 3,175 m
Major volcanoes
Mont Pelée, Martinique
1,397 m
Soufrière, St Vincent
1,234 m

Map labels:
UNITED STATES
Atlantic Ocean
Gulf of Mexico
Grand Bahama
Florida Keys
Straits of Florida
Yucatan Channel
THE BAHAMAS
Tropic of Cancer
MEXICO
CUBA
Turks and Caicos Islands
Great Inagua
BELIZE
Cayman Islands
DOMINICAN REPUBLIC
HAITI
PUERTO RICO
Virgin Islands
GUATEMALA
JAMAICA
St. Kitts
Nevis
Antigua
HONDURAS
Guadeloupe
Dominica
EL SALVADOR
Martinique
St. Lucia
NICARAGUA
Caribbean Sea
Pacific Ocean
Lake Nicaragua
Aruba
Curaçao
Bonaire
St. Vincent
Grenada
Barbados
COSTA RICA
Panama Canal
0 kilometres 500
(311 miles)
PANAMA
COLOMBIA
Lake Maracaibo
VENEZUELA
Tobago
Trinidad

Land height in metres
more than 2000
1000–2000
500–1000
200–500
less than 200

The Caribbean Sea stretches over 3,000 km
(1,900 miles) from the coast of Central America
to Trinidad and Barbados. When geographers
talk about the Caribbean, they usually include
all the islands around the sea, the Caribbean
coastlands of Central and South America, and
the countries of Guyana, Surinam and French
Guiana which do not touch the Caribbean Sea
but have strong links with the island chain.

Landscape and climate

The islands are sometimes called the West
Indies. Some of the islands are very large; others
are so small that no one lives on them. Some are
built up from coral reefs, and are so flat that
they hardly rise above the sea. Others have steep-
sided mountains, covered with thick rainforest,
two or three thousand metres high. Many of
these mountains are volcanoes. Some are still
active. Mont Pelée on Martinique killed over
30,000 people in 1902, and Soufrière on St
Vincent last erupted in 1979.

The Caribbean has a warm, tropical climate, but
it is never as hot as in the interior of Africa or
South America, because the islands are cooled
by breezes from the sea. In the mountains it is
quite cool. Rainfall is heavy, but comes in short,
violent showers, so there is plenty of sunshine
too. Most rain falls from June to November.
From February to April, it can be very dry. On
all the islands, there is much more rainfall in the
mountains than on the coast. Most of the time,
gentle winds known as the North-East Trades
blow across the sea; but occasionally, during
the rainy season, there is a violent storm known
as a hurricane. Hurricanes can cause very serious
damage.

Farming and mining

Many tropical crops thrive in the Caribbean
climate. Sugar cane, bananas, coffee, spices and
cocoa are all grown for export. Bauxite, from
which aluminium is extracted, is mined in some
islands, and there are also other minerals, such
as oil. Many ships sail through the Caribbean to
reach the Panama Canal, which joins the Atlantic
and Pacific oceans.

Tourism

Most of the Caribbean islands have a tourist
industry catering for holiday-makers from North
America and Europe who fly to the islands to
enjoy warm sunshine, tropical beaches and water
sports. ■

Caribbean history

Five hundred years ago the Caribbean islands were home for two groups of American Indians, the Arawaks and the Caribs. Today nearly all Caribbean people are descended from people who came there since 1492: Europeans, Africans and Indians. Many of them are of mixed race.

Arawaks and Caribs

Up to 50 Arawak or Carib families lived with their chief in a village. Every few years they moved their thatched huts and their sleeping hammocks to a new place for farming. They grew maize, sweet potatoes and peppers and caught fish. The Arawaks lived mostly in the western islands. The Caribs who lived on the South American mainland and in the eastern Caribbean used to raid other islands in their war canoes.

European empires

In 1492 Christopher Columbus sailed into the Caribbean from Spain. He hoped he had sailed round the world to the East Indian islands. Other explorers recognized that these were different islands, which they named the West Indies. The Spanish sent soldiers and traders to build an empire in the Caribbean and America. They killed many Arawaks by working them to death. Arawaks also died in thousands because they had no resistance to European diseases.

French, Dutch and English sailors, including Francis Drake, began to raid the Spanish empire and captured many islands, especially in the eastern Caribbean. There were many wars between the settlers and the Caribs. Today, only a few people on the smaller islands have Carib ancestors. New settlers arrived to grow crops to send to Europe. They tried tobacco, and then changed to sugar when they started to bring in slaves from Africa to do the work.

Slaves and sugar

In West Africa, men, women and children were captured and taken to the coast by traders who were Arab, African and European. European captains bought them and carried them across the Atlantic in the holds of their filthy ships. Many slaves died in this 'middle passage', but over 5 million were landed over a period of about 200 years and sold at auctions to plantation owners.

Slave life in the Caribbean

On the plantation, the slaves lived in huts near the owner's great house. New slaves were put into gangs for field work. They hoed the ground, planted sugar cane and cut it when the stems had grown thick. Other slaves worked in the sheds where the cane was crushed between rollers to extract the juice. Cane juice was boiled down to make sugar.

African customs continued while they were slaving for the Europeans. Slaves had their own stories such as the tales about the spider hero, Anansi. Many slaves were skilled at beating out rhythms on drums for the ceremonies they held when young people became adults, when old people died or when a season's work was done. They kept alive their belief in African gods such as Shango, the Yoruba god of thunder. Most plantations had a person who was skilled in African herbal medicine.

As time went on, these African traditions combined with the ways of the Europeans. Many Caribbean people today speak Creole languages with French or English words and mainly African grammar. The modern calypso comes from songs which poked friendly fun at people in village festivals. Beating and shaking instruments, and many of the rhythms used, still link African and Caribbean music. Forms of dance owe a great deal to the dance of the West Africans.

Amerindians is an alternative word for American Indians.

◀ An Arawak chief's stool, carved from wood.

▼ Although the slave trade had been abolished in 1807 and no new slaves were being transported from Africa, slaves were still being bought and sold 22 years later. This sale took place four years before the act abolishing slavery was passed by the British Parliament.

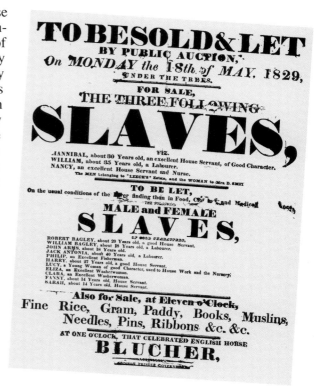

► Artists in Haiti have developed a distinctive style of painting which is colourful and stylized and often draws inspiration from their African roots. This painting of a boat below a bridge is by Préfète Duffaut.

▼ The Jamaican hero, Marcus Garvey, is commemorated on a postage stamp.

► Many West Indians volunteered to join the armed services in World War II. This recruiting poster shows a Jamaican air gunner in the British Royal Air Force.

Revolts and emancipation

Slaves often revolted. Some Africans, called maroons, ran away to live free in the mountains of Jamaica. In Haiti, an army of former slaves fought successfully against the French. Their most famous leader was Toussaint l'Ouverture. In 1804 Haiti became the first independent black country in the Caribbean.

In Britain, William Wilberforce led a campaign against the slave trade. The trade was ended in 1807 by the British Parliament. Slavery was becoming much less profitable and in 1833 Parliament ordered all slaves in the British colonies to be emancipated (set free). In fact slavery did not completely end until 1838. Slavery lasted in the French islands (Martinique and Guadeloupe) until 1848 and the Spanish islands (Cuba and Puerto Rico) until 1886. After emancipation the British took labourers from India to work on plantations in Trinidad and Guyana, where their descendants are known as 'East Indians'.

New ways of earning a living

Most ex-slaves wanted to leave the plantations. They started their own farms to grow new crops such as cocoa and bananas. Some became traders or craftsmen. However, Europeans kept the best land and did little to see that the black people had jobs, schools or health care. In 1865 Paul Bogle led a revolt against such unfair treatment in Jamaica. Other people had to emigrate to find work. Caribbean people helped build railways all over America and did most of the digging for the Panama Canal.

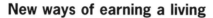

In the 20th century West Indies were still on the move. Many went to the USA and Canada, or to fight in the British army in both world wars. Marcus Garvey, who was born in Jamaica, had tried to bring these scattered people together as members of a single nation which had its roots in Africa. In 1914 he started his Universal Negro Improvement Association with the motto: 'One God! One Aim! One Destiny!' Garvey inspired many black people to work towards independence.

Independence

In the 1920s and 1930s, most people in the Caribbean were still desperately poor. Trade unions and political parties were formed to press for better conditions and, later, for independence. Jamaica, and Trinidad and Tobago, achieved independence in 1962. Most of the former British colonies are now independent countries, but the French islands are governed as if they were districts of France, and Puerto Rico is linked to the USA.

Most parts of the Caribbean have become much more prosperous since the 1950s. Tourism, bauxite mining, and oil and natural gas all bring money into the region. Many factories have been set up and farming has been modernized. There is now a strong North American influence on the way of life. Many people have relatives in the USA and Canada, travel there to study or on holiday, and watch American television programmes. But many people in the Caribbean are also now placing much more emphasis on their own culture and identity. ∎

Carnivals

Carnival is a big open-air festival which usually includes music, dancing, processions and colourful costumes.

Most Roman Catholic countries in Europe celebrate carnival just before the beginning of Lent. Lent is a period of repentance and prayer before Easter, and carnival was the last opportunity to sing and dance for six weeks. The word 'carnival' probably comes from the phrase *carne levare*, which means 'to take meat away', because in the past no meat could be eaten in Lent.

The history of European carnivals probably goes back to Roman festivals like Saturnalia, when masters and slaves behaved as equals for one day. In the Middle Ages, carnival was celebrated with songs, dances, masks and costumes. Control of a city might be handed over to a jester who was 'Lord of Misrule'. People could make fun of the rich and powerful with songs and plays which were full of double meanings.

Today, Fasching in Germany is probably the best-known European carnival. In Britain the carnival tradition did not really develop, but games which were played on Shrove Tuesday, just before Lent, may have been the origin of modern football.

In Roman Catholic parts of North and South America, slaves were often allowed a holiday while their owners celebrated carnival. The slaves came from Africa, where music, costume and dance generally play an important part in culture and religious belief.

Today, carnival in the Caribbean and America is a blend of African and European traditions. Carnival in Trinidad has 'steel band' and calypso competitions, and thousands of people join costumed bands which parade through the streets led by a 'king' and 'queen'. Carnival in Rio de Janeiro in Brazil, and 'Mardi Gras' in New Orleans in the USA, are also world-famous. A carnival with a strong Caribbean flavour is held at Notting Hill in London in late August. ■

See also
Bands

'Mardi Gras', the New Orleans carnival, means 'Fat Tuesday'. In the old days, people used to use up all the fats in their homes before the period of fasting during Lent began.

The world-famous carnival in Rio de Janeiro lasts for four days and most of the city's inhabitants join in the festivities.

▼ **Carnival procession, Port of Spain, Trinidad. The steel drums are carried under awnings to protect the drummers from the Sun.**

Carols

Carols are celebration songs. There are carols for all kinds of celebrations: birthdays, weddings, the start of the new year, and May Day. But the best-known carols are Christian songs celebrating the birth of Christ and telling the story of Christmas.

▲ Carol singers at Hampton Court, London, in the 1880s.

Carols can also celebrate other Christian festivals. 'This joyful Eastertide', for instance, is sung at Eastertime.

Singing carols from door to door is a custom that began only about 100 years ago. In the Middle Ages carols were danced as well as sung. Later they were sung as people moved in procession about the church. The words of many carols include a chorus, and bid all people to worship Jesus. 'Good Christian men, rejoice' and 'O come, all ye faithful' are carols of this kind. ■

See also
Christmas
Easter

Cartoons

Cartoons are simplified drawings that aim to poke fun. Unwanted details are left out and important features are exaggerated to make them look funny or silly. Caricatures are cartoon drawings of real people, such as particular politicians. Stereotypes are cartoons of a type of person, such as a typical horse rider.

Jokes and stories

A single cartoon makes a joke in just one drawing, called a single frame. A strip cartoon uses several frames to relate a funny incident.

Comic strips use many frames to tell a story. What the people say is written in speech bubbles that point towards the speaker's mouth. Thought bubbles have a row of circles linking the person's head to the words. Sometimes the action is described in a short commentary or narrative.

Film cartoons

Animation is the technique of making cartoon films. A person called the animator draws key pictures that show the main parts of the action and says how many frames are needed to show each stage of the movement in between.

There must be 24 frames for each second's worth of movement. Artists called inbetweeners draw these frames. Most of the background will be drawn separately and the individual pictures that show stages of

▶ In the Disney film 'Bambi', made in 1942, the animals' faces were made rounder and larger than in real life and the lengths of the deer's limbs were exaggerated to make the characters seem more appealing.

▼ 'Peanuts' by Charles Schulz is the most widely syndicated cartoon strip in the world. Since it began in 1950 it has appeared in more than 2,000 newspapers in 68 countries in 26 different languages.

movement will be put in the right place on top and photographed onto film. Finally, the film is projected at the rate of 24 frames per second to give the impression of continuous movement. Today, animators can use computers to speed up the drawing process.

Flashback

The original meaning of the word 'cartoon' is a simple drawing for a more complicated painting or tapestry. The artist would draw the picture as lines on a piece of paper, rub over the back with chalk, and then pin the paper over the canvas or wall. Drawing over the lines would leave an outline of the chalk on the surface underneath which the artist could follow when painting. ∎

See also
Comics
Drawing
Films

Cassette players

Cassette recorders can record and play back speech, music, or data for a computer. The cassette is a small plastic case containing magnetic tape and two reels. It fits in the front or top of the player. When the player is working, a rotating spindle called a capstan pulls the tape past a record/playback head. To record your voice, a microphone changes the sounds into electrical signals which are boosted and sent to a coil in the head. This puts a track of varying magnetism along the tape. During playback, the tape again moves past the head. But this time, the magnetic pattern generates electrical signals in the coil. The signals are boosted by electronic circuits and changed into sound by a loudspeaker. Stereo cassette players have two loudspeakers. They can record two separate tracks. ∎

Audio cassette
A cassette which is made for recording sounds, such as music or speech
First cassette of modern design
Manufactured by the Philips Company in 1963
Cassette numbers: C60, C90, C120
These tell you the playing time in minutes. The thinner the tape, the more will fit on a reel and the longer the playing time.

See also
Electronics
Recording

▼ This portable cassette player can record sounds and play them back.

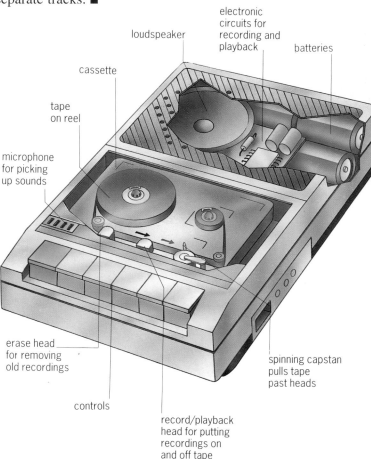

electronic circuits for recording and playback

batteries

loudspeaker

cassette

tape on reel

microphone for picking up sounds

erase head for removing old recordings

controls

record/playback head for putting recordings on and off tape

spinning capstan pulls tape past heads

Castles

▲ A castle under siege painted in an illuminated manuscript, in about 1400. The defenders are throwing huge stones down and one is shooting with a crossbow. The attackers are scaling the walls using ladders.

▶ King Edward I of England (1272–1307) built eight massively strong castles in North Wales. One was at Harlech, on rock high above the sea. When the castle was besieged supplies could be brought in by ship.

Castles are fortified buildings or sets of buildings. Most of them were once the homes of chieftains, kings or nobles. The best-known castles in Europe date from the Middle Ages. But fortified palaces existed in much earlier times. The Assyrians built one, in the mountains north of Nineveh, in the 9th century BC. The ancient Romans protected some of their country palaces and towns with high walls too. Even the Celtic tribesmen of Iron Age Britain had their own types of castle. These hillforts were defended by earthen walls and deep ditches. Much later, in the 8th century AD, the English built special forts (*burhs*) to protect themselves from Viking invaders.

Castles of the feudal age

In 10th-century France, the first true castles began to take shape. Many started as a simple wooden tower, built on a high motte (mound) and encircled by a wall. This wall could be of earth, or it could be a wooden palisade (fence). There might also be a surrounding ditch filled with water. This was called a moat. In time, some ground might be fenced in at the foot of the mound. This area was known as a ward or bailey.

Such *motte-and-bailey* castles were very popular with the Normans. During the 11th century they became common all over western Europe. In many places builders remade the wooden towers and outer walls in stone. This was to stop attackers from setting fire to them. Baileys became bigger too, so that more fortified buildings could be added. All this happened at the time when kings were ruling in a 'feudal' way. This meant that they lent out lands to their leading nobles, who then had to govern them in the king's name. The nobles would build castles on their lands and use them as their headquarters. They lived there with their families, and also with a force of trained knights. When an enemy army was in the area, the local people would take shelter in their lord's castle. But some castles were built to overawe the local people, as well as to protect them. This was one of the reasons why the Normans built the great Tower of London, in about 1078.

The search for improvements

Builders were always looking for ways to make their castles safer from attack. After 1100, they got many new ideas from crusaders who had seen the mighty fortresses of the Byzantine empire. Western Europeans copied the Byzantine style when they built castles. They made the outer walls much thicker, and often

added a second defensive wall inside. They built round towers to guard each section of wall. They protected the main gateways with double towers called barbicans. And they made baileys big enough to hold stables, gardens, a chapel and even buildings for making bread and beer.

Castles under siege

Enemy attempts to capture castles were called sieges. These could be very complicated. The army of attackers had to camp outside the walls. If there was a moat, they had to fill part of it with stones and tree trunks. Then they could get close enough to the walls, climb up to the battlements with ladders, and fight it out with the defenders. They might instead try to break down the sturdy castle gates with battering rams. They might tunnel their way beneath the walls, or even try to break them down by hurling stones from giant catapults. But all these approaches could take a long time. In 1215 Rochester Castle in Kent held out for almost two months, with only a hundred knights and men-at-arms inside. In 1266 Kenilworth Castle held out for half a year.

During a siege, a castle's defenders were on constant alert. It was possible to fire arrows at the attackers, through narrow slits in the walls. If they came closer, the defenders could drop heavy objects on them from hoardings. (These were covered wooden platforms fixed high up on the castle walls.) Sometimes the defenders sent out raiding parties of their own. They would leave by a small hidden gate, then take the attackers by surprise. And all the while, stonemasons and carpenters would busily repair any damage done to the defences.

◄ This is the splendid 'fairy-tale' castle of Neuschwanstein. It was built in the 19th century by King Ludwig II of Bavaria.

End of the age of castles

Some medieval sieges ended only when the defenders' food-supplies ran out. But during the 15th and 16th centuries, everything gradually changed. This was because gunpowder had been invented. Attackers could now batter down the walls with ease, or pour cannon shot into the heart of the castle. New, more solid forts had to be built, protected by guns themselves. These forts were usually controlled by kings, not by noblemen. Meanwhile, the nobles started to live in less fortified homes, which were also much more comfortable. Castles were still built, however, like the one above built in 19th-century Germany. But such castles were made to look beautiful, not to stand up to sieges. ■

The word castle comes from the Latin *castellum* a little fort. The Spanish word is *castillo* and the French *château*.

So many castles were built in Spain by both Christians and the Muslim Moors in the Middle Ages that central Spain became known as *Castilla* (Castile), the land of castles.

British royal castles

Windsor Castle was begun by William the Conqueror (1066–1087) and parts were rebuilt by Edward III (1327–1377). The whole castle was enlarged in the 19th century under George IV (1820–1830).

Balmoral Castle was built in 1855 on land that Prince Albert bought for Queen Victoria.

French nobles and merchants as well as kings built splendid *châteaux* in the Loire valley in the 16th century. They were not fortified and are more like palaces than castles.

See also
Feudal system
Hillforts
Middle Ages
Normans
Scotland's history (photo)
Welsh history

Caterpillars

▲ This caterpillar's bright colours and long hairs protect it from predators.

Looper caterpillars are also known as 'measuring worms' or 'inchworms'.

Phylum
Arthropoda
Class
Insecta
Order
Lepidoptera

Caterpillar is the name given to the larva (grub) of a butterfly or moth. It must spend all this stage of its life feeding and growing. To do this, it has a bag-like body, and scissor-like mouthparts to cut up its food. Most caterpillars feed on leaves. Usually they will eat only one sort of leaf.

Caterpillars can feed undistracted as their eyes and antennae are small, so they are aware of very little. They move slowly, for their three pairs of legs are tiny and all at the front of the body. To help support the long hind part of the body, they usually have little hooked suckers called prolegs. One big group of caterpillars has only two pairs of prolegs, near the back of the body. When they walk, they have to hump their bodies up into a loop, and then throw themselves forwards. They are called looper caterpillars.

Caterpillars have many enemies, such as birds, which would like to eat them. Some protect themselves by feeding at night, and being so well camouflaged by day that their enemies cannot see them. Some, usually the brightly coloured ones, taste nasty, and others have a coat of thick, stinging hairs, which stick in the throat. ■

◉ See also
Butterflies
Larvae
Metamorphosis
Moths

Cathedrals

A cathedral is a large church where a bishop (or archbishop) has his headquarters. It is the main church in the diocese (the area that is under the bishop's control). The Roman Catholic Church, the Church of England and the Episcopal Church of the USA all have cathedrals.

Services and festivals

Every day in the long life of a cathedral, at least two services are said or sung. Church festivals like Christmas and Easter have elaborate ceremonies, but important national days, like Remembrance Sunday, are celebrated too. Cathedrals provide a splendid setting for national events such as coronations, royal weddings and state funerals.

Cathedrals usually contain many precious works of art and beautiful furnishings. Many possess fine embroideries and metalwork, displayed in special rooms known as treasuries, or rare books and manuscripts kept in libraries.

In the Middle Ages, pilgrims used to flock to cathedrals because of the holy relics which they housed. Today cathedrals draw visitors from far beyond their diocese to marvel at their size and splendour.

All cathedrals have special choirs, and many have choir schools. With their vast spaces, they provide exciting concert halls for orchestras and musical performances.

▲ The bishop's throne in Canterbury Cathedral.

▲ Over 70 of the 176 stained glass windows at Chartres were paid for by local guilds of craftsmen. This window shows stonemasons at work on the statue of a saint.

▼ The spectacular Crystal Cathedral in California is a 20th-century 'television cathedral'. Viewers donated the $20 million needed to build it, and the cathedral's dramatic star-shaped design provides a perfect stage for televised services.

Catholics

▲ A church has existed in Chartres, France, since Roman times. Several times it was damaged by fire and rebuilt more splendidly than ever. The present cathedral was begun in 1194 and built in the Gothic style of architecture. Local people hauled carts full of building materials up the steep hill to the cathedral site, and the tradesmen's guilds made generous contributions to the cost of the great building.

See also
Christians
Churches
Gothic architecture
Middle Ages (Lincoln Cathedral)
Normans (Durham Cathedral)
Renaissance (Florence Cathedral)

The great age of cathedral building

Many cathedrals in Europe were constructed during the Middle Ages. In the space of just over three centuries, between about 1150 and 1500, these enormous, elaborate, expensive structures in the Gothic style were created in cities throughout Europe. They were designed and supervised by brilliant master masons, the architects of the time. The building process sometimes continued for over 100 years.

Cathedrals are still being built, especially in North and South America, and today's architects face the challenge of creating inspiring buildings which fulfil all the traditional roles of a cathedral. ■

Christians use creeds which say that the Christian Church is catholic. The word 'catholic' here means universal, belonging to all times and places. This is the ideal for all Christians.

The most common use of the word catholic, however, is for members of the Roman Catholic Church as distinct from other Christians. It is called Roman because it has its headquarters in the Vatican City in Rome, Italy. The bishop of Rome, the Pope, is its leader. Roman Catholics believe he is God's representative on Earth. The Catholic Church was the only form of Christianity in western Europe until the Protestants broke away at the Reformation. In Russia, Greece and eastern Europe the Orthodox Church had rejected the Pope's authority by 1054.

There are more members of the Roman Catholic Church than of any other Christian denomination. It has members all over the world. Each local church has a priest, who is usually called 'Father'. Roman Catholic priests are not allowed to marry. This means that they can give all their time and interest to the people. There are also many Catholic monks and nuns.

Like all other Christians, Catholics are part of a worldwide family and at least once a week on Sunday the members of a local church get together for worship and celebration. This ceremony is called the Mass. The priest blesses and shares bread and wine with the people. He reminds them of the real presence of Christ in the bread and wine, his body and his blood. They remember and feel they share the last supper Jesus had with his friends and become part of his life in the world.

Catholic churches are often decorated with paintings and statues to help people remember the saints in Christian history. ■

Roman Catholics live all over the world. They are the majority of Christians in these countries: Austria, Czechoslovakia, France, the Irish Republic, Italy, Poland, Portugal, Spain, parts of southern Germany, the Philippines and in all the countries of Latin America.

Cardinals are the most senior priests in the Roman Catholic Church. They are advisers and assistants to the Pope and they elect each new Pope.

An **archbishop** is a chief bishop of a province.

A **bishop** is a priest who is in charge of a diocese and has his headquarters at a cathedral.

In the Church of England (Anglican Church) there are bishops and archbishops but no cardinals.

See also
Christians
Churches
Festivals
Monasteries
Pilgrimages
Popes
Reformation
Saints
Vatican

Cats

Cats are among our favourite pets. They were first tamed by the ancient Egyptians at least 3,500 years ago. Now there are many breeds of domestic cat, which people have taken all over the world. They may look very different from each other. Some, such as the Persian cat, have long, fluffy hair and a short face. Others, such as the Siamese cat, have short, smooth fur and a long face and long legs. Domestic cats vary greatly in colour. They may be black, grey, white or various shades of brown, or a mixture of these colours. Their eyes may be golden, green or blue. Yet all kinds of pet cats can breed together. This shows that they all belong to the same kind (species) of animal and have all descended from the same wild ancestor.

Care of pet cats

Cats are more independent than most other domestic animals. Even so, they must be fed twice a day on high protein food, for cats need more meat in their diet than most other animals. They usually like to drink milk, but they must

Distribution
Wild members of the cat family are found in all of the continents except for Oceania and Antarctica. They do not occur on some islands.

Largest
Siberian tiger, which measures up to 2·8 m head and body length plus 95 cm tail length. Males may weigh as much as 360 kg.

Other great cats
Lion, leopard, jaguar, snow leopard, cheetah. These cats roar, but they have a throat structure which prevents them from purring except when breathing out.

Smallest
Black-footed cat of South Africa. This has a head and body length of not more than 50 cm and a tail length up to 20 cm. It may weigh as little as 1·5 kg, never more than 2·7 kg.

Other small cats
European wild cat, Pallas's cat, serval, marbled cat, golden cat, margay, fishing cat, jaguarundi, lynx, cougar. These cats do not roar, but can purr when breathing in as well as when breathing out.

Subphylum
Vertebrata
Class
Mammalia
Order
Carnivora
Family
Felidae

▶ Your cat behaves like its wild cat relatives. The garden is the jungle where it hunts. Its Latin name is *Felis sylvestris catus*.

See also
Cheetahs
Classification
Eyes
Flesh eaters
Leopards
Lions
Nocturnal animals
Teeth
Tigers

have water available as well. Although pet cats spend a great deal of time grooming themselves, they need to be brushed to get rid of any loose hair. This is particularly important in the long-haired breeds, where the fur can get tangled or matted if it is not properly cared for. Pet cats should be protected against illness such as feline enteritis and cat flu. A yearly visit to the vet for injections against these diseases enables pets to survive far longer than their wild relatives.

The cat family

Pet cats are members of the cat family. This is a group of 37 species including the great cats such as the lion, and the small cats such as the ocelot. Whatever their size, it is easy to see that they are closely related to each other.

Hunting and feeding

All wild cats are hunters depending almost entirely on their kills for food. They all have lithe bodies and strong legs, for their method of hunting is to ambush their prey and then make a brief dash or pounce for the kill. Most cats are very fast over a short distance, but give up if their quarry runs for more than a few metres.

They have large, forward-looking eyes set in the front of the face. This gives them the ability to judge distances accurately as they leap onto prey. A cat's toes carry sharp claws. These are normally sheathed in the pads of the foot so that they are not blunted as the animal runs, but they can be pushed out to hold and tear food.

Many cats hunt at night and have large whiskers which help their sense of touch in the dark. ■

◀ Siberian lynx yawning, showing its 28 teeth (most cats have 30). The small front incisors are for ripping and the large canines for stabbing and tearing. Its back teeth act like scissor blades for slicing meat off the bone.

When it has made a kill a cat wastes no time in eating its meal. At the back of its mouth it has scissor-like teeth which it uses for slicing its food. Like most flesh eaters, cats swallow huge pieces of meat which they can digest easily. Usually they do not have to share their food, for apart from lions, cats live on their own. Most mark out and defend large territories, and avoid others of their own kind. Any group of cats in the wild is likely to be a mother and her cubs.

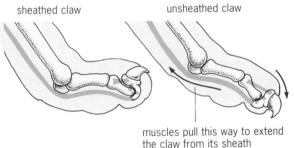

sheathed claw   unsheathed claw

muscles pull this way to extend the claw from its sheath

◀ A cat can retract its claws into sheaths in its paws so they are not worn and blunted when it walks. During an attack, strong muscles pull against the toe bones on which the claws grow, making them extend, like daggers, from their sheaths.

◀ Some cats, like this clouded leopard, live in cool parts of the world. They have beautiful dense soft fur. Cats have been hunted for their fur for many centuries, so that some species are now on the verge of extinction.

Cats' eyes

Cats' eyes are red where cars must not cross them. They are green for crossing, where a sliproad joins a motorway, for example.

See also
Roads

Cats' eyes are tiny rubber blocks set in the road, containing two specially shaped glass prisms. The prisms reflect the light from a car's headlamps back at the driver. It is much easier for drivers to follow the road at night or in fog when they can see a row of gleaming cats' eyes.

Cats' eyes were invented in 1934 by Percy Shaw, a motorist who was saved from an accident at night by seeing the gleaming eyes of a cat. Cats' eyes can blink! The rubber block is squashed every time a car drives over it. This makes the rubber wipe over the front of each prism and clean it. ■

Cattle

Distribution
Wild cattle south-east Asia
Domestic cattle worldwide
Size
About 1·8 m shoulder height; weight anything between 450 and 900 kg depending on breed
Number of young 1
A domestic cow may produce 5,735 litres of milk per year
Lifespan Over 20 years

Subphylum Vertebrata
Class Mammalia
Order Artiodactyla
Family Bovidae (cow family)
Number of species 5

▼ Wild cattle live in the forests of south-east Asia. This is a gaur, one of a species now very rare.

Cattle were originally wild, woodland animals. Few are left in the wild now, as their forests have been destroyed. The ancestor of almost all domestic cattle, the aurochs, became extinct in 1627. Wild species of cattle called the banteng and the gaur still survive in very small numbers in the forests of south-east Asia. In the wild the bull leads a group of about fifteen cows and their calves.

Cattle feed mostly during the daytime, each eating about 70 kg (150 lb) of grass, but they also browse on trees and shrubs. They are cud-chewing animals, which means they have complicated stomachs, made up of four parts. Grasses and other leaves are eaten, without much chewing, and swallowed into the rumen and reticulum where they are partly broken down (digested) by millions

of bacteria. The animal then 'chews the cud' by passing food back into its mouth and chewing it thoroughly. Chewed food is swallowed into the reticulum, then passes into the omasum and abomasum where more microbes complete digestion.

The bulls use their horns for defence, and domestic bulls can be quite dangerous animals. Cows also have horns, but are generally harmless, except when defending a calf. Domestic cattle are often dehorned, which makes them safer to deal with and less likely to damage each other.

Cattle were first domesticated about 8,000 years ago. Today there are about 200 breeds, which vary in size and colour. Some, such as the Jerseys, have been bred for the rich milk that they produce, and others for their meat and hides. Cattle are also used for pulling ploughs and heavy loads, and in some parts of the world their dried droppings are important as fuel. ■

▲ **Cows have complicated stomachs and their food is returned to the mouth to be chewed again after it has been swallowed.**

Cattle have cloven hooves, which means their hooves are divided into two toes. Deer, giraffes and camels are also cloven-hoofed.

Yaks are closely related to cows. Mongolians, Tibetans and other people of the high Himalayas keep them for wool, milk, meat and fuel, and to carry heavy loads.

See also
Antelopes
Bison
Buffalo
Deer
Domestication
Farming
Goats
Horns and antlers
Milk

Cavaliers

Cavalier was the nickname for Royalists, the people who fought for King Charles I in the English Civil War. It was a term of abuse used by their enemies, the Roundheads, who supported Parliament.

Cavalier comes from a Spanish word, *caballero*, which means a horseman or knight. Roundheads said that Cavaliers behaved like wild, cruel horsemen who stole and killed. But Cavaliers made the best of their name. Charles I said: 'The valour of Cavaliers hath honoured the name . . . it signifieth (means) no more than a gentleman serving his King on horseback.'

We may think of a Cavalier as a fine gentleman on a good horse, wearing a wide-brimmed hat, lace collar and cuffs, breeches and leather boots. Officers in the king's cavalry were usually rich men, and often looked like this. But not all Royalists wore such elaborate clothes, especially when they were fighting.

Many Cavaliers chose to fight for Charles I because they believed it was their duty to be loyal to the king, even though they did not always approve of the way he ruled.

Sir Edmund Verney was killed at the battle of Edgehill in 1642, fiercely defending the king's standard (flag). Before the battle, he told a friend that he thought King Charles ought to agree to the demands made by Parliament, but he could not betray the king because he had served him for 30 years and had eaten his bread and salt. ∎

Prince Rupert, son of Frederick V, the Elector Palatine and of Queen Elizabeth of Bohemia (Charles I's sister), joined the Cavaliers in 1642 and commanded the royal army.

See also
English Civil War
Roundheads
Stuart Britain

Biography
Charles I

Cavalry

Over the centuries, many soldiers have ridden horses to get from place to place. Cavalry are soldiers who actually fight on horseback. Before the days of motor vehicles, cavalry were the only mobile force a general could use.

The fierce tribesmen of central Asia, who spent most of their lives in the saddle, were among the earliest effective cavalry. From them, warriors such as Cyrus, King of Persia 2,500 years ago, learned the art of mounted warfare. In the hilly country of ancient Greece cavalry were of little use, but the Greek king Alexander the Great made good use of cavalry when he began conquering lands in Asia where there were wide, flat plains to charge over. The stirrup came into use from about the 3rd century and this made riding much easier.

In the Middle Ages knights in armour used to fight on horseback. But the weight of their armour made them anything but mobile. Cavalry came back into their own when heavy armour was discarded in the 16th century.

Cavalry horses had a very rough life. A troop of cavalry was always accompanied into battle by farriers, carrying gleaming axes. Their sad task was to put any seriously wounded horses out of their misery.

The great days of cavalry lasted until World War I, and a few cavalry units fought in the Soviet army during World War II. Generals used their mounted soldiers along with infantry for different purposes during battles. For one thing, cavalry

were ideal for pursuing a beaten foe retreating in confusion. Cavalry were also used for reconnaissance or sudden, daring raids behind the enemy lines.

A cavalry charge was a thrilling but bloodthirsty event. Men and horses, spears levelled or swords flashing, thundered down on their opponents. Faced with a charge, many groups of infantry (foot-soldiers) broke and fled. But gradually the infantry learned how to resist a cavalry attack. They used pikes, very large spears, with their butts resting on the ground, to make a spiked 'fence' on which a charging horse would be impaled.

As guns were improved, it was possible to bring down horses and riders from a distance. Finally, the development of the machine-gun and the tank made it impossible to use cavalry.

Since World War II, armies have used cavalry only for ceremonial occasions. The old cavalry regiments, with their proud traditions, now ride into battle in tanks and other armoured vehicles. ∎

▲ Painting of the 6th Mounted Brigade of the British Army in action against the Ottoman Turks in Palestine, 13 November 1917, during World War I.

A famous cavalry charge was the Charge of the Light Brigade at the battle of Balaclava in 1854, during the Crimean War. Owing to a muddle over orders, the Light Brigade charged straight at a battery of Russian guns. Of the 670 officers and men, 159 were killed and 121 were wounded; 325 horses were killed.

See also
Armies
Armour
Crimean War
Knights
Tanks
Weapons

Cave paintings

▲ In 1940 some schoolboys discovered the most famous cave paintings of all in the woods of Lascaux in the Dordogne area of France. Deep in the cave they found walls covered with a range of animals. The photograph shows bulls and horses painted between 15,000 and 14,000 BC.

The prehistoric hunting peoples of Europe made paintings and engravings on walls of caves from about 30,000 to about 8000 BC. They also carved in bone, antler and stone. The most famous caves are in south-western France and northern Spain, but there are other examples in Europe, as far north as Russia. In Africa and Australia, artists were still painting on cave walls into more modern periods.

▶ Painting in a cave shelter at Tassili, Algeria. Paintings like these were carried out by artists from about 1000 BC. The people were cattle herders.

▶▶ Cave painting of dancing girls in Tassili, Algeria.

 See also
Archaeologists
Hunter-gatherers
Prehistoric people

European cave artists

It is difficult to be quite sure why these hunters took so much trouble to paint animals and people on the walls of caves. Although there are some examples of paintings in shallow cave shelters, most are deep inside the caves. Some paintings are so difficult to reach that they could not easily be seen at all. Some archaeologists believe that the paintings were a form of magic or religion to make the hunters successful. Often, though, the artists did not paint the animals they were hunting. The hunters at Lascaux lived on reindeer but they did not paint them.

Cave paintings worldwide

Hunters in other parts of the world painted caves or engraved pieces of bone. The Bushmen in South Africa and the Aborigines of Australia are famous for their art.

The illustrations for this article, showing people herding cattle and the two dancing girls, come from caves in the Sahara Desert, at Tassili in Algeria. There are paintings in the Sahara by hunting peoples from before 5000 BC right through to the 3rd century AD. ■

Caves

The most spectacular caves are found in areas with lots of limestone, such as northern Yugoslavia or the Mendip Hills in England. The rock is made up mainly of calcium carbonate, which dissolves in rainwater. Water seeps through cracks and joints in this permeable (porous) limestone and gradually widens them. Rivers, which disappear into the limestone and flow above the impermeable (non-porous) rock, also wear the limestone away, leaving large caves where stalactites and stalagmites then form. Many limestone caves have rivers running through them, or evidence of old river beds.

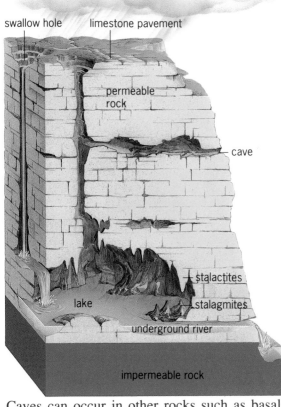

swallow hole   limestone pavement

permeable rock

cave

stalactites

stalagmites

lake

underground river

impermeable rock

Caves can occur in other rocks such as basalt (cooled lava). Liquid lava will flow like a river. The surface cools and hardens first. A tunnel or cave may be left when the lava underneath stops flowing. There are spectacular lava tunnels and caves in Hawaii. Sea caves are formed by pounding waves which hurl stones and rocks at the cliffs to form hollows. If the sea-level has changed, these caves may be high above the present beach. Weak parts of rocks that have been severely folded may be worn away to make caves. Small caves may be seen in central Australia, far away from the sea and from volcanoes or limestone. ■

Deepest cave
Réseau du Foillis, in the French Alps, 1,455 m deep.

Largest cavern
Sarawak Chamber, in Sarawak (East Malaysia), 700 m long, 300 m wide, 70 m high.

Biggest cave system
Mammoth Cave system, Kentucky, USA, with 345 km (214 miles) of caves and passages.

◄ A swallow hole is formed when water has made a tunnel deep down through the porous limestone rock. There are sometimes lakes in underground caves above the impermeable rock.

👁 **See also**
Erosion
Rocks
Stalactites and stalagmites

Celestial sphere

If you stand outside on a clear, dark night you can see lots of stars. Some are bright and some are faint but you cannot tell how far away they are. You could imagine that they are all on a big dome a very long way away. Centuries ago, people thought that the stars were on a huge crystal sphere around the Earth. They called this the celestial sphere. We now know that the stars are really scattered through space at different distances, but the best way to make a map of what the star patterns look like is on a globe.

The dome of the sky

Imagine travelling out into space until the Earth looks as small as the Moon. You can see there are stars all around and above and below you. Now you travel back to Earth. From the ground, you can see only half the stars you saw from space. Which stars you can see depends on where you land and varies from place to place. People who live south of the Equator, in Australia for instance, can see stars that are quite different from the ones people in Europe and North America can see.

Polaris (the Pole Star) always appears to keep the same position in the northern sky. It is almost exactly at the North Celestial Pole. There is no star bright enough to be seen at the South Celestial Pole.

▶ **People used to think that the stars lay on a huge sphere that turned slowly about the Earth. This was the 'celestial sphere'. We now know that the stars are at many different distances away, and it is the Earth which turns.**

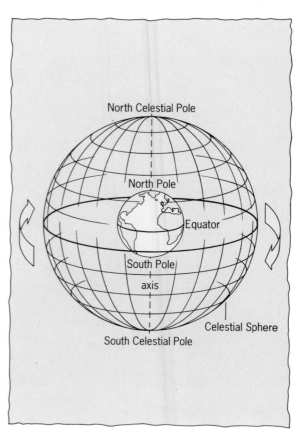

▶ **Star trails photographed near an observatory in Australia. The camera was kept still with its shutter open for several hours. The stars seem to move round the sky as the Earth spins.**

 See also

Constellations
Planets
Seasons
Stars

How the sky changes

We all notice that the Sun rises and sets. It is not so obvious that stars rise and set. Rising and setting happen because the Earth spins round once a day. One way to track the stars as they move across the sky is to take a photograph with the camera shutter left open for several hours. The stars make trails of light across the film. Some stars never set below the horizon but trace out complete circles in the sky. They are called circumpolar stars.

Another thing you might notice is that the stars you can see on a winter evening are not the same as the ones in the summer sky. The constellations change with the seasons. In fact, each star rises four minutes earlier every day.

Sometimes you can see bright planets or the Moon. They seem to move through the patterns of stars from night to night because they are very much closer to us than the stars. ■

Something to do

See if you can follow a star across the sky. Look through a window for a bright star and notice where it is over a building or trees. You could make a sketch and note the time. Stand in the same place an hour later and see how far that star has moved. Try again a few days later.

Cells

Cells are the tiny, living building blocks from which microbes, animals and plants are made. Microbes and some very simple plants and animals, such as amoebas, have only one cell. Most living things are made of large numbers of cells all grouped together. Your body is made up of billions of cells. Most of them are very small and can only be seen with a powerful microscope. A red blood cell, for instance, is only 0·007 mm (0·0003 in) across.

Cell structure

Most cells have the same basic parts. They are each surrounded by a cell membrane which holds them together. Inside this membrane the cell is divided into two parts: the nucleus and the cytoplasm. The nucleus contains the body's genes. The genes, which are made up of DNA, control the manufacture of protein. These, together with other chemicals, make all the substances in the body.

The cytoplasm surrounds the nucleus and contains a number of different cell 'organs' called organelles. These have a range of functions. Some, the mitochondria, enable the cell to combine glucose with oxygen to provide an energy supply for the cell (respiration). Others, called ribosomes, make proteins. They receive chemical messages from the DNA in the nucleus which tell them exactly which proteins to make. In plant cells green organelles called chloroplasts contain the substance chlorophyll. This traps sunlight energy, which the chloroplasts use to build sugars from carbon dioxide and water (photosynthesis).

Tissues

Groups of cells are called tissues. The cells that make up a tissue are of the same type. So, for instance, muscle tissue consists of cells packed with a bundle of protein fibres that can shorten (contract). Nerve tissue consists of cells with long thin nerve processes and a cell membrane that can transmit electrical nerve impulses.

Cell division

Cells reproduce by dividing in two. The genes in the cell's nucleus are linked together in long threads called chromosomes. When a cell is ready to divide each chromosome splits in two. Now the cell has two copies of its genes (DNA). The nucleus and the cytoplasm then divide in half, forming two new cells each with a complete copy of the cell's DNA. ■

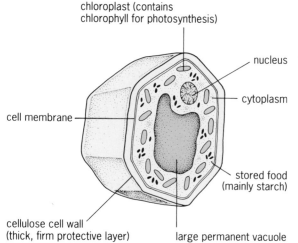

stored food (oil droplets and glycogen – animal starch)
nucleus
cytoplasm
cell membrane
small temporary vacuole

◄ A typical animal cell. Animal cells have a faint outline when seen under a microscope, because they are enclosed only in a thin cell membrane. The nucleus is often the only thing clearly visible inside the cell.

See also
Bacteria
DNA
Living things
Muscles
Nervous systems
Photosynthesis
Respiration

chloroplast (contains chlorophyll for photosynthesis)
nucleus
cytoplasm
cell membrane
stored food (mainly starch)
cellulose cell wall (thick, firm protective layer)
large permanent vacuole

◄ A typical plant cell. Plant cells are clearly visible under a microscope because they have a thick cellulose cell wall outside the much thinner cell membrane. Green chloroplasts, a nucleus and large vacuoles are clearly visible inside.

▼ Photograph of human heart muscle cells, many times enlarged.

▼ Photograph of human bone cells, many times enlarged.

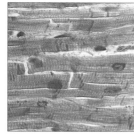
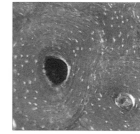

▼ Each chromosome splits in two to form a second set of chromosomes. The cell itself then divides in two and each new cell receives a full set of chromosomes. All human cells, except the sex cells, contain 46 chromosomes and divide in this way.

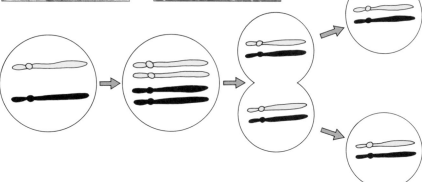

Celtic history

The Celts are an ancient European people. From about 500 BC the Greeks wrote about them as *Keltoi*. The Romans then called them *Galli*, 'Gauls' or 'Galatians'. We have to rely on what Greek and Roman writers said about them, for the pagan Celts themselves left no written records. This makes them seem rather mysterious, like a ghost people. But many Europeans are descended from the Celts. And Celtic place-names (such as London and Paris) and river-names (such as Rhine, Danube and Thames) are still very much in use.

► This bronze helmet was found in the River Thames by Waterloo Bridge, London. It is the only horned helmet that has survived in the whole of Europe. There are images of similar helmets carved in stone found in France and others shown on a cauldron from Denmark.

Conquest and defeat in Europe

The Celts' first homeland was probably in south Germany and western Czechoslovakia. They were warriors, farmers and traders, who used iron weapons to conquer more lands, and iron tools to farm them. By 400 BC Celtic tribes were settled in the British Isles, Spain, France and Italy. In 390 BC a Celtic army took and plundered the city of Rome. Fellow Celts were soon advancing into the Balkans, and about 276 BC a Celtic people even moved into Asia Minor (now Turkey).

It must have seemed, for a while, that the Celts would make all Europe their own. But they showed little interest in creating an empire, or in making a union of all their territories. And from about 200 BC, they rapidly lost ground: to the Germans in the north, the Dacians in the east and the Romans in the south. Roman armies led by Julius Caesar conquered the last great European realm of the Celts, in France. All this happened before Christ was born.

Celts in Britain

Celtic-speaking people started to come to Britain in about 700 BC. Tribes of invaders and settlers kept on migrating until the 1st century BC. They came from different parts of Europe, but they all shared the same culture. 'Their cities are the forests,' wrote the Greek historian Strabo, 'for they cut down trees, and fence in large circles of land. Inside, they build huts, and pen in their cattle for short periods.' These fortified places were usually on high ground, so we call them 'hillforts'.

Celtic survivors

Some of the tribes were more advanced than others. Their craftsmen made splendid works of art and traded goods with southern Europe. But each tribe had its own rulers and quite possibly its own gods. The tribes often fought each other, and did not join forces against the Roman invaders after AD 43. Many British Celts then became 'Romanized'. And, after the Roman

► This bronze mirror is decorated with abstract patterns that have been engraved onto the bronze. The other side is plain and would have been highly polished for reflection. No glass was then used in mirrors.

occupation, the new Anglo-Saxon settlers edged the Celts out too. Celtic culture did linger on in Cornwall, and the highlands of Wales and Scotland. It survived most strongly of all in Ireland.

Ireland was never invaded by the Romans or Saxons. It remained a Celtic country until the Vikings came, in the 9th century AD. So the Irish people went on speaking their Celtic or 'Goidelic' language. The modern form is Gaelic. ■

Celtic myths and legends

The Celts passed their myths and legends on by word of mouth. They avoided making statues or pictures of their gods, and did not write. Many people in Ireland, Scotland, Wales and Cornwall today tell the myths and legends, keeping them alive. The stories are about giants like Ysbadaden, who propped his eyelids open with pitchforks, wizards like Merlin, who helped King Arthur, and warriors like Geraint of Cornwall or Gawain of Wales.

Celtic gods and heroes

The Celtic people worshipped dozens of gods and spirits. Some gods were friendly; they looked after newborn babies, blessed crops and helped family life. Others were war-spirits, fierce and angry. The Celts believed that unless they were placated with warm blood before each battle, they would help the enemy. Celts also worshipped the Sun and Moon.

Celtic priests, called Druids, were skilled in making potions and medicines from plants. They told you a spell to say as you drank each potion. The spell was to make bad spirits leave you and good ones help you.

Cuchulain

The best-known Celtic hero is Cuchulain, 'the hound of Ulster'. He was an Irish prince, and his power was as dazzling as the rising Sun each morning. No human being could stand against him.

His enemies gathered an army from all Ireland to fight him, and he defeated them by a mixture of cunning, strength and battle-skill. It was not till the Morrigan (goddess of war) sided with his enemies, that Cuchulain was killed at last.

Other worlds

The Celtic people believed that this world was no more than a preparation for the next. After death, you began a second existence, in another world beyond mortal time and space. These worlds might lie anywhere: *Tir fo Thuinn*, 'Underwaves', was at the bottom of the sea; *Mag Mell*, 'Happiness field', was beyond the horizon; *Tir na nOc*, 'Land of youth', lay underground, and you reached it by pulling up a bulrush and slipping down the hole.

In these other worlds, there was no age, pain, hunger, want or cold. People spent their lives feasting, dancing and joking. In one of the lands, *Tir na nOc*, golden apples grew, and their presence gave immortality. Many Celtic folk tales tell of mortals who stumbled into other worlds by mistake, and returned to their earthly existence for ever changed. ∎

The *Mabinogion*, 'Tales', is a collection of stories from Celtic times. They were told hundreds of years ago in Wales. They tell of gods, giants, warriors, shape-changers and the lords and knights of King Arthur's court.

▲ Cuchulain, an Irish prince.

Some Celtic gods

The Dagda
His name means 'Father of all'. He was huge, pot-bellied and ugly. His club was so heavy that he dragged it behind him on a cart, and it made furrows the size of river-valleys. He owned a cauldron of plenty, and the whole world could feast from it without ever emptying it.

Lug
He was a shape-changer, a wizard able to take on any disguise he chose. He had every mortal skill, from harp-playing to stone-masonry, from poetry to fighting. He was armed with a spear and sling, and used them to make war on giants.

Macha, Morrigan, Badb
These three warrior-goddesses took part in battles. They were shape-changers, appearing as blinding mists, torrents, gadflies, wasps and wolves. If one of them took the form of a crow and perched on a warrior's head or shoulder, his death-hour had come.

⊙ See also
Arthur and his knights
Celtic history
Druids

Biography
Arthur

Cement

Cement is usually a soft material that can be used to stick two things together and which goes hard after a time. Paste, glue and solder are all cements. However, the name cement is most often used for the grey powder that builders mix with sand, gravel or crushed stone to make concrete.

How cement is made

Cement is made by grinding clay and limestone together. The mixture is then burned in a large oven or kiln. The burning is carried out at such high temperatures that the materials begin to melt. When they are cooled they form small lumps, called clinkers. These are ground to a fine grey powder. When mixed with water, this powder sets as hard as stone within a few hours. ■

See also
Concrete
Glue

Cemeteries

Cemeteries are places for burying the dead. The name 'cemetery' comes from a Greek word meaning a sleeping-place, and was first used by the early Christians in Roman times. People have set aside burial grounds for thousands of years. The name given to many ancient cemeteries is *necropolis*, which comes from a Greek term meaning 'city of the dead'.

At one time in Europe people were mostly buried in churchyards. Now the older churchyards are full, and cemeteries are generally provided by local authorities.

Most cemeteries have a chapel or other place where a short religious ceremony can be held. Many include crematoriums (places for burning bodies) and gardens of remembrance where the ashes are scattered.

Some countries have national cemeteries where members of the armed forces are buried. ■

Soldiers are generally buried on the field of battle where they fall. Many lie in mass graves, such as that at Waterloo, Belgium. After World War I 1,600 war cemeteries were dedicated and the dead were reburied there. Similar war graves exist for soldiers who fell in World War II.

US soldiers of World War II and the Korean War are buried in the National Memorial Cemetery of the Pacific, in Honolulu, Hawaii.

The United Nations maintains a cemetery at Pusan, Korea.

See also
Burial mounds
Churchyards
Funerals

Censorship

In wartime, governments appoint officials called censors whose duty is to read material that is to be broadcast or published, and delete anything that might help an enemy. Military censors do the same for letters written by members of the armed forces to make sure they give nothing away. Some governments apply censorship in peacetime in order to suppress political news and views from people who do not support them. ■

See also
Newspapers

Centipedes

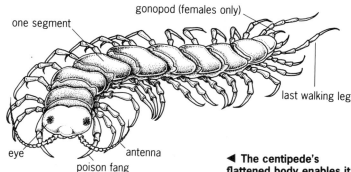

gonopod (females only)
one segment
last walking leg
eye
antenna
poison fang

The name centipede means 'hundred feet' though most centipedes have fewer than this. Many have as few as fifteen pairs of legs. Some have even less than this when they first hatch, but as they grow longer they develop more legs. Centipedes have been known to have up to 177 pairs of legs.

Centipedes' bodies are made up of a number of similar parts, called segments. Most of these have a single pair of legs. Centipedes have rather flat bodies, which enable them to squeeze through narrow spaces. They move fast, for they are hunters, tracking insects, grubs and worms which are their main food. They use poison fangs to overcome their prey.

Some tropical centipedes can give an unpleasant bite if they are handled, but most are entirely harmless to humans. ■

◄ The centipede's flattened body enables it to squeeze through narrow spaces in the soil or rotten wood. Its eyesight is poor, but its long antennae help it to track its prey. This is killed by poison from fangs formed from the first pair of legs.

Distribution
Worldwide
Smallest
About 5 mm in length
Largest
Over 30 cm in length. This species sometimes eats mice and lizards as well as insects.

Phylum
Arthropoda
Class
Chilopoda
Number of species
About 2,000

See also
Millipedes

Central African Republic

The Central African Republic is a country in the middle of Africa. The hot, rainy south contains large forests where timber is cut for export. The north has a long dry season from November to April. Grass covers most of this land. The country has many rivers and most transport is by boat.

More than 50 languages are spoken. Seven out of every ten people work the land growing such food crops as cassava, groundnuts, bananas, maize and sweet potatoes. Coffee, cotton and diamonds are the country's most valuable products, and the hardwood forests also provide timber for export.

France ruled the country from the 1890s until 1960, when it became an independent republic. ∎

Area 622,984 sq km (240,535 sq miles)
Capital Bangui
Population 2,775,000
Language French, Sango, Gbaya, Banda, others
Religion Traditional, Christian, Muslim
Government Republic
Currency
1 (CFA) franc = 100 centimes

◉ See also

Africa

Central heating

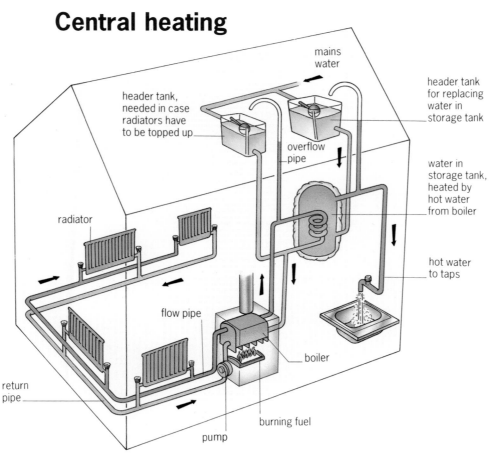

mains water

header tank, needed in case radiators have to be topped up

header tank for replacing water in storage tank

overflow pipe

water in storage tank, heated by hot water from boiler

radiator

hot water to taps

flow pipe

boiler

return pipe

burning fuel

pump

◀ A central heating system. Hot water from the boiler heats the radiators. It also heats the separate supply of water for the hot taps. The same water circulates through the boiler over and over again. This stops the boiler and its pipes scaling up like a kettle.

Central heating means that a whole building is heated by hot water or air from a single heat source. Most systems use water, because it is a very good material for storing and carrying heat. The water is heated in a boiler fuelled by gas, oil, electricity or solid fuel. It is circulated through radiators by an electric pump. The radiators heat the rooms. An adjustable valve at the base of each radiator controls the flow of hot water. The whole system is controlled by an electric timer. This automatically turns the heat on and off at the times you choose.

Hot water from the boiler is also used to heat the water for washing and baths. Some hot water from the boiler flows through a coiled tube in a storage tank. This heats the water in the tank, which is connected to the hot taps and shower. A pump is not needed for this purpose. Hot water rises naturally from the boiler. When it cools, it sinks back down to the boiler to be heated again. The same water circulates through the boiler over and over again. If fresh water were used each time, the system might scale up like a kettle. ∎

◉ See also

Houses
Insulation
Plumbing
Pumps

Cereals

Did you know that your main food is a type of grass? Since prehistoric times people have cultivated plants of the grass family to make what we now call cereals. The seeds are called grains. These are quite large and full of carbohydrate, which means that when they are cooked they can make a filling meal. They also contain some protein, vitamins and minerals and have plenty of fibre.

Cereals can be eaten whole or processed into flakes, such as those eaten at breakfast time in many countries, or they can be ground into flour to make bread, pasta, porridge and puddings. Different cereals grow in different parts of the world, depending on the climate and the soil conditions.

Wheat

Wheat is grown all over the world but it grows best in temperate areas. It needs moist cool days to start with, then dry sunny days for ripening and harvesting. Strong wheat, with a high protein content, is grown in North America and the USSR. It is good for making bread. Durum wheat is a special kind of strong wheat which is used to make semolina, couscous and pasta. Weak wheat, with a lower protein content, is grown in Europe.

There are almost 1,000 different varieties of wheat and wheat-like grasses known throughout the world.

Grains of wheat are tough and chewy, even when cooked, so most of it is processed in some way. In the Middle East the grains are soaked in water to make cracked wheat (bulgur or burgul). However, in most parts of the world wheat is ground or milled into flour.

Wheat flour contains a substance called gluten. When the flour is mixed with water, the gluten makes the dough elastic and allows leavened bread to rise.

Maize

In North America maize is usually called corn. It is the most important cereal crop grown in the USA and about three-quarters of the crop is cultivated in an area called the Corn Belt which is in the Midwest of the USA.

There are several thousand varieties of maize.

In Italy the thick, smooth porridge made of ground maize is called polenta. It is often served with a tomato sauce.

There are two main types of maize. One produces a head of large kernels known as sweet corn or corn on the cob. This is eaten fresh as a vegetable. The other produces smaller, more starchy grains. Maize contains fat as well as starch, and this is often extracted before the grains are ground into flour. It is used to make corn oil. Maize contains no gluten, so it cannot be used to make leavened bread.

Ground maize is used in East Africa and Italy to make a thick porridge which is served instead of potatoes or rice. In Mexico and South America it is made into flat pancake-like bread called tortillas. In Europe, North America and China it is used as a thickening and in cakes and biscuits.

Oats

Oats can grow in colder climates than wheat, rice or maize. Only the husk is removed in the milling, so oatmeal retains most of the fibre and all the nutrients of the grain. In northern Europe, ground or flaked oats are used to make porridge and oatcakes.

► maize

Rye

Rye also grows in colder climates where many other cereals will not survive. It is grown in Scandinavia, northern Germany and the USSR. Rye can be used in much the same way as wheat. Rye flour is usually whole grain and produces a darker and heavier bread than wheat.

Barley

This is another cereal which likes a cooler climate. In some northern countries whole grain barley is used instead of potatoes or rice. Polished or pearl barley is used in soup. Most barley, however, is either malted to use in making beer or whisky, or is fed to cattle.

Millet

Millet and sorghum are very similar cereals. They grow in drier and less fertile regions of the world. Both crops are very important in Africa because they grow very quickly in areas of drought. They can be used instead of rice, or be made into flour for porridge or unleavened bread.

Rice

Rice grows best in the warmer parts of the world. It is a very important cereal in Asia because farmers can raise two and in some places three crops a year. Over half the world's population eats rice as a staple food. In Bangladesh, Indonesia, India, Nepal and parts of China some people eat hardly anything else. Most rice is grown in flooded fields called paddies, but upland rice grows like any other cereal.

Wild rice is not really rice at all. It is the seed of a water plant which grows in the lakes of North America. It is rare and expensive.

Breakfast cereals

Ready-to-eat breakfast cereals are made mainly from corn, rice and wheat. Special machinery is used to blow up the grain for puffed wheat or rice crispies, to make flakes as in cornflakes, Weetabix and branflakes, or to make shredded products like shredded wheat. Some breakfast cereals such as shredded wheat use the whole grain and are therefore more nutritious than others like cornflakes which do not.

Flashback

The earliest cereals used for food by human beings were the seeds of grasses which grew in the Middle East. Prehistoric people gathered the seeds for food from about 10,000 BC. Perhaps about 1,000 years later, some people discovered that, if seeds were dried, they could be kept through the winter and planted the following year. As people moved, they took the seeds of the best plants with them and planted them in new lands. The best of these plants have become the cultivated crops of today. ■

◐ **See also**
Beer
Bread
Diets
Food
Grasses
Grasslands
Prehistoric people
Rice
Yeasts

First breakfast cereal
Shredded Wheat produced in 1893

First flaked cereal
Granose Flakes produced in 1895 from wheat

Cornflakes
First produced in the USA in 1898 by W. K. Kellogg

Muesli
Invented in Switzerland by Dr Bircher-Benner

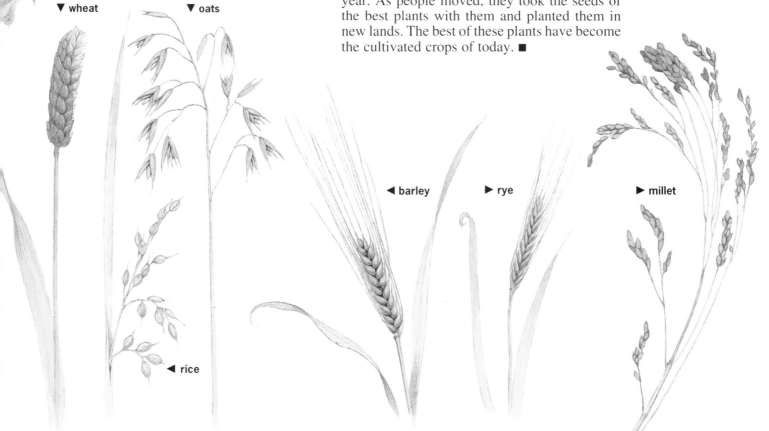

▼ wheat ▼ oats ◀ barley ▶ rye ▶ millet ◀ rice

Chad

See also
Africa   Arabs
African history Sahara

Chad, a large country in north-central Africa, is named after Lake Chad, which the country shares with Cameroon, Niger and Nigeria. Much of Chad lies in the burning hot Sahara. The south has enough rain for grasses and trees to grow.

Many northern people are Arabs, while most people in the south are black Africans. In dry areas, people rear livestock. Crops, such as cotton and groundnuts, are grown in the wetter south.

Around 1,200 years ago, Chad became part of the Kanem empire. Kanem grew rich by trading ivory and other goods with items from North Africa, Europe and Asia. France ruled Chad from the 1890s until it became independent in 1960. ∎

Area 1,284,000 sq km (495,750 sq miles)
Capital N'Djamena
Population 5,018,000
Language French, Sara, Arabic, Maba, others
Religion Muslim, Traditional, Christian
Government Republic
Currency 1 (CFA) franc = 100 centimes

Chamber music

▲ A string quartet at rehearsal.

Chamber music means 'room music', to be played in a room in a private house.

See also
Classical music
Musical instruments

Biography
Bach
Beethoven
Haydn
Mozart
Schubert

Chamber music is classical music for small groups of instruments. With such small numbers there is usually no need for a conductor. The musicians work together to create the right sound. Each player has a separate line of music or 'part', and the beauty of the music is in the interplay of sounds rather than the brilliance of any one solo part.

In the 16th and 17th centuries, richer families would often spend their evenings playing music. Early chamber music was written for such intimate musical occasions. In the 18th century, chamber music was often too difficult for amateur musicians. It was written to be played by professionals in a concert setting.

Duo or duet (two instruments). Usually for a wind instrument (such as a clarinet) or a string instrument (such as a violin or cello) with piano.

Examples are Beethoven's 'Spring' Sonata (violin and piano) and Poulenc's Sonata for Flute and Piano.

Trio (three instruments). A string trio is violin, viola and cello. A piano trio is piano, violin and cello.

Examples are Dvorak's 'Dumky' Trio and Ravel's Piano Trio.

Quartet (four instruments). The best-known kind is a string quartet: two violins, viola and cello.

Examples are Haydn's 'Emperor' Quartet and Beethoven's three 'Rasumovsky' Quartets (Opus 59).

Quintet (five instruments). A favourite kind of quintet is one wind instrument, or piano, plus a string quartet.

Examples are the Brahms Clarinet Quintet and Malcolm Arnold's Three Shanties for Wind Quintet.

Sextet (six instruments). Usually two violins, two violas and two cellos.

An example is Brahms's Sextet in G.

Septet (seven instruments). Usually a string quartet plus wind instruments, horn and/or piano.

An example is Beethoven's Septet.

Octet (eight instruments). This usually consists of string and wind instruments.

Examples are Schubert's Octet, and Mendelssohn's Octet (for double string quartet).

If there are more than nine players, the performers are usually called a 'chamber orchestra'. This has the same instruments as a large orchestra, but there is usually only one player for each line of music. Examples of music for chamber orchestra are *Siegfried Idyll* by Wagner and *Divertissement* by Ibert. ∎

Chameleons

Distribution
1 species in southern
Europe, the rest in Africa,
Madagascar and southern
Asia
Largest About 30 cm long

Subphylum Vertebrata
Class Reptilia
Order Squamata
Family Chamaeleontidae
Number of species 85

Chameleons are small lizards. In the wild they are hard to see, as they match their background amazingly well because they can change colour. In brilliant sunshine they are a rich green, whilst at night they become paler. Their colour changes are complex, and a frightened chameleon may turn pale, while an angry one goes a blackish green. If an enemy, such as a snake, should find it, a chameleon wraps its tail around a twig and clings tightly to it with its hands and feet.

A chameleon's eyes are like little turrets on the top of its head. Each eye can look in a different direction, and if one spots an insect, the lizard stalks its prey. It moves so slowly, rocking with each step, that it looks like a leaf stirring in the wind. When the prey can be brought into focus

with both eyes, the chameleon shoots out its sticky tongue, which is often nearly as long as the rest of its body, and pulls the insect into its mouth. ■

▲ **Three-horned chameleon catching a cricket using its long sticky tongue. It steadies itself on the branch with its prehensile (gripping) tail.**

See also
Camouflage
Lizards
Reptiles

Channel Islands

Languages
English, French,
Norman-French

The Channel Islands were part of the Duchy of Normandy at the time of the Norman conquest of England. The English kings later lost their lands in France but the Channel Islands remained attached to the English monarchy.

Four main islands make up the Channel Islands, which are in the English Channel just off the north-west coast of France. The largest island, Jersey (117 sq km, 45 sq miles) is about 20 km (12 miles) from the French coast. The islands are part of Britain but they have their own government. Many Channel Islanders speak both English and French, and many of the place names are French. The islands have a mild climate and are popular with tourists. Spring flowers, and vegetables such as tomatoes, are produced and exported to Britain and France. Most people live on Jersey and the second largest island, Guernsey. Alderney has a population of 2,000 most of whom live in the only village on the island. The island of Sark is just 5·5 sq km (2 sq miles) and the only transport is by horse and cart or tractor, because cars are not allowed. ■

See also
Normans

Charities

Charities are groups or institutions formed specially to provide help for people in need. Most charities help one particular group of people, such as children or the blind. Many rely for their funds on money given to them by the public.

In most countries there are laws which govern the way in which a charity can operate. In Britain, organizations which wish to become charities must register with the Charity Commission, which is a government department. There are laws about how they spend their money and keep their accounts.

There are over 165,000 charities registered in England and Wales. Legally each falls into one of these four categories: for the advancement of religion; for the advancement of education; for the relief of poverty; or for some other purpose that benefits the community. ■

Famous British charities
Age Concern
British Heart Foundation
Cancer Research Campaign
Childline
Christian Aid
Mind: the National
    Association of
    Mental Health
National Society for the
    Prevention of Cruelty to
    Children (NSPCC)
National Trust
Royal National Lifeboat
    Institution (RNLI)
Royal Society for the
    Prevention of Accidents
    (RoSPA)
Royal Society for the
    Prevention of Cruelty to
    Animals (RSPCA)
Royal Society for the
    Protection of Birds (RSPB)
St John Ambulance Brigade
    (St Andrew in Scotland)
Save the Children Fund
Spastics Society

See also
Aid agencies   Red Cross
Oxfam   Salvation Army

Chartists

The 1830s was a bad time for ordinary people in Britain. Wages were low and there was much unemployment. Only rich people had the vote; it seemed difficult to change things.

So a group of people in London drew up a 'Charter' of six points which would enable ordinary people to vote and to get into Parliament. Then they could make laws to improve their lives.

Some Chartists believed violence was the only way to make people listen to them. There was a serious riot when Welsh miners tried to capture Newport in 1839, and there was talk of a general strike.

Chartists organized three monster petitions to Parliament. The last one was in 1848, the year of revolutions in Europe. The government was frightened and employed 150,000 special policemen. They allowed a meeting in Kennington, London, but the Chartists had to take the petition to Parliament quietly in three taxi-cabs. It had two million signatures, but they included those of such unlikely people as Queen Victoria. The Chartists did not succeed. But five of the Chartists' six aims became law in Britain later. ■

The People's Charter 1838

1 A vote for every adult male, but not for women, criminals or mentally ill people.
2 Secret voting.
3 MPs should not have to own property.
4 MPs should be paid a salary.
5 Constituencies should be all the same size.
6 Elections for Parliament should be held every year.

All the Chartists' aims except the last one have been achieved.

Chartist leaders
William Lovett
Feargus O'Connor
Francis Place

See also
Parliaments
Poor Laws in Britain
Tolpuddle Martyrs
Trade unions
Victorian Britain

Cheese

Most cheese is made from cow's milk, but the milk of other animals such as sheep, goats, buffalo, camels, yaks and reindeer is also used. Making cheese was a way of using extra milk in the days before there were refrigerators to store it. Simple fresh cheeses are made by heating milk with lemon juice or vinegar. These acid liquids cause the particles of fat and protein in the milk to stick together and form curds (solids) which separate from the water or whey.

Hard cheeses such as Cheddar and mature soft cheeses such as Brie are made by adding rennet. The curds are cut, heated, drained and spooned into moulds. They may also be pressed. The cheeses are then left to ripen and mature for a few days, a few months or even a year. Each cheese has its own exact recipe which gives it its character.

Most cheese has a high fat content of around 40–50 per cent. Cheese is also a good source of protein and calcium as well as the vitamin B complex and vitamins A, D and E. A piece of cheese 5 cm x 3 cm x 2 cm will give the same amount of calcium as 10 slices of bread and nearly as much as ½ pint of milk. ■

In 16th-century Sweden the local vicar took the rent for the church pasture in the form of milk or fresh cheese. A Swedish cheese called Prästost, meaning parson's cheese, is a reminder of the old custom.

Rennet is an enzyme extracted from the stomach of a young calf or lamb. Plant rennets are sometimes used for vegetarian cheeses.

See also
Farming
Food
Milk
Nutrition

Cheetahs

Cheetahs are animals of the grassy plains and are now very rare. They hunt the smaller antelopes and the young of some larger ones. Cheetahs are the fastest moving of all mammals and often run down their prey with a tremendous burst of speed. A cheetah can sprint at about 96 km/h (60 mph) but only for a short time. An average chase lasts 20 seconds. A cheetah's claws are blunt, so it kills its prey by knocking it off balance and throttling it. This is very successful and about half of its chases end in a kill. ■

Distribution
Africa, south Asia, Middle East
Size
Head and body length 112–150 cm; tail length 60–80 cm; height at shoulder 70–90 cm
Weight 39–62 kg
Number of young
3–5 cubs
Lifespan
Up to 12 years in the wild

Subphylum Vertebrata
Class Mammalia
Order Carnivora
Family Felidae (cat family)
Number of species 1

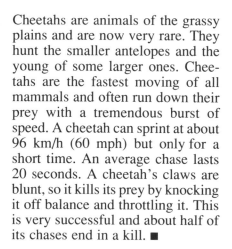

▶ Cubs must learn how to hunt. If they are taken from their mother before 15 months they are unable to make a kill even when strong enough to do so.

See also
Cats

Chemicals

When people talk about chemicals, they usually mean substances used in chemistry. There are thousands of these. Some, such as calcium and carbon, are solids, and some, such as sulphuric acid and ethanol, are liquids. Others, such as hydrogen and oxygen, are gases. When chemicals combine, they make new substances. For example, when hydrogen and oxygen combine, they make a brand new chemical called water. The whole world is made of substances on their own or combined with others. So really, every substance is a chemical.

The chemical industry gets its chemicals from many sources, including the sea, plants and rocks. Many of our most important chemicals are produced in factories from materials found in oil and coal. Chemicals have many uses. Some are medicines, some kill germs, while others stop food going bad. Some, called fertilizers, help plants to grow better. Others are needed to help make metals and plastics. ∎

Chemists

Chemists study all the different substances found in the world. They are interested in what things are made of and they do experiments to study how chemical substances behave under different conditions: when dissolved; when heated; when other chemicals such as acids and alkalis are added to them. Chemists also synthesize new substances such as plastics, fertilizers and medicines.

Organic chemists work with chemicals such as oil and plastics which contain carbon. Inorganic chemists study other chemicals such as alkalis and metals. Biochemists look at the chemical processes which go on in living things, such as the way food is digested in our bodies and set to work in different ways. ∎

Chess

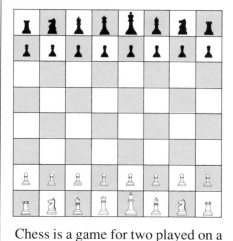

◀ This diagram shows how the pieces are placed on the board at the start of a game. White always moves first.

king

queen

bishop

rook

knight

pawn

Chess is a game for two played on a board of 64 squares. Each player has an army of sixteen black or white pieces with which to fight a battle.

Each of the pieces has its own special way of moving. For example a queen, which is the most powerful piece, may move any number of squares backwards or forwards, sideways or diagonally, in a straight line. All pieces except the kings can be captured.

The aim of the game is to trap the enemy king so that he is attacked and cannot escape. This is called 'checkmate'. The player who checkmates his opponent's king is the winner.

One of the skills of the game is moving the pieces to squares where they may be strong in attack or solid in defence. Another skill is in deciding on a plan of action for the battle. Yet another is in looking ahead and calculating sequences of moves.

Flashback

Nobody is sure when chess was first played. In ancient India they played the war game of 'chaturanga' on a board with pieces representing the king, his wise man, and the four sections of the army: elephants, chariots, horsemen and infantry. It is thought that this game was passed on by the Persians and Arabs, but the rules changed before the game arrived in Europe in the 8th century as the ancestor of today's game. ∎

Children

Childhood is the time when babyhood is over and you are not yet adult. How long you are thought to be a child depends on the society in which you live. The end of childhood is marked by the beginning of puberty. But in some cultures the end is set legally as the age at which you can vote in elections.

Growth or development

Childhood is a time of rapid growth. Fastest growth takes place during the first two years of life and again between 10 and 15 years for girls and from 12 to 17 years for boys. Growth and change take place in the brain too, so that children gain more and more control over their bodies as they get older.

▲ Young children often play on their own. By 4 years old they can already run, jump, and climb. Catching can be difficult unless a big ball is thrown slowly and straight into their hands.

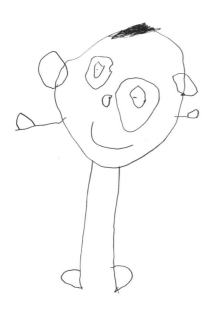

A portrait of Thomas by Thomas

▲ James is 5 years old. He can control a pencil but does not yet draw all the parts of his body in the right position. He draws what is important to him. He understands that by writing you can give messages. Sometimes he gets letters the wrong way round.

▲ Thomas is 11 years old. His self portrait is very detailed. All the body parts are shown in the right position. Younger children often draw the clothes after they draw the body so the body parts show through. Thomas's writing is well controlled. His letters are joined up, and are small and even.

Skills and ideas

Skills and ideas develop through learning, as your body and brain grow. You are able to control all kinds of movements more accurately. Language also develops rapidly. You are able to think about the future and plan and predict what may happen. Reading and writing are important skills you learn during childhood. Ideas about right and wrong develop through the example and teaching of adults.

Play

Playing is one of the main ways of exploring and learning about the world. In play you can practise and improve your skills. You can practise for real life situations by pretend play. Young children play alongside each other. As you get older you learn to play together, to take turns and share toys. You learn to sort out quarrels by talking things over and without fighting. Friends become very important and some children have a special friend.

Independence

Small children are dependent upon their parents, or other adults they know well, to make them feel safe and happy. In some countries older brothers and sisters or grandparents look after the younger children. By the time they reach their teens children need to become more independent. They have gained the confidence and experience to take some responsibility for themselves. They can go shopping, use public transport and arrange their own social life. Many enjoy going away from home on school trips or to stay with friends. It is still helpful to have caring adults to support and advise.

Children's rights

In 1959 all the countries then belonging to the United Nations agreed on the Declaration of the Rights of the Child. This states that all children have the right to love and understanding, to food, housing, medical care, education and play facilities so that they can grow and develop in a healthy way. Every child has the right to

▲ Older children can play together without adult help. They can concentrate and co-operate in games with complex rules. They can control the speed and direction of movement for dancing and running, and can judge distance and height for throwing and catching. Better balance means they can ride a bicycle or skate.

protection and those who are handicapped or orphaned should be given particular care.

In 1979 the United Nations set up a group to consider further the needs of children and to write a Convention. A Convention states what governments *must* do if they accept it. The Convention of the Rights of the Child was published in 1990. It extended the children's rights and set up a Committee to check that governments keep their agreement. Only 61 out of 159 countries in the United Nations have, so far, said that they intend to accept the Convention. Meanwhile millions of children all over the world still lack the basic rights of food, education and freedom from abuse.

These laws apply to children in England and Wales.

At 5 you must	go to school
	pay a child's fare on public transport
At 10 you can	go to a U or PG film alone
	be convicted of a crime
At 12 you can	buy a pet
	get a part-time job but for not more than two hours on schooldays and Sundays
At 14 you can	go inside a pub but not buy or drink alcohol
At 16 you can	get married with your parents' permission
	leave school
	get a full-time job
	buy fireworks
	have a licence to drive a moped
you must	pay full fare on public transport
At 17 you can	be sent to prison
	have a licence to drive a car
At 18 you can	vote

You are legally an adult.

Flashback

Till about 200 years ago, most children worked with the rest of the family in the fields or at home, as soon as they were old enough. Young children pulled up weeds, picked up stones to make the ground easy to plough, or scared birds away from the growing crops. They hardly ever went to school. Children in Europe who lived in towns often left home at about 7 years old, and went to live with a craftsman or shopkeeper. They worked for him and learnt his trade, and were called apprentices.

During the Industrial Revolution many families moved to the cities to find work in the new factories. Children worked for very long hours, near noisy, dusty and dangerous machinery. They were often unhealthy, and as they had little or no education, they had few chances to live better lives when they grew up. Gradually Parliament passed laws to stop children working in factories and mines, and to provide schools for all the nation's children.

Rich children

In the Middle Ages boys from noble families often left home early. They went to live in another noble household when they were about 7, to learn hunting and fighting skills, good manners, and, as time went on, reading and writing. From about 1450, schools were started for some of these boys. By the 19th century most boys from well-to-do homes went away to boarding school. Girls usually stayed at home to learn how to run a big house, and prepare for a good marriage.

Changing attitudes

It is difficult to find evidence to tell us what it was like to be a child at different times and in different places in the past. Certainly, till the last 50 years, most children were brought up more strictly than they are now. They had fewer chances to play, and were usually expected to be 'seen and not heard'; beating was a common punishment. Families were bigger, but many children died from disease, often before they were one year old. ■

Laws for England and Wales

1842
No child under 10 to work in a coal mine.

1870
Elementary schools were to be provided for all children between 5 and 10.

1880
Children had to attend school, or the parents would be fined.

1891
Parents no longer had to pay fees for elementary schools.

1899
School leaving age raised to 12.

1918
School leaving age raised to 14.

1947
School leaving age raised to 15.

1973
School leaving age raised to 16.

◄ Many children worked in coal mines in the early 19th century, as this picture drawn in 1842 shows. 'Trappers' could be only 5 years old. They sat alone in the dark all day, opening and shutting the ventilation doors for the 'hurriers'. These were older children who pushed heavy carts full of coal along the narrow winding passages of the mine.

Chile

Area 756,945 sq km
Capital Santiago
Population 12,074,000
Language Spanish
Religion Christian
Government Republic
Currency One Chilean peso
= 1,000 escudos

Chile is the longest country in the world, measured from north to south. Squeezed between the snow-covered Andes Mountains and the Pacific Ocean, it stretches down the west coast of South America. No person in Chile lives more than 400 km (250 miles) from the ocean.

You can find almost every kind of climate in Chile because the country extends from the hot tropics to within 850 km (530 miles) of the icy Antarctic continent. In the north is the Atacama Desert, the driest place on Earth. Some parts did not have rain for 400 years. The desert contains the world's largest deposits of copper and is rich in sodium nitrate, a salt used in explosives and fertilizers.

Most Chileans are descended from early Spanish settlers who married Indians. There are still more than 100,000 Araucanian Indians in Chile. Most of the people live in the central region and the capital Santiago is here. This is a green land of sunshine, farms and vineyards, but there are frequent earthquakes. Farther south, cold, damp forests fringe a wild and windy coastline. Chile proclaimed its independence from Spanish colonial rule in 1810. ∎

▲ A modern skyscraper stands next to the 400-year-old cathedral in Santiago in the city's main square, the Plaza de Armas.

See also
American Indians
Andes
South America
Spanish colonial history

Chimpanzees

▲ Chimpanzees safe in a sleeping nest made from springy branches.

Chimpanzees are apes closely related to human beings. Like us, they dislike being alone. Small groups travel together through the African forests looking for the fruit and leaves which are their main food. They may also eat insects and grubs, and some chimpanzees hunt young antelopes or monkeys, though meat is only a small part of their diet.

Chimpanzee language includes at least 24 sounds each with its special meaning. They also use gestures and facial expressions to give information, mainly about how they are feeling, to other members of the group. Chimpanzees use some tools, such as crumpled leaves as 'sponges' for collecting water, and twigs to 'fish' termites from their nests. At night they rest at a safe height above the ground in nests which are like springy mattresses made of branches.

The small groups of chimps often split up and change, for they are part of a much larger number, which forms a clan. These animals wander through an area of about 120 sq km (45 sq miles) of forest. They usually avoid the members of neighbouring clans. ∎

Distribution
Tropical rainforest in Central and West Africa
Size
Up to 1.7 m when standing upright
Weight
Males up to 80 kg; females smaller
Number of young 1

Subphylum Vertebrata
Class Mammalia
Order Primates
Number of species 2

See also
Apes
Evolution of people
Gibbons
Gorillas
Human beings
Monkeys
Orang-utans
Primates

Biography
Goodall

China

China is the third largest country in the world. It is about the same size as all the countries of Europe put together. Only Canada and the Soviet Union are larger. It has the world's largest population; over 1,000 million (one billion) people live there. This is about one-fifth of the population of the world.

The vast majority of the people who live in China speak Chinese, but there are many different dialects of the language and northerners and southerners cannot understand one another's speech. There are also 55 minority groups with their own languages, including Mongolian, Tibetan, Kazakh and Uighur.

China is still a rather poor country. It has so many people to feed, but much of its land is mountains or desert. North-east China is an important wheat-producing region, but winter temperatures can fall as low as –40°C (–40°F). Nomadic Mongols and Tibetans live in tents made of felt or animal hair and raise flocks of sheep on the north-western grassland plains.

Soft yellow dust, called loess, is carried south from the Gobi Desert by the strong Siberian winds, where it enriches the soil for cotton, tea and rice growing.

In the south the climate is tropical, hot and humid, which makes it possible to produce three harvests of rice there each year.

Area
9,596,961 sq km
(3,705,408 sq miles)
Capital
Beijing
Population
1,160,000,000
Language
Chinese, Manchu,
Mongolian, Uighur, Tibetan,
others
Religion
Confucian, Buddhist, Taoist,
Muslim
Government
Republic
Currency
1 yuan = 100 fen

◀ **Landscape in southern China.**

▼ **Many people move around the grasslands of Xinjiang in western China by horse.**

► The poster is encouraging people to have just one child, part of the effort to control China's massive population.

▼ China's land border is 22,800 km (14,160 miles) long and is shared with eleven other countries, as can be seen on the map.

Food, work, homes

Most Chinese live in the countryside and work on the land. They rise with the dawn. After a breakfast of rice-porridge with vegetables and steamed bread they work until nightfall. Lunch might be boiled rice with stir-fried vegetables and perhaps a little meat. Supper is often the same as breakfast or lunch. For eating they use a pair of wooden or plastic sticks, called chopsticks, which they hold in one hand and use to pick up pieces of food, or to scoop portions of rice into their mouths. The Chinese drink lots of green and black tea, without milk or sugar.

Many Chinese live in small houses or flats with only one or two rooms. They often have to

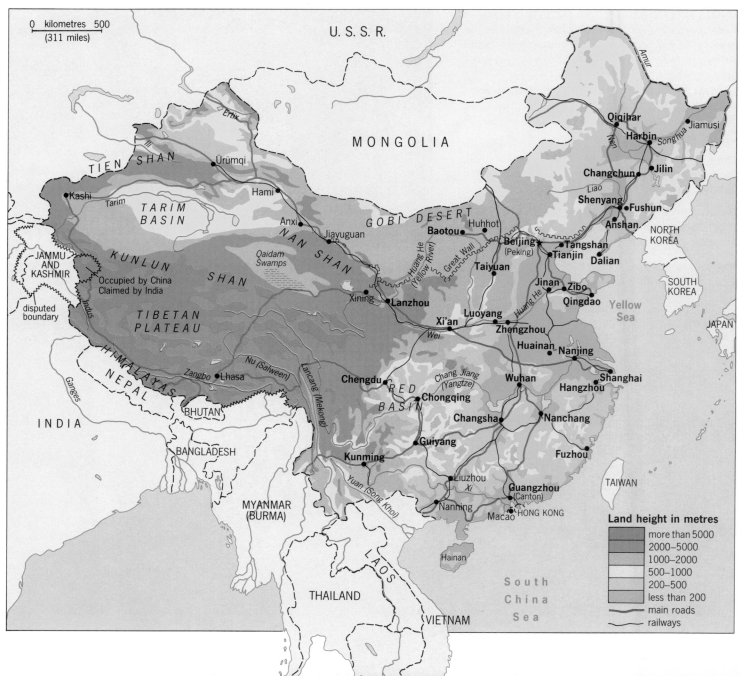

Land height in metres
- more than 5000
- 2000–2000
- 1000–2000
- 500–1000
- 200–500
- less than 200
- main roads
- railways

◀ A meal in Shanghai.

In the north, the capital Beijing (Peking) is a flat, dusty, drab city the size of London. At its centre is the fabulous Forbidden City, the former home of the Chinese emperors. Its magnificent halls, temples, houses, pavilions, pagodas and gardens can take a day to walk through. The buildings are roofed with exquisite golden yellow ceramic roof tiles, and the whole 'city' is enclosed inside a series of enormously thick and high walls. Today the Forbidden City is open to the public and has been renamed the Palace Museum.

share toilets and communal bath-houses with other families. In the countryside many still live without electricity in their homes and have no running water. It has to be collected from the village well or pump. Very few Chinese people own a car. They use public buses or trains. The fares are very low. More than half of all Chinese families own at least one bicycle.

Cities of China

There are several very large cities in China. Shanghai, for example, is bigger than London, Birmingham, Manchester and Liverpool all put together. It is a busy, noisy city full of bell-ringing cyclists and horn-blowing buses and trucks. It is not unusual to see elegant, traditional junks with their dark red sails, slipping past enormous, modern supertankers in Shanghai's thriving harbour.

▼ Part of the Forbidden City, Beijing.

As a developing country, China is keen to improve its agriculture, industry, education and defence. Foreigners are now encouraged to visit China, and Chinese specialists go abroad to learn new ways to tackle their problems. These contacts have made many Chinese anxious to make their country more free and democratic, which has led to disturbances in China. ∎

◀ Workers walk their bicycles across a bridge in Guangzhou (Canton), southern China.

China's history

China today is a republic ruled by the Communist Party. Between 1912 and 1949 it was a republic ruled by a nationalist government. For 2,000 years before that it was an empire, and even when the first empire was founded it carried on many traditions which went back another thousand years or more. No other country can trace its language, or its ways of life and traditions, over such a long period.

Dynasties	Starting date
Xia	about 2000 BC
Shang	about 1500 BC
Zhou	about 1030 BC
Qin	221 BC
Han	206 BC
Time of the three kingdoms	AD 220
Sui	581
Tang	618
Five dynasties	907
Song	960
Yuan	1260
Ming	1368
Qing (Manzhou)	1644
Nationalist Republic	1912
People's Republic	1949

Early times

Before 1912, the Chinese divided all their history into dynasties, the periods of time when the country was governed by rulers from the same family or group. A lot of what we know about the Xia dynasty comes from legends. The best-known stories are about Prince Yu, who struggled for many years to help his people stop the Huang He (Yellow River) from flooding their fields. We do not know if Yu was a real man, but the first Chinese farmers did live by the Huang He. Archaeologists have dug up their stone tools and the clay pots they used to store their main food which was millet (a kind of cereal). The Xia people also grew mulberry bushes for silkworms to feed on.

▶ The simple drawing for the word 'cart' changed over the centuries to the characters used for the word.

The Zhou, Qin and Han dynasties

The Chinese called their emperor the 'son of heaven' and described their country as the 'middle kingdom'. They believed that the people outside the middle kingdom were barbarians and the Zhou people built walls to keep them out. In 221 BC a man called Zheng gave himself the title 'The First Emperor' and started the Qin dynasty. He ordered 300,000 peasants to go to the north and join a series of walls into one, the Great Wall of China.

▶ Bronze tripod from the 7th century BC, made in the shape of a deer. People of the Shang and Zhou dynasties used such pots for cooking and storing food and drink used in religious ceremonies.

The Great Wall was made longer in the Han dynasty to protect the way to the silk road. Merchants from Arabia and Asia used this track to carry silk from China over mountains and deserts into the Roman empire. In the year AD 2 the Han emperors had a count of all the people in China. There were 59 million, more than in all the countries of the Roman empire.

Scholar gentry

The Han emperors needed hundreds of thousands of officials to rule so many people. They came from the scholar gentry. (Europeans later called them 'mandarins'.) A boy who wanted to join the scholar gentry had to study for years to read and write 40,000 characters of Chinese script. This way of writing went back to the Shang dynasty when priests had kept records on strips of bone. They wrote in columns and used a simple drawing for each word or idea. There was no alphabet to help spell out the words. Later the characters in the script became less like pictures.

cart

The scholar gentry had to pass examinations in books written in Zhou times by Kongzi (Confucius) and other men. He was a scholar who travelled about to teach the sons of noblemen how countries should be ruled. The ideas of Kongzi were wise rules about how people should live together and most Chinese believed they should follow them. Another group of teachers, the Taoists, believed that the wisest way was to live simply, in harmony with nature.

All Chinese gave great respect to the spirits of their ancestors, who they believed watched over their daily lives. Every family had a shrine for these spirits. Many Chinese also worshipped in Buddhist temples. Buddhism was originally an Indian religion which was brought to China in Han times.

Peasants' lives

Homes in a village courtyard were usually huts made of mud-bricks. In the cold north everyone slept on a *kang,* which was a brick platform heated by a stove. The main crops in the north were millet and wheat. In the warmer south, rice was grown in muddy paddy-fields.

Families lived in a group of houses arranged around a courtyard. One house was for the oldest people and others for their sons. A father chose his son's wife by making an arrangement with her father. The wife always came to live in her husband's household. In a peasant's household she had to obey all the men, do all the work in the house and help in the fields.

Most peasants had to pay rents to a landlord who owned the fields. The state officials collected taxes from them and ordered men to do work for the empire. Some would be sent for many years to guard the Great Wall against barbarians. Others would have to repair the roads or help in digging the huge canals which linked up north and south China. When life became too hard the peasants rebelled. Most dynasties came to an end because of a rebellion. This was an opportunity for 'barbarians' to try to get into China. It happened when horseback warriors from Mongolia broke through the wall and started the Yuan dynasty. An Italian merchant, Marco Polo, spent seventeen years at the court of the Yuan emperor, Kublai Khan, who was the first to put the capital in Beijing (Peking). After the Ming emperors turned out the Yuan in AD 1368 they built new palaces in a part of Beijing called the 'Forbidden City'. Only the emperor's family and top officials could enter. The 'sons of heaven' ruled China from this forbidden city until 1912.

◀ During the Ming and Qing dynasties young girls in rich families had their feet strapped so the bones were crushed. They grew up with tiny 'lily' feet which were thought to be beautiful. This practice continued well into the 20th century.

The last emperor

1905 Pu Yi born

1908 Made emperor

1912 Left dragon throne after revolution

1932–1945 Japanese made him emperor of Manchuria

1945 Captured by Russians

1950 Handed over to Chinese

1950–1959 In prison in China

1959–1967 Gardener and librarian in Beijing

1967 Death of Pu Yi

◀ The First Emperor's bodyguard. In 1974 archaeologists were excavating near the Huang He to uncover the capital city of the First Emperor, who died in 210 BC. They found a vast tomb with life-size models of 6,000 soldiers placed there to serve the emperor in the afterlife.

▶ Chinese sailors were using compasses made of lodestone, a magnetic rock, in the 1st century AD.

Inventions

1st century AD
Magnetic compass
Ship's stern rudder
Canal locks
Seismograph

2nd century
Paper

3rd century
Wheelbarrow

5th century
Horse-collar harness

6th century
Suspension bridge

9th century
Gunpowder

11th century
Movable type printing
Mechanical clock

Inventions

Paper was made in China, out of rope, tree bark and fishnets, as early as AD 105. It took more than 1,000 years for information about how to do this to reach Europe. Before then the Chinese had learned how to print on paper using a separate block for each character. (The first European to develop a printing press using movable type was Johann Gutenberg in Germany in the 15th century.) In the Song dynasty Chinese soldiers used gunpowder to set off rockets in bamboo tubes. Many other Chinese inventions made work easier for peasants in their fields or when they were building canals. China's sailors were the first to use compasses.

▼ The Chinese first made porcelain from fine white clays in Tang times. This dish was made in the 14th century.

Rich Chinese homes had plates and vases made of porcelain, pictures on silk, furniture painted in coloured lacquer (varnish) and patterned wallpaper. In the 18th century merchants brought these things back to sell to rich British people for their country houses. The Chinese said these merchants from Europe were a kind of barbarian or 'foreign devil'.

Foreign devils

The Portuguese were the first foreign devils to reach China by sea, in the early 16th century. Then Dutch and British trading ships came. The Chinese said they could build warehouses on the water's edge but not travel about through the country. Few Chinese could afford English-made goods and in any case they did not see the need for them.

The British began to smuggle opium, grown in poppy fields in India, to sell. The Chinese forbade this because opium was a drug which ruined the health of people who became addicted, and made a misery of the lives of their families. The British government supported their traders by sending warships and troops to force China to accept the opium. In the Opium War (1839–1842) British steamships sank the Chinese fleet of sailing vessels and soldiers occupied Shanghai in south China. The emperor was forced to hand over the island of Hong Kong to Britain and let her carry out trade there and in other ports.

This was the start of the 'opening of China'. Britain asked for more business rights, and France, Germany, Russia, Japan and the USA wanted the same. European traders and missionaries were eventually allowed to travel anywhere. They built railways and sent the money they made back home, and even collected taxes from the Chinese.

Worst of all, Europeans often treated the Chinese as an inferior people, good only for hard work as 'coolies'. In 1900 the anger of some Chinese was so great that they joined in attacks on Europeans, led by the Boxers, which was the European name for the Society of Harmonious Fists. Six European states and the USA and Japan sent troops to deal with the Boxers.

End of the empire

The Chinese often blamed their emperors for the misery caused by the foreign devils. They already hated the Qing rulers because they came from Manchuria in the far north, which the Chinese looked on more as a barbarian land than part of the true China. It was the Manzhou (Manchus) who made all Chinese men follow their custom of wearing pigtails.

On 10 October 1911 a revolution broke out overthrowing the Manzhou rule. China became a republic led by a president. But soon the country was divided among warlords whose armies fought each other.

◀ A painting showing soldiers on the Long March.

Chinese time
Years are reckoned in cycles of twelve years. Each has the name of an animal, such as a rat or dog. Each year has twelve or thirteen lunar months of 29 or 30 days. That means that New Year's day is different each year but is usually in January or February.

The Nationalists

In the south of China, Dr Sun Yixian (Sun Yat-sen) started the Guomindang (Nationalist) Party. He collected an army to fight the warlords, but then he died. His place was taken by General Jiang Jieshi (Chiang Kai-shek) who defeated the warlords and set up a Guomindang Government.

Jiang had been helped by peasants and trade unionists who followed the ideas of the Communist Party in Russia, which promised to make workers and peasants the most important people in the country. Communist agents had gone ahead of Jiang's armies to turn people against the warlords and their friends. After his victory, Jiang Jieshi feared that the communists would turn against him. He ordered his troops to massacre large numbers of their supporters in 1927.

Mao Zedong and the communists

A peasant's son called Mao Zedong escaped the massacre and helped peasants set up a Soviet in the middle of China, where they ruled themselves. Jiang Jieshi sent troops to attack them. Mao Zedong and the communists set off on their famous Long March to escape to the north through the high mountains in the west of China. Jiang Jieshi's armies and warplanes attacked them for most of the 9,600 km (6,000 miles). Many were killed, but even more died from the lack of food, the cold or sheer exhaustion. 100,000 people set out in 1934 and only 20,000 were alive a year later.

Between 1931 and 1945 Japan attacked and occupied parts of China. Jiang Jieshi's armies retreated, but the communists sent men and women to help fight the invaders. In 1945 Japan was beaten in World War II and had to leave China.

The armies of Mao Zedong and Jiang Jieshi then fought a civil war. Jiang lost and fled to the island of Taiwan. In 1949 Mao Zedong set up the People's Republic and a communist government ruled all China from Beijing.

The communists took away all the landowners' fields and gave them to communes where the whole village owned the land together. The government also took over all the factories, mines and banks and drove the foreign businessmen out of China.

Mao Zedong's government made important improvements in the way that the Chinese lived. Women had equal rights to men for the first time ever. Many diseases were wiped out. Children and adults were taught to read and a new simpler way of writing was used.

Mao Zedong died in 1976. The new leaders were still communists who tried to see that the Chinese people had more food to eat and more goods to buy in the shops. They welcomed foreign tourists and traders and no longer feared that foreign devils would harm China as they had in Manzhou times. But a movement led by students for greater democracy was brutally suppressed in 1989. ■

Writing Chinese in the Roman alphabet
Before 1956 Westerners used the Wade-Giles system. Today they use Pinyin which is closer to the sounds spoken by Chinese people.

Pinyin	Wade-Giles
Beijing	Peking
Mao Zedong	MaoTse-tung
Qin	Ch'in
Zhou	Chou
Guomindang	Kuomintang
Sun Yixian	Sun Yat-sen
Jiang Jieshi	Chiang Kai-shek

◉ See also
Buddhists
China
Confucians
Great Wall of China
Taoists
Writing systems
Biography
Deng Xiaoping
Jiang Jieshi
Kongzi
Mao Zedong
Polo
Sun Yixian
Zhou Enlai

Chivalry

Chivalry comes from an Old French word for horsemen. To begin with, it just meant all men who were knights. Later it was used to describe the way that Christian knights should behave. These rules of behaviour became known as the 'Code' of chivalry. Most agreed that a true knight should be brave, strong and a skilful fighter. He should be generous, kind and polite. He should protect the weak, be loyal to his lord and always serve God and the Church. The Code was meant to help to tame knights who terrorized the ordinary people of Europe in peacetime.

Many knights loved hearing stories of chivalry, like the ones about King Arthur and his Knights of the Round Table. But they did not always act in a chivalrous way in real life. Some historians none the less call the years from about 1100 to 1400 'The Age of Chivalry'. Even before it ended, most knights had stopped taking the Code seriously. Instead of serving God and protecting the weak, they busied themselves with tournaments or with fighting duels of honour. ∎

▶ These knights are jousting with long lances at a medieval tournament. The earliest tournaments were practice battles between two picked sides. They were rather like miniature wars, and men were often badly hurt. Jousting was more like a mock duel between individual champions.

See also

Arthur and his knights
Crusades
Heraldry
Knights

Chocolate

The slab of chocolate you may buy from a shop comes from cocoa (cacao) beans. So does the powder used to make drinking chocolate or cocoa, and the chocolate used in cooking.

Before chocolate can be made, the cocoa beans must be fermented. Whole cocoa pods containing the beans are stored in boxes or under leaves until the flesh begins to ferment. The beans are then dried in the sun and roasted until the shells fall away. The remains are called 'nibs'. These nibs are ground until the fat in them liquefies. The resulting dark liquid (cocoa mass) is heat-treated and then cooled in moulds or rolled into bars.

The main ingredients of dessert (plain) chocolate are cocoa mass and cocoa butter, which both come from the cocoa bean, and sugar. Milk chocolate has had powdered milk added. ∎

Dessert chocolate contains up to 40% fat and 50% sugar. It is often taken on expeditions, as it is a high energy food taking little space.

First factory-made slab of dessert chocolate
Produced by François Louis Cailler at Vevey in Switzerland in 1819.

▶ Cocoa beans are harvested and fermented before being shipped to a factory to be made into chocolate.

See also
Cocoa

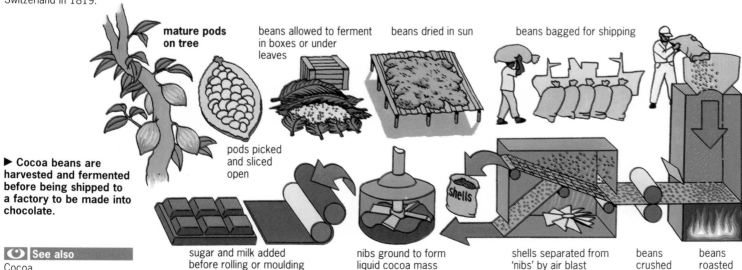

mature pods on tree

beans allowed to ferment in boxes or under leaves

beans dried in sun

beans bagged for shipping

pods picked and sliced open

sugar and milk added before rolling or moulding

nibs ground to form liquid cocoa mass

shells

shells separated from 'nibs' by air blast

beans crushed

beans roasted

Choirs

Choral singing is one of the simplest ways of making music. Over the centuries, men and women have sung together at work, at religious ceremonies, to entertain people and above all to enjoy themselves. Choirs can have over a thousand voices or as few as eight, but most have between 20 and 60 members.

Singing in unison and singing in parts

When members of a choir have voices of a similar pitch, such as choirs in primary schools, everyone sings the same line of music. Mixed choirs of men and women usually sing in harmony at the most suitable pitch for their voices. At the top are the sopranos (women) or trebles (boys), then come altos who are usually women, and the male voices, tenors and basses. In music scores the parts are often written with the initials as SATB, SSAATB and so on.

Ethnic choirs

In many parts of the world, including most of Asia and Africa, traditional music has not been written down, and modern choirs may sing the music of their own people as it has been sung for centuries. One common way is for one voice to lead and a larger group to sing an answering phrase, so that there is a kind of musical conversation going on, often telling a story. In the past this kind of singing was used for work songs or special occasions like weddings, but now choirs sing like this for entertainment. In Britain and the USA, gospel choirs give this kind of performance to Christian hymns and spirituals, often bringing in jazz and soul rhythms.

Church choirs

Singing has always been a way of bringing a religious message to the congregation. Some of the most beautiful and complex choral music has been written for highly trained church choirs in Christian cathedrals or abbeys. Choir schools provide musical training and an all-round education for musical boys and some girls, from the age of eight.

Chamber choirs

Many of the songs that we now sing were written by their composers for small groups of singers. Some of the earliest of these were madrigals, where four or more voices interweave in intricate rhythms and melodies, usually on the subjects

▲ A Ukrainian choir in concert, wearing national dress.

of love and war. Madrigals were first sung in Italy, but around the time of Queen Elizabeth I most English composers took time off from church music to write a set of madrigals. At the time, the home entertainment of most upper class households included playing and singing, and a visitor would be expected not just to listen to a madrigal but to join in, often with one person to a line of music. Today, madrigals are among the music sung by small choirs, which are often called chamber choirs.

Male voice choirs

Male voice choirs have been popular for centuries. In the Middle Ages, Scandinavian and German university students formed male voice choirs to sing drinking songs. In 18th-century Britain, men at glee clubs sang about drinking, feasting and flirtatious love. Many 19th-century composers including Schubert, Mendelssohn and Brahms gathered groups of their friends together and wrote songs for them to perform. In Wales at about the same time, male voice choirs established a high reputation for their performance of folk and religious music.

Choral societies

Choral singing was very popular in 19th-century Britain, especially in the industrial Midlands and the North. Most towns had their choral society, which could be anything from 50 to 500 in size. The societies performed locally, and competed in musical festivals and competitions which were largely devoted to choral works. The music included ambitious performances such as Handel's *Messiah* and Mendelssohn's *Elijah*, as well as folk music, sentimental ballads and songs by Gilbert and Sullivan. ■

Famous works for choirs

Madrigals
'Lasciate me morire' by Monteverdi, 'Now is the Month of Maying' by Morley, 'Draw on, Sweet Night' by Wilbye
18th century
B Minor Mass by Bach, *Messiah* by Handel, *Creation* by Haydn, *Requiem* by Mozart
19th century
Symphony No. 9 (Choral) by Beethoven, Requiem by Verdi
20th century
Dream of Gerontius by Elgar, *Belshazzar's Feast* by Walton, *Carmina Burana* by Carl Orff, *A Ceremony of Carols* and *War Requiem* by Britten

◉ See also

Singing and songs

Christians

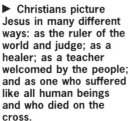

▶ **Christians picture Jesus in many different ways: as the ruler of the world and judge; as a healer; as a teacher welcomed by the people; and as one who suffered like all human beings and who died on the cross.**

1 Mosaic from Byzantine church, Istanbul
2 A statue of Christ is held on a donkey in the Palm Sunday procession, Peru.
3 Sculpture of the crucifixion, Ibadan, Nigeria
4 Painting of Jesus healing a blind man, India

The story of the birth of Jesus is told in the article on Christmas.

When Jesus was born, the Romans dated years from the legendary foundation of Rome (*ab urbe condita*). About 500 years after Jesus lived, Christian scholars worked out a new system counting from what they thought was the year of his birth. Their calculations were not accurate. Later historians realized that Jesus was born four years earlier. AD is short for *Anno Domini*, in the year of our Lord.

The Christian religion began with the life and teaching of Jesus. He was a Jew who lived in Palestine from about the year 4 BC to AD 29. Within a hundred years of his death, missionaries including St Paul had taken Christian teachings to many countries around the Mediterranean Sea. There are now Christians in most parts of the world.

Who was Jesus?

Jesus was born into the Jewish religion. Like many Jewish prophets before him he criticized the way some people were living, particularly those who were rich and powerful. Crowds came to hear him teach and see him perform miracles of healing. People began to say that he was more than a prophet. Many believed that he was the Jewish Messiah, called 'Christ' in the Greek language. This worried the Romans and those Jewish families such as the Sadducees who helped the Romans to rule. Many Jews thought that the Messiah would lead an army against foreign rule and oppression.

So the Romans and Sadducees arrested Jesus and the Romans decided to execute him on a cross. Christians believe that Jesus was a prophet and the expected Messiah, but they believe even more than that. They say that on the third day after he was crucified and buried he rose from the dead. He was able to do this because he was more than an ordinary human being; he was God himself who loved the world he had created so much that he came into it to live as a human

being and share human suffering. Christians believe that Jesus' death was a sacrifice for the wickedness of the world and that it helps people who want to love God to be closer to him.

The teaching of Jesus

Jesus taught through his own example of love for other people and self-sacrifice. Even as he was dying on the cross, he prayed to God to forgive the soldiers who had nailed him there. He encouraged his followers not to worry about food, clothes and homes, but to depend on God and care for one another. People can be part of a kingdom where God is the ruler. He rules like a loving father who asks his children to trust him. The sort of people who are happy in this kingdom are those who make peace, who know about sadness, who are gentle, who are poor and who are fair to others. This happiness begins on Earth but continues after death in heaven. Jesus talked about the kingdom of God in many parables. It has small beginnings, like a mustard seed which grows into a great tree. It is precious, like a pearl, and it involves celebration, like being given an invitation to a party. It also involves using what talents you have as well as you can.

Writing it down

The first written accounts of Christian belief are the letters Paul wrote to help groups of Christians in Corinth, Ephesus, Rome and other places around the Mediterranean Sea. The four gospels which record the events of Jesus' life and his teaching are named after Matthew, Mark, Luke and John and were written when the first generation of followers of Jesus was beginning to die out after about AD 65. Mark probably got a lot of his information from Peter, and Luke had travelled with Paul.

The spread of Christianity

The Acts of the Apostles tells the story of the spread of Christianity from Palestine, through parts of Greece and other Mediterranean lands to Rome. Gradually Christianity spread throughout the Roman empire. But the early Christians were harassed and persecuted for their beliefs. Some were even killed to amuse the Roman crowds. The first emperor to accept the teachings of Christ publicly was Constantine. In AD 313 he allowed Christianity to be recognized and persecution ended.

◄ Many Christians honour the memory of saints by pilgrimages or processions. This procession is in southern Italy.

▼ Baptism being celebrated in the sea in the Bahamas. John the Baptist baptized Jesus in the waters of a river and many Christians have continued the tradition of baptism in the sea, lakes or rivers.

Rome continued to be the headquarters of the Western churches and Constantinople (Byzantium, now Istanbul) became the centre for the Eastern Orthodox churches. It was Greek monks who took Christianity to Russia, where it became the official religion in 988.

There were Christian churches on the north coast of Africa, which was part of the Roman world, from at least the 2nd century. Hundreds of years later, from the 15th century, European traders and missionaries took Christianity into this vast continent where there are now many independent African churches.

In South America, Spanish and Portuguese soldiers and missionaries established Roman Catholic Christianity from the 16th century onwards. The Pilgrim Fathers took Protestant Christianity to North America in the 17th century.

The Christian way of life

Most Christians marry and have children; others believe that God wants them to be unmarried priests, monks and nuns. The most important thing for all Christians is to love God and to care for other people around them. Jesus is their example and they feel close to him when they feed the hungry, visit and heal the sick. When doubts arise about decisions to be made, they ask: would Jesus have done that, said that, behaved like that?

Christians try to study the Bible and learn to listen to God as well as talk to him through prayer, every day. On Sundays they usually go to church or chapel with other Christians because Sunday is the day of Jesus' resurrection.

In their services Christians remember the last supper which Jesus had with his friends, the twelve apostles, before he died.

The four gospels, the Acts of the Apostles and the Epistles of St Paul are found in the New Testament of the Bible.

One of the best guides to Jesus' teaching is found in St Matthew's Gospel, chapters 5–7. This is known as the Sermon on the Mount.

▼ A missionary teacher in Zimbabwe is instructing a group of children in the art of drumming.

▶ A Greek Orthodox bishop in rich vestments (clothes) in procession among his people at the liturgy.

This service of remembering and sharing in these events is called the Mass, Holy Communion, the Eucharist or the Lord's Supper. The main part of this worship is sharing bread and wine that has been blessed. This is one of the sacraments. Sacraments are outward actions which show an inner relationship with God. Baptism is another sacrament.

Christians celebrate many festivals linked with Jesus' life, such as Christmas (his birth) and Good Friday and Easter (his death and resurrection). They also go on pilgrimages to places connected with his life, such as Jerusalem and Bethlehem, and with the lives of Christian saints.

There are three main groups of Christians today. Eastern Orthodox Christians live mainly in the USSR, Greece, Romania and Bulgaria. Their history goes back in an unbroken line to the beginnings of Christianity. The ancient city of

▼ A Roman Catholic priest raises the host (the bread) at a celebration of Mass. Roman Catholics believe that Christ is present in the bread and wine.

▶ A Protestant pastor (minister) in Germany preaches the good news from the Bible to his congregation.

Constantinople was an important centre for them. Eastern and western forms of Christianity drifted apart for some centuries before there was a break in 1054 over the authority of the Pope and the exact words used in the creed.

The distinctive feature of the Orthodox churches is their colourful and majestic form of worship (the liturgy). Orthodox churches are full of icons, special pictures of Jesus, his mother Mary, or of a saint. People believe that these holy pictures have the power to do good and channel God's grace into the world. They are honoured by Orthodox Christians with candles and a kiss.

The Catholic Church was the official form of Christianity in the West from 1054 till the time of the Reformation. For most of the time its centre of authority has been the Vatican in Rome, where the Pope lives. For hundreds of years Catholics sang the Mass and said prayers in Latin because this was the language of educated people in western Europe. Today Roman Catholics use their everyday language for worship.

Protestants believe that at the time of the Reformation in the 16th century they returned to beliefs and a way of life closer to that of the Bible. They did this in protest at some practices of the Roman Catholic Church. There are now very many different kinds of Protestant churches and denominations because of their emphasis on individual interpretation and commitment rather than an acceptance of a traditional form of Christianity. ■

Christmas

Christmas is a Christian festival which celebrates the birth of Jesus. We do not know the date of his birth but most Christians hold the celebration on 25 December. Russian Orthodox Christians celebrate on 7 January. The whole 'season of Christmas' lasts from Advent (the coming), which starts four Sundays before Christmas, to Epiphany (showing Jesus to the wise men) on 6 January.

The story of Christmas

The story of the birth of Jesus is found in the gospels of Matthew and Luke in the New Testament of the Bible. His mother, Mary, and Joseph her husband had to travel to Bethlehem to be entered on the lists for paying taxes to the Romans. Bethlehem was crowded and there were no rooms in any of the inns (hotels) in the town. Mary and Joseph found a stable, which was either a shed or a cave used for cattle. Here Mary gave birth to Jesus. She used a feeding trough called a manger as his crib and he slept on a bed of hay.

Christians believe that Jesus was not an ordinary baby but the son of God who came into the world to help people. Many stories are told of the days after his birth. Angels visited shepherds looking after their sheep in the fields outside Bethlehem. They told them that someone who would save the people had been born nearby and that they should visit him. Wise men (magi) from the east saw a very bright star and followed it. It stopped over the stable in Bethlehem, and the magi gave to the baby gifts of gold, frankincense and myrrh. They believed that the star announced the birth of a very special person.

Christmas customs

Celebrations at Christmas are a mixture of Christian and pre-Christian activities. Extra eating and drinking and decorating houses with holly, mistletoe and evergreen trees are part of the way Europeans try to get through the darkest and coldest time of midwinter. Giving presents is a way of remembering that Jesus was a gift to the world.

Santa Claus

St Nicholas is the patron saint of children. He was a bishop who lived in the 4th century and has come to be known as Santa Claus or Father Christmas. His feast day of 6 December is a day for giving presents in many parts of Europe.

Carols and the crib

There are always special Christmas services in churches and chapels, when Christmas hymns called carols are sung. In the 13th century, Francis of Assisi made a kind of model of the stable where Jesus was born. Since that time, people have made a Christmas crib for their church with models of Jesus, Mary, Joseph, an ox, an ass and visiting shepherds and wise men. ■

◄ Children act out the story of Jesus' birth in a school nativity play.

The first **Christmas card** was made in England in 1843. The message read: 'Merry Christmas and a Happy New Year to You'.

The custom of decorating **Christmas trees** started in Germany. Prince Albert, husband of Queen Victoria, took the idea to England. German settlers in Pennsylvania in the 19th century took the custom to America.

Frankincense is a fragrant gum resin. It has been burnt since ancient times as an incense in religious services.

Myrrh is a gum used for incense and perfumes and to embalm the dead.

◄ A choir sings Christmas carols under a huge Christmas tree decorated with lights in Trafalgar Square, London.

Churches

The word 'church' originally meant a group of Christians in a particular place or the whole Christian family throughout the world. Now it also means a building specially designed for Christian worship.

A **cathedral** is the church where a bishop has his headquarters. An **abbey** is a church attached to a monastery. A **chapel** is the word used for some Protestant places of worship. Quakers use the term 'meeting-house'.

Christians can worship anywhere. Originally they met in each other's homes and many Christians still prefer 'house-churches'. The early Christians used the underground burial passages, called catacombs, in Rome when they were being persecuted by the Roman emperors. When persecution stopped, Christians began to build special places.

Styles of building

The style of many early churches was based on the Roman hall called a basilica. These had a rounded end called an apse. This style has continued to be used in some church buildings. Many Eastern Orthodox churches are in a style named after the city of Byzantium (Constantinople). Byzantine churches have a ground plan like a cross with four equal arms. They often have a

central dome in which there are mosaics or paintings of Jesus as ruler of the world. There are few windows and inside there is a special sense of being separate from ordinary life.

The most common shape for a church in the West is the Latin cross, where one arm is longer than the others. In the Middle Ages, churches and cathedrals were built in a style called Gothic. Gothic churches have tall pillars and pointed arches and are often decorated with elaborate carvings both inside and out. They may also have tall towers or spires which could be seen

▶ The Eastern Orthodox church of St Anna in Moscow. The gilded onion-shaped domes are found on Orthodox churches throughout Russia.

▲ Plan of a basilica.

▲ Plan of a Byzantine church.

▶ A modern church at Ronchamp, France. The famous architect, Le Corbusier, was inspired by the shape of the headdress worn by an order of nuns.

▼ The parish church in Burford, Oxfordshire, was built in the Gothic style in the Middle Ages.

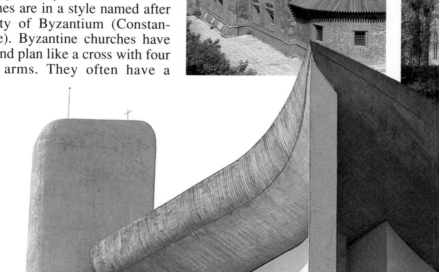

◄ This three-dimensional plan shows how the interior is arranged in most churches built in the Gothic or Classical styles.

choir stalls

pulpit

aisle

nave

lectern

chancel

altar

font

aisle

vestry

transept

for miles around when the church was the biggest building in a district. These spires reminded people of the presence of God. The tower often contained bells which told people the time and called them for services. The size and decoration of Gothic churches show the wealth and importance of Christianity at the time when they were built.

Today churches are built in many exciting new styles. The architect of the cathedral in Brasilia, Brazil, designed it in the shape of a crown of thorns, symbolizing the crucifixion of Jesus.

Inside a church

Some churches are dark and mysterious, with the kind of atmosphere in which people want to be on their own and pray quietly. Churches can also be light and airy and bustling with activity, places to meet friends and feel part of the Christian family.

Some Christians like statues and paintings in their churches; others prefer no decoration at all, except perhaps some fresh flowers. Eastern Orthodox churches have many specially painted pictures of saints called icons. These remind worshippers of Christians who have lived in God's way. In Roman Catholic churches, statues do the same.

The altar is the most important part of the Eastern Orthodox, Roman Catholic and Anglican churches. An altar is a special table where the priest or vicar re-enacts the last supper that Jesus had with his followers. In an Eastern Orthodox church the altar stands behind a screen of icons, at the eastern end of the church. In some Roman Catholic and Anglican churches, altars have been moved towards the middle of the church so that the priest and people can stand round it together as a family. The traditional position for the altar is at the east end.

For Protestants the most important part of the church is the pulpit. The minister stands there when he or she preaches and teaches the Bible to the people. Most churches have a font for baptisms; this might be a small one for babies or a larger one set in the floor for the total immersion of adults. In most Christian worship there is music and singing and there are often choir stalls and an organ. ■

The Normans built many churches with rounded, not pointed arches. The style is known as Romanesque, because it copied the style of the ancient Romans.

In the Renaissance, architects revived the style of the Romans and developed a fresh classical style.

See also

Bible
Cathedrals
Choirs
Christians
Gothic architecture
Icons
Mosaics
Normans
Renaissance
Worship

Biography
Le Corbusier
Wren

Churchyards

A churchyard is a Christian burial place, and is literally the yard or plot attached to a church. In the days before Christianity people used to bury their dead in sacred places, and indeed some European churches today stand on sites that were used for pagan religious worship. Many churchyards are older than their churches, which were formed around wooden preaching crosses set up by missionaries.

In the Middle Ages churchyards were used as meeting-places, as well as for burials. Fairs, markets, and court hearings were held there.

Old churchyards

The oldest graves in a churchyard are generally on the sunny south side of the church, which was built towards the north of the graveyard so that its shadow did not fall on the tombs. However, if the church was once part of a medieval monastery, the graveyard may be to the east or north of the church, the south side being a cloister. Some tombs are found inside a church. This custom began in the monasteries, where it was common to bury the founder or patron saint of the monastery inside the church.

The custom of burying people in holy ground around a church was taken by Europeans to other lands when they founded colonies there. In North America the oldest burial grounds were near farms and other settlements. Then when people were able to build churches, churchyard burials became common.

Many English churchyards have ancient yew trees growing in them. These sites were probably sacred groves in pre-Christian times. In Italy and other Mediterranean lands the common churchyard tree is the cypress, which was a symbol of death to the Romans.

A churchyard is often referred to as 'God's acre', a term that originated in Germany. The term 'the potter's field', however, strictly means a burial ground for strangers. It comes from the Bible story of the chief priests in Jerusalem, who used the 30 pieces of silver returned to them by Judas to buy the local potter's field for that purpose. The American West term 'boot hill' refers to the fact that many men were buried with their boots on.

Churchyards today

In England people still have a legal right to be buried in their nearest churchyard. However, many churchyards can no longer be used for burials because they are full. But years ago people were buried without coffins, and their remains quickly returned to dust. So new graves were dug on top of old ones. For this reason, many old churchyards stand 1–2 m (3–6 ft) above the floor-level of their churches.

You can learn a lot about local history from the tombstones in old churchyards. Some family names go back for generations. Many people are commemorated in verses, which often describe their occupation. ∎

Since the 14th century every church has had people whose job it is to look after the church and churchyard. These churchwardens are chosen, usually at Easter, by the minister of the church and the congregation.

In the American West men who 'were buried with their boots on' had usually died a sudden or violent death, possibly in a gunfight.

In the 19th century people became worried by the sanitation problems that might be caused if too many bodies were buried in churchyards. Cemeteries then began to be built away from churchyards.

▶ **This very well tended churchyard is in Norfolk in the east of England.**

◐ **See also**
Burial mounds
Cemeteries
Funerals

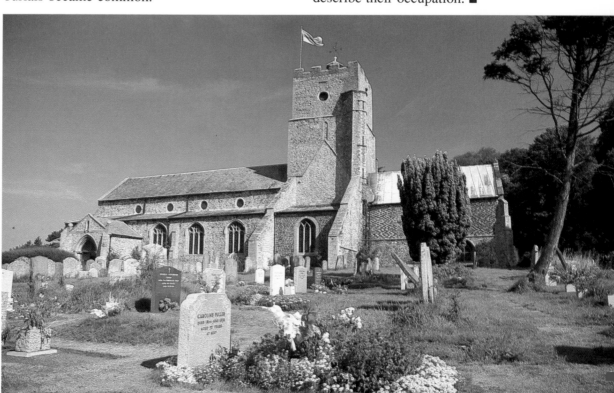

Circuses

◀ Acrobats on cycles at the Moscow state circus.

▲ Two clowns from a German circus.

A circus is a show. The audience sit around a circular space called the circus ring, where people perform tricks and feats of skill. There are jugglers, acrobats, trapeze artists, plate-spinners, tightrope-walkers, magicians, knife-throwers, fire-eaters, sword-swallowers, and many more. There are also some animal acts, such as performing horses.

Between more serious circus acts, clowns rush into the ring. Clowns dress in silly clothes and spiky wigs, and have grinning, made-up faces. Everything they do goes wrong. They trip over. They drive cars which fall to pieces. They try to decorate a wall, and cover each other with wallpaper paste. In a favourite trick, one clown chases another with a bucket of water. The clown being chased ducks as the other clown throws the water at him, and it seems as if people in the audience are going to get hit instead. But the bucket does not have water in it at all. It is full of confetti or paper flowers.

Many circuses in Britain and Europe are travelling shows. The circus ring and the audience are all housed in an enormous tent called the Big Top. The Big Top travels from place to place with the circus. There are not many large travel-ling circuses left in Britain, but in the USSR and eastern European countries circuses flourish and are housed in permanent buildings. In Moscow there is a world-famous school for training circus performers.

Flashback

Circuses began in ancient Rome. Some Roman circuses included feats of skill, like chariot racing. In others the audience went to see wild animals fight each other, or fight people armed with spears and nets. In the most bloodthirsty Roman circuses, human fighters, called gladiators, fought each other to the death.

The modern circus developed from the late 18th century when ex-sergeant-major Philip Astley began giving horse-riding displays in London. He opened an area called 'Astley's Royal Amphitheatre for the Arts'. There were soon similar shows elsewhere in England and Europe.

The really big circuses developed in America. Barnum and his partners opened their first show in Brooklyn in 1871. In 1880 they joined forces with the rival Bailey and Cooper circus to form Barnum and Bailey's Circus. ■

Circus is a Latin word, meaning ring or circle.

The character of the English clown was created by an actor called Joseph Grimaldi at the start of the 19th century. He invented the clown's costume of baggy trousers, wig, and big shoes. He was nicknamed Joey, which is why many clowns are still called Joey.

Cities

▶ You can see different parts of the city structure of Paris in this photograph: buildings of various sizes and heights, parks, roads and a bridge over the River Seine.

Metropolis and megalopolis
Sometimes the word 'metropolis' is used for a large city such as London. The London police force is called the Metropolitan Police. When cities grow into one another, as in the north-east of the USA, the word 'megalopolis' is used to describe the supercity.

A city is an important town where lots of people live and work. It is likely to be bigger than other towns and may have some things small towns do not have. Cathedrals, for example, are usually only found in cities.

People and transport

About one third of the world's people live in cities. Some cities have very large populations, including a few that have more than 10 million inhabitants. Most of the people work in the city but it can take them a long time to travel from home to work. Roads become so congested that traffic is very slow moving. To get round this problem some cities, including London, Paris, Prague, New York, Tokyo and Moscow, have underground trains (subways).

Buildings

All cities are built up. This means that most of the available space has to be used to provide homes, business premises and civic buildings including city halls, schools and hospitals. Space is saved by building very tall blocks called skyscrapers. These will tower above older buildings that may be centuries old. Many cities have a mixture of ancient and modern buildings because they have grown and developed over a very long time.

Structure

If you were to take a map of a city and colour in all the homes in one colour, all the shops another and so on for every different type of building, you would probably see a pattern. This pattern is called the structure of a city. For example, there are usually more houses and flats around the outside of a city than in the middle. The centre is often full of offices and shops, although there are also shops in among outer areas of housing. The main roads in and out of your city may show a pattern: leading to other cities, or avoiding high hills, for example. Factories may be together on one side, not in the centre.

Growth rates

Cities are always changing. Bus stops are moved, new shops may open, buildings are demolished and new ones built in their place. The number of people living in a city also changes. In many developing countries the cities are growing very

fast. But in Europe and North America, some cities are not growing at all. Some are even losing people.

Capital cities

Every country has a capital city. This is where the government of the country can be found. If you want to know the capital city of any country, just look up the name of the country in this encyclopedia and you can find it in the margin.

The capital city is often the most important in the country, with the most people and more businesses, shops, and factories than anywhere else. This is not always so, because some countries have built their capitals specially, such as Canberra in Australia and Brasilia in Brazil.

Mexico City: Population 12,932,116

Mexico City is the capital of the country of Mexico. More people live in Mexico City than in any other city in the world. It is very large and very crowded. The buses are often so full that some people have to hang on to the doors outside. Driving in Mexico City can be dangerous; many of the cars have had accidents. Air pollution is a serious problem in the city, because of exhausts from cars and buses, and also because of factories. The government has tried different ways of tackling the problem, for example by stopping people from using their cars one day a week. People can travel on electric trolley buses that don't produce exhaust fumes, or they can use the underground (the 'metro').

▲ This map shows all the cities in the world with a population of over one million people. The cities which are named have more than five million inhabitants.

The largest office building in the world is in Chicago, USA. The Sears, Roebuck and Company Headquarters there is over 400 metres high. The tallest building in the UK, the National Westminster Bank, is small by comparison, being only 180 metres high.

This is the estimated population of Mexico City under the city administration. The population of the city with the suburbs is about 18,748,000.

• 1–5 million inhabitants
● over 5 million inhabitants

On the metro, people can travel long distances between the places where they live and the places where they go to school or work. The trains are very quiet, because they run along wide, flat tracks on inflated rubber tyres. At weekends and on holidays, thousands of people leave the city to visit other places, yet Mexico has some beautiful spots and areas of historical interest.

▶ One of the many grand buildings in the centre of Mexico City.

There is a very big park called Chapultepec near the centre of the city, with a zoo that is free, pony rides and boating lakes where many people like to go. Around the Zócalo (central square) are some fine buildings in the Spanish colonial style. The cathedral here has sunk into the ground over the years, because the city was built on seven lakes. Only one now has water in it. It is called Xochimilco, and is a favourite place for Sunday afternoon picnics where boats decorated with flowers are paddled about, some selling maize to eat, others carrying bands playing music. Aztec ruins have been uncovered next to the cathedral, and to the north of the city are spectacular temples and pyramids which are over 1,000 years old.

▶ Life is hard for this family living in the slums around Mexico City. This is their house. There are no toilets and no running water.

Planned cities

Sometimes governments decide to build a new city in a new place. Often these planned cities are built especially to be the capital. Brasilia, the capital of Brazil, was founded in 1960. Many of the modern buildings are for the government, but there is a new cathedral, the round roof of which is designed to look like Christ's crown of thorns. In the Central American country of Belize the capital was moved from Belize City on the Caribbean coast, inland to a new city called Belmopan. Belmopan was specially built to be the capital. One of the reasons for putting Belmopan away from the coast was because Belize City suffers from hurricanes.

▼ The planned city of Brasilia in Brazil.

São Paulo: Population 8,490,763

São Paulo is the largest city in Brazil but is not the capital (which is Brasilia). The city centre is modern and affluent, with skyscrapers, wide streets and spacious parks, but thousands of poor families live in the *cortiços* (slum areas) without running water and proper sewage systems. The city has grown very rapidly this century because of immigration from Italy, Germany, Japan as well as other parts of Brazil. The Paulistas (as residents are called) manufacture textiles, motor vehicles, clothing, footwear, plastics and other goods. These are exported, along with coffee and other agricultural produce through the Atlantic port of Santos.

Tokyo: Population 8,156,000

Tokyo, the capital of Japan, is on Honshu island, the largest of the islands which make up Japan. The Sumida River flows through the city and links with a network of canals. Marshy land around Tokyo Bay has been reclaimed. The transport system is very efficient and the city's flourishing industries use the most advanced technology.

The city was called Edo until 1868 when it was renamed Tokyo, meaning 'eastern capital'. In 1923 an earthquake and fire destroyed half the city. Tokyo was again severely damaged by bombs in World War II. As a result the majority of buildings are modern, but some fine Buddhist temples have survived.

Seoul: Population 9,645,932

Seoul is the capital of South Korea (the name Seoul means 'capital'). Most buildings in the centre have been put up since World War II, particularly the enormous stadium built for the 1988 Olympic Games. Seoul dominates the commercial, educational, industrial, and political life of South Korea, and includes one-fifth of the country's population.

Moscow: Population 8,967,000

Moscow, the largest city in Europe, is the capital of the USSR. It is also capital of Russia, one of the republics that make up the Soviet Union. The most famous part of the city is the Kremlin, which was originally a walled citadel. Here, surrounded by 15th-century walls are four cathedrals, several large palaces and the main government buildings. Beside the Kremlin is Red Square and the great 16th-century Cathedral of St Basil. Outside its historical centre Moscow is a modern city. There are wide avenues crossed by ring roads and lined with concrete blocks of apartments. The Moscow subway, opened in 1935, has splendid, spacious stations.

New York: Population 7,262,700

New York is the largest city of the USA but is not the capital (the centre of government is in Washington). It is built at the mouth of the Hudson River, and extends across Manhattan Island, Long Island and the mainland. There are five boroughs : Manhattan, the Bronx, Queens, Brooklyn and Staten Island. New York is famous for the Statue of Liberty, its skyscrapers (especially the Empire State Building and the United Nations Building), Central Park, Wall Street (the financial centre), Broadway (theatres), and 5th Avenue (expensive shops). Dutch colonists bought Manhattan for $24 worth of trinkets in 1626 and named it New Amsterdam. The English seized it from the Dutch in 1664 and renamed it New York. The city expanded as immigrants arrived in the late 19th and early 20th centuries. Subways were built from 1904.

London: Population 6,770,000

London is the capital and largest city of the United Kingdom. It lies on the lower reaches of the River Thames, which led to Roman invaders settling there some 2,000 years ago. The area of the Roman settlement is now an international financial centre, known as The City. London has a thriving tourist industry, attracting visitors to the shops, theatres and museums in the West End; and to historic buildings such as Buckingham Palace, Westminster Abbey, St Paul's Cathedral, and the Tower of London. From about 1800 until World War II, London was the world's biggest city.

Jerusalem: Population 493,500

Jerusalem is the capital of the state of Israel. Most government departments are based there but the United Nations does not recognize it as Israel's capital. For twenty years from 1947 to 1967 it was divided between Israel and Jordan. Israel captured the whole city in 1967. Jerusalem is a holy city for Christians and Muslims as well as for Jews. The Muslim quarter of the Old City contains the shrine of the Dome of the Rock and the Mosque of al-Aksa. Close by is the Wailing Wall. This is the only remaining part of the Temple of Solomon and is sacred to Jews. Within the Christian quarter is the Via Dolorosa where Jesus is supposed to have carried the cross, and the Church of the Holy Sepulchre. ■

Large cities generally have two population figures. A smaller figure shows the number of people living in the area controlled by the city's local government. The figures used here are for the population under the city administration.

Metropolitan area populations are often used to decide which are the world's largest cities. It is very difficult to compile population figures that include the city plus its suburbs and parts of other towns that belong to the wider metropolitan area. Population of the metropolitan areas are approximately:

São Paulo 16,832,285
Tokyo 19,040,000
New York City 18,000,000

For London, there are no figures given for the metropolitan area.

Subways
London Underground has the most track (more than 400 km); New York has the most stations (466); and Moscow has the most passengers (more than 6 million a day).

See also
Hong Kong
Singapore
Town planning

Civilization

The word 'civilization' originally meant 'living in a city'. Today it means an advanced way of life, in which people have an organized government, good housing, fine public buildings, education and laws. They also have all the things such as music, dance, art, literature and religion which are described by the term 'culture'.

We also use 'civilization' to describe the way of life of a group of people. For example, 'Chinese civilization' means the culture and habits of the Chinese people. ∎

Civil rights

Civil comes from the Latin word *civis* meaning 'citizen', that is 'one who lives in a city'.

Every person ought to have certain rights: the right to own property, speak freely, not to be imprisoned without being charged with an offence, and to be treated fairly by other people. We call these rights civil rights.

In dictatorships, people do not have all these rights. In democratic countries, civil rights are set out in the law of the land. Britain's civil rights are laid down in the Bill of Rights of 1689. In the USA, civil rights are set out in the first ten amendments to the Constitution. But having things written down does not always mean that they are carried out. In many countries minority groups have to overcome prejudice and disadvantages to gain their rights.

In the USA, the Civil Rights Movement, led by people like Martin Luther King, tried to get laws passed in the 1960s which would guarantee the rights of black people.

In the 1970s and 1980s, many people in Eastern European countries began to demand their civil rights, such as freedom of speech and the right to start their own political parties. Charter 77 in Czechoslovakia was one such civil rights group. By the end of the 1980s these demands had become so powerful that a number of communist governments handed over power or were overthrown. ∎

◉ See also
Afro-Americans
American Constitution
Democracy
Dictators

Biography
King

Civil service

Governments are run by politicians who are usually elected by the public, but the politicians need people to carry on the daily work of running the country. These people belong to the civil service.

Civil servants do all sorts of jobs. Some work in government factories and offices; others do scientific research; and the highest civil servants help politicians to make important decisions about government policy. ∎

◉ See also
Government
Politicians

Clans

Clans are groups of people who claim to be related, and are led by a chief. The most famous clans are those of the Highlanders of Scotland, and the name comes from a word in the old Highland language, Gaelic. This word is *clann*, and it means 'children'.

Members of a Scottish clan often have the same surname as the name of the clan, such as Hay or MacDougall. Some clans have several different surnames.

Each Highland clan has its own tartan (cloth woven with a criss-cross pattern). The tartan is an essential part of Highland dress, which for men includes the kilt, a heavy pleated skirt.

The term clan is also used for similar groups of people in other parts of the world. In many clans, for example those within American Indian nations, members must not marry people in the same clan. ∎

◉ See also
Kinship

Mac means 'son'.

▼ Tartan is worn as an emblem of clan membership.

Classical music

The composer John Cage wanted to make people aware of the many different sounds going on around them, sounds that they normally would not notice. So in 1952 he wrote a piece of music called *4 minutes 33 seconds*, in which a pianist sat and played nothing at all.

To most people classical music means symphonies, chamber music, operas, and concertos. Writers of classical music include some of the most famous composers in history: people such as Bach, Mozart, Beethoven, and Schubert who lived and worked in the 18th and 19th centuries. But classical music can also mean any music that has a lasting quality. Some of the Beatles' songs are classics of their kind.

Classical music for orchestra

Symphonies are large-scale works for orchestra. They often have four contrasting sections, called movements. In a concerto, a soloist or small group of soloists show off their skill, with accompaniment from the orchestra. Suites were originally collections of dance pieces, but the name came to mean a series of contrasting movements.

Solo and chamber music

Solo music features one instrument. Often this is a keyboard instrument, usually the piano, which can accompany itself with chords and harmonies, but there are solo pieces for other instruments. Long works for a solo instrument, or for an instrument with piano accompaniment, are called sonatas. Chamber music is for small numbers of instrumental players. No one instrument is singled out; it is the interaction between the instruments that is important.

Songs, choral music, operas and oratorios

Schubert, Schumann and Brahms wrote some of the best classical songs.

Songs are for solo vocalists, often with accompaniment from a piano or other instruments. Choral music is for much larger groups of singers, called choruses or choirs. Operas are stories told entirely through music and acting. Oratorios are musical stories, usually on religious themes, but the singers do not act the stories out as in opera. Soloists and choirs sing oratorios. ■

See also
Ballet
Chamber music
Choirs
Composers
Concertos
Operas
Orchestras
Sonatas

Classics

This word has several different meanings. Thousands of books are published each year and most are quickly forgotten. Those special ones that survive, such as *Gulliver's Travels* and the novels of Jane Austen, for instance, are called classics. The classical languages are ancient Greek and Latin. They have survived even though they are not spoken by people today. 'Classics' can mean the study of Latin and Greek. Classical architecture, like St Paul's Cathedral in London, is the style that copies that of the ancient Greeks and Romans. ■

See also
Classical music
Greek ancient history
Roman ancient history

Classification

All over the world, people have always given names to the plants and animals that live around them. As they discovered more and more, they saw that some of these living things resembled each other in certain ways. So, ever since ancient times, human beings have tried to classify (group together) similar things.

Today, all biologists use a system of classification which puts together plants or animals that are similar in their structure. Each group is then assembled with others which are like it in some way. This was first suggested by an Englishman called John Ray, but the idea was perfected by a Swede, Carl von Linné, usually known today as Linnaeus.

Many people have tried to find other systems of classification for plants and animals, but the Linnaean system continues to be used, as it is so simple and so flexible that any new discovery can be fitted into the known pattern of life. The names are always latinized, since Latin was the language of scholars in the time of Linnaeus. An animal family name always ends with '-idae'; plant family names end with '-aceae'. ■

An example of classification

Kingdom *Animalia* includes all animals.
Phylum *Arthropoda* includes all invertebrate animals with an outer skeleton and jointed legs.
Class *Insecta* includes all insects.
Order *Coccinellidae* includes all of the ladybirds and their close relatives.
Genus *Coccinella* includes about 40 closely related species.
Species *Coccinella septempunctata* (the seven-spot ladybird)
The full species name always includes the generic (from genus) name, which is a bit like a surname and is always written with an initial capital letter, plus the specific name which is always written with an initial small letter.

See also
Animals
Libraries
Plants

Biography
Linnaeus

Climate

The climate of any place or region can be thought of as the yearly average of the daily weather. In Britain, for example, the weather often changes from day to day. This changeability of the weather is typical of Britain's climate. Other climates are much less changeable. A hot desert climate, for example, often has many days and weeks on end when the weather is hot, cloudless and sunny.

Elements of climate

When we talk about climate we use the words: temperature, rainfall, wind, pressure, humidity, cloud, sunshine, fog and many others. These are the elements that make up climate.

Tropical climates are the rainiest. The rainiest town on Earth is Cherrapunji, in India, with an average rainfall of 11,437 mm (450 in) a year. That is over 17 times the average rainfall of London. The hottest places in the world are in deserts. Timbuktu, in Mali, has an average annual temperature of 29°C (84°F).

The coldest climates are at the poles. The Siberian town of Verkhoyansk, inside the Arctic Circle, has an average annual temperature of –17 °C (1½°F).

Polar climates can be very harsh. In Antarctica winds of 145 km/h (90 mph) can blow continuously for 24 hours. When these winds pick up snow a 'whiteout' occurs, and it is possible to get lost even a few metres from camp. The poles are also very dry. Scientists think that it has not rained in the dry valleys of Antarctica for 2 million years.

Seasons

Another important part of climate is the way in which weather changes through the course of a year. Winter, when snow may fall, is of course colder than summer. In the northern hemisphere winter is at the end of the year, roughly from November to February in Britain, but these are the summer months in the southern hemisphere.

Towards the Equator the seasons are not cold and hot, but are often divided into a rainy season and a dry season. The climate of an area affects every part of the inhabitants' lives. Seasons are very important for crops, which need particular times of rain, sunshine and the right temperatures to grow well. ■

In the northern Sahara Desert a place called Al Aziziyah in Libya has recorded a temperature of 58°C (136°F).

The lowest temperature ever recorded at Verkhoyansk was –68°C (–90°F).

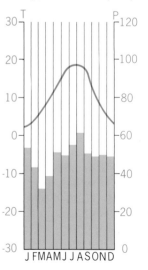

T:temperature (°C)   P:precipitation (mm)

Paris, France
Height 53 m

Alice Springs, Australia
Height 584 mm

Yellowknife, Canada
Height 208 m

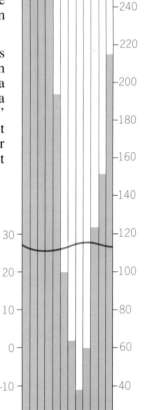

Manaus, Brazil
Height 44 m

Climbing

Climbing is the sport of climbing and exploring mountains, using the right methods and equipment. It began to catch on as a popular sport after the successful ascent of Mont Blanc in the late 18th century.

Two different kinds of climbing are rock and ice climbing. In both kinds, two or three people are usually roped together for safety. In rock climbing they look for secure places to put their feet and hands, keeping their bodies as far as possible away from the rock. They use iron spikes called 'pitons' which they hammer into cracks in the rocks. They then fasten a steel snap-link, called a 'carabiner', to the end of the piton. They thread a nylon rope through the carabiner, to hold them if they should fall.

In ice climbing they use special equipment such as ice axes, for cutting steps in the ice. They also use 'crampons'. These are steel frames with eight to twelve sharp spikes on them. Climbers strap them to their boots to give them a better grip on the ice.

Coming down a mountain, a climber 'abseils' over steep spots. This is a method of controlling the speed of descent by means of a rope looped round the body. ■

▲ A climber uses a tiny crack in the rock face to edge up the left wall of Cenotaph Corner, which overlooks Llanberis Pass in north Wales. This is one of the most famous climbs in Britain.

▶ Here you can see the safety rope attached to a harness around the climber's waist. Essential equipment, such as pitons and carabiners, is attached to the harness, leaving the hands free to seek out holds in the rock.

See also
Mountains

Biography
Bonington
Hillary
Tenzing

Clinics

◀ A mother bringing her baby to a public clinic in Zaïre.

Clinics are centres which people attend for medical treatment and advice. Nowadays, clinics often concentrate on preventing disease. Mothers expecting babies can go to clinics for advice on keeping healthy. Mothers with babies can go to 'well-baby' clinics that help them to prevent problems. In Britain and the USA, clinics often specialize in one or two things. In the USSR there are 'polyclinics' that deal with a whole range of treatments. In some countries such as Nigeria and India, mobile clinics are used to take medical services to rural areas.

A clinic can also mean teaching medicine at the bedside. Medical students must receive some 'clinical' teaching before they become doctors. 'Clinician' has become another word for a doctor who looks after patients in hospital.

Flashback

Clinics began in Britain in the 18th century as places where medical care was given as charity to poor people. The patients were not put in beds, but came in for treatment and then left, so they came to be known as 'out-patients'. Later, many clinics became hospital out-patient departments. ■

First clinic in the English-speaking world
The London Dispensary, founded 1696, to give medicines to the sick poor.

First antenatal clinic
Set up by A. Pinard at the Maternité Baudelocque in Paris in 1890 for pregnant women.

First health centres
Opened in 1910 in Pittsburgh and Wilkes-Barre, Pennsylvania, USA. These were multiple clinics offering a wide range of treatments.

World's most famous clinic
The Mayo Clinic in Rochester, Minnesota, a centre for diagnosing diseases.

See also
Doctors
Hospitals

Clocks and watches

Clocks and watches are used for telling the time. The mechanical sort with an hour hand and a minute hand were not made until the 17th century, but people have used timekeepers for many thousands of years.

The first clocks

Shadow sticks have been used since at least 3500 BC. The length and direction of the shadow cast by the Sun changes as the Sun moves through the sky. Sundials are a kind of shadow clock. You can read off the time by where the shadow falls on the dial. The stick that casts the shadow is called a 'gnomon'.

► On a sun-dial, the shadow changes position as the Sun moves across the sky. The position of the shadow tells you the time.

Water clocks (*clepsydras*) were used in Egypt from about 1400 BC. Time was measured by how long it took water to flow out of holes in a container. The Greeks and Romans made more complicated water clocks, like a cylinder into which water dripped from a reservoir. The time was read from a float.

Lamps, where the level of oil got lower as it burnt away steadily, and candles were used for centuries to tell the time. King Alfred the Great of Wessex is said to have used candles for timing in the 9th century.

Sand-glasses have been used from the Middle Ages. They are still often used as kitchen egg-timers. Large ones were made to time periods of half an hour or more.

Galileo discovered that a swinging pendulum keeps regular time, but only used it to make a little instrument for doctors to count a patient's pulse beats. His son, Vincent, was the first to try and make a pendulum clock.

The first successful pendulum clock was made in 1657 in The Hague on instructions from the scientist Huygens. It can be seen in a museum in Leiden, Holland.

◉ See also

Candles
Pendulums
Time

Biography
Hooke
Huygens

Mechanical clocks

The first mechanical clocks were made in the 14th century. They did not have hands or a dial but made an alarm ring every hour. Striking clocks started to be put in public places in large cities in Europe. Soon, smaller versions were made for homes. The time was kept by a heavy bar, pivoted at the middle, that swung to and fro.

Pendulum clocks were invented in the 17th century. They were more accurate, because a swinging pendulum keeps regular time. To start with, the pendulums were short. The first long-case ('grandfather') clocks were made in 1670.

► Modern watches can be bright, colourful and inexpensive. With electronics to make them work, they are also extremely accurate.

▼ 16th century sand-glass. Turned so that all the sand was in the top half, it would take 15 minutes for the sand to flow through to the bottom.

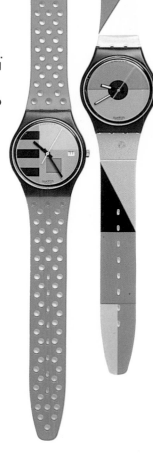

▲ Probably the oldest surviving working clock in the world is at Salisbury Cathedral in Wiltshire. It dates from 1386 and most of it is thought to be original. It has no face but signals the time by chimes.

Watches

Pocket watches became possible after the invention in about 1500 of the mainspring (a tightly wound coil) to give the power. Wristwatches started to get popular around 1900, when they were made mainly in France and Switzerland.

▼ Watches that use hands and a dial to show the time are called analogue watches. This watch is reading a quarter to four, or 3.45. When you look at the hands it is easy to see that there are fifteen minutes to go before four o'clock.

▼ Watches that use numbers to show the time are called digital watches. They keep time very accurately. This watch is also reading 3.45, but you cannot see at a glance how long it is until four o'clock. You have to work it out.

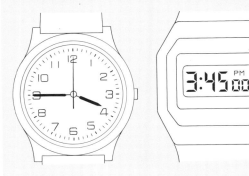

Modern clocks and watches

Mechanical clocks get their power from a weight that slowly falls or a spring that has to be wound up from time to time. In the 19th century, clocks driven by electric power were first made and by 1918 they could use the signal from mains electricity to keep time.

Today, many clocks and watches use the natural vibrations, 100,000 times per second, in a quartz crystal to keep time and their power comes from batteries. Even a small watch can be like a tiny computer, with a built-in alarm and stop-watch and the time shown by a digital (that is, in numbers) electronic display.

Famous clockmakers

Thomas Tompion (1638–1713) was renowned for the quality and accuracy of the clocks and watches he made. He made the first watch with a balance spring to keep time, an idea invented by the scientist Robert Hooke.

John Harrison (1693–1776) took up the challenge of making a chronometer, a particularly precise clock, that would keep accurate time on long sea journeys. Such a clock was desperately needed to help mariners navigate. In 1772 he was awarded a £20,000 prize as the first successful maker of a chronometer. ■

The first electric clock was invented in 1843 by Alexander Bain, but it was not very reliable.

Atomic hydrogen masers are the most accurate timekeepers. They are accurate to within one second in 1,700,000 years.

Clones

A clone is a group of organisms which are exactly the same as each other and their parents; that is, they have the same genes. Clones are more common in plants than animals. When a new variety of rose is bred, the grower needs to produce a large number of identical plants. He can do this by taking cuttings. When they grow into new plants they are clones of the original plant.

In England elm trees were very common because new plants called suckers readily grew from the roots of the parent tree. Botanists think that most English elms came from one or two parent plants. These had little resistance to Dutch elm disease and as the plants in a clone are identical most trees died.

Female greenfly and blackfly are able to give birth without mating and the hundreds of young are identical to them. Scientists have been able to produce clones in animals that do not normally clone, such as frogs. ■

Cloning of animals really began in 1962 when Dr Gurdon of Oxford University produced a group of frogs that were genetically identical. This was achieved by removing the nuclei of frogs' eggs and replacing them with nuclei from the tissue-lining of the intestines of one frog. All the eggs then had identical genetic information and grew into identical little frogs.

◖ **See also**

Aphids
Genetics
Reproduction

Clothes

Most people in the West today buy ready-to-wear clothes which are mass-produced in factories or workshops, and choose styles for comfort or to put over a particular image to other people. In Europe, Australia and North America, fashion styles are often similar, since both textiles and designs are exchanged in trade, and many people can afford to buy new clothes as the fashions change.

In some countries, including India, Pakistan, some countries of the Far East and much of Africa, traditional national dress is worn every day. In Japan and parts of eastern Europe, on the other hand, national dress is for special occasions, and most people usually wear western-style dress.

Design

Designers decide what clothes will look like, and also plan how they will be manufactured. The choice of shape and the type of material will depend upon whether the clothes are intended to be fashionable, casual, for sport or for work. They will consider how a fabric looks and feels, and whether the clothes need to be shaped for ease of movement or for fashion and how they look. The sort of weather they are designed for will determine what weight the material should be, and whether the garment should cover the whole body or just parts of it.

To make a prototype pattern, the designer drapes the fabric over a dummy and cuts and pins it into shape. The pieces of material are then taken

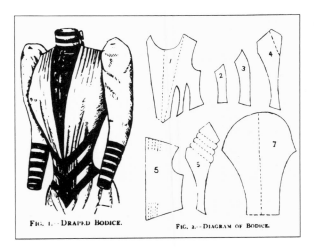

FIG. 1.—DRAPED BODICE.   FIG. 2.—DIAGRAM OF BODICE.

off the dummy, flattened out, and the shapes are traced to make a pattern. The pattern has to be fitted together very tightly onto the flat material to make sure that as little as possible is wasted. Each section is cut out, several layers of material at a time, with electric cutters or lasers. Today, computers can help to work out pattern shapes and how they can be fitted together on the material.

Manufacture

The pieces are then sewn together, often by a number of workers. One may sew up the main body of the garment; another puts in the sleeves; a third does the collar and cuffs, and so on. In some factories where hundreds of the same garment are made daily, one machine may put together particular parts such as pockets. However, machines cannot be changed quickly enough to meet the demands of fashion, so automation is used less in the clothing industry than in other manufacturing industries.

When all the pieces of a garment have been sewn together it must be pressed to take out creases or put in pleats and mould it into shape. The finished garments are carefully checked before they are sold, often to a wholesaler who sells them on to the retail shop or market stall.

Flashback

Until the 17th century outer garments were made by men tailors, and women only made shirts and underwear. Gradually, women started to make women's clothes, but men continued to make corsets, riding habits, and men's clothes.

Everything had to be sewn by hand, because the sewing machine was not available until the 1850s. Once the sewing machine had been invented and manufactured, dressmakers could work more quickly. ■

▶ An Edwardian pattern for a draped bodice. Dotted lines on the pattern pieces show where the material is to be folded or gathered to make pleats or give shape to areas like the shoulders.

National and ceremonial dress is described in the article on Dress. European clothes worn in the past are shown under Costume.

Haute couture designs may be ultra-fashionable or classic in style so that they do not go out of fashion.

The 'rag trade' is a term used for the cheap end of the clothing industry.

▶ By the late 19th century, there were thousands of women who lived by sewing.

◯ **See also**
Costume
Dress
Fashion
Hats and head-dresses
Sewing
Shoes

Clouds

There is lots of water vapour in the Earth's atmosphere. But since the temperature in the air is not always the same everywhere, the water vapour sometimes changes back to a liquid by condensation. Clouds are formed when water vapour condenses to become small droplets in the air. These droplets are so small they are not heavy enough to fall to earth as rain. They stay in the air and come together to form clouds.

Cirrus clouds look like wisps of hair, and usually lie 12 to 15 km (7–9 miles) up. At this height the temperature is always below freezing-point, so these clouds consist always of ice.

Cirrocumulus looks rather like the ripples in the sand on the seashore. It is often seen at the approach of fair weather after a depression. One form of cirrocumulus is the well-known 'mackerel sky'. The appearance of this cloud means that rain is on the way.

Altocumulus are layers of blob-shaped clouds arranged in groups, in lines or waves. In summer this cloud can often be seen in late evening or early morning. **Stratocumulus** is a lower and heavier form of altocumulus.

Altostratus is a veil of even, grey cloud through which the Sun can be seen dimly. It gives a 'watery sky' and is an almost certain sign of rain, because it is usually caused by a current of warm, moist air flowing up over a 'cold front'.

Stratus is the lower type of cloud, often blotting out all high ground. Many mountaineers and hikers have got into difficulties through the sudden appearance of this cloud. It may thicken and turn to fog, drizzle or rain.

Nimbostratus, the cloud which gives us most of our heavy rain, also hangs low. It is dark grey and threatening.

Cumulus are heavy, cauliflower-shaped clouds with flat bases. They are formed by convection currents of rising air, warmed by reflection of heat from the earth's surface.

Cumulonimbus is the thundercloud of hot, still summer weather. ■

Cumulus means 'heap' in Latin.

Cirrus comes from a Latin word meaning 'curl'.

Stratus comes from a Latin word *stratum* which means 'something spread or laid down'.

Nimbus means 'storm cloud'.

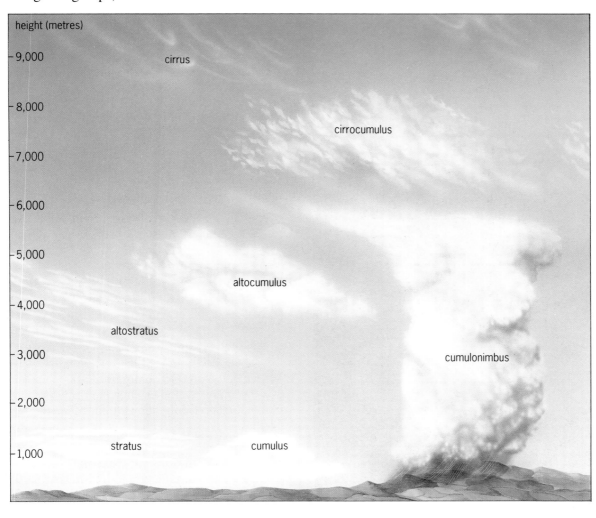

◄ Different types of clouds form at different heights above the ground. Low means below 3,000 m (9,800 ft). Medium means from there to about 6,000 m (19,700 ft). Cirrus clouds are the highest and may form up to 14 km (8 miles) above the ground.

See also
Atmosphere
Depressions
Rain
Snow
Water

Coal

The heat energy which is produced by burning a piece of coal comes originally from the Sun. This is because coal is the fossilized remains of plants. These plants grew with the aid of the Sun's energy millions of years ago.

How coal is formed

It takes a very long time for trees, ferns and other plants to turn into coal. Dead plants usually decay completely, leaving no remains. But in swampy areas the process of decay is very slow. Dead plants pile up and form the spongy material known as peat. In places such as Ireland and Scotland, peat is dug out of the ground and dried. It burns quite well but is rather smoky.

Many of the peat bogs that formed in geological time were close to the sea, often near the mouths of rivers. The sea washed sand, clay and gravel over the peat. The weight of these materials made the peat sink, squashing it. Other layers of peat and sand formed above the first. Eventually the sand, clay and gravel turned into rock. The peat was so compressed that it too became hard, turning into coal.

▶ To reach the coal, different types of mine are needed depending on where the coal seams are.

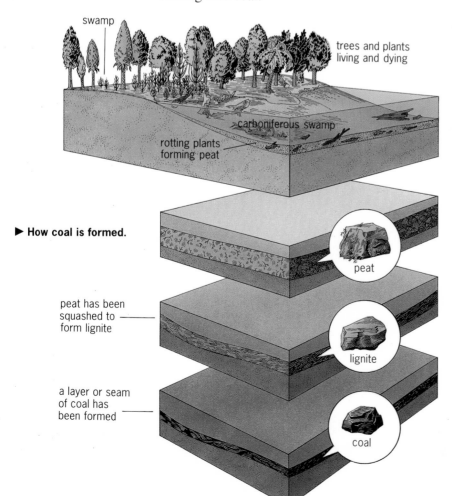

▶ How coal is formed.

Types of coal

Not all coal is hard, black and shiny. Peat that is not too compressed produces lignite, a coal that is soft and brown. This is mined in large quantities in Germany, the USSR and Australia. The most common kind of coal is called bituminous coal. This black coal is easy to use because it does not crumble like lignite, and it burns easily. Where the peat is highly compressed, it produces anthracite, which is hard and black. Anthracite is difficult to set alight, but once on fire, it burns slowly with very little smoke.

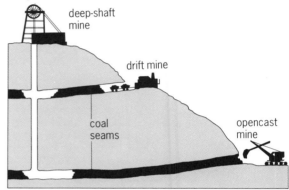

Opencast and drift mines

Where coal occurs near the surface, it is dug up by opencast quarrying. Giant machines cut a trench through the soil and surface layers of rock to reach the coal seam. Smaller mechanical shovels then dig out the coal. Although opencast quarrying is cheap, it can ruin the landscape.

Coal seams are often found one above another, sandwiched between other rock strata, rather like a layer cake. Where part of a coal seam reaches the surface of the ground, for example on the side of a hill, miners can tunnel horizontally straight into the seam. This type of mine is called a drift mine.

Shaft mines

Most coal seams are found far below the surface. To reach them, two vertical shafts are dug. One of the shafts is used to carry the miners up and down, and the other to lift the coal and to provide a second way out in an emergency. The shafts are also used to ventilate the mine. One pumps in fresh air and the other extracts stale air and dangerous gases. Galleries or 'roads' are cut from the shafts to the coal face.

Nowadays most coal is mined mechanically. A machine slices the coal away from the face of the seam with a rotating cutting-head. A conveyor belt carries the coal away to the foot of the shaft. The coal is then loaded into the lift and taken to the surface. The roof of the mine immediately behind the coal face is supported by hydraulic props made of steel. When the coal reaches the surface, it has to be washed and sorted. Different sizes and qualities of coal are used for various purposes.

Uses of coal

Some coal is simply burned as fuel, not only in household fires but also in power-stations, to produce electricity. Much coal is also turned into coke. In this process the coal is baked instead of burned. The gases given off are collected and used to make a number of important chemicals. Coke is a valuable smokeless fuel. It is also used in making iron from iron ore.

When coke is made, coal tar and ammonia are also formed. Many chemicals are present in coal tar, and these are used to make a wide range of products, including plastics such as nylon, explosives, the wood preservative creosote, and even cosmetics and medicines such as aspirin. The ammonia is made into fertilizers.

Flashback

Coal mining has always been dangerous. Until quite recently much of the work in mines was done by the muscles of people and animals. The coal was dug out from the seam by men with picks and shovels. In many early 19th-century mines, young children dragged heavy tubs of coal along the underground passageways. Later, ponies did this work. Many miners died from the effects of poisonous gases or explosions, or because the roofs of mines collapsed on them.

Today, machines do most of the work. Electric lights have replaced oil-burning lamps, and electric railways and conveyor belts do the work once done by ponies. Yet the miners' life is still dangerous, with the ever-present risk of fire, rock falls and other accidents, and the unhealthy effects of dust-laden air. ■

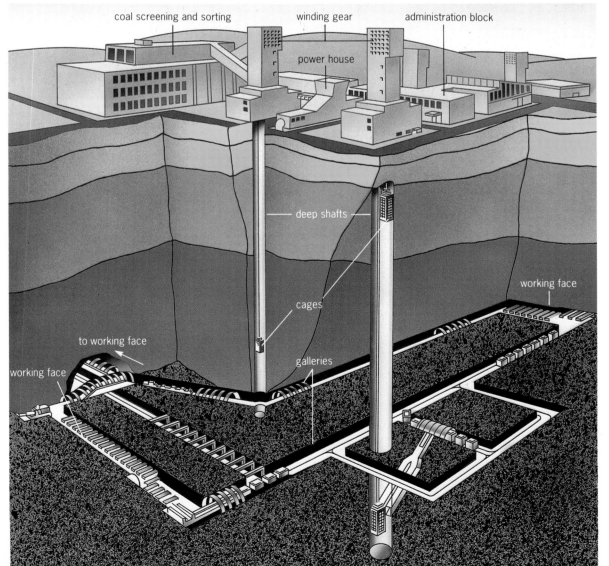

coal screening and sorting   winding gear   administration block

power house

◀ Main features of a deep-shaft mine.

deep shafts

working face

cages

to working face

galleries

working face

◖ See also
Children (picture)
Electricity supply
Fossils
Geological time
Mining
Plastics
Rocks
Welsh history (photo)

Coasts

Any map of the world is really a map of coasts, the boundaries where land meets sea. The world has about 312,000 km (194,000 miles) of coastlines, but their pattern is constantly changing as some coasts are worn away by the sea and others are built up by mud and sand.

► Powerful waves crash into the coast near Port Arthur in Tasmania. Over the years they cut back the cliffs to bring the overhang tumbling into the sea.

▼ The direction of the waves causes sand and pebbles to move along a beach in a zigzag pattern called longshore drift. Waves carry sand up the beach, but as they retreat the sand is dragged back towards the sea. Groynes slow down longshore drift and widen the beach.

groynes

waves come up the shore at an angle

► Coastlines are changing all the time. Some are being cut back. Others, like this coast in Donegal, Ireland, are being built up with eroded sand washed in by the waves.

◐ See also
Erosion
Rivers
Sea

Erosion

Waves are amazingly powerful forces. The force of a large breaking wave is rather like dropping a 10-tonne weight onto a square metre of rock. During storms, the waves become even more powerful, and can move rocks weighing more than 1,000 tonnes. So it is not surprising that waves can carve out cliffs and caves.

The waves wear away the rocks at the base of the cliffs, until the weight of rock overhanging the beach becomes so great that it breaks off under the strain. It crashes onto the beach below, to be further pounded into smaller and smaller pieces. These pebbles are swept by the current along the coast, helping to wear away more rocks. In the process they are worn down to sand and deposited as beaches.

Deposition

Rivers bring billions of tonnes of sand and silt to the oceans every year. More sand is produced when cliffs are worn away by the sea. The faster water is moving, the more sediment it can carry. As the breaking waves rush up the beach, they carry with them sand and shingle. Once their force is spent, the water drains back down the beach into the sea, but it is now flowing more slowly, so some of the sand and shingle is left behind to build up the beach. If the wind blows towards a sandy shore for most of the year, it may pile up the sand to form sand dunes.

Sand or shingle may continue to drift along the beach in a straight line even if the coast curves. It piles up to form long ridges called spits. Where spits reach from one headland to the next, they trap water to form a lagoon behind them.

Inlets of the sea

In some parts of the world the land is sinking or rising relative to sea-level. Added to that, during the last 18,000 years the sea-level has risen about 120 m (400 ft). This has led to some river valleys being drowned by the sea to form long inlets of the sea called rias or fjords. (These form very jagged coastlines on the west coasts of Europe and North America.)

Where rivers enter the sea, the flow of the water is slowed down, so the rivers drop their sediments. If a lot of sand or mud is dropped, it may build out the coast to form a huge fan-shaped delta. The deltas of the Mississippi River and the Nile are examples. ■

Cockroaches

The oriental cockroach originally came from Asia, but has been spread all around the world with shipments of food.

Distribution
The warmer parts of the world
Phylum Arthropoda
Class Insecta
Order Dictyoptera
Number of species 3,500

See also
Beetles
Insects

Most cockroaches live in tropical forests, feeding on whatever dies on the forest floor. A few species have become pests. They thrive in buildings where food is stored and can make themselves at home almost anywhere.

Cockroaches might be mistaken for beetles, for they have thickened front wings which fold back to protect large, fragile back wings.

Unlike true beetles, however, they beat both pairs of wings in flight. Cockroaches have very long, slender antennae made up of a large number of small segments, whereas those of beetles are made of a small number of large segments. ■

Cocoa

▲ **Fruits growing on a cacao tree in Brazil.**

Cocoa beans were also used as money by the Aztecs.

Cocoa was a fashionable drink in the late 17th and during the 18th centuries.

See also
Aztecs
Chocolate

Cocoa is the powder made from the crushed seeds of the cacao tree. Other ingredients, like powdered milk, sugar and flour, are sometimes added to make hot chocolate (drinking chocolate). The powder is mixed with hot milk or water to make a rich drink.

The cacao tree grows wild in the tropical rainforests of Brazil. It is now also cultivated in West Africa and Indonesia. The seeds or beans are the size of almonds. They are enclosed in fruit rather like small cucumbers, which grow out straight from the tree trunk. These seeds are fermented, dried, treated to remove some of the fat, and powdered.

Flashback

The Aztec Indians used the cocoa beans to brew a drink called *chocolatl*. They called it the 'food of gods'. The Spaniards, who took cocoa to Europe from Mexico in the 16th century, kept the recipe for making drinking chocolate a secret for nearly 100 years. In the 17th century other Europeans learned how to make it. ■

Codes and ciphers

Codes and ciphers are two ways of turning ordinary written words into secret messages. The process is called encryption and the messages are called cryptograms. They can be decoded or deciphered only by people who have the key to the system. The government, the armed forces and businesses may use cryptograms to protect new or important information.

Cipher systems involve a set of rules for turning the ordinary words, called plaintext, into their secret form and a key for understanding them. Transposition ciphers use the letters of the original plaintext but rearrange the order. Substitution ciphers keep the letters of the plaintext in the same order but use one letter in place of another. The rules can be very complex.

Code systems are a special form of substitution that works rather like a made-up secret language. The people who use it need a code book that lists each word in plaintext and its code equivalent to put messages into code. They need another list of the code words and the plaintext translation to decode messages.

Today, a great deal of information is handled electronically by computers. Experts write computer programs to create cipher systems that put this data into a secret form. This process is called data encryption.

Codes and ciphers encrypt written symbols. There are also ways to encrypt radio signals, television signals and fax messages by scrambling timed bits of the signals.

The ciphers shown here are easy to use but also quite easy for an expert to solve. For the Playfair Cipher, instead of using a jumble of letters in the grid which the person reading the message needs a copy of, you can use a word (with no repeated letters) and then the rest of the alphabet in order. ■

A transposition cipher

DON'T TELL THE SECRET TO ANYONE

C	H	I	P	S
D	O	N	T	T
H	T	S	L	E
E	A	E	C	R
N	S	T	T	E
N	Y	O	O	E

DOHET NTLSA NOELT ECTYO TRENE

Use a secret word to set the width of a grid (CHIPS). Write this way on the grid. Transpose this way. Write the letters in blocks of five. A person who knows the system can write the jumbled letters in a blank grid and then read the message. You can change the format of the grid by choosing a different secret word. You can enter the letters and transpose them in any order you choose, such as up and down or spiralling inwards.

A substitution cipher

The Playfair Cipher uses the letters of the alphabet arranged in a five-by-five block (I and J are together). The plaintext is divided into groups of two letters. Choose substitute letters this way:
Pairs on a row: move to the right of each.
Pairs in a column: move down.
Pairs diagonally opposite: use the other diagonal.

B	G	M	O	IJ
S	V	Y	Z	W
A	P	D	R	L
F	X	H	K	U
N	C	T	Q	E

GO AND EAT
GO AN DE AT

GO MI
AN FB
(the next letter down is the top of the same column)
DE LT
AT DN

Coffee

▶ Each coffee berry has two seeds or beans inside. They must be ripe before being picked by hand, as unripe berries would spoil the quality.

👁 See also
Brazil
Jamaica

Coffee is an aromatic (strong-scented) drink made by pouring boiling water over the roasted and ground beans (seeds) of the coffee plant. It

contains a stimulant called caffeine. There are two main types of coffee: arabica, which grows mainly in South America, and robusta which grows mainly in Africa. Each has its own distinctive aroma and flavour.

Coffee grows in the warmer parts of the world. It once grew wild in Ethiopia, but it is now cultivated in places as far afield as Brazil, Nicaragua, Indonesia, the Ivory Coast, Kenya and the West Indies. Some coffee is grown on large plantations, but much of it is grown on small holdings. It is best grown on slopes between 600 and 1,800 m (2,000 and 6,000 ft) above sea-level.

A single coffee tree usually provides only enough coffee a year to fill a ½-kilo bag, although the yield varies greatly from year to year. The fruit is collected and soaked in water or dried in the sun to release the beans. These are then dried, sorted and roasted. The degree of roasting affects the flavour of the coffee. ■

Coins

▶ The front (obverse) and back (reverse) of a coin from Lydia of about 550 BC.

▲ Chinese copper coin with a square hole from 212 BC.

▲ Silver coin of Julius Caesar, Dictator of Rome, 44 BC.

👁 See also
Money

▲ Gold coin of the time of Alexander the Great. The head is that of Athena.

▶ Modern British 20p piece. The 'code' reads Elizabeth II D. G. REG. F. D. which is short for the Latin DEI GRATIA (By the Grace of God) REGINA (Queen) FIDEI DEFENSOR (Defender of the Faith).

Coins are just one form of money. We think that coins were first made in Lydia (now part of Turkey). They were made from a metal called electrum, which is a mixture of gold and silver.

The idea of using coins soon spread. The Greeks used coins from the early 6th century BC and so did the people in what is now Bulgaria. Coins were being used all around the Mediterranean by the 5th century BC.

In the last two centuries BC the Celtic and German tribes who had close contact with the Romans and with Greek traders made coins for themselves. At first they copied Greek ones. Then they made their own designs, making abstract shapes from heads, chariots and horses.

The Chinese used cowrie shells at first as coins. Then they made bronze coins in the shape of cowrie shells, and of other things such as hoes and knives. Coins that we would recognize today were introduced by the First Emperor of the Qin dynasty in 212 BC.

Making coins

Coins have usually been made by striking a piece of metal with a punch which has the design of the coin on it. The Chinese cast their coins in a mould. We call the place where coins are made a 'mint'. Later coins usually have writing as well as pictures on them. The writing is often in a kind of code, to save space. ■

Cold

The molecules which make up all substances move more slowly when cooled. Energetic whizzing water molecules bounce off each other in steam, but slow down and turn into liquid droplets when they condense on a cold window. At an even lower temperature the water molecules move more slowly and the water freezes into solid ice. Chemical processes become slower: for instance, sugar dissolves more slowly in cold tea than hot tea. Food takes longer to cook in a cool rather than a hot oven, and if the temperature is not high enough the cake will not bake.

People and hedgehogs

The chemical processes which enable animals and plants to grow, move and keep alive are all slowed down when they are cold. But we are lucky. We are able to keep our blood warm and do not need to bask in the sun like lizards and snakes before we can get moving. Our bodies have special chemical processes that are switched on to keep us warm enough to function even on cold days. However, in newborn babies this system is not working properly, so they must be well wrapped up. Old people are also not very good at producing their own body heat and without extra warmth in cold weather they can suffer 'hypothermia' and fall into a deep sleep and perhaps die. Hedgehogs and dormice stop moving when they become cold and go to sleep, hibernating through the cold winter months. ■

Absolute zero
The coldest possible temperature, when the molecules cannot move any slower, is 273°C below 0°C (–459°F).

Lowest temperature
Recorded in Antarctica, 80°C below 0°C (–112°F).

Body temperature
Hibernating hamsters' temperature is just above 0°C (32°F).

⊙ See also
Energy
Heat
Hibernation
Hypothermia
Molecules
Superconductivity
Temperature

► These bacteria, which cause food poisoning, stop growing in extreme cold. This is why food stays fresh in a freezer. If the food is left in a warm place, the bacteria will quickly increase in number and produce substances that are poisonous to us.

Cold war

When two countries are political enemies but are not actually fighting each other, they are said to be in a state of cold war.

The most important cold war was the tension between the USSR and other communist countries on one side, and the USA and its allies on the other. It began in 1945, as soon as World War II ended. By 1988 relations between the Russians and the Americans had improved so much that the Cold War seemed to be over. ■

Colds and coughs

Colds are not caused by exposure to cold, but people used to think that they were, because colds happen more often in winter. Colds are caused by a germ called a virus, and they are spread by people who carry the virus.

A cold begins either with a sore feeling at the back of the nose or throat, or with sneezing and a runny nose. Then the nose becomes blocked so that you are forced to breathe through the mouth. The nasal discharge changes to a slimy mucus. For a few days someone with a cold may have a higher than normal temperature and some headache. The infection may spread to the chest and cause a cough.

There are no medicines to prevent or cure a cold, but there are some that make you feel more comfortable. If possible, people with colds should stay away from crowds to prevent the cold spreading. When you are about to sneeze, you should press a handkerchief against your nose and mouth until the sneezing has stopped, as the virus may be carried in droplets blown out by the sneeze. ■

⊙ See also
Diseases
Viruses

Collages

Collage is a way of making pictures by sticking different materials or objects onto a background support. The word collage comes from the French word *coller* 'to glue'. All kinds of materials, magazine pictures, newspapers, fabric scraps, stamps, buttons and matchsticks, can be used to make a collage picture or pattern.

To make a collage using materials like these you will need a strong support on which to work. You could use thick paper or thin card. A reliable and quick-drying glue is essential. An acrylic-based adhesive is ideal.

You can also experiment and make a collage using papers of contrasting colours, patterns and textures. Very thin papers (such as tissue paper) can be used either flat or crumpled. For paper collage, wallpaper paste can be used.

When more than one type of material is being used the picture is called an 'assemblage'. Often these pictures are three-dimensional, with projecting objects giving thickness or depth to the design. You could also try to make a collage or assemblage using natural materials: sand, seeds, dried leaves and grasses, bark, feathers and even shells. ■

▼ *Toy Shop*, an assemblage by Peter Blake. We are invited to look into the shop window with its selection of 1950s toys. The window may make us want to go inside the shop through the closed door and see more, though we know that the shop does not really exist.

Colleges

Famous specialist colleges
Royal College of Art
Royal College of Music

See also
Schools
Universities

A college consists of a group of students and teachers who come together to study and learn. Generally students go to college for further education after they leave school. In Britain, Colleges of Further Education provide a wide variety of courses. You can enrol for technical subjects, business or secretarial studies, nursery nursing, hairdressing and many other vocational (meaning related to a job) courses. They also run evening classes for adults. In the USA, college usually means the same as university. In Britain some universities, including Durham, Oxford and Cambridge, consist of a number of separate colleges. ■

Colombia

Colombia is a country in the north-western part of South America. It has many types of landscape and climate. The snow-covered peaks of the Andes Mountains run up the western side of the country. To the east and south is tropical rainforest, and grasslands make up the central region.

About three-quarters of Colombians live in cities. Bogotá, the capital, is high in the Andes. Colombia's main export is coffee which is mostly grown on large plantations. Peasant farmers, on the other hand, often have very little land. The crop that they can sell for the highest price is from the coca bush. The leaves are chewed by Indians to fortify themselves against the hard mountain life. Today coca leaves are made into the drug cocaine illegally and exported secretly for large profits.

Flashback

Colombia's original people were Indians who have lived there for more than 6,000 years. The Spanish arrived in 1499. Colombia's Indian tribes were great craftsmen. The Chibchas, who lived in the area around what is now Bogotá, made jewellery from gold and emeralds. European explorers heard stories of a fabulous city, rich in gold. They named it El Dorado (the gilded one) but no such city was ever found. The legend probably came from the Chibchas' ceremony in which the chiefs covered themselves in gold dust and dived into a sacred lake to cleanse themselves. ■

Area
1,138,914 sq km
(439,737 sq miles)
Capital Bogotá
Population 26,525,670
Language Spanish
Religion Christian
Government Republic
Currency
1 Colombian peso = 100 centavos

Simón Bolívar liberated the country from the Spaniards in 1819.

◯ See also
American Indians
Andes
Coffee
South America
Spanish colonial history

Biography
Bolívar

▼ **The dangerous illegal drug cocaine comes from the coca bush grown on the terraced mountain slopes.**

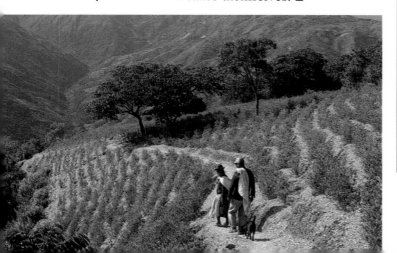

Colonies

Colonies were places where people from a distant country came to settle. Their home country ruled the colony, and usually gained wealth from it. Very often colonists took the land from the people who lived there. Colonists risked dangerous journeys to unknown lands for many reasons.

The ancient world

The ancient Greeks were short of land, so Greek cities encouraged people to start colonies in southern Italy, Sicily and North Africa. They even drove colonists away by force if they tried to come home again.

European settlers

From the 16th century onwards, new trade routes led to European colonies in the Far East and the New World. Explorers and merchants settled where they could do business. Soldiers went to protect them. Some colonists, like the Pilgrim Fathers, went to America to escape persecution. Poverty in Scotland drove some to a new life in Canada. Others did not go freely: unemployed and homeless people were kidnapped and sent to work as indentured labourers in the colonies. Later Africans were captured and sent to work as slaves in Caribbean and American colonies. People convicted of crimes in Britain were forced to sail to Australia.

In the 19th century, Europeans began a desperate race for colonies in Africa. They wanted raw materials for their industries, and thought they were bringing 'civilization'. They brought railways, Western education, and hospitals, but they robbed Africa of its resources and often destroyed ancient cultures.

Colonies do not last for ever. In the 20th century, native peoples have reclaimed their land from European colonists in Africa, South America and the Far East. ■

The Latin word *colonia* was used to describe the communities of Roman citizens who were sent out to guard the coast of Italy. In this way Rome could defend itself without having a large fleet.

Colonists in South America sent back vast amounts of gold and silver to Europe. Unfortunately the arrival of all this wealth caused a major problem of inflation. In England, for instance, prices rose by 250% between 1500 and 1650.

Colonies introduced many new products into Europe during the 17th century, such as tobacco from America, chocolate from Mexico and potatoes from South America.

Some land in the colonies was bought from the original inhabitants. In 1624 the Dutch bought Manhattan Island from the Indians for $24.

◯ See also
African history
American colonial history
Australia's history
British empire
Canada's history
Indian history
Pilgrim Fathers
Spanish colonial history

Colour

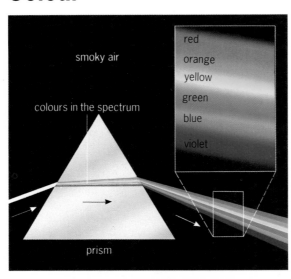

smoky air

colours in the spectrum

prism

red
orange
yellow
green
blue
violet

▶ A glass prism splits white light into all the colours of the rainbow. The spread of colours is called a spectrum. It shows up easily in the smoky air.

Light rays themselves are invisible; we can see them only when they bounce off things. In the diagram we see the light bouncing off specks in the glass or smoke particles in the air.

▶ When mixing light beams, the colours are added together. By mixing red, green and blue in varying amounts, other colours can be made.

▼ Mixing of light to give secondary and complementary colours.

We live in a world full of colour. Perhaps the most beautiful sight is a rainbow arching its colours across the sky. But how do we see all this colour?

All light travels to us like the waves that ripple across a pond when you drop a stone in. The distance between the top of one ripple and the top of the next is called the wavelength. Light of different colours has different wavelengths. Red light has the longest wavelength and violet the shortest. The wavelength of the light makes us see different colours, but that is not the whole story. The brain has an important part to play. Nobody knows exactly how we see all the shades of all the different colours.

White light

The light from the Sun or a lamp bulb seems colourless, but it contains all the colours of the rainbow. Whenever our eyes receive a mixture of all the colours of the rainbow we see this as white light.

Coloured light

To make beams of light of different colours, you can put sheets of transparent coloured plastic (filters) in front of a torch beam of white light. A red filter gives you a red light beam. A green filter gives you a green light beam. If you shine the red beam and the green beam onto a sheet of white paper, you will see yellow where they overlap! When light is added together in this way we need only three basic colours: red, green and blue, in different proportions, to make all

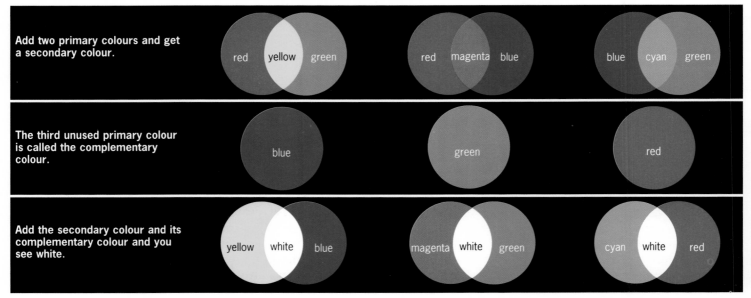

Add two primary colours and get a secondary colour.	red yellow green	red magenta blue	blue cyan green
The third unused primary colour is called the complementary colour.	blue	green	red
Add the secondary colour and its complementary colour and you see white.	yellow white blue	magenta white green	cyan white red

other colours. Scientists call these three basic colours the primary colours. Television uses only these colours to produce colour pictures.

Paints and dyes

Perhaps a room has blue walls and a red carpet. These colours come from paints and dyes. But mixing paints (or dyes) gives different colours from mixing beams of light. When you mix beams of light the colours are added together. But, when you mix paints, colours are taken away. White light shines on the paint on the walls and the paint absorbs most of the colours. You see only what is left: in this case colours in the blue part of the spectrum. In the same way the carpet looks red becase all the other colours in the blue part of the spectrum are absorbed by the dye. If you were to mix red and blue paint, the result would be very dark because, between them, the red and blue paint would absorb almost all the light.

Artists and printers can make most colours by mixing paints or inks of three basic colours: magenta, yellow and cyan (which they sometimes call primary red, primary yellow and primary blue). They are the same as the secondary colours you get when you mix light.

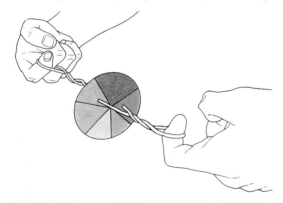

Something to do

A whizzer is easily made. Carefully cut out a circle of thick card. Draw six lines from the centre of the circle so that you have six equal sections. Paint each section a different colour of the rainbow. Thread string through holes on either side of the centre of the circle. Hold the whizzer as in the diagram. Turn the circle round and round so that the strings become tightly twisted. Pull the loops apart and watch it spin. Try painting the whizzer red and green, or other colours, and see what happens.

◀ **Printers use three basic colours and this shows what happens when they are mixed. Yellow takes away the blue light and cyan takes away the red light and so if they are mixed we are left with green. If you mix all three basic colours, then red, blue and green are all taken away and the result is almost black.**

You cannot accurately describe colours but you can match a colour to one on a chromaticity colour chart. These charts have thousands of different colours, and for each they state the exact proportions of the three primary colours needed to make that particular colour.

Telling colours apart

Not everyone is good at telling colours apart. Some people cannot see the difference between any colours. They are colour blind. Others have difficulty telling red from green. About one boy in ten is born with red–green colour blindness, though hardly any girls are affected. Colour blindness is something which people inherit. When darkness falls, everyone has problems telling colours apart because the bits of the eye which pick up colours work properly only if there is plenty of light.

In everyday life, colours are often used to give warnings or other messages. For example, red may mean 'stop' or 'danger', while green may mean 'go' or 'all clear'. This can cause problems for colour blind people. With traffic lights, they have to look at the position of the light (top or bottom) to know whether it means stop or go. Colour blind people also find it difficult to work with electric cables. In most cables, the wires are in different colours so that electricians can work out which connections to make. Mains cables usually have three wires in them; one of which is a safety wire (called an earth wire). In many countries, the earth wire is striped so that people do not have to rely on a colour to tell them which one it is. ■

Colours used to describe people and their moods

red	angry
green	jealous
blue	depressed
yellow	cowardly
white	pure
grey	uninteresting

See also

Dyes
Eyes
Light
Paint
Paintings
Printing
Rainbows
Symbols
Television

Comets

▶ Halley's Comet in March 1986. The coloured dots are stars. They look coloured because the photograph is actually made up from three separate coloured pictures, one red, one green and one blue.

A bright comet in the night sky looks like a hazy patch with a long wispy tail. Comets bright enough to be seen easily by eye are quite rare, but astronomers using telescopes find 20 or 30 every year.

Comets are made of ice, gas and dust. They are out in space between the planets, travelling in orbits round the Sun, and they shine because they reflect sunlight. The long tails only grow when comets get near the Sun. They are caused by the light and streams of atomic particles from the Sun.

When a comet comes near Earth, it gets brighter over a few weeks. A check from night to night shows that it moves slowly among the stars. Then it gradually fades and disappears.

Most comets are seen only once. They are pulled towards the Sun by the force of its gravity but afterwards they vanish into distant space. Others get trapped by the gravity of the Sun and planets so that they keep going round the Sun in long oval orbits. The most famous comet of all, Halley's Comet, is like that. It can be seen from the Earth every 76 years. The last time was in 1986. The comet is named after Edmund Halley, who saw it in 1682. He was the first person to realize that it came back regularly. He used old records of observations going back to 1301. The earliest definite observation of Halley's Comet that we know about was made in China in 240 BC. ■